Multinationals, Technology, and Industrialization

Multinationals, Technology, and Industrialization

Implications and Impact in Third World Countries

Katherin Marton
Fordham University

Lexington Books
D.C. Heath and Company/Lexington, Massachusetts/Toronto

Library of Congress Cataloging-in-Publication Data

Marton, Katherin.
  Multinationals, technology, and industrialization.

  Includes index.
  1. International business enterprises—Developing
countries. 2. Technology transfer—Developing countries.
I. Title.
HD2932.M37   1986   338.8'881724   86–7218
ISBN 0–669–13209–8 (alk. paper)

Published simultaneously in Canada
Printed in the United States of America
Casebound International Standard Book Number: 0–669–13209–8
Library of Congress Catalog Card Number: 86–7218

The paper used in this publication meets the minimum requirements of
American National Standard for Information Sciences—Permanence of
Paper for Printed Library Materials, ANSI Z39.48–1984. ∞™

86 87 88 89 90 8 7 6 5 4 3 2 1

To My Father

Contents

Preface and Acknowledgments

F ew economic issues in international relations raised greater controversy and recrimination during the 1960s and 1970s than the role and
activities of multinational corporations in Third World countries, particularly in the developing countries in Asia, Africa and Latin America. With
several countries in Asia and Africa achieving independence from colonial
rule during the period from 1947 to 1967, economic and industrial issues
assumed a new urgency and dynamism. Varying degrees of economic
nationalism emerged, especially regarding the exercise of sovereignty over
natural resources, and the operations of multinational corporations from industrialized economies came increasingly under scrutiny and criticism. These
developments led to considerable changes in the relationships between
multinational corporations and Third World governments in several important sectors of industrial production.

The past two decades have also seen the emergence and application of
significant technological innovations in most industrial sectors, the impact of
which has often extended beyond the particular industry involved. These
technological developments have taken place almost entirely in industrialized
countries, and major innovations in microelectronics, genetic engineering,
and other such fields not only have revolutionized communications and production processes in several industries but have also resulted in an increased
technological gap between industrialized economies and Third World countries. At the same time, there has been considerable technological diffusion
and fairly rapid growth of industrial and technological capability in a number
of developing countries. With increased industrial diversification in most of
these countries, the demand for industrial technology will grow at a rapid
pace and will have to be met mostly through alternative arrangements with
technology owners, suppliers, and licensors from industrialized countries.

Historically, the major sources of foreign industrial technology in Third
World countries have been the multinational corporations operating on a
global basis. Consequently, the behavior and response of these corporations
will, to a large extent, determine the pattern of industrial technology flow

and the terms and conditions of transfer to developing countries. In several fields of industry, the natural resources, the labor and other factor conditions, and the relatively unsaturated markets of developing countries provide substantial scope and potential for investment and local production activities. Nevertheless, there has been a growing feeling in most developing countries that production by subsidiaries of multinational corporations has not contributed adequately toward self-sustained technological development and that remedial measures have to be incorporated in national policies on foreign direct investment and technology.

This book deals principally with the changing roles and relationships of multinational corporations in Third World countries, particularly as they relate to industrial and technological development in these countries. Although the environment for multinational corporations in most of these countries is significantly different from that of two decades ago, regulatory measures and other policies are having a major impact on the operations of these corporations.

This book discusses various implications and aspects of commercialization of technology by multinational companies in developing countries and the ways in which such corporations have responded to changes in the socioeconomic environment, both internationally and in individual developing countries in which substantial industrial development has taken place. The book also examines the nature and impact of technology transfer through multinational companies, especially with respect to the growth of technological capability and the absorption and adaptation of foreign technology and know-how in various industrial sectors. The most important aspects covered here relate, however, to the role and effects of national policies in host developing countries and their impact on the activities of multinational corporations regarding investments and technology transfer in these countries. The recent operations of multinational corporations in important industrial sectors and the evolution of national policies toward multinational companies in several developing countries are analyzed. In addition, the nature of these policies and their effectiveness and limitations are examined in some detail. In the light of this analysis, certain trends and prospects are discussed with respect to alternative forms of MNC participation and the nature of industrial technology transfer to Third World countries during the coming decades. This is all viewed within the framework of the objectives and policies in these countries and the changing role of multinational corporations in various industrial sectors.

Acknowledgments

I should like to express my appreciation and gratitude to the many government officials and members of research, academic, and other institutions in various Asian, African, and Latin American countries, and to the representatives of multinational corporations and state-owned and private sector corporations who spared considerable time discussing the problems of technological development and the role and impact of multinational corporations in their respective countries.

I am grateful to Fordham University, which granted me a sabbatical year and two summer fellowships to complete my research and writing. My thanks also go to the Alexander von Humboldt Stiftung, which allowed me to spend a term at the Free University of Berlin, where several members of the Economics Department gave me valuable help and suggestions.

Finally, I am obliged to Mr. Rana K. Singh, who was kind enough to read my manuscript and make valuable comments and suggestions.

Part I
Technological Development and Industrialization

1
Role of Industrial Technology in Developing Countries

The last decade has witnessed significant revolution in several Third World developing countries in the basic approach to development planning and industrialization. With great diversity in factor endowments, size of markets, levels of economic development and varying socio-political systems, industrial strategies in these countries have differed considerably and have also been modified substantially from time to time. Nevertheless, certain common trends have emerged, particularly in developing countries that have achieved significant industrial growth. One important trend has been the growing importance of, and emphasis on, the role of industrial technology as a critical element in the process of economic and industrial development. It is increasingly recognized in these countries that an essential prerequisite to industrialization is the rapid development of technological capability in the use, absorption, and adaptation of foreign technology and in the growth of indigenous techniques and processes.

Despite this, in most countries, only during the last two decades have specific policies been adopted that directly affect the application and development of technology, particularly at the level of production enterprises. Previously, technological development was mainly promoted by institutional programs for technical education and training, on the one hand, and by the establishment and operation of government-owned or supported research institutions in selected fields, on the other. It was generally considered that capabilities for the application, use, and development of technologies in various industrial sectors would emerge as an integral part of the process of industrialization and that policies designed to accelerate this process would, at the same time, ensure technological development. Thus, policies and programs designed to establish production capacity in various sectors were also expected to result in the necessary flow of production technology and management techniques. Only in recent years has the pattern of technological development—including issues of foreign technology transfer and its absorption and adaptation, and development of indigenous technological capability—become an important feature of current policies and programs in many developing countries. These aspects are, in turn, closely linked with policies toward foreign direct investment and the role of activities of multinational corporations (MNCs) in these countries.

Initially, it is necessary to define the concept of industrial technology in relation to technological development. Technological development may be viewed either as the overall level of scientific and technological knowledge in a community at a particular time or as the level of technological application, adaptation, and innovation in a particular production or service sector. Similarly, industrial technology may relate either to the technological capability in a branch of industry or to the specific production process or technique required for the manufacture of a certain product. A broad definition is used by Merrill, for example, who conceives technology to be "a body of knowledge and procedures for making, using and doing useful things."[1] Baranson, on the other hand, refers to technology as "the package of product designs, production and processing techniques and managerial systems that are used to manufacture particular industrial products."[2] The United Nations Industrial Development Organization defines technology or know-how as "the sum of knowledge, experience and skills for manufacturing a product or products and for establishing an enterprise for this purpose."[3]

Industrial technology must initially include the knowledge and capability to operate machinery and equipment that have technology embodied in them. In several branches of industry, the capacity to operate the necessary machinery and equipment is quite adequate for manufacture of various products. With the increasing complexity of products and their designing and manufacturing processes, however, technology has assumed a broader connotation that includes the specialized knowledge and techniques necessary for producing and marketing specific products or for performing certain technical services. This may take the form of blueprints or manufacturing drawings or formulas, but may also be in a form that can be communicated only through training programs. The specialized information may be covered by patents or other industrial property rights, may be unpatented but nevertheless proprietary to a particular corporation or individual, or may be in the form of unpatented know-how. The process of technological development involves appropriate application and development of such industrial technology and development of the capability to plan and implement programs that achieve the necessary growth of technical skills in planning, production, and management in various industrial sectors. This includes project planning, production technology, and management expertise in different fields of industry and covers the technological requirements at various stages of industrial planning and project implementation.

The transfer of industrial technology relates to the transfer of specialized production or management know-how among different parties, generally industrial enterprises. Where technological knowledge is embodied in machinery and equipment, information on machinery operations would itself constitute transfer of operational technology. In international business activities, however, transfer of technology is viewed as a specific but broader concept and is related to the transfer of specialized know-how, either patented or nonpatented, from one enterprise to another. Such transfer comprises the transmission of knowledge for production and associated activities that enable recipient enterprises to manufacture a particular product or provide a specific service. According to Baranson, "transfer generally implies a sustained enterprise-to-enterprise relationship necessary to reproduce production capabilities at the desired levels of quality standards and cost efficiencies."[4] This definition probably comes closest to the common conception of what transfer of industrial technology involves, particularly as viewed by technology suppliers. In this definition, it is interesting to note that the objective is considered to be reproduction of production capabilities. Thus, effective transfer should enable the recipient enterprise to produce the goods and services in question in accordance with quality and cost parameters. This does not imply, however, that the process of technology transfer should enable the recipient enterprise to achieve rapid absorption of the technology or to undertake significant adaptation or innovations on the technology transferred. This aspect assumes special importance in the case of complex and advanced technology, in which the transfer of knowledge on basic designs and processes may be necessary for modifications and adaptations that suit particular situations and factor endowments. The transfer of basic technical knowledge and design capability that would enable technology-recipient enterprises or licensees (as they are commonly known) to adapt and develop the production or process technology does not normally form part of the existing pattern of industrial technology transfer. Such transfer is usually limited to the knowledge and use of production processes and know-how utilized by the technology supplier.

It is important to emphasize, however, that technology transfer is a broad concept. Its scope depends on the arrangements between the enterprises concerned and may extend considerably beyond technical information on a particular production process. To assess the extent to which transfer is actually achieved, it would be necessary to differentiate the knowledge, skills, and capabilities that are developed through transfer of a particular technology. These skills might be limited to the level of machinery operations or might relate to development of production and marketing capability. They also might extend to the development of design and engineering capability to undertake further research and to develop adaptations and innovations on the licensed technology. Furthermore, technology transfer can, and often does, comprise various stages that precede production, such as project formulation, feasibility studies, and detailed project planning and implementation, and the postimplementation stage of management, including production planning and marketing.

It would be useful, at this point, to digress and look at the expression *technology transfer,* a term that is accepted by technology suppliers (or licensors) and licensee enterprises as well as by the countries concerned in these arrangements. Semantically, the notion of *transfer* implies that something is given or granted to another party. In the case of industrial technology, however, the knowledge is retained and continues to be used by the technology supplier and only certain defined elements of that knowledge are transferred, for commercial considerations. Consequently, a more appropriate term for the communication of technological knowledge between enterprises would be *commercialization of technology,* because this process is motivated primarily by commercial and profitability considerations.[5] The references to technology transfer should be viewed, therefore, in the context of commercialization of technology and know-how. Regardless of whether the transfer takes place between affiliated companies or between unaffiliated parties, it is principally a commercial transaction. When technology is transferred internally within a company, usually from the parent company to its subsidiaries, no direct payments specifically for use of technology may be involved. Such transfer would, nevertheless, be motivated by profitability, which would be reflected in the profits and returns accruing to the parent company from its subsidiaries and affiliates. There has also been an increasing trend to specify payments by subsidiaries and affiliates to parent corporations for the supply of know-how and technical services. In the case of transfer between unaffiliated companies, the commercial nature of the transaction is obvious and is clearly demonstrated by the payment and other contractual conditions governing the acquisition and usage of the transferred technology.

Despite the obvious commercial character of technology transfer, the term *sale of technology* is not generally used, except in relation to the outright purchase of a specific technology. The notion of sale would normally imply that the buyer or technology-receiving enterprise would own the technology and that payments for technology would entitle the recipient enterprise to ownership of the technology in question. This is not the case in industrial technology, where proprietary knowledge and rights are retained by the technology supplier or licensor, which often views the transfer process primarily as a lease for the use of its technology by the licensee during the period of agreement. Certain contractual provisions that were commonly incorporated in technology agreements, particularly with licensee enterprises from developing countries, attest to this approach on the part of the licensors. These provisions generally involved two areas: the restricted conditions of use during the period of agreement and prohibition on the use of the technology after expiration of the agreement. However, in recent years, this position has changed significantly in several developing countries with the introduction of regulatory measures concerning technology agreements. A clearer and more equitable picture has now emerged on the concept of technology transfer, both in terms of the principles and contractual conditions governing the transfer and because knowledge that is once transmitted cannot later be withdrawn nor can its use be restricted after the period of the contract, except under legal rights relating to industrial properties.

In Third World developing countries, industrial technology has largely been of foreign origin, but in recent decades there have been certain adaptations and development of new techniques and processes in some industrial sectors. The major channels of foreign technology transfer have ranged from MNCs investing in subsidiaries in these countries or in supplying technology and know-how through licensing arrangements with domestically owned companies to foreign suppliers of machinery and equipment and foreign consulting engineering organizations performing specific technical services. Traditionally, foreign technology has been transferred largely through MNC subsidiaries, which have been either wholly owned by parent corporations or which have foreign majority holdings.[6] With the gradual implementation of industrialization programs, the supply of machinery and equipment to developing countries also increased considerably, and transfer of operating know-how by machinery suppliers has also constituted an important channel of technology transfer. As large infrastructure and industrial projects have been undertaken in these countries, considerable use has also been made of foreign consulting and engineering companies that have provided various technological services, including planning and construction of turnkey projects.

Although considerable dependence on MNC subsidiaries and affiliates for technology and know-how and on foreign machinery suppliers and consulting organizations continues, in most developing countries this pattern is undergoing certain changes. The growing emphasis on national ownership and increased local capital participation has led to the formation of MNC affiliates with minority foreign holdings in several developing countries. With the growth of domestically owned enterprises, both in the state-owned and private sectors in these countries, technology licensing by technology suppliers without foreign equity holdings has also increased. Predominantly, however, technology licensors have been MNC parent companies and their subsidiaries located in industrialized countries. Domestic production of machinery and equipment has also increased significantly in developing countries such as Brazil, India, Mexico, and the Republic of Korea. Nevertheless, machinery exports to developing countries from industrialized nations have continued to increase.[7] In several developing countries, local consulting engineering capability has also developed in certain production sectors, which has resulted in the gradual replacement of foreign consultancy organizations. However, for most large and complex projects, foreign consulting engineering companies continue to be utilized.

The use of particular channels of technology transfer has varied according to specific country and industry situations and to the nature of the technology involved. National policies on foreign investment and regulatory measures for the acquisition of foreign technology and use of foreign consultants have also had considerable impact on the channel of transfer. In industrial sectors where production technology is mostly embodied in machinery and equipment, as in sugar plants or cement factories, the channel of transfer has primarily been the supplier of plant and equipment. The machinery supply arrangements often include plant erection and machinery installation and programs for the training of local personnel on machinery operation and maintenance. In cases involving foreign capital participation, technology supply is one of the principal functions of foreign partners, which are also generally responsible for technical services and for the supply of various elements that are not manufactured locally. In developing countries where domestically owned companies have achieved significant financial and entrepreneurial capability, foreign technology is being increasingly acquired through licensing arrangements or joint ventures, with the conditions of transfer defined in contractual agreements.

Consulting engineering companies from industrialized countries also have constituted an important channel of technology transfer to developing countries.[8] These companies have assumed an expanded role with the increased differentiation between engineering design and production functions, leading to greater autonomy of engineering and design companies. Their growth has also been favored by the increasing complexity of construction techniques, the development of continuous production processes, and the larger size of plants and industrial complexes. Such companies have often specialized in the integration of large industrial complexes in various socioeconomic and techno-economic environments. Engineering consulting companies have also specialized in various functions, such as project engineering, work preparation, maintenance activities, and other operations in industrial projects. The services of such companies may range from advice by an individual consultant on a specific technical issue to the complete planning and supervision of construction of large projects employing hundreds of engineers and technicians. They may practice in a narrow field of specialization or cover a wide range of engineering functions. For the construction of such major infrastructure projects as electrical power plants, irrigation projects, highways and bridges, and the like, foreign consulting services have been utilized extensively for various stages of planning and implementation. Similarly, in the case of large industrial projects, including petroleum refineries, fertilizer, petrochemical, steel and aluminum plants, set up by governments in the public sector, the services of foreign technical consultants have been used to a considerable extent. In certain developing countries, however, local consultants and personnel have been increasingly participating in these projects, and such association has been an important channel for transferring planning, engineering, and construction skills to local engineering companies.

The nature of the foreign technology package obviously varies considerably from case to case, extending from supply of manufacturing drawings and production technology for relatively simple products to turnkey arrangements for the planning, installation, and initial operations of major infrastructure projects and industrial plants. Foreign technology inflow may take place through various channels, and often there may be various combinations in different technology-supply sources. In most cases, however, MNCs continue to be the principal channel of technology transfer to developing countries.

Foreign technology transfer to industrialized countries generally differs both in scope and magnitude from that to developing economies. In industrialized countries, the needed technology is often patented or proprietary know-how. The advanced technological capabilities of recipient companies and their ongoing research and development (R&D) activities enable these companies to absorb and adapt the licensed technology once the basic technical details and the right to use the proprietary information have been acquired. Often, they improve on the licensed technology and make innovations. Licensor and licensee companies are operating in a similar technological environment and local suppliers and subcontractors can manufacture required inputs once technical specifications have been furnished. Also, the requirements for a qualified and skilled labor force seldom pose major problems. Because of the similarity in the usage conditions of the technology and of the final product manufactured under the licensed foreign technology, major process or product adaptations may not be necessary.

In the transfer of industrial technology to companies in developing countries, however, the technology package is usually much larger. These enterprises often need not only product design and production know-how but a much broader range of technological functions. Because of significant gaps in the availability of intermediate materials and inputs, the technological requirements generally extend considerably beyond the acquisition of basic designs or a specific technology. The licensee company would usually also need various forms of technical assistance in the preparation of feasibility and market studies, project planning, specification of inputs and machinery, and expertise at various stages of project implementation and initial operation. Often, quality control techniques for locally purchased inputs and foreign sources of intermediates would have to be defined by the licensor. The production know-how required may often be nonproprietary to the licensor and may even be common knowledge in industrial countries in the specific industrial sector. In developing countries, however, effective utilization of foreign technology would also require the transfer of such industry-specific technology. The assimilation of foreign technology and the adjustment to different factor endowments and conditions in these developing countries is a far greater task for enterprises than it is for licensees in industrialized economies. Besides the production function, much greater support is required in managerial and marketing operations. Therefore, the technological needs of enterprises in developing countries tend to be of a composite nature and cover various stages of project preparation, implementation, and operation.

It is against this background of diverse technological needs and the nature of industrial technology transfer to developing countries that the technological objectives of these countries have to be considered. In broad terms, the basic objective may generally be defined as the achievement of technological self-reliance and rapid growth of technological capability in various production and service sectors.[9] Self-reliance, however, should not be viewed as technological isolationism and the development of industrial technology from its initial stages in each field. Enterprises and institutions in developing countries should avail themselves of technological developments and innovations in other countries and should effectively participate in the process of acquisition and sharing of technological knowledge at various stages of technological development. In fact, an important feature of contemporary global industry is the rapid increase of technology trade and exchange between corporations and institutions in different countries. Considerable technological interdependence is emerging in most production sectors, and technology licensing and cross-licensing between companies within a country and internationally are becoming increasingly common. The concept of self-reliance, therefore, should be conceived principally in terms of the development of the necessary technological capability to determine technological needs and to ensure that these needs are adequately served by appropriate technological choice and that processes and techniques necessary for and suitable to such needs and to domestic factor endowments are acquired and developed. The process of effective acquisition and development of technology also implies the ability to absorb and adapt technological processes and to develop innovative capability. Thus, technological objectives must be viewed in terms of both the exercise of effective choice and the establishment of a capability for technological absorption, adaptation, and innovation.[10] Increased technological self-reliance should also be concerned with the achievement of greater parity with enterprises in industrialized economies in the process and practice of technological trade and exchange. This is becoming an increasingly intricate field, and the negotiation of suitable terms and conditions and the process of absorption and adaptation necessitate the growth of considerable capability on the part of recipient institutions and enterprises.

Unpackaging of Technology

In the past two decades, there has been very rapid growth in technology transfer agreements between enterprises in different countries, largely through the activities of MNCs. Industrial technology is more frequently emerging as a marketable commodity, within MNC operations and through various contractual arrangements for the provision of technology and services to unaffiliated companies. The commercialization of technology, mostly in the form of lump-sum fees and royalties for technical services, has increased considerably. Though most of these transactions have taken place between enterprises in industrialized countries, payments by developing-country enterprises have increased signficantly in recent years. The channel of transfer in most cases, has been MNCs, and transactions have largely been between the parent and the affiliated companies. Consequently, policy objectives of Third World developing countries have to be harmonized with those of MNC investor and technology suppliers in these countries.

In this context, an important objective in several developing countries is the unpackaging or disaggregation of the various components of foreign investment and technology. Often, in the past, such proposals were presented in an aggregate or composite form, and it was extremely difficult to assess the financial and other implications of the different elements of investment and technology. For technology alone, a lump-sum fee was often quoted for a turnkey operation. In other cases, fees and payments for overall technical assistance and supply of technology were sought without full details of the nature of the technological support to be provided. It is in this context that unpackaging of the composite technology package has been considered necessary in several countries, so that the costs and implications of various elements can be evaluated to a greater extent. This also enables an effective assessment of the extent to which locally available inputs in terms of materials and services can or are proposed to be utilized. Since the various elements of technology in a major industrial project can be considered under various categories—such as feasibility study, detailed engineering, machinery selection and purchase, production know-how, plant erection and machinery installation, training, and start-up operations, unpackaging requires a detailed breakdown of the costs of each stage. To the extent that these activities could be performed by local enterprises, the supply from external sources could be reduced or modified.

Unpackaging of technology has been undertaken in developing countries such as Argentina, Brazil, India, and Mexico as part of the process of negotiating or reviewing foreign technology agreements. It has resulted in considerable increase in the use of local technical services and equipment. As domestic consulting engineering and other technical-service capabilities have developed in these countries, the use of foreign consultants has been substantially reduced. The purchase of domestically produced machinery, both at the initial stage and subsequently, during production operations, has also been ensured to a much greater extent when the various technological elements have been clearly identified. Also, local inputs have been utilized to a much larger extent because more technological information has been available as part of the disaggregation process. Technology unpackaging has obvious limitations and constraints. In a number of cases, foreign technology and investments are closely interlinked in that a technology may not be available at all unless it accompanies foreign investment. To disaggregate these two elements would not be really useful in such cases. In many instances, various technological elements go together; if these are separately considered and evaluated, there may be serious practical difficulties. Thus, a particular technology may require the use of a special type of engineering or a very specialized operational capability. Also, certain components and intermediate products may be available only from a single source. It is important, therefore, that the concept of technology unpackaging take the special features of that particular technology into full account.

Although varying degrees of technology unpackaging in project planning and engineering, production know-how, and technical services have been implemented in some developing countries, with unpackaging becoming an important feature of technology regulation, the fact remains that industrial technology supplied to developing countries still comprises several technological elements. Even in countries such as India and Mexico, technology agreements that relate solely to the use of patents and do not extend to various aspects of know-how are fairly limited and constitute a small percentage of the agreements. A notable exception is Brazil, where various categories of agreements are listed separately but patent licensing is often accompanied by separate agreements relating to supply of know-how or services.

Foreign Investment and Technology Flow

Because MNCs have been the major channels of technology transfer to developing countries, there is a close relation between transfer of industrial technology and foreign direct investments by MNCs. The flow and stock of foreign investments in developing countries serve as one indicator of the magnitude and rate of growth of foreign technology inflow. The flow of direct foreign investments from developed market economies to all receiving countries increased from $4.1 billion in 1960 to $12.1 billion in 1970 and to $41.8 billion in 1980. Of these, investments in developing countries accounted for $1.8 billion in 1970 and $7.6 billion in 1980, at current prices.[11] This indicates that investments in developing countries have been approximately 30 percent of total foreign investments during the last two decades. More than 50 percent of such investments have been from the United States, although the proportion of investments in developing countries from Japan and the Federal Republic of Germany has been increasing in recent years. The total stock of foreign investments from Organization for Economic Cooperation and Development (OECD) countries, including reinvested earnings, in developing countries was estimated at $32.3 billion in 1967 and $89 billion in 1978.[12]

The close relationship between investment and technology flows is also indicated by the large share of receipts for technology from affiliated companies out of total payments received for technology and technical services. In 1983, for example, in U.S. corporations, 78 percent of receipts from technology were from affiliated companies. This ratio showed relatively little variation throughout the 1970s.[13] For U.K. corporations, 55 percent of technology receipts were from affiliated companies during the late 1970s, indicating the greater propensity of U.K. companies to license their technology to unaffiliated companies.[14] While technology licensing is increasing rapidly, payments for technology and technical services, which are usually compiled by government agencies, may provide a closer approximation of international technology flows.

The measurement of technology transfer, whether for enterprises or for countries, poses major methodological difficulties. For the quantification of technology transfer, technology payments in the form of fees and royalties are viewed as a commonly accepted measurement, both by suppliers and recipients. Such payments, however, indicate only the financial implications and consequences and do not measure the nature or extent of the technology transfer. The level of technology payment reflects the value of a particular technology at a specific time. There is no established international price for a specific technology; the determination of a particular payment or rate of royalty is influenced by several factors, especially the availability of alternatives and the knowledge of the buyer. In certain technologies, monopolistic or oligopolistic market situations increase the bargaining position of technology owners and the price of the technology in question. On the receiving side, government policies generally influence the permissible payments by setting maximum levels, which may differ to a varying extent from the market value of a particular technology. In some countries, legislation may also prohibit payments for proprietary technology by MNC subsidiaries and affiliates to parent corporations. In others, permissible payments by affiliated companies may be considerably below the rate allowed to nonaffiliated enterprises. Licensors may also supply their technology for relatively low payment, if the expected profitability can be achieved through exports of associated inputs, such as intermediates and components. These factors make technology payments a very inadequate measurement for the value of the technology transfereed. The measurement of technology transfer by the number of agreements entered into is also a rather weak indicator of the substantive nature of transfer. Technology agreements vary widely in their scope; some may cover a narrowly defined area, such as the production of certain parts or the assembly of imported components. They may relate primarily to the use of foreign brand names or to the supply of specific technological services. On the other hand, such agreements can cover the entire range of technological requirements for the establishment of a production enterprise, including the use of foreign patents and trade names, production technology and know-how, and various technical services. In view of the wide variations in such agreements, and in the absence of any better measurement, although technology payments might be used as an indicator of technology flows, the severe constraints and limitations of such measurement should be considered in interpretation and evaluation.

The quantification of technology flows at a national level by government agencies—often compiled primarily for balance of payment purposes—is also not uniform in different countries. For example, in some countries, such as the United Kingdom, receipts from all turnkey arrangements are measured under exports.[15] Furthermore, several technology transactions among companies are undertaken on a technology-exchange basis that does not involve money flows and thus is not reported in the balance of payments.[16] Despite the various limitations of technology payments as a measure of international technology transfer, the overall payments for and receipts from technology transactions do provide broad indicators of the trend in technology flows and their destinations and sources of origin. Technology payments of a country over a period of time also provide a useful indicator of the long-term trends in foreign technology inflow, for the economy as a whole and for particular industrial sectors.

During the past two decades the volume of payments for technology and technical and management services has increased significantly. In 1965, technology receipts of five developed countries, notably the United States, the United Kingdom, France, West Germany, and Japan were $1.93 billion; by the early 1980s, they reached approximately $12 billion.[17] The highest receipts, $7.66 billion in 1983, which were obtained by the United States, rose from $1.53 billion in 1965.[18] Throughout the 1970s, the share of payments from developing countries in the total technology receipts of these major licensor countries increased, with the exception of Japan and West Germany. In the case of the United States, the share of developing countries in technology payments, 21.2 percent in 1970, increased to 26.9 percent in 1983; for the United Kingdom between 1970 and 1978, this share increased from 21.5 percent to 28.8 percent; and, during the same period, France's share increased from 13.4 percent to 24.3 percent.[19] Although, in the United States and Western European countries, technology payments from developing countries accounted for about 20 percent of total technology receipts, until the mid-1970s these countries were the major sources of licensing revenues in Japan. In 1972, for example, they accounted for 55.5 percent of total technology receipts in Japan. With the growing expansion of Japanese MNCs to Western Europe and the United States, the share of developing countries decreased to about 47 percent by the late 1970s.[20]

The overall trend of foreign investment and technology flows to developing countries indicates substantial increase during the past two decades. This growth has partly been the result of expansion of global operations of MNCs, reflecting the growing internationalization of capital and technology flows, which also has increasingly extended to developing countries. Developing countries, however, on the whole, still account for only about one-third of investment flows and 10 to 15 percent of global technology trade. The global trends in these flows, however, do not reflect the significant changes that have taken place during the period in the nature, composition, and direction of both foreign investments and technology transfer to these countries. These changes have been very significant with respect to the sectoral orientation of such investments and accompanying technology and in the types of technologies that have been transferred to developing countries. This period has also witnessed an increasing polarization among developing countries both in terms of the magnitude of investment and technology inflows and in the nature of MNC activities in these countries. Such differences have primarily been related, on the one hand, to individual developing country market conditions and, on the other, to the various strategic interests of MNCs in their internationalization of activities. These market conditions have been largely determined by the nature of industrialization strategies that have been pursued by host governments, which have created both opportunities and constraints for MNCs as suppliers of capital and technology. The next chapter discusses alternative strategies for industrial growth, particularly with respect to their impact on the technological development and the growth of technological capability in these countries.

Notes

1. R. Merrill, "The Study of Technology," in *International Encyclopedia of the Social Sciences,* ed. D. Sills (New York: Macmillan & The Free Press, 1968), vol. 15, p. 576.

2. Jack Baranson, *International Transfer of Industrial Technology by U.S. Firms and Their Implications for the U.S. Economy* (Washington, D.C.: U.S. Department of Labor, December 1976).

3. *Guidelines for the Acquisition of Foreign Technology in Developing Countries* (Vienna: United Nations Industrial Development Organization, 1973).

4. Baranson, *International Transfer.*

5. This point is argued, for example, in C.V. Vaitsos, "The Process of Commercialization of Technology in the Andean Pact," in *International Firms and Modern Imperialism,* ed. H. Radice (Harmondsworth, England: Penguin, 1975).

6. The traditional pattern of technology transfer through wholly owned foreign subsidiaries is discussed, for example, in J. Baranson, "Technology Transfer through the International Firm," *American Economic Review* 60(May 1970): 435–40.

7. Capital goods exports from OECD countries to developing countries increased from $16.7 billion in 1970 to $122.6 billion in 1980 at current values (Paris: OECD, *Trade in Commodities,* 1983).

8. For the growing role of consulting engineering firms in technology transfer to developing countries, see J. Perrin, "Consulting Engineering—A New Form of Technological Dependence in Developing Countries," in *The New International Division of Labour, Technology and Underdevelopment,* ed. D. Ernst (Frankfurt am Main and New York: Campus Verlag, 1979).

9. The role of technological development objectives of developing countries is presented in detail in *Technological Transformation of the Third World—Issues for Action in the 1980's,* UNCTAD/TT/9 (Geneva: UNCTAD, 1978). The relationship between technological self-reliance and technological development was the subject of the 24th Pugwash Symposium, "Self-reliance and Alternative Development Strategies," Dar-es-Salaam, June 1976. The concept of technological self-reliance is discussed in detail in F.R. Sagasti, "Technological Self-reliance and Co-operation among Third World Countries," *World Development* 4(1976): 939–46.

10. Most recently, technological objectives and needs of developing countries in the context of self-reliance were the subject of the Jamaica Symposium. See *Mobilizing Technology for World Development* (Washington, D.C.: International Institute for Environment and Development, March 1979).

11. *Transnational Corporations in World Development—Third Survey* (New York: United Nations, 1983).

12. Ibid.

13. U.S. Department of Commerce, *Survey of Current Business* (Washington, D.C.: U.S. Government Printing Office, various issues).

14. "Overseas Royalties and Similar Transactions in 1977," in *Trade and Industry* (London: Department of Trade and Industry, 1980).

15. Publications on intrafirm technology payments by the Board of Trade in the United Kingdom indicate the following limitations on the data. Statistics on the share of intrafirm technology payments from the total payments are assessed on the basis of a sample of 1,200 companies contacted, rather than on the total number of companies engaged in technology. Payments are not assessed when they form part of payments incorporated in the contract price of capital goods. According to the Board of Trade, this omission is most significant in the case of large contracts, such as turnkey projects for the erection of plants, in which the technology transfer is part of the total agreement and receipts from the entire contract would appear under export revenues rather than licensing revenues. See "Overseas Royalties and Similar Transactions in 1975," in *Trade and Industry* (London: Department of Trade and Industry, 12 April 1977), 293; also, W.B. Reddaway, S.J. Potter, and C.T. Taylor, *Effects of U.K. Direct Investments Overseas* (Cambridge: Cambridge University Press, 1968).

16. The Deutsche Bank states, for example, "Technology receipts do not give a complete picture because not every transfer of technological know-how is connected with corresponding flow of money. In many instances, enterprises exchange technological know-how without statistically recordable payments or accounting involved. Sometimes, various companies interested in the results share in the research costs. Payments for such future know-how are made as contributions to costs and not as licence payments." See "Patents and Licence Transactions with Foreign Countries," *Montly Report of the Deutsche Bank* 28(April 1976).

17. Data for the United States are from U.S. Department of Commerce, *Survey of Current Business,* various issues; for Japan, *Annual Report of Foreign Technology Initiation, Office of Science Technology* (Tokyo: Office of Science Technology, 1981), 56; and *Costs and Conditions of Technology Transfer through Transnational Corporations,* ST/ESCAP/283 (Bangkok: United Nations), table 1.

18. U.S. Department of Commerce, *Survey of Current Business,* various issues.

19. *Technology Transfer to Developing Countries,* Analytical Study No. 2, DSTI/SPR/79.32 (Paris: OECD, October 1979), 51; for the United States, U.S. Department of Commerce, *Survey of Current Business,* various issues.

20. OECD, *Technology Transfer to Developing Countries,* 1979.

2
Industrial Strategy
and Technological Development

Although the importance of technological development has been increasingly recognized, few developing countries adopted explicit policies toward industrial technology until the late 1960s. It was generally believed that policies designed to achieve industrial growth would also result in technological development. Although this chapter is not intended to cover the wide range of economic and industrial policies for accelerating industrialization in these countries, it does examine the impact of certain industrialization strategies on technological development. These strategies have been considered under the two broad categories of import substitution and export-oriented industrial development. Import substitution has been a major objective in most developing countries from the early stages of industrial development. In recent decades, however, export-oriented industrial growth has received increasing attention in many countries, and a wide range of policies have been adopted for this purpose. Governmental policies and measures for import substitution and export-oriented manufacture have influenced not only the pattern of industrial investments but also the development of technological capabilities in various industrial sectors. Most industrial production in these countries, except for cottage and small-scale industries, has been based on foreign technology, which has been either embodied in machinery and equipment or transferred as part of foreign investments and through contractual arrangements for the supply of technology or technological services. The impact of alternative industrial strategies on technological growth has obviously varied from sector to sector and has depended on the nature of the industry, the complexity of the technology and know-how involved, the level of domestic technological infrastructure available, and the relationship between foreign suppliers of technology and domestic production enterprises. Nevertheless, the effects of import-substitution policies, with their emphasis on reduction of imports of finished products, components, and intermediate products, tend to differ from those of export-oriented industrial strategy. Of course, most developing countries have emphasized the development of exports of manufactured products over a period of time, but the initial strategy at early stages of industrialization has had considerable effect on technological development. Another important aspect of industrial strategy, which will also be examined in this chapter, is the growth and impact of state-owned enterprises and expansion of private-sector industrial groups in these countries. Regional integration efforts and their constraints among groups of developing countries are reviewed also.

Import Substitution

Policies for import substitution have constituted a basic framework for industrialization in most developing countries. With a shortage of foreign exchange and expanding local demand, there has been a growing emphasis on import substitution, both to conserve foreign exchange and to expand the local industrial base. These policies were initiated in several countries during the 1950s and 1960s and were extended to consumer durable and nondurable goods as well as to other intermediate products. As a result, manufacturing activities were diversified considerably in several Latin American countries, in South and Southeast Asia, and, to a lesser extent, in some African countries.

Most Third World developing countries have provided a wide range of incentives for the establishment of new industries and the expansion of existing enterprises. In countries where local entrepreneurial initiative has been lacking, MNC subsidiaries have played a critical part in setting up production capacity to meet local market demand where initially they had focused mainly on consumer-goods manufacture and on the establishment of industries designed to utilize the natural resources of these countries. Foreign investments were generally encouraged and, apart from various fiscal and tax incentives such as tax holidays, accelerated depreciation provisions, loan capital on favorable terms and duty-free imports of machinery and equipment, locally produced goods were protected by import restrictions or high tariffs. The flow of industrial technology accompanied foreign investments in most cases, with choice and extent of use of particular technologies being determined by user MNC subsidiaries and affiliates.

Generally, import substitution was initially undertaken for nondurable consumer goods and gradually expanded to the manufacture of durable consumer goods such as electrical appliances. In several countries, domestic manufacture was further extended to the production of simple industrial products from pumps and electric motors to automobile and truck assembly. Foreign subsidiaries and affiliates played a major role in import substitution in a number of countries. Their strong position was favored by the access to financial and technological resources of their parent companies and financial institutions and by market acceptance for their products in developing countries, which had been built up through earlier exports to these markets. Whether the locally manufactured products were consumer or industrial products, they were largely based on foreign technology and used foreign trademarks and brand names. This was so not only for foreign subsidiaries and affiliates, but also for domestically owned companies, which gradually obtained licenses and production technology from foreign technology suppliers. The acquisition and use of foreign technology was necessary in most cases, and utilization of foreign brand names by these companies improved the marketability of their products significantly.

As import substitution progressed from the manufacture of nondurable consumer goods to certain intermediate products and industrial machinery, the local content of such manufacturing activities began fairly low, and most of the initial transfer of foreign technology was largely for assembly operations and for production of simple engineering parts and components. In mining and resource-based industries, local production was mostly confined to the initial processing of ore and other natural resources. These activities were mostly undertaken by foreign subsidiaries, though, in some countries, joint ventures with local industrial groups also gradually became fairly common.

Low vertical integration of production by foreign subsidiaries requires a relatively small investment for the parent company to meet local production requirements. At the same time, the supply of parts and components and other inputs from the parent company compensated the MNC substantially for the loss of export markets for finished products, which resulted from import substitution policies. For the MNCs, local assembly operations or the local production of only a relatively small proportion of the final product also limited the need for transferring comprehensive technological capabilities to their foreign subsidiaries.

Over a period of time, however—particularly during the late 1960s and early 1970s—national governments in several developing countries, especially in Latin America and parts of Asia, began to exert greater pressure for increasing the local content of production. In most cases, these measures were primarily aimed at reducing the growing import bill that had resulted from the high import intensity of production by foreign subsidiaries and domestic companies. Although both had high import propensity, empirical evidence suggests that, in the same field of production, the import propensity of foreign subsidiaries exceeded that of domestically owned companies.[1] This has been partially due to the relatively limited size of most developing country markets, which prevented efficient production of various parts and components with the mass-production technology available to MNCs. Partly, however, this resulted also from the MNC's strategy of utilizing existing production facilities in the home country or of subsidiaries (usually located in industrialized countries) in order to limit investments in developing country markets. The rapid growth of imports in the earlier stages of import substitution in most developing countries resulted not only from foreign sourcing of capital goods but, even more significantly, also from the continuous imports of parts and components and various intermediate products in sectors where local production had been undertaken.

Under government pressure, partly as a result of the growing local markets, local content in most import-substitution industries has increased considerably in these countries. This has taken place either by extending vertical integration of local manufacture—requiring larger investments by the enterprises concerned—or through a process of greater horizontal integration, which has involved local purchase of inputs from domestic supplier industries. With extended vertical integration, increase in the depth of production by local subsidiaries and affiliates required additional technology and know-how, usually supplied by the MNCs concerned. To achieve a higher local content by purchase from local suppliers, these companies had to establish subcontracting relationships with domestic firms and to import technology and know-how for specific parts and components. In either case, there was greater need for technology transfer and, since MNCs played an important role in such manufacturing activities, the technological requirements were primarily for foreign techniques and processes.

With increased industrialization, the demand for various industrial machinery and equipment has grown rapidly in most countries, and an important aspect of import substitution in several developing countries involves the degree to which the manufacture of industrial machinery, such as electrical and mechanical equipment, is undertaken locally. The demand for machinery and equipment has also grown considerably as a result of efforts to modernize agriculture through increased mechanization and extensive irrigation systems. This has resulted in much greater demand for agricultural machinery such as tractors and harvesters, along with pumps, diesel engines and other agricultural equipment. In most countries, however, the efforts to extend import substitution to the capital goods sector have encountered considerable difficulty in a slow and gradual process. Several factors have accounted for this: Besides the large capital investment required for machinery production, a long gestation period is also necessary for the development of specialized production skills. The domestic market for machinery and equipment in most developing countries has been small and often comprises mostly replacement equipment. Furthermore, industrial and import policies to promote import substitution in the consumer and intermediate-goods sectors often exempted imported machinery and equipment from tariffs. In the absence of protection, local foreign and domestically owned companies could not expect to compete with duty-free imports in the initial years of production and thus refrained from undertaking local production of capital goods. Also, local manufacturers of consumer and intermediate goods, particularly foreign subsidiaries but also domestically owned enterprises, preferred to import their capital goods even if similar machinery was being manufactured by local industry. This tendency was further strengthened by the provision of foreign supplier credits, which domestic manufacturers of capital goods could seldom offer.

It is only in a relatively few developing countries that substantial import substitution has been achieved in the capital goods sector. These countries include Argentina, Brazil, India, the Republic of Korea, and Mexico, though more recently, much export-oriented machinery production has also developed in Hong Kong, Singapore, and Taiwan. In these countries, import substitution in machinery and equipment production has followed a rather similar pattern. In most of these countries, which include those with the highest level of industrialization among developing countries, there was already a fairly strong indigenous base for production of engineering goods by domestic companies, usually in the small or medium-scale industrial sector. Such companies manufactured various types of commonly used machinery and equipment, mainly by copying imported equipment and adapting it to local market conditions. With the extention of import substitution into more complex machinery and parts, however, technology acquisition through such reverse engineering became more difficult and local companies turned to foreign licensors. The result was considerable inflow of technology and a heavy reliance on foreign sources of technology.

The growth of domestic production capacity in machinery and engineering goods manufacture in developing countries serves as a useful indicator of the level of industrial technological development, apart from the impact on import substitution. These sectors have significant backward and forward linkages with other production sectors and have a large potential for subcontracting and promoting the growth of auxiliary industries.[2] The creation of such linkages may be singled out as a fundamental element in development.

As a result of import-substitution policies that promoted local manufacture by foreign subsidiaries, MNC subsidiaries and affiliates have penetrated significantly into most industrial sectors in developing countries. The extent of foreign penetration was the strongest during the 1960s and early 1970s in Latin American countries, with the major share of foreign direct investments being made by MNCs from the United States. In Mexico, for example, MNCs increased their ownership and control in most technologically advanced industrial sectors and, by the 1970s, the estimated market share of foreign subsidiaries was 84 percent in rubber, 80 percent in tobacco, 79 percent in electrical machinery, 67 percent in chemicals, and 62 percent in nonelectrical machinery.[3] In 1972, about half of the 300 largest manufacturing firms were foreign controlled. In Brazil, the share of production of MNCs increased signficantly in most industrial sectors during the 1960s, often through takeovers of local enterprises. By the early 1970s, MNC subsidiaries occupied a dominant position in most technologically advanced fields of production.[4] In 1974, for example, foreign subsidiaries held a major share of the assets in several sectors: 100 percent in automobile manufacture, 85 percent in pharmaceuticals, 61 percent in rubber, 55 percent in machinery and equipment, and 45 percent in chemicals.[5] In the early 1970s, MNCs controlled 49 percent of the 300 largest Brazilian manufacturing firms.[6] In Argentina, sales by foreign subsidiaries in the manufacturing industry increased to 31 percent in the early 1970s from 18 percent in 1955.[7] Sales by such companies accounted for 96 percent in petroleum refining, 85 percent in motor vehicles, 82 percent in nonelectrical machinery, and 75 percent in the production of rubber.[8] By the mid-1970s, similarly high foreign ownership and control had taken place in smaller Latin American countries such as Chile,[9] Colombia,[10] and Peru.[11]

Although the role of MNCs expanded rapidly in early phases of import substitution in most developing countries, the nature and extent of MNC participation varied considerably. Major investments and transfer of complex technology and production skills took place only in the relatively few countries where large and growing internal markets allowed sufficient returns on investments. Apart from consumer good production, MNC participation focused mainly on certain industrial sectors, such as manufacture of chemicals, rubber, transport equipment, and certain electrical and nonelectrical machinery. MNC subsidiaries and affiliates, with their easy access to parent-company technology, parts and internal intermediates, had considerable technological advantage over local enterprises competing in the same or similar fields. This enabled foreign subsidiaries to develop a dominant market position in several sectors in most developing countries. Although, after the mid-1970s policy measures were gradually introduced in a number of developing countries to strengthen the position of domestically owned enterprises and to increase local capital participation in foreign-owned subsidiaries, the production, technological, and marketing leads already established by foreign subsidiaries have often strongly constrained the growth and expansion of domestically owned companies in a number of manufacturing sectors. The two major exceptions have been the state-owned enterprises established in several developing countries and the large private sector industrial groups, which have emerged in most industrially advanced Third World countries and are challenging the role of MNCs in several industrial sectors. Both these categories have, to a large extent, depended on industrial technology from an external source, but the nature and pattern of technology flow and acquisition have been significantly different from those of MNC subsidiaries.

State-Owned Public-Sector Enterprises

An important development with considerable impact on import substitution and domestic technological development in several developing countries, introducing new dimensions to corporate relationships, has been the growth of state-owned corporations that have been established even in countries where industrialization has primarily taken place through the private sector. State-owned enterprises have been set up in several critical manufacturing sectors such as steel, machinery and equipment, and electronics in countries such as Algeria, Brazil, Egypt, Iran, and Mexico and in mining and resource-based industries in Brazil, Burma, India, Indonesia, Mexico, Peru, Tanzania, and Zambia. There are also petroleum exploration, refining, and distribution in a number of developing countries.

State-owned enterprises in Third World developing countries have been established to ensure state control of the pattern of growth and to allow adequate channeling of investment in critical sectors of the economy. In some countries, mostly those with socialist orientation, public sector ownership has been primarily motivated by the belief that certain key sectors of the economy should be owned and controlled by the state, with the state-owned enterprise as the mechanism for the implementation and operation of industrial activities. In these countries, state-owned or public sector enterprises were either new or were established following the nationalization of foreign-owned companies. The nationalization of foreign companies, however, has not always been related purely to ideological considerations but more often has reflected the desire for national ownership and control over critical sectors of the economy. This was particularly so in the nationalization of foreign assets in utilities, transportation, and in the petroleum and mineral sectors. National ownership in infrastructure activities and in basic industries was considered necessary for the provision of effective control over vital economic activities and for the achievement of broader development objectives. In market-oriented economies, public sector enterprises were also established to cover major production and technological gaps in the economy and, to that extent, supported the growth of the private sector. Consequently, in the last two decades, several basic industries were set up through state-owned undertakings in a number of developing countries. Most of these industries required large initial investments and long gestation periods. Private sector investments would not have been forthcoming for most of these projects. Then, too, in several developing countries, state-owned enterprises have been established for the production of equipment and specialized products required for defense and military activities.

During the 1970s, the activities of state-owned enterprises in these countries extended into various fields of manufacture. The same policy principles were applicable in this extension of production activities. However, another form of state participation also developed during this period, with government financial institutions playing a more active role through their participation in equity capital of private sector companies. Financing institutions participated both in foreign and domestic companies in various industrial branches. Institutions such as Nacional Financiera in Mexico, the Banco

Nacional de Desenvolvimento Economico (BNDE) in Brazil, the Industrial Finance Corporation and, later, the Industrial Development Bank in India and parastatal financial institutions in Kenya and other African countries have played an increasingly important role as partners in ownership to cover the gap in industrial investments, particularly in sectors considered to be essential to the country's development. The role of government financing institutions has generally been confined to capital participation and other financial assistance, rather than to active participation in management, although some of these institutions are paying much greater attention to investment and other important decisions by enterprises in which they have substantial holdings. In several instances, initial investments by development banks have also often been undertaken with a view to divesting these investments to the private sector once the profitability of the operations has been established.

In terms of their impact on import substitution, public sector enterprises can broadly be considered under four categories. First, state-owned units generally deal with infrastructure activities, particularly electricity generation and rail transport. Second, they have been set up in basic industrial sectors—for example, steel production or resource-based industries such as petroleum, fertilizers, and petrochemicals, and mining and mineral-based industries. Third, these enterprises have been established in high-priority industrial branches, including those requiring large capital outlays and long gestation periods, such as the manufacture of machinery and equipment. Fourth, state-owned firms have also been established for various service activities, including consulting engineering, hotel operations, and the like. In all these fields, these enterprises have had considerable impact on import substitution and the level of technological development.

In most developing countries, electricity generation and distribution is undertaken through state-owned enterprises. This is because this constitutes a basic infrastructure for industrial growth and because it involves large capital investment that can best be provided by government. Thus, Electrobras operates as a utility holding company in Brazil, coordinating the plans for major generation and transmission facilities. These functions, including the responsibility for the bulk supply of electricity, in certain cases, are performed in Egypt by the Egyptian Electricity Authority; by various State Electricity Boards in India, since power generation and distribution falls under the jurisdiction of state governments, though coordinated by the Central Electricity Authority; by the Perusuhaan Listric Negava (PLN) in Indonesia; by the Comision Federal de Electricidad in Mexico; and by the Electricity Generating Authority (EGAT) in Thailand. Only in a few developing countries—for example, the Philippines—are any major utility concerns still privately owned. Apart from achieving better planning of power generation and transmission, state enterprises in this sector have played an important role in import substitution through development of local production of electrical equipment and in increasing local technological capability in planning and executing large thermal, hydroelectric, and nuclear projects for electrical power generation. In transportation, rail transport is generally operated by state-owned agencies, leading to considerable import substitution for railway equipment. This has been successfully achieved in India, where the state-owned railway organization has itself undertaken the manufacture of most of its railway equipment requirements, including railwagons, steam and diesel engines, electrical equipment, signaling machinery, and other items for rolling stock—to the extent that India's entire demand is fully met through domestic production and some products such as railwagons have also been exported to several countries. In Mexico, too, several items of railway equipment are manufactured by a state-owned enterprise. This is likely to emerge as an important trend in other developing countries also.

The production of iron and steel has often been undertaken by public sector corporations in several developing countries—in Brazil by Compania Siderurgica Nacional, in India by Hindustan Steel, in Mexico by Altos Hornos de Mexico S.A. (AHMSA), and in state-owned steel plants in Egypt and Libya. This not only has resulted in substantial import substitution but also has led to considerable growth of skills and technology in a basic metallurgical industry. It is, however, in the fields of petroleum and minerals that state-owned enterprises have played the most critical role. During the last two decades, petroleum operations, including drilling, processing, and refining, have been nationalized in a number of countries. During the 1970s, state-owned corporations also entered into the manufacture of petrochemicals in OPEC countries and in other developing countries such as Bangladesh and India. The establishment of state-owned companies in these fields represented an important stage in economic development. Through these enterprises, it was possible to increase earnings from petroleum and petroleum-based industries as well as to develop local technological skills in various stages of production and operations. Although the operations of state-owned petroleum companies in OPEC countries did not directly result in greater import substitution, they have had a major impact on the balance of payments and are gradually bringing about significant restructuring in global petroleum and petrochemical production. The development of production-sharing agreements and service contracts with oil companies from the United States and other industrialized countries by the state petroleum companies of OPEC and other developing countries also represents an important stage in the development of contractual arrangements between resource-rich developing countries and MNCs from industrialized countries. In mining, several agreements entered into during earlier periods, even those with former colonial regimes, were renegotiated to provide a greater share of income and participation in decision making to state-owned institutions and enterprises in host countries. An important aspect of renegotiations in these cases has been forward linkages in ore processing, which could be undertaken locally. This could have a significant impact on the balance of payments of these countries.

Besides their influence on such basic industries as iron and steel, public sector enterprises in several developing countries have played an important role in the production of fertilizers and chemicals and the manufacture of machinery and equipment. Fertilizer manufacture has been undertaken through state-owned corporations in several developing countries in Asia and the Middle East, resulting in much import substitution in these agricultural economies. Production facilities have been established in the public sector in India, Bangladesh, Indonesia, and the Middle East. In petrochemicals, public sector enterprises in Algeria, Saudi Arabia, Kuwait, Indonesia, Mexico, and other oil-producing countries, together with state-owned corporations such as Petrobras in Brazil, the Indian Petrochemical Corporation in India, and state-owned companies in Pakistan, Thailand, and other oil-importing countries, are playing an increasingly significant role in import substitution in the development of production and technological capabilities.

Another important production sector covered by state-owned corporations is machinery and equipment. Capital goods production (including machine tools and mechanical and electrical equipment) was undertaken through state-owned undertakings in the 1950s by Nasser in Egypt. The largest import substitution in the capital goods sector through domestic machinery manufacture by state-owned corporations, however, was achieved in India during the 1960–80 period. A number of state-owned enterprises were established to cover major production gaps in electrical and mechanical equipment and major parts and components; during the past two decades, these companies have established production capacities for the local manufacture of most of the country's domestic needs in various categories and ranges of machinery and equipment. In other developing countries—for example, Algeria—the role of state enterprises has been very significant in import substitution in electrical machinery, electronics, and other high-technology industries. State enterprises are also operating in several other production areas, including pharmaceuticals, coal, copper and aluminum production (in India), plantations (in Sri Lanka), and agricultural and food-processing industries (in Bangladesh and in Tanzania). In a number of countries, the range and coverage of these enterprises has expanded considerably in recent years.

Along with the achievement of a great deal of import substitution, the establishment of state-owned enterprises and the channeling of substantial investments through such enterprises has had a major impact on the development of production and technological capabilities in these countries. The large size of the production facilities operated by these enterprises has led to considerable development of specialized skills in the concerned sectors. In some of the firms, skill development has been a very slow process, and production capacity has not been adequately utilized for several years at a time. Nevertheless, the foreign technology on which these enterprises have been based has been gradually absorbed, and with the basic production facilities in position, these enterprises are likely to become increasingly productive in the next few years. In many cases in the past, the criticism often leveled at these enterprises for being inefficient and badly managed have been justified, but gradually the managerial and other weaknesses that have plagued many of these enterprises have been overcome. The fact that there is no foreign partner has often enabled state-owned companies to acquire foreign technology from several sources, which has been a great advantage. The bargaining strength of these companies, which generally occupy monopolistic or oligopolistic positions in their countries, has been much stronger with foreign technology suppliers than has the bargaining power of private sector licensees from the same country. Since the fields in which these enterprises operate are generally closed to foreign investors and imports, the only avenue by which MNCs can enter these markets is through technology licensing to these enterprises. Although several MNCs had reservations about public sector companies during the 1960s, it is now recognized that these enterprises have come to stay and provide an effective channel for technological participation. With greater experience in negotiations for the acquisition of technology and know-how and after evaluation of various alternatives, most state enterprises generally show well-negotiated agreements. It has also been possible for such enterprises to have greater flexibility in the regulatory norms and guidelines applied to foreign technology inflow in their respective countries. Although such norms are applicable to government-owned enterprises also, exceptions are often made in their cases, partly because they are state-owned and partly because they often are engaged in specialized production fields that are usually not covered by private sector companies.

In many cases, local governments have promoted the technological development of public sector enterprises by giving them preferential treatment in the acquisition of required foreign technology, and prevailing regulations regarding foreign technology have not been applied so rigorously as they have been to private sector companies. This has, however, also been partly related to the fact that public sector companies operate in priority or key industrial sectors, and considerable flexibility is often necessary in these sectors if adequate technology inflow is to take place. Political pressure by public companies and other government bodies has, however, also played a role. As a result, public sector companies have often been permitted to make higher payments for technology than would have been allowed to private companies. Contracts of public sector enterprises also contain export restrictions that otherwise would have been prohibited. Production by public sector enterprises, however, at least during the initial years of production, is aimed mainly at covering domestic demand; therefore, certain export restrictions for limited periods do not severely affect the operations of such companies. In most cases, global export restrictions have not been allowed, usually to ensure that exports within the particular geographical regions are permitted. In countries where rather strong foreign-exchange control measures are applied, public sector enterprises have been given the highest preference in the required foreign exchange for technology payments and for imports of associated machinery and equipment.

Apart from their role in acquisition and absorption of foreign technology, many of these enterprises have played an important part in technological adaptations. They have been able to diversify into various product lines of increasing complexity by acquiring foreign technology from new sources and by undertaking local adaptations. The initiatives taken in this regard by PEMEX (Mexico), Petrobras (Brazil), and the Fertiliser Corporation and Hindustan Steel (India) exemplify the opportunities available to such organizations for adaptive research. Close contact has also been maintained by these enterprises with local R&D institutions.

The favorable position of state-owned enterprises in acquiring foreign technology has had both positive and negative results. Their access to foreign exchange for acquisition of technology has allowed them to obtain a wide range of technologies from various sources, including some of the most advanced technologies in their respective fields of operation. Though in-house technological R&D capabilities have developed rather slowly, particularly in early stages of operations, there has been fairly rapid absorption of foreign technology and its adaptation to local conditions. The pattern of technology acquisition by public sector companies has also gradually changed over time. During the early period of their operation, their relatively low technological capability made these companies focus on the effective absorption of foreign technology and production know-how. At that time, technological services of foreign suppliers mostly involved assistance with production and engineering problems. Gradually, however, capabilities in design and technological adaptation have been acquired. Also, the necessary time for absorption of foreign technology has been reduced, often allowing project completion within the prescribed contractual duration.

Although state-owned companies have had certain advantages in technology negotiations and much greater freedom to select from available technological alternatives, the fact that technology and know-how are obtained solely through licensing arrangements and without any foreign equity participation has also been an important constraint. Without any foreign partner, the responsibilities for effective technological absorption have rested wholly on these companies, with their foreign licensors functioning purely within the terms and conditions of their agreements. Training programs in particular have posed considerable problems and have often proved inadequate, leading to a slow pace of absorption. After a particular technology has been absorbed, there has also been a tendency to continue with the same know-how for indefinite periods. While this may be adequate for internal markets, it can become obsolete and unsuitable when applied to exports.

State-owned enterprises have had considerable impact on the domestic development of technological services. When these plants were initially established, it was often on a turnkey basis, with foreign manufacturers and consulting engineering companies being responsible for various stages, including feasibility studies, detailed engineering, production know-how, and plant installation and start-up.[12] As recently as the early 1970s, product-in-hand agreements were being entered into by Algerian state enterprises and foreign parties. These agreements extended beyond the turnkey concept and required that the final product be produced by the contractor according to the specifications of the agreement. The supply of turnkey projects was often accompanied by foreign credits and tied aid that covered the initial financial requirements for foreign equipment and inputs. Turnkey supply arrangements were entered into both by companies from Western industrialized countries and by state enterprises from the Soviet Union and Eastern Europe.

There has, however, been considerable development of technology service capability in many developing countries, and state enterprises have played an important part.[13] In several countries, consulting engineering organizations have been set up by governments, either for general industrial consulting services or for consulting engineering in particular sectors, although the provision of technological services through state-owned corporations in developing countries has been a relatively recent development. Certain construction projects of the People's Republic of China, such as the Tanzania-Zambia railway, and some projects of Indian consortia in the Middle East were undertaken, however, through the public sector. It was not until the 1970s that state-owned consulting engineering organizations were established in some developing countries. In India, these included Engineers India for chemical and petrochemical projects, MECON for steel plants, and National Industrial Development Corporations (NIDC) for a number of medium-sized industrial projects. Organizations similar to NIDC have been set up in several developing countries, primarily to draw up feasibility and technical studies for local projects. In many of these organizations, however, basic engineering and detailed engineering work is done largely through linkages with foreign consulting organizations. Nevertheless, the provision of consulting services through state-owned bodies has provided considerable technical support for industrial projects aimed at import substitution and has also directly brought about considerable import substitution in an important service sector.

Major state enterprises have also developed their own technological service capabilities and are directly taking up project planning and engineering and assessment of technological alternatives, besides assuming supervisory responsibilities in various stages of implementation and operations. This has been particularly evident in organizations dealing with electricity generation and distribution, where considerable in-house capabilities have been developed by state-owned utilities and other government agencies. Although foreign consulting and management companies will continue to play an important role in most developing countries, there is a considerable increase in local capabilities in technological services, often through state-owned enterprises.

The overall pattern of technological development in state-owned enterprises in developing countries, however, still indicates considerable dependence on foreign sources of technology for the manufacture of new products or applying new processes. In several countries, though, the rapid development of technological capabilities and R&D activities by such enterprises in recent years often constitute the major local efforts toward industrial research. The role of state enterprises is likely to become increasingly important during the next decade. In some of the large developing countries, such as Brazil, India, and Mexico, major investments have already been made through these enterprises, which are likely to expand further in sectors such as petroleum, steel, chemicals and fertilizers, mineral development, and capital goods manufacture. In other developing countries, also—for example, in Algeria, Bangladesh, Egypt, and Tanzania—the activities of state enterprises will continue to grow, since a number of these enterprises have already been established in various sectors. In countries where the level of industrial development is still relatively low, state-owned enterprises may have to be set up to channel industrial investments in important sectors of the economy if private sector investments are not forthcoming, particularly in sectors where import substitution is possible and desirable from a techno-economic viewpoint. In these countries, technological development may be increasingly led by such companies.

Private Industrial Groups

A significant feature in most Third World developing countries where considerable industrial growth has taken place has been the rapid expansion of several large, private sector industrial conglomerates, which are usually composed of a number of companies wholly owned by a family or group of national shareholders. These companies have emerged as important mechanisms for local technological development and for absorption of foreign industrial technology through licensing arrangements or joint ventures with MNCs. When industrialization programs were launched in these countries, these companies, which were usually family groups, took most of the initiative and embarked on major industrial expansion. Some of the companies concentrated on particular sectors, but most of these large, domestic companies and groups diversified in various fields of production and emerged as large and medium-sized conglomerates. With national policies geared toward increased domestic participation in ownership, these companies and groups took the lead in establishing joint ventures with MNCs and also increasingly acquired the holdings of local MNC subsidiaries as they were gradually divested and sold to local shareholders. In certain fields, national governments gave considerable financial and other support to these industrial groups, which remain fairly dominant in fields where foreign subsidiaries are not operating. In some cases, certain industrial groups have become identified with particular regimes, and their strength has largely derived from their association with particular leaders and political groups, causing difficulties when the regime changed. In most cases, however, the rapid growth of these companies has largely been the result of the exercise of greater entrepreneurial initiative at various stages of industrialization and in the acquisition and adaptation of foreign industrial technology. Thus, groups such as Alpha in Mexico, Industria Villares and Industria Matarozzo in Brazil, Tatas, Birlas and several others in India, and Hyundai, Samsung, Daewoo, and others in the Republic of Korea have grown very rapidly in a relatively short period of time and have extended their operations in several fields in response to growing industrial opportunities in these countries. As these locally owned industrial groups expanded their relationships with foreign companies, these linkages mainly took the form of joint ventures with minority foreign holdings or technology licensing agreements without foreign holdings.

The rapid growth of large domestic private sector groups, usually those controlled by particular families, has had varied response in certain developing countries. Although domestic companies were initially given every encouragement to undertake industrial investments, the rapid expansion of certain industrial groups has led to considerable concentration of economic and industrial power in the hands of a few family groups and may have further accentuated existing inequalities. Their domination of local industry in particular sectors has often been at the expense of small and medium-sized local companies. They have had close links with and support from banking institutions, both foreign and domestic, an important factor in their growth. In some cases, this has also led to overextension of their activities, resulting in the financial difficulties recently faced by the Alpha group in Mexico and the Matarozzo group in Brazil. One country that has imposed curbs on further expansion of these industrial groups is India, which, since the 1970s, has regulated the establishment of new production facilities by these groups and their subsidiaries and has limited their expansion mostly to certain core industries or export-oriented production. In some other countries, such as

Pakistan and Egypt, restrictions were imposed on certain industrial groups after changes in the regime. In other countries, however, particularly in Brazil, Mexico, and several Southeast Asian countries, the growth of domestic and foreign companies continues to be encouraged in the same manner, and no special facilities are provided to local industrial groups. In other countries, such as the Republic of Korea and the Philippines, these domestic industrial groups have received greater consideration and support, especially from government-owned or affiliated financial institutions.

The growth of domestically owned industrial groups and conglomerates in developing countries has been important in providing a strong domestic entrepreneurial and technological base, one that can usually compete effectively with MNC subsidiaries. The growth of such large private sector companies has led to increased domestic capital accumulation, along with technological and managerial know-how, in a number of production sectors. Although most of these companies base their production on foreign technology, the extensive inflow of technology through these companies constitutes an important factor in technological development. These private sector companies provide technological leadership in several fields and are able to compete with MNC subsidiaries in these sectors. With the access that such companies have had to local investment funds and financial institutions, they have had the necessary entrepreneurial and financial base for industrial expansion. The principal gap they have faced has been in industrial technology and production know-how. Once this was obtained through joint ventures and licensing agreements, these companies were able to expand their industrial operations rapidly. Although these private sector groups have performed valuable functions as conduits for technology inflow, their activities have resulted in a high degree of concentration of industrial and technological capability among relatively few locally owned enterprises in most of these countries.

Technological Impact of Import Substitution

The strategy for import substitution has had varying impact on technological development and the growth of technological capability in Third World countries. Although industrial investments and production have undoubtedly resulted in considerable technology transfer, application, and absorption in various fields, the overall technological impact has depended on several factors. These include the levels of skills and technological infrastructure available in the host country, the industrial sectors where such import substitution has taken place, the extent of domestic integration in manufacture in these sectors, and the nature of the relationships between local production enterprises and foreign suppliers of technology and know-how.

The technological impact of import substitution has, to a large extent, depended on the levels of industrial skills, as has entrepreneurial and managerial initiative in host developing countries. Where such skills have been totally lacking or available only to a minimal extent, the process of technological absorption has been very slow and has been mainly limited to simple technological applications. On the other hand, in countries such as Argentina, Brazil, Chile, and India, where the technological infrastructure was fairly well developed, the pace of technological absorption and adaptation has been quite rapid, enabling competitive production capacity to be developed in several fields, including those involving complex technology and know-how. Although the technological infrastructure is an essential prerequisite, however, it has to be combined with policies specifically designed to achieve technological development, including increased domestic integration.

The impact on local technological development has inevitably been limited to the sectors where import substitution has taken place. Since such substitution has mostly occurred with consumer goods and certain intermediate products, technological absorption and usage has been mainly in these fields. On the other hand, the overall impact on domestic technological development tends to be considerably greater in producer goods, particularly in the manufacture of machinery and equipment. This is so because more extensive technological absorption and diffusion are required for the variety of skills and know-how, which extend to supplier industries and user enterprises. In countries where there is little capital goods manufacture, the type of machinery imports by import-substitution industries also often determines the nature of technology utilized by these industries.

The manufacture of consumer and intermediate goods within the framework of import-substitution programs has been largely based on foreign technology and technical services, which have been used extensively by both MNC subsidiaries and domestic companies. The technological impact of such production has varied from country to country. In countries where only the final stage of production or assembly was undertaken locally, the extent of technology transfer remained extremely limited and was largely confined to that particular stage. However, as the degree of local integration in manufacture increased, the extent of technology application and absorption also became much greater in most industrial sectors. Foreign capital and technology have both played a critical role in import substitution, and MNCs have often been major participants in these programs. In several developing countries, where the inflow of foreign technology has not been regulated, the establishment of production facilities for import-substitution industries has often not taken adequate account of the need for development of local technological capability.

An important aspect of the import-substitution concept is the replacement of previous imports by local production. Narrowly conceived, this implies that the major participants in import-substitution activities are the previous exporters to those countries. These usually have been MNCs, which, under the pressure of import-substitution policies, have used their technology and expertise to establish local production. If local companies should wish to compete with such foreign subsidiaries, it would be necessary for them to acquire foreign technology and foreign trademarks to meet the competition of local MNC subsidiaries and the local preference for foreign brand names. Thus, the concept of import substitution, particularly as it was conceived and implemented in Latin American countries throughout the 1950s and 1960s, had a built-in bias for promoting the entry of MNC subsidiaries.

A high degree of technological dependence on their parent companies has characterized the operations of MNC subsidiaries in most import-substitution industries. This is also common, however, for most domestic companies because of their much weaker bargaining position in relation to foreign technology suppliers. The tendency in most of these companies has been to rely as far as possible on their foreign technology suppliers and licensors. The degree of continuing dependence on foreign sources of technology has tended to be much less, however, in the case of most state-owned enterprises. It is also less in the case of some of the large, privately owned industrial groups and companies in these countries, though initial operations are generally based on foreign technology. Their strong position in the local market and the government support, often in the form of permission to hold a monopolistic position, has enabled several of these large, nationally owned enterprises to increase domestic integration and, at the same time, retain effective control while acquiring most of their technological needs abroad. In the case of state-owned enterprises, however, there is criticism of the fact that technological capabilities have often been created at very high costs to national governments and that the cost-benefit ratio in most of these cases has been unsatisfactory. In the case of large, private sector industrial groups in these countries, although they have absorbed foreign technologies more rapidly than other private sector licensees, their strong market power has tended to limit the growth of a strong medium-scale sector, which can be an important feature of successful import-substitution programs.

It is inherent in the nature of import substitution that such industrial development is insulated from foreign competition, at least for a period of time. In the absence of effective competition, local manufacturers, both foreign-owned and domestic, have not had any strong motivation for acquiring or developing improved technologies and processes. The level of domestic integration in manufacture has tended to be slow also, except where governmental pressure has forced the pace. In most cases, this would have involved additional investments for new machinery and retooling, for training of the labor force, and for the acquisition of technology either from external sources or through internal development. Since foreign competition did not threaten loss of local markets, such expenses have generally not been incurred by local manufacturers. Insulation from external competition has also usually resulted in high-cost local production, at the expense of local consumers. The acquisition and development of the latest technologies for local markets and for exports may be essential and unless this can be ensured, import substitution may well lead to the continued use of obsolete processes and techniques. Access to technological innovations and development would also be essential if it would lead to higher productivity and to the manufacture of more efficient products. Import-substitution programs have not generally given adequate attention to the acquisition or development of technological improvements and have often resulted in technological capabilities becoming static and frozen at the level of initial import or acquisition.

Export Promotion

Policies and measures designed to achieve a higher degree of exports of nontraditional and manufactured products have received considerable attention in recent years. Most developing countries regard greater participation in global exports as essential for economic development. This focus of industrial strategy has been related partly to the experience with import-substitution policies and their limitations in several areas and partly to the increased foreign-exchange requirements of most of these countries. The dramatic growth of world trade in manufactured goods compared to primary commodities during the post–World War II period also clearly indicates that the increased export of manufactured goods constitutes a major factor in economic growth. In island economies, such as Hong Kong, Singapore, and Taiwan, an export-oriented strategy has been successfully pursued for over three decades because the small internal markets provide very limited scope for efficient import substitution, while favorable conditions, particularly cheap labor and geographic location, provide considerable potential for the local production and export of manufactured products. In most other countries, however, greater emphasis on exports of manufactured goods is more recent and has usually been combined with import-substitution policies in various industrial sectors.

Most developing countries have adopted a wide range of policies to increase the export performance of their enterprises, and companies engaged in export-oriented production can generally avail themselves of various fiscal and financial incentives, including direct export subsidies, import entitlements, and special facilities for import of capital goods, intermediates, and other inputs required for production. The first stage of manufactured exports from developing countries generally comprises textiles, shoes, wood, and leather products, which have become quite competitive in global markets and have secured substantial markets in industrialized countries. The export of more complex products, such as consumer durables, machinery and equipment, and engineering goods, from these countries has been far more difficult but has been achieved in several industrial bɪ .nches, especially in engineering goods and equipment. For example, a considerable range of electrical equipment and appliances and electronics products are exported from the Republic of Korea. Similarly, plant equipment, machine tools, hea y mechanical and power equipment, and other engineering goods are being exp ɔrted from India. Automobiles and other transport and mechanical equipment are exported from Brazil, along with a large variety of manufactured goods. Flour milling machinery and other equipment are being exported from Mexico. At the same time, engineering goods exports from Hong Kong, Singapore, and Taiwan have also registered a substantial increase. Exports of such products require international standards for quality and price as well as access to foreign distribution channels and to global markets. With well-known foreign products using trademarks and brand names that enjoy favorable market acceptance, manufacturers of similar products from developing countries have had to establish similar reputations over a period of time. This has required the use of modern industrial technologies and specialized marketing expertise, which is often acquired through MNCs operating in these markets. At the same time, in those developing countries that are exporting manufactured goods, considerable local marketing capability has developed, and it is largely production technology that is acquired from foreign sources.

Export-oriented manufacture, whether undertaken by domestically owned companies or by MNC subsidiaries, has relied heavily on foreign technology, more so than has production for the domestic market.[14] Domestic manufacturers often have acquired foreign technology in conjunction with the right to use the technology licensor's brand names in export markets. In most developing countries, however, domestically owned companies have not had adequate technological capability to produce a large variety of manufactured goods for exports. Their limited knowledge of export markets and problems of foreign distribution and service facilities have been additional constraints. Consequently, it is often expected in these countries that MNC subsidiaries and affiliates must play a major role in increasing nontraditional exports of manufactured goods. This has required some reorientation of policies toward foreign direct investments. Although, in most developing countries, the trend has been toward exercising greater regulatory control over the activities of foreign companies, an important and overriding exception has been made in the case of MNCs whose local production is largely designed for exports. Export-oriented operations have often been exempted from regulations that are applicable to foreign investments and are evaluated mainly on their contributions to a country's foreign exchange revenues.

Regulatory provisions for increased domestic integration are often not applied in such cases, and special facilities are given for imports of intermediate products, components, and other inputs. Thus, foreign subsidiaries engaged in export-oriented production have often been given exemption from regulations related to permissible fields of operations and have been allowed to retain 100 percent foreign holdings or foreign majority holdings. Besides relaxation of regulatory provisions for the entry of foreign investments, ownership structure, local content, and other such aspects, export-oriented companies have also been eligible for a comprehensive package of incentives that have been available to foreign subsidiaries, whether operating within or outside of export-processing zones.

Since the late 1960s, there has been much greater response by MNCs to incentives offered by developing countries for export-oriented production because of the rapid increase in labor costs in industrialized countries and the availability of cheap skilled and semiskilled labor in developing countries. MNCs that relocated some of their production activities to developing countries with the aim of utilizing these units for exports are primarily from industrial sectors where the production process (or certain stages of production) involves highly labor-intensive operations.[15] During the 1970s, a number of manufacturers in the electrical and electronics industries and producers of precision instruments and optical products established foreign subsidiaries, particularly in Southeast Asia. This was in addition to the export-oriented production of ready-made garments and other consumer products, which also increased considerably during this period. A number of production operations were also set up by U.S. companies along the U.S.-Mexican border. Favorable government policies toward foreign investments, relative political stability, and cheap, semiskilled and hardworking local labor enabled the manufacture of such products or components at a much lower cost than in industrialized countries. Usually, MNCs undertook such production to reduce product costs by decreasing the labor-cost component, a factor that has largely determined the type of export-oriented production by foreign companies and the extent of technology transfer. In these aspects, export-oriented foreign subsidiaries tend to differ from those producing mainly for import substitution in local markets. Since production is entirely or mostly for exports, the activity of the foreign subsidiary is fully integrated within the MNC's production and distribution strategy, and the unit operates as a part of the parent company.[16] Generally, these export-oriented units manufacture only one stage of the product, often assembly or parts that are exported to the parent company and to other foreign subsidiaries. This usually requires the transfer of the most recent technologies available, so as to meet competition in the home country of the parent company and in global markets. The technological needs of the subsidiary are limited, however, only to the production know-how for the specific task it performs, rather than for the entire product or for its design. Often, this narrow production task of the foreign subsidiary continues indefinitely—unless the subsidiary diversifies its production to other areas—since export-oriented foreign subsidiaries generally are not subject to the progressive increase in local content requirements.

The participation of MNCs in export-oriented strategy of developing countries has been uneven.[17] Most of these subsidiaries have been concentrated in a few countries, particularly in Southeast Asia and along the U.S.-Mexican border. Manufacturing activity has been in the relatively few industries that use labor-intensive processes not easily amenable to automation. Partial production is characteristic for most of this manufacture, except for relatively simple items, such as consumer electronics products, in which the entire product is manufactured.

The role of foreign technology has continued to be dominant in the export-oriented production of Third World developing countries. Although all the technological needs of export-oriented foreign subsidiaries are met by parent companies, MNCs have also been the major suppliers of technology and know-how to domestically owned companies producing for export, except for products such as textiles and shoes, for which local technology is adequately available. In countries where domestically owned industry has developed a substantial export capability, as in the Republic of Korea, Taiwan, Hong Kong, and Singapore, local companies have often entered into subcontracting relationships with MNCs and have manufactured parts, components, and intermediate products to their specifications. In such relationships, the required designs and production know-how, together with quality control, are usually provided by the foreign company.

Significant export capability for manufactured products has also been developed by large, domestically owned industrial groups and companies in a few countries, such as Brazil, India, the Republic of Korea, and Mexico. In most of these cases, the development of export capacity has been an extension of production and technological capability achieved initially through import substitution. In most instances, the initial technology was acquired from abroad and absorbed and adapted over time. License agreements for foreign technology have expired in many cases, and local companies have been free of contractual conditions restricting exports. Some of the important exporters of machinery and equipment have also been state-owned enterprises, for example, Bharat Heavy Electricals Ltd. (BHEL) and Hindustan Machine Tools Ltd. (HMT) in India. Often, domestic export-oriented companies have been the leading manufacturers, and their domestic sales have supported lower pricing for exports. In recent decades, these companies have also acquired and absorbed necessary foreign technology and expertise in their respective fields of operations to varying extents. They may not, however, be as efficient as the latest technologies in industrialized countries, and this may be a limiting factor in export efforts. With the increase of regulation of foreign technology in the countries, technology agreements containing global export restrictions are generally not permitted, and this may have considerable impact on acquisition of the latest techniques and processes.

In small and medium-scale companies in developing countries, however, limited access to the latest foreign technologies required for competing in global markets has been a major constraint. The latest technologies are generally difficult to obtain through licensing without equity participation, more so in the case of small and medium-sized companies that have relatively small scales of production. These companies have also had inadequate information on available foreign technological alternatives and development, often acquiring technology that is considerably behind recent technological developments. Rather slow absorptive abilities have further constrained such companies in fields such as electronics, where rapid technological changes have been occurring. At the same time, several medium-scale units from certain developing countries have been very successful in the more traditional exports, such as carpets and textile, where indigenous technology has been fully adequate.

In all but a few developing countries, exports of manufactured goods have grown relatively slowly and have fallen below earlier expectations. The slow progress has been partly due to import-substitution policies, which have insulated most of these markets from foreign competition, and partly due to increasing global competition in industrial products with a fairly standardized technology. Since the mid-1970s, with the growing foreign-exchange shortage in most countries, rapid increase in export revenues has assumed new urgency. Several host country governments have exerted pressure on MNC subsidiaries and affiliates in their countries to increase export activities and to make export commitments. Often, specific export performance has been prescribed for foreign subsidiaries. In some countries, these quotas have been related to imports by the subsidiaries. For example, in Brazil and Mexico, and earlier in India, imports by foreign subsidiaries must often be balanced by exports of the same or similar value.[18]

Export Processing Zones

During the last decade, several developing countries have established export processing zones (EPZs) as part of their industrialization strategy. The broad objectives for the creation of EPZs has been to accelerate industrialization, create employment, and develop exports. In several countries, more specific contributions, such as increased use of local raw materials, inflow of foreign capital and technology, and development of export skills have also been expected.[19] It has also been argued, though mostly by economists and representatives of industrialized countries, that EPZs would be a step toward interdependence between rich and poor countries and a hopeful sign that MNCs and developing countries can work together for mutual benefit.[20] It has also been considered that the location of such zones away from metropolitan centers can play an important role in the regional dispersal of industries, as in the Bataan Zone of the Philippines.

EPZs, similar to industrial estates, have been developed by host country governments by the establishment of infrastructure and other production facilities for prospective investors. In the case of EPZs, however, production in the zone is mainly restricted to foreign companies in most countries. When domestic companies are permitted to operate in the zones, they are usually involved in joint ventures with foreign companies. Besides providing infrastructure and related services, the government attracts foreign companies by providing a comprehensive package of incentives. This usually includes suspension of the regulations on foreign direct investments and technology, as well as on foreign-exchange control.[21] Capital goods, intermediate products, and raw materials can be imported free of duty to the zone where operation takes place in a bonded area. Often, foreign companies can use the facilities of the zone, including electric power and housing, at a subsidized rate and enjoy various fiscal and financial incentives, such as tax holidays, reduced tax rates, and subsidized interest rates for local borrowings.

Since EPZs have been expected to promote the implementation of several development objectives, there was a rapid increase in the creation of such zones during the 1970s, often through significant investments by local governments. In 1980, fifty-five developing countries had operating EPZs and about another twenty EPZs were in the process of construction.[22] About twenty of the existing zones are located in the Caribbean and Latin America and twenty are in Asia. MNCs using labor-intensive processes in production have taken considerable advantage of the incentives and facilities in the EPZs and the relatively low cost of labor. In several countries, companies operating in the zone have also been exempted from prevailing labor laws on minimum wage and working hours.

The activities of foreign subsidiaries in the zones have been concentrated mostly in a few industries. In the earlier stages of creation of such zones, most of the manufacturing activity was in the textile and garment industries. Since the mid-1970s, however, several MNCs manufacturing electrical and electronics products have established subsidiaries in various EPZs, particularly in Southeast Asia and along the U.S.-Mexican border. These subsidiaries produce mostly parts and components, such as semiconductors and chips, and assemble final products for the consumer electronics industry and, to a smaller extent, for industrial applications. These offshore operations are closely integrated within the MNC system; they receive required inputs from parent companies or other subsidiaries, and their final products are exported back to their home countries or to other export markets. The rapid growth of the global electronics industry, with its attendant labor-intensive and assembly operations, has caused this sector to emerge as the fastest growing industry in the EPZs. In Asian EPZs, for example, it is estimated that about

300,000 workers, or approximately half of the total labor force employed in the zones, are employed by the electronics industry.[23] In Mexico's Border Industries Program, about 60 percent of the *maquiladoras* are engaged in the assembly of electrical and electronics products.[24] Further activities in the zones include manufacture of parts and components and assembly of precision instruments, metal products, and leather and plastic goods. In 1981, the total labor force employed in the various EPZs of developing countries was estimated at about 1 million, 70 percent of whom were Asian.[25]

Technology transfer by foreign companies to their subsidiaries in the EPZs has been directly related to the type of operation. Such production has been characterized by a high import propensity and the specialization of the subsidiary in a narrowly defined production process, such as the manufacture of specific parts and components or the assembly activity. Although, with the rapid growth of the electrical and electronics industries in these zones, there has been a shift to the manufacture of more sophisticated products than the traditional textiles and garments, the specific phase of production of such goods has been very narrow in scope and has usually been confined to the simplest stages of production or assembly, with the more technologically complex activities completed in the home country of the MNCs. In semiconductor manufacture, for example, mask making and wafer fabrication, which are two sophisticated stages of production, are performed mainly in the home countries of the MNCs concerned.

Since production in these zones is for export rather than for domestic sales, the technological skills that are imparted to the labor force are seldom relevant to the needs of local industry. In the majority of EPZs, over 70 percent of the labor force is women, and most of their tasks as operators can be learned in one day to two weeks.[26] Such skills are mainly for a specific production phase of a component or product. Generally, these skills do not have a high degree of transferability to other industrial applications in the host country. Relatively low and routine skill development of the labor force has characterized the garment and textile industries and the transferred knowhow is also mostly partial and related to a specific production stage, as it is in the electrical, electronics, and precision instrument industries.[27] The firm-specific nature of the skills imparted further limits their transferability to other production activities.

Although limited technology transfer characterizes most EPZs, there has been some progress beyond this level in countries that have been able to be more selective in the industrial activities of these zones. In Singapore, Taiwan, and the Republic of Korea, for example, foreign companies intending to locate in the EPZs for the manufacture of light industrial products, such as textiles and garments, are not encouraged. At the same time, incentives are given to foreign manufacturers of more sophisticated products, such as engineering goods and industrial machinery. As a result of these policies, in the Masaan EPZ of the Republic of Korea, for example, manufacture of machinery and equipment has increased rapidly in recent years and well-diversified production has developed in the zone. This has been accompanied by a gradual increase in the share of locally manufactured inputs used by companies in the zone. In the Masaan Zone, imports amounted to 72 percent of exports in 1972; in 1978, this share decreased to 52 percent.[28] A similar increase in the usage of local inputs was found in Malaysia and in a number of other areas.[29] Although an increase in local value added through domestic suppliers makes important contributions to local industry, its direct impact on technological development is more difficult to measure. In Malaysia, for example, the local content provided by domestic suppliers covered a wide spectrum of products with varying degrees of technological sophistication, such as chemicals, steel, plywood, yarns, fibers, and leather. Increased production by local industry for subsidiaries in the zone may have encouraged domestic companies to meet the technological specifications of MNC subsidiaries and to achieve international standards. In such cases, however, the nature and extent of technology transfer by subsidiaries to local suppliers has not been studied in detail.

In a few countries, where export-oriented production has been pursued for two decades, diversification of production in the zone has gradually become more pronounced. In most of the EPZs, though, two principal factors have limited the technological contribution of foreign companies to local industry. First, since zones function largely as enclaves in the economy, their production is only marginally linked with domestic suppliers and users, prohibiting significant technological spillover to local industry. Second, since the functions of the offshore subsidiaries are narrowly defined and are closely integrated within the MNC system, the role of the subsidiary itself is defined very narrowly. Decisions on products, technology, and sales are made by the parent company and, consequently, such capabilities need not be transferred to the offshore subsidiary unit. The technology transferred to EPZ subsidiaries primarily takes the form of the training of the labor force, often predominantly female labor, for performance of firm-specific assembly or routine production activities.

Since production techniques imparted in the zone usually tend to be very limited, little export-marketing capability has been developed. With EPZ subsidiaries producing for the parent company and other subsidiaries, sales are intrafirm, and the need for the development of international marketing skills does not arise.

Technological Impact of Export-Oriented Production

The impact on technological application and adaptation of an export-oriented industrial strategy has been significantly different from that of import substitution. Export-oriented production must necessarily avail itself fully of the comparative advantages of local production—in most cases, the availability of much cheaper labor and particular resources or raw materials in developing countries. The type of technology to be utilized in export-oriented production must be geared to competitive factors in the external markets it is seeking to serve. The need to use the latests technologies for export-oriented production has increased the dependence on foreign technology. At the same time, technology owners seldom license their latest technologies to unaffiliated companies; these are usually transferred on an intrafirm basis, tending to increase the potential role of MNCs in export-oriented sectors.

Export-oriented production by MNC subsidiaries has been rather narrow in terms of both industrial sectors and production processes. Industrial sector activities are mainly limited to a relatively few, labor-intensive industries, while production processes are usually confined to a specific stage of production. Consequently, the technology transfer to export-oriented foreign subsidiaries has been very uneven among industrial sectors and has been directed mainly to meet their specific, narrowly defined needs.

Since export-oriented manufacture has to meet international quality and price competition, host countries have not imposed pressure on such companies to increase their local content. Thus, export-oriented production, particularly in the technologically advanced sectors for complex, high-technology components, and intermediate inputs has been highly import-intensive. So far as export-oriented, high-technology industries are concerned, local suppliers do not have the production and technological capabilities to supply most intermediate inputs for these subsidiaries. Because of the enclave characteristics of export-oriented foreign subsidiaries, even more in the export processing zones, technological linkages with local industry have been rather weak and are often absent.

The technological operations of export-oriented domestic companies tend to be different from those of MNC subsidiaries setting up production facilities primarily for exports. In the case of domestic companies, export capability has been achieved with greater knowledge and experience of production and technological development. Such companies do not always have access to recent production techniques, but they have been able, in several industries, to absorb and adapt foreign technology to their scales of production and other factor conditions, and they have been able to develop considerable export potential in several manufactured products. Although MNC subsidiaries engaged in export manufacture operate from the latest technological base, it is for a narrow field of production specialization and, in most cases, the technological impact on the host economy is very limited. Domestic companies exporting manufactured products, on the other hand, function from a production base covering most stages of production and from a broad technological base, often initially based on foreign technology but with limited access to latest technological development. From the viewpoint of technological development, this access can be of much greater significance.

Regional Integration

The efforts toward import substitution on a fairly broad and comprehensive scale have been a feasible industrial strategy only for countries with relatively large internal markets. In most developing countries, however, the small domestic market, among other factors, prohibited the establishment of industries that require large-scale production, because projected demand was significantly below the output of minimum efficient plant sizes. This was so for durable consumer goods, for several intermediate products, and for most categories of machinery and equipment. To overcome the limitations posed by inadequate local demand and to achieve closer economic and industrial links, efforts were made to establish certain industries on a regional basis through programs of regional integration. These programs have varied in scope and have ranged from free trade in a region for specific products to more comprehensive cooperation, including common industrial programming for certain sectors. Through such integration, it was intended to achieve both import substitution and closer industrial linkages on a regional basis in products that could not be produced efficiently at a national level. Although most efforts at regional integration have not been successful, the experience of Latin American countries is of special interest.[30]

The limitations in market size, sought to be met through regional programming, were not the only constraints to industrial development in most Latin American countries. The establishment of new industries in various industrial sectors, which integration aimed to promote, required not only new investments but also necessary technology and managerial expertise, which were often not available in these countries. Also, in several industrial sectors, MNC subsidiaries, which often considered the region as a single market, had already set up production. It was easier for these companies to expand to meet the increased demand than it would have been to establish new production facilities, particularly by domestically owned companies. To some extent, domestic enterprises were participants in the joint ventures set up in the region; in any case, most of them were dependent on foreign technology and expertise.

Some studies of integration efforts in Latin America and Africa suggest that although integration had aimed to accelerate industrialization in the region and to reduce external dependency, it has tended, instead, to increase the dominant role of MNCs in the member countries, and such companies have been the major beneficiaries of such programs.[31] This pattern has characterized the Union Douaniere des États d'Afrique Central (UDEAC), the

Latin American Free Trade Association (LAFTA), the Central American Common Market (CACM), and the Andean Pact. Because of the relatively weak domestic production and technological capabilities, MNCs were able to take advantage of the growing export possibilities in the region and, through their access to capital and advanced technology, have dominated the newly established industries under the various complementary agreements.

In 1974, in the LAFTA region, for example, it was noted that under Complementary Agreement No. 10 and 11, which related to office equipment, more than 97 percent of the exports were undertaken by MNCs.[32] A major shift of the exports of other products was also dominated by MNCs.[33] Similarly, in Central America ten years after the formation of the market, MNC subsidiaries had increased their exports from 40 to 60 percent of the region's exports.[34] The dominant position of MNC subsidiaries in the region emanated from their strong technological capabilities, their ability to mobilize financial means, and their organizational structure, which permitted them to utilize free trade within the region for exports to their own affiliates. In the absence of efficient industrial planning in the member countries, the MNCs' ability to allocate their production according to each country's own efficiency, size, and so forth, their technological expertise, and their access to export markets made them more competitive than domestic companies.[35]

Drawing on the experience of earlier regional integration efforts, the region adopted a more comprehensive approach toward the treatment of foreign direct investments and technology and toward industrial programming in the formation of the policies of the Andean Group. A common policy and regulatory approach to foreign investments and technology by member countries was considered necessary to counteract the behavior of MNCs, which often tended to take maximum advantage of the incentives in the region and, consequently, reduce the bargaining position of member countries. Such a coordinated approach was new to regional integration in developing countries and to regional industrialization. The concepts underlying the approach of the Andean Group were also motivated by the member countries' objective of reducing the region's dependence on imports, foreign capital, and technology and allowing the region to progress toward self-sustained development.[36]

The Andean Group was set up by Bolivia, Chile, Ecuador, Peru, and Venezuela, although Chile later withdrew from the group. By the early 1970s, fairly detailed programs were developed for regional allocation and assignment of production for the metalworking and petrochemical industries, the first two programs approved by the members of the Andean Group. In 1970, Decision 24, "Common Treatment of Foreign Capital, Trademarks, Patents, Licensing Agreements and Royalties" was approved.[37] Industrial programming within the region, together with a common regulatory approach toward foreign investments and technology, were intended not only to channel foreign capital and technology according to the priorities of the region, but also to improve the bargaining position of domestic companies in relation to MNCs and to pursue self-reliant development.

Subsequent studies on the performance of the metalworking and petrochemical industries in the region, however, have shown the various constraints and difficulties encountered in the pursuit of self-reliant production and technological development.[38] Several factors have accounted for the limited success of this program for regional industrial integration. Some of the factors concerned failures in planning in the allocation of projects to member countries; others arose out of the limitations in existing production and technological infrastructure. Thus, in the programming of the metalworking industry and the allocation of production activities, the underlying concept was that the countries with the lowest technological capabilities should produce the more sophisticated industrial goods and products. Through such production, they might achieve rapid technological development, then gradually reduce the technological gap existing between the more advanced member countries and those with lower industrial and technological capabilities. Bolivia, for example, with the least-developed technological infrastructre, was assigned nine metalworking projects, seven of which had high levels of technological sophistication.

Because of limited technological capabilities, manufacturers had to turn to foreign technology suppliers for their technological requirements. Often, such technologies were available only in conjunction with substantial foreign equity participation. Because of the low absorptive capacity of local manufacturers, foreign equity participation usually also was necessary to ensure effective transfer and absorption of foreign technology. In the petrochemical industry, which requires sophisticated process and production technology along with substantial capital outlays and large scales of production, reliance on foreign capital and technology became even more pronounced. Since ownership of technology in several subsectors of the petrochemical industry is confined to a few MNCs, foreign companies enjoyed strong negotiating positions with local governments and, in several subsectors of the industry, agreed to provide technology to their own subsidiaries. As a result of technological dependence, the progressive implementation of regional industrial programs in metalworking, and more obviously in the petrochemical industry, has brought an increased participation by MNCs in the Andean Group subregion. Their role has been predominant, not only as technology suppliers but also as investors in foreign-majority subsidiaries and in affiliated joint ventures with domestic companies.[39]

The intent of host governments had been to compensate for the strong position of MNCs by the establishment of state-owned enterprises. When state-owned enterprises were formed for the implementation of assigned projects—for example, Monomeros, a company jointly owned by the Colombian and Venezuelan governments—they also relied heavily on foreign engineering services for the planning and implementation of projects and for the provision of production technology, because their implementation was very limited. Little use was made of the unpackaging of various elements of the required technology, except in a few cases. The experience of several state-owned public sector projects within the region also suggests that ownership by the state did not, by itself, significantly affect choice of technology or increase the knowledge of alternatives or the ability to unpackage technology. National participation has similarly been rather limited in joint ventures between state-owned enterprises and foreign firms. In most of the Andean Group projects, decision-making powers for technology selection and use have been largely left to the foreign partners.

Beyond the promotion of MNC entry because of local conditions and constraints, regional industrialization programs also facilitated the operations of MNC subsidiaries in several other areas. Thus, to achieve the rapid buildup of production capabilities in the relevant fields, the governments relaxed local content requirements of production with the result that, in many cases, only assembly operations were developed by MNCs and most of the inputs were imported. In general, in most sectors of the metalworking industry, the local content continued to be very low. Subsequent analysis of the implementation of the metalworking and petrochemical industrial programs in the region indicate that industrial programs by the member governments has often created opportunities for MNCs that might not otherwise have existed and, despite the regulatory measures aimed at foreign direct investments and technology in the region, foreign subsidiaries had been the major beneficiaries of regional integration.[40]

The achievement of self-reliant technological development was, however, also hindered by the behavior of nationally owned firms, particularly in the private sector. For the manufacture of assigned products by the industrial program, companies invariably turned to foreign technology suppliers for most of their technological needs, and little attempt was made to utilize or develop local capability. The intent of Decision 24, to promote the acquisition of appropriate technologies by local industries and to accelerate their assimilation and absorption, was not pursued vigorously by local industry. In their technology acquisition these companies have generally been motivated by the reputation of brand names and trademarks of foreign technology suppliers and their market acceptance. Local companies also do not appear to have made major efforts to adapt foreign technologies or to undertake R&D for local innovations in order to reduce their continuing dependency on foreign technology.[41]

Another effort toward regional industrial programming is being attempted in the ASEAN group of countries in Southeast Asia. The objectives are more modest, however, and it is recognized that MNC subsidiaries and affiliates could play an important role in this program. Regional industrial programming is extremely difficult to formulate and even more difficult to implement, largely because national interests and policies are often different within the region or subregion. At the same time, despite its history of limitations and constraints, it may nevertheless have potential in the future, particularly in technology planning and development for the necessary technological infrastructure in various groups of countries.

Although efforts at regional integration have so far had limited effect on the technological development of the regions concerned, the impact of national industrial strategies of import substitution and export development on the operations of MNCs in developing countries, as investors and suppliers of industrial technology and know-how, has been very significant. The nature of MNC operations, particularly in Third World countries, is discussed in some detail in Part II, which deals with MNCs and technology transfer in key industrial sectors and covers commercialization and transfer of technology through various forms of MNC participation, as well as the impact on local technological development in various critical sectors. Part II also discusses the background and rationale for various regulatory and other policies, in respect to foreign direct investments and technology licensing and to contractual arrangements. The response of MNCs to regulatory measures in several developing countries is also of considerable significance. The effectiveness of these measures in changing certain basic features and aspects of MNC activities is also examined in the following chapters.

Notes

1. A study of the import propensity of foreign and domestic firms in 1973 in Peru showed that, in the same activity, foreign subsidiaries have higher import content. See C.V. Vaitsos, *Employment Problems and Transnational Enterprises in Developing Countries: Distortions and Inequality* (Geneva: International Labour Office, 1976). Also, in the case of the Brazilian power equipment industry, the import propensity of foreign subsidiaries was about twice as high as that of domestically owned companies. See R.S. Newfarmer, "International Oligopoly in the Electrical Industry," in *International Oligopoly and Development,* ed. R.S. Newfarmer (Notre Dame, Ind.: University of Notre Dame Press, 1984). Similarly, in the case of South Korea, the import content of foreign firms exceeded that of local firms. See Sung-Hwen Jo, *The Impact of Multinational Firms on Employment and Incomes: The Case Study of South Korea,* Working Paper No. 12 (Geneva: International Labour Office, World Employment Programme, 1976). In the late 1970s in Mexico, the import propensity of a sample of foreign subsidiaries was 26 percent and that of comparable national firms was 17 percent. See K. Unger, "Market Structure, Transfer of Technology and Performance in Mexican Manufacturers" (Mexico City: Colegio de Mexico, 1982, mimeographed). A comprehensive review of the import propensity

of foreign subsidiaries is presented by S. Lall, "Transnationals, Domestic Enterprises: A Survey," in S. Lall, *The Multinational Corporation* (New York: Macmillan, 1980).

2. The critical role of linkages in development is presented in the classic book by A.O. Hirschman, *The Strategy of Economic Development* (New Haven: Yale University Press, 1958).

3. F. Fajnzylber and T. Tarrago, *Las Empresas Transnacionales* (Mexico City: Fondo de Cultura Economica, 1976). The share of foreign subsidiaries in the Mexican economy during the 1960s and early 1970s is also discussed in B. Sepulveda and A. Chumacero, *La Inversion Extranjera en Mexico* (Mexico City: Fondo de Cultura Economica) and in R. Newfarmer and W. Mueller, *Multinational Corporations in Brazil and Mexico: Structural Sources of Economic and Non-economic Power* (Washington, D.C.: U.S. Government Printing Office, 1975).

4. Newfarmer and Mueller, *Multinational Corporations in Brazil and Mexico*. In the case of Mexico, for example, between 1956 and 1967, only 34 percent of the U.S. subsidiaries entered the market by establishing new plants; 66 percent entered by takeover of national firms. See Fajnzylber and Tarrago, *Las Empresas*.

5. "Quem e Quem na Economia Brasileira," *Visao* (August 1975); *Investing, Licensing and Trading Conditions Abroad—Brazil* (New York: Business International Corporation, various issues). The role of MNCs in the Brazilian manufacturing industry is also analyzed in Newfarmer and Mueller, *Multinational Corporations in Brazil and Mexico*.

6. "Quem e Quem na Economia Brasileira,"

7. J.V. Sourrouille, *El Impacto de las Empresas Transnacionales sobre el Empleo y los Ingresos: El Caso de Argentina,* Working Paper (Geneva: International Labour Office, World Employment Programme, 1976).

8. Sourrouille, *El Impacto de las Empresas*.

9. The share of foreign subsidiaries in the various industrial sectors in Chile in 1978 is presented in F. Latrera, "Presencia y Participacion de las Empresas Transnacionales en la Economia Chilena" (Santiago: Economic Commission of Latin America, mimeographed), tables 58, 59.

10. For Colombia in 1974, see M. Mortimore, *Foreign Participation in Colombian Development: The Role of Transnational Corporations,* Working Paper No. 14 (Santiago: Economic Commission for Latin America, Joint CEPAL/CTC Unit, June 1979), table 19.

11. For Peru in 1974, see Virgil F. Gonzales, *Capital Extranjero y Transnacionales en la Industria Peruana* (Lima: Centro de Investigacion y Capacitacion y Editorial Horizonte, 1982).

12. Studies on the Latin American experience found that managers of public sector enterprises look for safety in their purchases and aim to reduce the risk of buying equipment and industrial installations on a turnkey basis from foreign suppliers rather than depackaging the foreign technology package; thus, they utilize local resources to a maximum extent. See A. Araoz, J.A. Sabato, and O. Wortman, "Purchase of Technology by the Public Sector" (Unpublished mimeograph); a Spanish version of this paper appeared in *Comercio Exterior* (Mexico), February 1975.

13. For the extensive dependency of public sector enterprises on foreign technology and services, Algeria is a good case. With the growing acquisition of foreign technology, mostly in the form of turnkey arrangements in various industrial sectors, not

only has the dependency on foreign capital goods intensified, but the need for foreign technical services for maintenance and operation of sophisticated plants has increased rapidly. See A. Benachenhous, *Foreign Firms and the Transfer of Technology to the Algerian Economy* (Geneva: International Labour Office, 1976).

14. The importance of foreign technology for export-oriented production by Korean manufacturers is analyzed in L.E. Westphal, Y.W. Rhee, and G. Pursell, "Korean Industrial Competence: Where It Came From" (Washington, D.C.: IBRD, 1980, mimeographed).

15. This new phenomenon in international investment and trade flows, which started in the late 1960s, is discussed in G. Adam, "New Trends in International: World-Wide Sourcing and Dedomicilling," *Acta Economica* 7(1971): 349–67. Also see G.K. Helleiner, "Manufactured Exports from Less-developed Countries and Multinational Firms," *Economic Journal* 83(March 1973): 21–47.

16. The far-reaching integration of export-oriented foreign subsidiaries within the MNC system and the resultant limited decision-making power is analyzed in C.A. Michalet, "The International Transfer of Technology and the Multinational Enterprise," *Development and Change* 7(1976): 154–74.

17. For the participation of MNCs in export activities of developing countries, see Helleiner, "Manufactured Exports."

18. In Mexico, where such policies were adopted, there is some evidence that they succeeded in achieving the expected results only partially, because MNCs often failed to comply with the established export targets. This is demonstrated for the automobile industry in D. Benett and K.E. Sharpe, "La Industria Automotriz Mexicana y la Politica Economica de la Promocion de Exportaciones; Algunas Problemas del Control Estatal de las Empresas Transnacionales," in *Industrializacion e Internacionalizacion en la America Latina,* ed. F. Fajnzylber (Mexico City: Fondo de Cultura Economica, 1981).

19. Such objectives are identified, for example, in *Mexican Border Industrializacion Programme* (Mexico City: Secretaria de Industry y Commercio, 1971) and *Export Processing Zone Karachi: Scheme and Objectives* (Karachi: Department of Industry, n.d.).

20. R.W. Moxon, *Offshore Production in Less Developed Countries: A Case Study of Multinationality in the Electronics Industry,* Working Paper (New York: New York University, July 1974).

21. A detailed description of the various types of incentives granted by governments to foreign companies operating in the zone is given, for example, in T. Kelleher, *Handbook of Export Free Zones,* UNIDO/IOD.31 (Vienna: United Nations Industrial Development Organization, 1976); also in J. Currie, *Investment: The Growing Role of Export Processing Zones* (London: Economist Intelligence Unit, 1979).

22. *Export Processing Zones in Developing Countries,* Working Paper on Structural Changes, No. 19 (Vienna: United Nations Industrial Development Organization, August 1980).

23. H.K. Ping, "British of the Second Generation," *Far Eastern Economic Review* (May 1979).

24. M.P.F. Kelly, "Mexican Border Industrialization, Female Labor Force Participation and Migration," Paper presented at the Annual Meeting of the American Sociological Association, San Francisco, 1978.

25. United Nations Industrial Development Organization, *Export Processing Zones.*

26. The composition, activity, and training of the labor force in the export processing zones are discussed in *Women in the Redeployment of Manufacturing Industry in Developing Countries,* Working Paper on Structural Changes, No. 18 (Vienna: United Nations Industrial Development Organization, July 1980).

27. The limited scope of training and skill development in the electronics industry imparted by MNCs is also presented in L.Y.C. Lim, "Multinational Firms and Manufacturing for Export in Less Developed Countries: The Case of the Electronics Industry in Malaysia and Singapore," Unpublished Ph.D. dissertation, University of Michigan, 1978.

28. United Nations Industrial Development Organization, *Export Processing Zones.*

29. A. Van Naerssenm, *Location Factors and Linkages at the Industrial Estates of Malacca Town,* Publication No. 10 (Nijmegen, Netherlands: University of Nijmegen, Department of Geography and Physical Planning, 1979).

30. For a comprehensive review of the issues involved in regional integration, see C.V. Vaitsos, "Crisis in Regional Cooperation-Integration among Developing Countries: A Survey," *World Development* 6(June 1978).

31. Ibid.

32. R. Tomasini, *Acuerdos de Complementacion de ALALC y la Participacion de las Empresas Transnacionales: Los Cases de Maquinas de Oficina y Productos Electronicos,* Document No. 3 (Santiago: United Nations Eonomic Commission for Latin America, July 1977).

33. Ibid.

34. G. Rosenthal and I. Cohen, "Algunas reflecciones en torno al marco conceptual de la integracion economica Centroamericana," (Mexico City: CEPAL, 1976, mimeographed).

35. These issues are analyzed in depth in C.V. Vaitsos, "The Role of Transnational Enterprises in Latin American Economic Efforts: Who Integrates, and with Whom, How and for Whose Benefit." Paper presented at the United Nations Conference on Trade and Development, Geneva, 1978).

36. L.K. Mytelka, *Regional Development in a Global Economy* (New Haven: Yale University Press, 1979).

37. A detailed description of Decision 24 is presented in L.K. Mytelka, "Regulating Direct Foreign Investment and Technology Transfer in the Andean Group," *Journal of Peace Research* 14(1977).

38. Mytelka, *Regional Development.*

39. Ibid.

40. This is argued, for example, in Vaitsos, "The Role of Transnational Enterprises."

41. Such a conclusion was reached from the survey of the technology acquisition process of forty-seven metalworking and forty-three chemical firms in Peru, Ecuador, and Colombia in L.K. Mytelka, "Licensing and Technology Dependence in the Andean Group," *World Development* 6(1978).

Part II
Multinational Corporations and Technology Transfer in Key Industrial Sectors

3
Pattern of Technology Transfer through MNCs

The utilization of specialized industrial technology and control over its application have been important features of the corporate strategy of multinational firms. They have been critical factors in the international production of oligopolistic industries in which MNCs have tended to concentrate. The capability on the part of MNCs to mobilize capital resources, combined with their ownership and control of specialized technology and know-how has, in general, led to the internationalization of corporate activities, initially through sales and subsequently through production operations in different countries. The growth of proprietary technology, covered by patents and industrial property rights, or held as commercial secrets and know-how, has served as a major barrier to new entrants in most technology-intensive industries and has led to an oligopolistic market structure in favor of the holding of proprietary technology and know-how by MNCs.

In the internationalization of production, the ownership of specialized, unique, and proprietary technology has been a major factor in ensuring successful production operations in different countries. The technological advantage of MNCs in specific fields over domestic companies, both in industrialized and in Third World countries, has consequently been a major competitive advantage in their entry and dominance in foreign markets. The ownership of specialized technology and know-how has also enabled MNCs to commercialize other elements, such as management and marketing expertise and other technical knowledge and capability, that may also be available to other companies and that might otherwise have had much lower market value.[1]

The production operations of MNCs are generally structured around specialized products and techniques that have provided a technological advantage to these companies over others in the same or related fields. The MNCs seek to maintain this lead with increased operational skills and know-how, dependent on expansion in production, combined with applied industrial research and application by the parent corporation. Products are covered by trademarks or trade names. In production technology, part of the technology may be covered by patents, while other elements of production know-how may be unpatented but proprietary in nature, including production and trade secrets that are closely guarded and protected. Although the extension of production activities beyond national boundaries is determined by several factors, including national policies and market and factor situations in host countries, an important determinant is also undoubtedly the nature of the technology and the extent to which similar products and techniques are available from other sources. Certain criteria have been developed to determine stages of technological application when particular manufacture or utilization of particular technical processes is undertaken in other countries.[2] Regardless of the basic motivations, however, there can be little doubt that specialized technology and know-how, combined with the capacity to mobilize financial resources, have been major factors in multinational industrial operations. With growing commercialization and trade in industrial technology, there has also been a rapid increase in technology licensing between industrial enterprises in different countries. The competitive position of individual MNCs can be maintained only if they retain their technological advantage, either through company-internal research or through licensing, cross-licensing, and various forms of technology-pooling arrangements. The scope and magnitude of such arrangements have increased considerably in recent years, with the rapid expansion of trade in technology. In the case of U.S. companies alone, income from technology fees and royalties increased from $2,787 million in 1971 to $6,275 million in 1983.[3] Of this, $1,594 million and $4,056 million respectively, comprised receipts from developed market economies, while income from developing countries amounted to $537 million in 1971 and $1,278 million in 1983.[4] Figures on technology income and payments in the form of fees and royalties in other industrialized market economies also indicate a similar pattern with the much greater proportion of technology trade taking place among enterprises from industrialized countries, and with only 15 to 20 percent of such trade between these enterprises and companies coming from Third World countries.

The ownership of industrial technology may be related to a specific product, or to the special features of a particular product, or to a production process or technique that is unique or specialized and that leads to competitive production costs and efficiency. In many instances, however, no clear-cut distinction can be made between product and process know-how and the two are closely interrelated. Taken either separately or together, the ownership of such know-how provides varying degrees of monopolistic control over production operations in particular fields, with corresponding advantages in terms of returns and profits. It also provides corporations with greater flexibility in determining the pattern of production and marketing on a global basis, since they are in a strong bargaining position in fields where alternative sources of industrial technology either are not available or are limited. This is reflected in the nature of the investment made in different countries, the structure of ownership, the extent of vertical integration to be achieved, and the corresponding import content and several other aspects of international corporate decision making. In oligopolistic industries, where a substantial proportion of global production is controlled by a few corporations, it has been possible for these corporations that possess proprietary technology to extend production operations to different countries.[5] This has been done to increase global production and marketing operations and also to achieve efficient international division of labor through subsidiaries and affiliates in various countries. This procedure has had important implications for Third World countries in different sectors of production. In petroleum and minerals, for example, MNC operations were largely limited to exploration and extraction of petroleum and mineral ores, with refining and processing operations largely located in industrialized economies. In the manufacturing sector, although certain goods were produced for local markets, local production of durable consumer goods and equipment was largely confined to the final stages of assembly and partial assembly of imported components. In recent years, a different pattern has emerged in the electronics industry, where considerable production of components and assembly operations are taking place in export-processing zones in several developing countries. The production operations of MNCs in Third World countries have differed considerably from their activities in other industrialized economies in various production sectors, and this has had considerable impact on the nature and pattern of technology transfer.

With ownership or knowledge of specialized technology constituting a key factor in an MNC's competitive position in national and external markets, the generation of new technology has received considerable emphasis in most corporations. Research expenditures by corporations have increased considerably in the effort to ensure that companies retain and develop technological advantage in their respective fields. Outlays on research have generally been much higher in the case of the larger corporations and have often been more a feature of the size of a corporation and its principal fields of operations than of the extent of its global activities. It is estimated that in the United States in the 1970s, the 200 largest corporations in terms of sales, mostly MNCs, spent 80 percent of nongovernmental R&D expenditure.[6] The total R&D expenditure through such corporations includes substantial research funding provided by governmental bodies.[7] In the case of U.S. corporations, for example, total annual R&D expenditure in the late 1970s was over $20 billion.[8] In certain production sectors, such as chemicals, pharmaceuticals, and electronics, the pace of research and technological innovation has been much more rapid than in fields, where products and manufacturing technologies have remained fairly stable. Even in the latter, however, considerable technological improvement is constantly taking place in the use of new materials and production processes, and in the degree of automation and the like. These developments, which are the result of applied research activities of individual corporations, have generally been utilized internally by these companies, though they have also been licensed to other companies at various stages, particularly when improvements have been well-defined and covered by industrial property rights.

The extent of licensing and cross-licensing has been much greater in the case of the larger MNCs in various sectors, largely because of the size of their operations.[9] With increased costs of research, corporations in the same field have tended to acquire user rights to technological developments by other companies through the process of licensing. The extent of technology licensing, especially patent licensing, has increased considerably in industrialized countries during the last two decades. In several instances, large corporations have acquired smaller companies with specialized technological expertise. In other instances, they have resorted to cross-licensing arrangements, which enable corporations to share the results of technological research undertaken by participating companies. In the manufacture of electrical power equipment, for example, major manufacturers in Japan have cross-licensing linkages with U.S. corporations, which, in turn, have a number of licensing agreements with Western European countries.[10] A similar pattern prevails in most industries that involve large-scale assembly or partial assembly operations, where technological developments relate not only to final products but also to a large variety of components and subassemblies. Technological linkages among corporations, which are embodied in licensing and cross-licensing agreements, have also been extended to various types of technological cooperation and coproduction arrangements. Thus, companies may enter into agreements to share technology for the production of certain parts and components and allocate their research costs, as well as the resultant production, among themselves. This has been done in the automobile, aircraft, and several other industries. The rising costs of machinery and equipment and of industrial research have had significant effect on costs and on the economic scale of manufacture in most fields, motivating closer technological cooperation among manufacturers located in different countries. This has also taken place through mergers and acquisitions within various industrial sectors, although in some industrialized countries, greater concentration of industrial production can run into problems with antimonopoly regulatory bodies. Coproduction and technological cooperation agreements have also taken place extensively, especially among companies located in the countries of the European Common Market. The generation and development of industrial technology has also taken place through joint ventures in these countries in several high-technology fields, such as aircraft, computers, military-related equipment, and also in capital goods production, particularly where governmental agencies are the principal or sole buyers. Government policies in industrialized countries have also promoted the development of high-technology and other key industries through various incentives and support measures, including direct grants and subsidies for defense-oriented or specific high-technology research and preference in government purchases for locally produced machinery and equipment, computers and related products, military equipment, railways and rolling stock, and other such products. In several countries, protectionist measures, both direct and indirect, have also made it difficult for foreign manufacturers to export to these markets.

There has also been a growing trend toward joint ventures between enterprises in industrialized countries.[11] Such arrangements have proved to be rewarding for both technology licensors and licensees. Licensors receive earnings from technology for the period of the agreement and life of patents, whichever may be applicable, while licensees obtain access to the use of required technology. For licensors, however, licensing always contains an element of risk, because the result can be the creation of competitive capability, since licensees can rapidly absorb and adapt licensed technologies. In such instances, unless the technology licensor is able to further improve on the licensed technology, the new competition may pose a problem, and although there may be significant earnings from licensing, existing markets of licensor enterprises may be threatened. The most notable examples in this regard are provided by Japanese corporations, which obtained considerable technology through licensing arrangements, especially with U.S. corporations, and through technological adaptations and gradually became major competitors in global markets for products manufactured through such technologies.

The generation of new industrial technologies in industrialized countries has not been confined to corporations; extensive research activities have been undertaken in research institutions funded either entirely or partially by national authorities. Defense-oriented research has also received extensive financial support from governments, especially in the United States, as have fields such as computer applications, nuclear research, laser-beam technology and the like. This has often paved the way for major innovations in technological applications. Such funding has, for the most part, been channeled through corporations and has provided considerable resources for innovative technological research. However, regardless of the source of funding for scientific and technological research, the industrial application of such research has taken place through companies and in global production operations, mostly through MNCs.

There is also a close relationship among technological applications in different sectors. In the textile industry, for example, a large proportion of synthetic materials are manufactured from chemical derivatives by companies producing chemicals. Consequently, some corporations, such as Imperial

Chemical Industries in the United Kingdom, have become involved in the production of synthetic fibers, while some chemical companies have developed close technological linkages with major manufacturers of synthetic textile materials. The impact of technological developments in microelectronics has been very significant, not only in the electronics sector but also in the instrumentation and control mechanisms in various production areas, including machine tools and automobile production. The developments in biotechnology and genetic engineering are similarly likely to have considerable effect on chemicals, pharmaceuticals, and agriculture. Research in new materials, including ceramics, would also have significant impact in several industries. The cross-sectoral linkages and effects of technological research are further increased by the constant movement of senior research personnel from one field of industrial research to another.

Generation of new and applied industrial technologies has also taken place, especially in process industries—including petrochemicals and fertilizers—through specialized engineering companies.[12] These companies also operate internationally and provide consulting engineering services for process plant designs and construction, including proprietary process knowhow. The multinational operations of consultancy engineering companies are, however, largely concentrated at the plant construction stage. Manufacturing MNCs also often utilize the services, processes, and construction know-how of such specialized engineering companies during the planning and construction of new plants.

Considerable emphasis has also been given by national governments in certain industrialized countries, particularly Japan, to the acquisition and generation of advanced industrial technology by nationally owned enterprises. Governmental policies and guidelines were supportive of the large flow of industrial technology to Japanese companies during the 1960s and 1970s; this is continuing, reflecting the importance given to acquisition of the latest technologies that might provide the base for the adaptation and generation of new products and processes. Most of this flow was through licensing arrangements, which enabled Japanese companies to absorb these techniques and to adapt them for new and globally competitive products. In Western European countries, on the other hand, the post–World War II period witnessed the establishment of a great many subsidiaries of MNCs from the United States, since there were few or no restrictions on foreign direct investments by MNCs. At the same time, the need for the generation of new technologies by local manufacturers was recognized and direct and indirect assistance was provided to such companies, particularly in the United Kingdom and France. In recent years, such assistance has been particularly marked for computers, microprocessors, and various branches of machinery manufacture. An alternative pattern has been the formation of joint ventures, as was the situation between France and the United Kingdom for aircraft, and among European corporations in various other fields for joint research and product development in high-technology industries. Most of the ventures involving such joint research have received financial and other support from the national governments concerned.

Although the acquisition and generation of industrial technology have become a critical aspect of corporate planning, an equally important issue has been control over industrial technology once is has been acquired or developed. Control over the dissemination and application of technology may be necessary in order to retain technological advantage in domestic and foreign markets and to secure adequate returns on investments in research and technical development. Such control may be exercised through various means, ranging from constraints in the use of technology in production activities of subsidiaries, affiliates, and licensees, to restrictions in diffusion and utilization of such technologies by other companies—including through imitations and copying of the products and processes involved.

Several strategies and measures are utilized by corporations to ensure effective and continuing control of their respective technologies and production techniques and processes. One important measure is to ensure that most MNCs, even those with significant foreign operations, concentrate all or most of their R&D activities in their home country.[13] The centralized location of R&D activities also has other advantages, such as proximity to major markets, better knowledge of the scientific infrastructure, and the availability of research and other institutions on which the company can draw for research. This also enables significant economies of scales in research activities, a factor of growing importance in view of the rising costs of research and development. Most important, however, the centralization of major R&D activities in the home country of the corporation allows far greater control over the innovation process and reduces the potential for leakage of technological developments. MNCs from the United States have tended to spend 80 to 90 percent of their R&D expenditure in the United States,[14] though some of the larger MNCs have also set up research facilities in Western European countries. In 1977, U.S. corporations spent 89.8 percent of their research expenditures in the United States, 9.5 percent in other industrialized countries, and only 0.7 percent in developing countries.[15] MNCs from other industrialized countries also have usually centralized their research activities in the countries of parent corporations, although there have been certain exceptions, such as Ciba Geigy's research center on tropical diseases in India and Nestlé's research activities in Mexico. Some major MNCs, such as Unilever, have also undertaken research programs in developing countries, but principally for the purpose of making product adjustments to suit local tastes and markets. Research efforts have also been made in certain developing countries to locate materials and products as substitutes for imported materials, which are in short supply. By and large, however, research activities of MNCs in developing countries have generally been for the purpose of making adjustments to local markets and for factor conditions, or for certain products that are produced only in these countries, such as tea, processed coffee, tropical drugs, and the like.[16] This is mostly because product development and research on basic technologies, which involve large capital investments and require highly skilled research personnel, can be most conveniently conducted at one or two centralized research centers. In the same manner, centralized research in research operations, technological applications of research results, and maintenance of confidentiality can be controlled more efficiently. Consequently, despite the fact that the costs of research are much lower in countries such as Brazil, Mexico, or India compared to the United States and Western Europe, MNCs have not made significant investments in R&D in developing countries so far.[17] The dependency of MNC subsidiaries and affiliates on R&D in their parent corporations applies in almost all sectors and countries,[18] ranging from the bauxite industry in Jamaica[19] to export-oriented electronics production in Malaysia.[20]

Protection and control over proprietary technology and know-how have been ensured by most MNCs in their global operations through specific patterns of expansion of foreign production. In several sectors, this pattern is closely linked to the product life cycle. Empirical material relating to the foreign operations of U.S. companies indicates that technological innovations have been exploited initially through exports, then only gradually through foreign production operations that were first undertaken in other industrialized countries, and only subsequently in some developing countries.[21] This not only minimized technological diffusion, it also provided relatively higher returns on investments compared with other ways of serving external markets. In recent years, however, there have been several exceptions to this pattern. In several production sectors, particularly in electronics, it has been more advantageous to undertake foreign manufacture of a large proportion of components immediately after the innovation stage in low-wage countries. With greater technological diffusion and with the continuance of major wage-rate differentials, several Third World countries continue to be attractive alternatives for the location of labor-intensive industries that involve relatively unskilled and semiskilled labor.

The legal means for protection of proprietary industrial technology are through patents, which secure proprietary rights on a worldwide basis. Consequently, MNCs engage actively in international patenting of innovative products and production technology, even in countries where they do not undertake or envisage local production. The protection afforded by patents has resulted in high levels of patent registration in developing countries, with actual utilization rates often falling below 1 percent of registered patents. In Colombia, for example, of the 3,513 patents registered in the late 1960s in the chemical industry, only ten were used in industrial production.[22] Similarly, in 1975 in Peru, the patent utilization rate was below 0.5.[23] Recent legislation adopted in some developing countries has sought to modify the structure of patent rights. The patent law of Mexico (1976), for example, has sought to reduce the time span of patent validity, but implementation of this legislation was held up for several years. The Brazilian patent law, which prohibits patents in sectors that are vital to national development, such as food processing, aims to limit the power based on the ownership of proprietary technology in certain sectors. The Indian patent law restricts the life of patents in food products, drugs, and other essential products to a shorter period. International patenting not only confers protection for the innovation; it also gives patent holders the right to export to these foreign markets.[24] Although patents have generally provided effective protection for technological innovations, there can be several limitations on the use of patents for exercising control over technology. First, several production processes may not be patentable, since they may comprise a series or combinations of operations that are not necessarily innovative. Second, it may not be in the interest of the corporation to take out patents on certain trade secrets, such as soft-drink concentrate formulas. Third, in some countries, only processes can be patented; in others, patents are not valid in certain fields, such as drugs, or have a limited duration. In some countries, governments have prescribed compulsory licensing provisions in areas considered vital for national development. These aspects do circumscribe the role and effectiveness of patents to some extent, but patents still constitute the principal protection for technological innovations. The marketing of innovative products is controlled through trademarks, and trade and brand names also serve as important instruments of control over product marketing. Other industrial property rights include copyrights and trade secrets, which also provide considerable protection for innovative technological development.

In the case of foreign markets, control over technology is often achieved through control over investments and the enterprise using the technology. This takes place not only in the case of wholly foreign-owned MNC subsidiaries or foreign-majority companies, but also in joint ventures in which owners of proprietary technology are able to exercise effective control over technology use through contractual and other arrangements. In these cases, the technology is transferred internally within the MNC and its external operation and is not shared fully with local joint-venture partners. In a number of sectors, MNCs are willing to transfer advanced technology only if they can operate through wholly owned subsidiaries or foreign-majority holdings.[25] Control of the technology and ownership aspects of foreign operations can thus be closely interrelated. In the case of joint ventures and licensing agreements, the technologies involved often do not comprise the latest technological innovations of the licensor company that are critical to their competitiveness. As the extent of ownership of subsidiary operations is reduced for owners of technology, the technologies transferred would be more in standardized technology, rather than in the latest innovative development. This continues to be true in several sectors, although the transfer of more advanced technologies to joint ventures and unaffiliated companies has been increasing considerably in recent years.[26] In such arrangements, MNCs utilize various operational practices and contractual arrangements to limit technological diffusion to the extent necessary to meet the requirements of their foreign operations.

In international technology transfer, an important element of control over technology may lie in the partial nature of the transfer.[27] This is quite common both with MNC subsidiaries and affiliates and in contractual arrangements for technology licensing. Partial technology transfer can be understood in two ways. First, in the case of complex products involving a wide range of production technology and know-how, technology transfer in a foreign undertaking may relate to only a small part of production, with other intermediate parts and materials being supplied from external sources. Such partial technology transfer prevents the foreign undertaking from acquiring or developing complete technological capability for final products. Although this pattern of technology transfer is related to other MNC motivations, such as limited local production and maximum imports of intermediate products, it also results in effective control by MNCs over technology for production of the final product. The second aspect relates to the fact that what is transferred is production know-how, rather than the capability for design and innovation. In the case of company-internal transfer, such know-how is not required by the subsidiary, because designs and continuing technical support are provided by the parent company. In the case of joint ventures and licensing agreements, this aspect assumes much greater significance. The withholding of design know-how may be motivated to control technology and may constitute a major constraint in technology transfer.

In licensing agreements between unaffiliated companies, the concept of control over technology assumes a different significance, since the licensor's objectives have to be achieved through contractual provisions that are designed to limit exports or that provide tie-in conditions for obtaining intermediate products and other inputs from licensors. These contractual conditions have often significantly restricted the operation of licensees and prevented them from emerging as competitors in global markets, along with ensuring a secure market for sales of parts and components for technology suppliers and licensors.[28]

It is against this background of technology generation and the measures for control over technology by MNCs that the issues of technology transfer by MNCs to Third World countries should be considered. In most developing countries, where significant industrial growth has been achieved in recent decades, MNCs have undoubtedly played a critical role in the initial process of transfer of industrial technology and know-how. Transfer of technology was closely linked with foreign direct investment and, as MNCs extended their investments in these countries, technological know-how and expertise were transferred through branches and subsidiaries, which, until the 1960s, were mostly wholly owned by parent corporations from industrialized countries. The establishment of MNC subsidiaries and the features of technology transfer to these entities followed a fairly similar pattern in most production sectors. In the last two decades, however, the nature of the corporate relationships between MNCs and their affiliates in Third World countries has undergone considerable change. With greater emphasis on national participation and control, and on joint ventures and licensing arrangements not involving foreign equity participation, the implications of industrial technology transfer have acquired somewhat different dimensions than in the past and have to be viewed against a broader framework of alternative arrangements.[29] The form and pattern of MNC investment and participation has differed considerably in various developing countries and also varies from sector to sector. Nevertheless, certain broad features of foreign direct investments are applicable to several production sectors of special importance to developing Third World countries.

Foreign direct investments by MNCs have contributed significantly to industrial growth in most Third World market-economy countries, and such investments have historically been the major source of inflow of foreign industrial technology. Prior to World War II, these investments were largely in the infrastructure and in extractive and resource-based industries, such as petroleum and minerals, and in the processing of agricultural and other natural resources, as well as in consumer goods industries in several developing countries. In the last three decades, however, MNC investments in these countries have extended to various fields of manufacture, most of which have involved the inflow of more complex technology. As in industries such as textiles, cement, durable consumer goods, and the like, considerable foreign investment has also taken place in sectors requiring more sophisticated production technology and know-how, such as chemicals, petrochemicals, and various branches of machinery and engineering goods manufacture, especially in countries with large internal markets or those with special-factor endowments.

Foreign investments in developing countries increased by about 15 percent annually during the 1970s.[30] The distribution of such investments was uneven, however, and most of the investments were concentrated in a few countries. Thus, during the 1970s, 57 percent ($4.9 billion) of the total $7.9 billion foreign direct investments in developing countries was invested in Latin America, mostly in Brazil and Mexico.[31] In the same period, MNCs invested $2.4 billion in South and East Asia, mostly in Hong Kong, Singapore, and Malaysia.[32] During this period, MNC investments in the manufacturing sector remained very limited in most African countries other than South Africa and was also very low in the Caribbean and in the smaller Latin American countries. Foreign investments in northern Africa, for example, accounted for only 2 percent of the stock of such investments in developing countries.[33] Certain significant changes have also taken place in the last two decades in the sectoral distribution of MNC investments in developing countries. Traditionally, the major share of such investments was in the extractive sector and in resource-based industries, but there has been a gradual shift to investments in the manufacturing sector, resulting in increased flow of various types of industrial technology. This was largely because of the process of industrialization in several of these countries, which provided increased opportunities for investments in various fields of manufacture and services, but it was also partly due to the increased emphasis on state ownership and control over petroleum, minerals, and natural resources in several of these countries. The entry of Japanese MNCs also channeled foreign investments from another source to developing countries in South and East Asia and Latin America, in such sectors as textiles, iron and steel, engineering goods, and other manufactured products.

Sectoral MNC investments in Third World countries, though varying from country to country, have generally followed a similar pattern in particular sectors. Such investments have depended not only on market considerations and factor endowments but also on national policies of host countries, which are playing an increasingly determinant role in channeling MNC investments in certain sectors and in structuring the nature of such investments. Thus, in petroleum and minerals, although foreign investments are governed primarily by location and the availability of resources, the establishment of state-owned corporations in several countries with such resources has circumscribed the role and activities of MNCs. In consumer goods industries, such as food and beverages, textiles, pharmaceuticals, durable goods, and the like, and in metal fabrication and the production of simple engineering goods, MNCs have invested in production enterprises in a large number of developing countries, including small countries in Latin America, South and East Asia, and North Africa. However, in sectors involving large capital investments and complex technology, such as the manufacture of chemicals and fertilizers or heavy mechanical, electrical, and transport equipment, MNC investments have been limited only to countries with large internal markets or to those from which products can be exported, either because of cheap labor or essential raw materials.

The motivations that have led MNCs to establish production operations in Third World countries, as distinct from MNC subsidiaries that deal solely with marketing and distribution, have differed from country to country and from sector to sector. In extractive industries, the motivation is obvious, although the extent of local processing activities can differ considerably, depending on the scarcity of the raw material concerned, the overall market situation, and the policies of the host country. The production of consumer goods in several developing countries, especially of agricultural goods, foods and beverages, fats and oil, and the like, has been undertaken largely to meet the demand of growing markets in these countries. It is with respect to more sophisticated fields of manufacture, such as those involving large capital outlays and a higher degree of technological and managerial know-how, that MNC motives become more complex and varied. They may range from response to host country policies and the protection of existing markets or entry into new markets to situations where certain technologies and products may have become increasingly available from alternative sources or may be emerging in the public domain, or when factor conditions in certain Third World countries are more favorable for certain types of production. The varying motives of MNCs have, nevertheless, led to MNC investments in most sectors of industry and manufacture in a number of developing countries, especially in recent decades.

The strategy of MNCs up to the 1960s was to operate principally through wholly owned subsidiaries and most MNC foreign production operations were through such subsidiaries, with technology transfer taking place internally between parent MNCs and their branches and subsidiaries in different countries. Even at present, it is generally considered that MNCs prefer 100 percent ownership of foreign affiliates.[34] This enables the internalization of benefits from specialized technological know-how and capability, and retains technology within the corporation.[35] The technology required by the subsidiary is fully transferred, on a continuing basis, together with the results of research conducted centrally by parent MNCs. This standard pattern of full ownership of their foreign subsidiaries and affiliates by MNCs changed significantly during the 1970s, principally as a result of host country policies in Third World countries, which either prohibited or discouraged wholly foreign-owned production operations. Consequently, since the 1970s, there has been a growing trend toward joint ventures between MNC affiliates and local enterprises in these countries. This has been further facilitated by the entry of Japanese MNCs into ventures in these countries.[36] In many countries, especially in Latin America and in South and East Asia, governments have encouraged joint ventures by granting higher incentives to such companies than to wholly owned subsidiaries. In other developing countries, however, including Brazil and several countries in Africa and Asia, there have been few or no restrictions on the establishment or continuance of foreign-owned subsidiaries.

Even in countries where foreign investment is regulated and joint ventures are preferred, varying degrees of flexibility have been exercised and foreign-owned subsidiaries have been allowed to be set up or to continue in various sectors, especially in those that are export-oriented or that involve complex and sophisticated technology. These exceptions have increasingly been viewed as part of the "new pragmatism" of developing countries in the implementation of policies toward foreign direct investment. In several of these countries, the rigidity initially imposed through regulatory policies regarding MNC investments have gradually been modified or toned down because of experience that shows that MNCs are often not willing to transfer complex, proprietary technology unless they can retain control over its use and diffusion. Apart from control over proprietary technology, MNC ownership over foreign operations also allows them to control global production operations. In certain instances, costs of transfer of certain complex technologies may be fairly high in terms of training and development of local skills, and MNCs may be willing to incur these costs only if they can appropriate full and adequate profits from the operations.

For MNCs, foreign production operations can be justified only if they yield adequate returns. In the case of joint ventures, since profits have to be shared with local partners, increased returns may be sought through payments for technology, technical services, centralized research activities, and transfer pricing of inputs supplied by parent companies or other subsidiaries and affiliates. Both with subsidiaries and in joint ventures, overall returns to MNCs include such payments, apart from dividends on capital invested. The fact that MNC investments in Third World countries are generally in oligopolistic industries, where they have major technological advantages, enables them to assume dominant or even monopolistic positions in these fields.

The acceptance of joint ventures by MNCs, as opposed to wholly owning subsidiaries, often depends on the proprietary and exclusive nature of the technology involved, except for situations—such as in petroleum and scarce minerals—where host countries are in a strong bargaining position and joint ventures constitute the only method of entry. In the manufacturing sector, MNCs have been willing to participate in joint ventures mainly in sectors in which production technology is well established and standardized or may enter the public domain. When the technology has been proprietary and exclusive, there has been considerable reluctance on the part of MNCs to set up joint ventures. Thus, joint ventures by U.S. firms in the 1970s were set up mostly in fields such as textiles and apparel, plastics, nonferrous metals, simple equipment, and industrial chemicals; to a much lesser extent in food processing, pharmaceuticals, office equipment, computers, and the like, where the prevalent form of MNC investment continues to be through wholly owned subsidiaries.

An important exception to this pattern has been the state-owned enterprises in developing countries. Although there was initial reluctance on the part of most MNCs to participate in joint ventures with government enterprises, a large number of such ventures were established in the 1970s, and early 1980s, not only in industries based on natural resources but also in those in the manufacturing sector. In Brazil, for example, by 1981, there were sixty-nine such joint ventures between MNCs, state-owned enterprises, and local companies in the production of petrochemicals, heavy metallurgical products, and other fields of manufacture.[37] In many instances, foreign companies involved in joint ventures in developing countries have not been the most dominant MNCs in their respective fields, but they have possessed the requisite technology and have participated in such ventures to improve their global competitive position.[38] In many cases, MNCs from the United States, Western Europe, and particularly Japan, late-comers to developing-country markets, have been willing to transfer technology and to participate in joint ventures with local companies, both state-owned and privately owned, in order to enter these markets.

Despite the increasing trend toward joint ventures, foreign direct investments in developing countries continued to be mainly through wholly owned or majority foreign-owned MNC subsidiaries in the late 1970s. In the case of MNCs from the United States, for example, the proportion of investments in wholly owned or majority-owned MNC subsidiaries has continued to be very high—for example, 78 percent in Ghana, 81 percent in Hong Kong, 76 percent in the Philippines, 68 percent in Singapore, 52 percent in Thailand, 80 percent in Argentina, 90 percent in Brazil, 83 percent in Chile, 66 percent in Mexico, 84 percent in Panama, and 79 percent in Trinidad and Tobago.[39] In several countries, MNCs have obtained exemption from local capital-participation regulations by assuming export commitments or by providing specialized technology in priority sectors in these countries. Thus, in Malaysia, for example, in 1981, about 50 percent of approved foreign investments were in wholly owned MNC subsidiaries, but the proportion was much higher in the machine-building industries.[40] In some developing countries, although MNC subsidiaries still constitute the prevalent form of foreign investment, there has been a gradual shift to the production of more technologically complex products by such companies. Thus, in the Republic of Korea, although the proportion of foreign investment through wholly or majority foreign-owned subsidiaries remained over 70 percent during 1968 to 1980, the ownership composition in several sectors changed significantly. In textiles, for example, the share of minority foreign-owned companies decreased from 34 percent to 13 percent, in petroleum from 65 percent to 14 percent, and in the hotel sector from 86 percent to 19 percent. At the same time, in agriculture and fisheries, the share of minority foreign holdings increased from 6 percent to 60 percent.[41]

Along with the trend toward joint ventures, there has also been an increased trend toward technology licensing by MNCs to nonaffiliated companies in developing countries. Although technology licensing to nonaffiliated companies has been commonly practiced among companies in industrialized countries for several decades, such licensing has also increased to a substantial extent in enterprises in developing countries. During the 1970s, as state-owned and privately owned industrial enterprises proliferated and developed capability for rapid technological absorption in several of these countries, restrictions were also imposed on foreign investments. As a result, licensing to domestic, nonaffiliated companies provided the only means of entering and deriving revenues from these markets. The extent of licensing by MNCs to nonaffiliated companies in developing countries has varied considerably and has largely been concentrated in a few countries, such as Brazil, Argentina, and Mexico, in Latin America and India, the Republic of Korea, and some South and West Asian countries. In the Republic of Korea, for example, locally owned firms accounted for 74 percent of all licensing agreements with foreign companies by 1980.[42] In India, out of 2,833 cases of foreign technical collaboration in the period from 1969 to 1979, 2,418 cases related to technology licensing to nonaffiliated local companies and only 15 percent of the cases had foreign equity participation, usually minority holdings of up to 40 percent.[43] At the same time, in most African countries, in the smaller Latin American countries, and in the Caribbean, there have been relatively few cases of technology licensing to local nonaffiliated companies.

Most technology licensing by MNCs to unaffiliated Third World companies has taken place in the areas of standardized production technology, and trademark agreements have accompanied such licenses. The licensing of mature, standardized technologies by MNCs has not threatened to erode their worldwide competitive position. Most of these technologies involve industry-specific know-how for the manufacture of durable consumer products and various engineering and other goods, and they involve process and production techniques for metalworking and metalforming, besides transfer of designs and know-how that have already been extensively utilized in industrialized countries. Products manufactured under such licensing agreements generally involve relatively simple industrial products, such as refrigerators, motors, pumps, and the like. For most of these products, the basic patents have long since expired and the license agreements mostly provide for technical production assistance and services to licensees. A large share of such licensing agreements are also accounted for by trademark and brand agreements, which were sought by developing country licensees to improve local sales of their products.

In many instances, technology licensors have improved the basic know-how, utilizing the improvements in their home countries and thus enabling either the reduction of production costs or the manufacture of higher quality final products. Such improvements have seldom been transferred to unaffiliated licensees in developing countries unless specific contractual commitments have been made. Technology license agreements to developing country enterprises have also often imposed certain restrictions on the operations of licensees, either explicit or implicit, if such practices are prohibited by local regulations. These restrictions have generally limited the export activities of licensees in the licensor's major markets. At the same time, the licensing of standard technologies to domestically owned companies has provided MNCs with revenues from markets where local regulations limit foreign investments in certain sectors, or where MNCs are not interested in undertaking production because of the limited size of the local market.[44]

In recent years, there has been a growing trend toward technology licensing by MNCs to nonaffiliated enterprises in Third World countries for several reasons, including for transfer of complex and sophisticated technology. This has been partly because of the increased financial and technological capability of enterprises in several of these countries, combined with host country restrictions on foreign investments. It has also been due to increased technological diffusion in several sectors and the availability of technology and know-how from alternative foreign sources. Technology licensing and terms and conditions of transfer have, however, varied considerably in different production sectors, as is discussed in subsequent chapters.

While technology licensing by MNCs to unaffiliated companies has increased in the past two decades, such technology transfer constitutes only a very small share of global technology transfer if it is measured in terms of payments. To the extent that revenues from licensing activity approximate technology inflows, the published data on the origin of licensing revenues by host countries allow some quantification. In the case of U.S. companies, for example, in 1983, from total receipts of $6.3 billion from fees and royalties, payments by developing countries amounted to $1.27 billion.[45] From this amount, approximately 15 percent came from unaffiliated companies in developing countries. Although licensing revenues from developing countries have increased about 10 percent annually during the 1970s, the share of revenues from unaffiliated companies has not increased over the decade. In fact, in 1960, unaffiliated companies accounted for 18 percent of the total revenues paid by developing countries; by the late 1970s this decreased to 15 percent.[46] In the late 1970s, U.S. receipts from unaffiliated licensees in developing countries accounted for only 2 percent of total worldwide licensing fees and royalties.

The transfer of industrial technology through MNCs to Third World developing countries is of signficance in all industrial sectors, but it is particularly relevant in certain fields that are of special interest and priority to most developing countries. First, the efficient utilization of natural resources, particularly petroleum and minerals, and the nature and extent of technology transfer in petroleum and mineral-processing industries is of special significance. The operations of MNCs in these fields has been a source of considerable controversy and has led to major changes in MNC involvement and relationships with host developing countries. Second, technology transfer in food industries, including food processing and food and beverage production, and in the pharmaceutical sector are of particular importance, since they impinge directly on the basic needs for food and medicines. Third, with the growing demand for machinery and equipment in developing countries, it is necessary to review the trends in production and technology transfer through MNCs as they relate to electrical power equipment, agricultural machinery (especially tractors), mechanical equipment (including machine tools and diesel engines), and automobiles and trucks in developing countries. Finally, it is important to analyze recent trends in high-technology areas, particularly in microelectronics and the technological impact of MNC activities in developing countries.

The coverage of the sectoral analysis deals initially with the concentration of production and technological capability among MNCs in the particular sector and with the nature and extent of their participation in production activities and technology transfer to developing countries. The participation of MNCs not only has varied in different sectors but has also differed considerably in the channels used to transfer industrial technology. Such differences resulted partly from the global strategy of MNCs and the respective techno-economic aspects of operations, and partly from local conditions. At the same time, in formulating their global strategy, corporations have adjusted their operations in the light of worldwide competition, which has increased considerably in most industrial sectors and developing countries. Thus, growing availability of technologies has increasingly motivated MNCs to engage in alternative modalities of technology transfer. Apart from an overall review of operations of MNCs in host developing countries, the sectoral analysis in the following chapters examines various aspects of MNC operations that directly or indirectly relate to technology transfer. These include the extent of domestic integration or local content in assembly or partial assembly production, the development of competitive export capability, and the development of a local capability for adaptation and self-sustained technological development, including R&D and the designing of facilities in developing countries. Although there are several variations in MNC activities in various countries and sectors, and although there have been major changes in recent years, certain general features and characteristics of technology transfer through MNCs can be identified that are relevant and applicable to most industrial sectors.

Notes

1. Although there is a significant body of literature on the role of technology in foreign direct investments, this idea is presented explicitly in C.V. Vaitsos, "Transfer of Resources and Preservation of Monopoly Rents," Report No. 168 (Boston: Harvard

University, Center for International Affairs, 1970, mimeographed). A similar conclusion is arrived at in J.N. Behrman and H.W. Wallender, *Transfer of Manufacturing Technology within Multinational Enterprises* (Cambridge, Mass.: Ballinger, 1978).

2. Probably the earliest conceptualization of the relationship between foreign direct investments and various market imperfections (including those in technology markets) was in S. Hymer, *The International Operations of National Firms: A Study of Direct Foreign Investment* (Cambridge, Mass.: MIT Press, 1976). Various further developments of this theme are reviewed in A.L. Calvet, "A Synthesis of Foreign Direct Investment Theories and Theories of the Multinational Firm," *Journal of International Business Studies* (Spring-Summer, 1981). A different approach is presented by Vernon, whose empirical study of U.S. corporations related foreign direct investments to the life cycle of the products and the availability of technology at various stages. See R. Vernon, "International Investment and International Trade in the Product Cycle," *Quarterly Journal of Economics* (May 1966): 190–207.

3. U.S. Department of Commerce, "Fees and Royalty Payments of U.S. Affiliates and U.S. Parents," *Survey of Current Business,* various issues.

4. Ibid.

5. The relationship between oligopolistic market structure and the multinationalization of the firm is presented in the classic article by R.A. Caves, "International Corporations: The Industrial Economics of Foreign Investment," *Economica* (February 1971):1–27.

6. W.K. Chung, "Technology-Related Activities of U.S. Multinational Companies," in *U.S. Multinational Companies: U.S. Merchandise Trade, Worldwide Sales and Technology-Related Activities in 1977* (Washington, D.C.: U.S. Department of Commerce, Bureau of Economic Analysis, 1983).

7. In most OECD countries in 1977, for example, over 50 percent of the R&D funding came from government sources. See *International Survey of Resources Devoted to R and D by OECD Member Countries* (Paris: OECD, 1980).

8. Chung, "Technology-Related Activities."

9. Studies in the late 1970s in the United States showed, for example, that cross-licensing agreements have been used most heavily in the chemical and pharmaceutical industries. Often such agreements are done informally, without entering into contractual agreements, to avoid potential antitrust legislation. See *International Licensing* (New York: Business International Corporation, 1977).

10. A comprehensive review of such agreements is given in *Transnational Corporations in the Power Equipment Industry* (New York: United Nations Centre on Transnational Corporations, 1982).

11. Based on several case studies, this trend for U.S. corporations is discussed in J. Baranson, *Technology and the Multinationals: Corporate Strategy in a Changing World Economy* (Lexington, Mass.: Lexington Books, 1978). For Western European countries, see L.G. Franco, *The European Multinationals* (London: Harper & Row, 1976), ch. 5.

12. The role of consulting engineering companies in transferring technology to developing countries is discussed in J. Perrin, "Consulting Engineering, a New Form of Technological Dependence in the Developing Countries" (Grenoble: Universite des Sciences Sociales de Grenoble, Institut de Recherche Economique et de Planification,

July 1978, mimeographed); and M. Brown, *International Aspects of Engineering Activities—Implications for Local Autonomy* (Paris: OECD Development Centre, 1978).

13. The various reasons for centralized R&D activity by MNCs are discussed in J.N. Behrman and W.A. Fisher, *Overseas R and D Activities of Transnational Companies* (Cambridge, Mass.: Oelgeschlager, Gunn & Hain, 1980).

14. An exception from the general pattern—seven U.S. MNCs that conducted a significant share of their R&D expenditures abroad—is discussed in R. Ronstadt, *Research and Development Abroad by U.S. Multinationals* (New York: Praeger, 1977).

15. Chung, "Technology-Related Activities," Similar results were also found in a study by D. Creamer, *Overseas Research and Development by United States Multinationals, 1966–1975: Estimated Expenditures and a Statistical Profile* (New York: The Conference Board, 1976).

16. For coffee in Kenya and tea in India, see R. Kaplinsky and S. Chishti, "Multinational Corporations and Transfer of Technology: Some British Multinationals in Kenya and India," in *Transfer of Technology by Multinational Corporations*, Vol. II, ed. D. Germidis (Paris: OECD, 1977). For tropical drugs in Brazil, see C. De Faro Passos, "Multinational Corporations and the Transfer of Technology: The Case of Brazil" in Germidis (ed.), *Transfer of Technology.*

17. To the extent that subsidiaries are engaged in local R&D or product development, they maintain very limited linkages with local technical and scientific institutions, mostly for confidentiality reasons. This was found, for example, in the case of twenty-three foreign subsidiaries in Mexico in the capital goods, petrochemical, and food industries in A. Nadal, *Instrumentos de Politica Cientifica y Technologica en Mexico* (Mexico City: El Colegio de Mexico, 1977).

18. The very limited R&D activity of foreign subsidiaries was also corroborated by the studies of Mytelka in the metalworking and chemical industries in the Andean Pact countries. See L.K. Mytelka, "Licensing and Technological Dependence in the Andean Group," *World Development* 6(1978): 447–59.

19. R.K. Bardouille, "Technological Aspects of the Bauxite Industry in the Caribbean" (Mona, Jamaica: University of West Indies, Institute of Social and Economic Research, 1977, mimeographed).

20. K.C. Cheong and K.C. Lim, "The Electronics Industry in Malaysia: Issues in Transfer and Development of Technology," *Asian Economist* (December 1981): 136–50.

21. Vernon, "International Investment."

22. C.V. Vaitsos, "Patents Revisited: Their Function in Developing Countries," *Journal of Development Studies* 9(October 1972).

23. M.A. Zevallos y Muniz, *Analysis Estadistico de las Patentes en el Peru* (Lima: Consejo Nacional de Investigacion, 1976). Analysis of statistics on the share of patents registered by nonresidents shows a similarly high level of foreign ownership. In most developing countries, nonresidents accounted for 80 to 99 percent of the registered patents. (Based on statistics in *Industrial Property* [Geneva: World Intellectual Property Organization], various issues.)

24. The disadvantages of the prevailing international patent system for developing countries are discussed in R. Penrose, "International Patenting in the Less-

developed Countries," *Economic Journal* (September 1973): 768–87. Also see *The Role of the Patent System in the Transfer of Technology to Developing Countries* (New York: United Nations, 1975).

25. In the case of Japanese MNCs, for example, it was shown that during the earlier phases of foreign expansion, when most of the production activities of foreign subsidiaries involved use of mature technologies, joint ventures were quite common. As it did in the 1970s, such investment shifted to technologically more advanced products and export-oriented production; parent firms have increasingly used wholly owned subsidiaries. See J.H. Dunning and R.D. Pearce, "Some Observations on the New Forms of International Resource Transfer" (New York: United Nations Centre on Transnational Corporations, January 1982, mimeographed).

26. Several case studies for the release of recent and advanced proprietary technologies by U.S. MNCs to nonaffiliated companies in the aircraft, automobile, consumer electronics, computer, and chemical engineering industries are presented in J. Baranson, *International Transfer of Industrial Technology by U.S. Firms and Their Implications for the U.S. Economy* (Washington, D.C.: Developing World Industry and Technology, 1976). The trend is discussed further in J. Baranson, *Technology and the Multinationals: Corporate Strategy in a Changing World Economy* (Lexington, Mass.: Lexington Books, 1978).

27. The partial nature of technology transfer that takes place internally—generally from the parent company to its foreign subsidiaries—is analyzed in C.A. Michalet, "The International Transfer of Technology and the Multinational Enterprise," *Development and Change* 7(1976): 154–74.

28. For the various restrictions in licensing agreements between U.S. MNCs and their licensees, see F.J. Contractor, *International Technology Licensing* (Lexington, Mass.: Lexington Books, 1981), table 4–4. (Findings are based on a survey of thirty-four U.S. MNCs with 1,581 foreign licensees in 1977.)

29. These issues are presented in Rana K.D.N. Singh, "Long-term Needs and Expectations of Developing Countries in Technology Licensing," Paper presented at the Seventeenth Annual Meeting of the Licensing Executives Society, Atlanta, 1981.

30. Based on *Balance of Payment Yearbook* (Washington, D.C.: International Monetary Fund, various issues).

31. Ibid.

32. Ibid.

33. Based on *Development Co-operation* (Paris: OECD, various issues).

34. An important item of evidence for this statement is the fact that the majority of foreign direct investment is still undertaken through wholly owned subsidiaries.

35. These benefits of company-internal transfer are analyzed in D.M. Teece, *The Multinational Corporation and the Resource Costs of International Technology Transfer* (Cambridge, Mass.: Ballinger, 1976). Similarly, such an assumption underlies the appropriability theory conceptualized in S.P. Magee, "Technology and the Appropriability Theory of Multinational Corporations," in *New International Economic Order,* ed. J. Bhagwati (Cambridge, Mass.: MIT Press, 1976).

36. The study of 180 United States–based MNCs showed that although during the 1951–66 period only 12.3 percent of the subsidiaries were minority owned by the MNCs, by 1973–75 this share had increased to 19.4 percent. See D. Curhan, W. Davidson, and R. Suri, *Tracing the Multinationals* (Cambridge, Mass.: Ballinger,

1977). By the early 1970s, the ownership patterns of 211 subsidiaries not owned by the United States showed that they were formed with minority ownership. Computation is based on *Transnational Corporations in World Development: A Re-examination* (New York: United Nations, 1978), table C.13. More recently, this trend of increased willingness on the part of MNCs to operate in joint ventures with domestic companies is quite substantial in various fields, and nonequity relationships have also become quite common. See Dunning and Pearce, "Some Observations." Also see G. Vickery, "New Forms of Investment: Evidence from Balance of Payments Accounts of OECD Countries, 1970–1980," Paper presented at the OECD Meeting, "Changing International Investment Strategies," Paris, March 1982. In the case of Malaysia, see Tan Siew Ze and M. Kulansingnam, *New Forms of Foreign Investment in Malaysia—A Preliminary Survey* (Paris: OECD Development Centre, March 1981.)

37. E.A. Guimaraes, P.S. Malan, and J. Tavares de Araujo, *The "New Forms" of Foreign Investment in Brazil* (Paris: OECD Development Centre, 1982).

38. This trend for United States–based subsidiaries is discussed in L. Franco, *Use of Minority and 50-50 Joint Ventures by United States Multinationals as Indicators of Trends in "New Forms" of International Investment* (Paris: OECD Development Centre, 1982).

39. U.S. Department of Commerce, *U.S. Investment Abroad* (Washington, D.C.: U.S. Government Printing Office, 1981).

40. Tan Siew Ze and Kulansingam, *New Forms of Foreign Investment,* tables 10, 12.

41. Bohn-Young Koo, "Status and Changing Form of Foreign Investment in Korea" (Paris: OECD Development Centre, 1982, mimeographed), tables 27, 28.

42. Ibid., table 35.

43. *Foreign Collaborations in India* (New Delhi: Government of India, Indian Investment Centre, 1985).

44. Motives for licensing technology to unaffiliated companies are analyzed in P. Telesio, *Technology Licensing and Multinational Enterprises* (New York: Praeger, 1979). See also F.J. Contractor, "The Role of Licensing in International Strategy," *Columbia Journal of World Business* (Winter 1981): 73–81.

45. U.S. Department of Commerce, "Fees and Royalty Payments of U.S. Affiliates and U.S. Parents," *Survey of Current Business* (Washington, D.C.: U.S. Government Printing Office, 1984).

46. Computations are based on *Legislation and Regulation on Technology Transfer: Empirical Analysis of their Effects on Selected Countries* (Geneva: UNCTAD, 1980).

4
Petroleum, Minerals, and Processing Industries

I n developing countries in recent decades, there has been growing emphasis on exercising sovereignty over the exploitation and use of natural resources, particularly petroleum and minerals.[1] In several instances, this resulted in nationalization of foreign-owned enterprises during the 1960s and early 1970s. Even where nationalization did not take place, comprehensive regulatory legislation and measures were introduced to achieve this purpose, and state-owned corporations were set up in several developing countries to exercise regulatory and supervisory functions and to participate in the development and exploitation of such resources.

Petroleum Exploration and Development

Petroleum technology includes the techniques and processes involved in petroleum exploration and development up to the stage of transportation and refining. Although the basic technology for petroleum development has remained fairly stable, major technological innovations have been constantly taking place in various operations relating to petroleum exploration, refining, and marketing. These include technological development in seismic and geophysical surveys; drilling to greater depths; offshore operations; improved recovery, separation, and collection processes; liquefaction and transportation; and various stages of refining. Technical improvements in these fields became greatly intensified during the 1970s, following the oil crisis, and new technologies and practices were rapidly introduced. These were principally designed to enable exploration and drilling activities in especially remote and difficult regions, and also to substantially enhance the efficiency of various operations, including the maximization of recovery from existing oil and gas fields.

The process of technology transfer to developing countries in petroleum exploration and development has historically been a function of the relationships between governments of host countries and MNCs, which played a dominant role in the past. These relationships have changed significantly during the last two decades, and traditional petroleum concessions granted to MNCs in earlier decades have, in recent years, been gradually replaced by production-sharing arrangements and service contracts in several of the Third World countries with petroleum reserves or potential.[2] The changes in contractual arrangements have had considerable effect on the nature of technology transfer and indigenous technological development in this sector.

Till the 1950s, petroleum operations in developing countries were dominated by major oil corporations, except in Mexico, where these operations were nationalized in 1938. The major corporations—Exxon (U.S.A.), Royal Dutch Shell (Netherlands/UK), Mobil, Texaco, Gulf Oil and Socal (U.S.A.), and British Petroleum (UK)—had a major share in the exploitation of global petroleum resources, with intensive and diversified activities spread over a large number of countries and with highly vertical operations, extending from geophysical surveys and drilling to world-wide marketing and refining. These MNCs, together with Philips, Occidental, Atlantic Richfield, and several others, operated largely through petroleum concessions covering extensive areas over long periods. The function of host governments was mostly confined to the receipt of royalties and taxes, and MNC operations in the concession areas were wholly controlled by the corporations. The techniques and processes utilized, were, for the most part, state-of-the-art technology used by the parent corporation in its global operations. The extent of local technological absorption was limited and was generally confined to the operation of machinery and equipment. This was further circumscribed by the nature of the operations in each country and the extent to which local personnel were employed by the MNC subsidiaries.

The structure of petroleum operations in developing countries changed significantly during the 1960s and 1970s. Certain state-owned enterprises from industrialized countries that had no petroleum resources expanded their exploration activities in developing countries, with a major role being undertaken by ENI (Italy) and ELF-ERAP (France). Technical assistance was also supplied by the USSR and Rumania to some developing countries, including India, in oil exploration and refinery establishment. The most important development was, however, the establishment of state-owned corporations in a number of Third World countries, companies that over the years have become responsible for petroleum operations and development in their respective countries. These state-owned enterprises were set up both in oil-producing countries and in countries with a potential for petroleum production. Their establishment marked an important stage in the growth of institutional technological capability in these countries. Gradually, most of these enterprises have assumed varying degrees of responsibility for the formulation of national programs for petroleum development and for supervising the implementation of such programs.[3] In certain developing countries, such as Mexico and India, state petroleum enterprises have assumed direct responsibility for the exploitation of petroleum and gas reserves, using MNCs and specialist companies mainly to perform specific technical services. State-owned corporations from certain developing countries have also undertaken petroleum exploration and development in other developing countries, such as PETROBRAS (Brazil), the Oil and Natural Gas Commission (India), and SONATRACH (Algeria). In other developing countries, such as Indonesia, state-owned enterprises function as national partners in joint ventures and in production-sharing and other contractual arrangements. Although the extent of direct participation by state enterprises in petroleum operations differs from country to country, these organizations have undoubtedly emerged as key institutional factors in the growth of local technological and managerial capability. National petroleum companies have also emerged as major traders and suppliers of crude oil and natural gas.

The shift in ownership in the oil industry from MNCs to the producing developing countries was most pronounced in the early 1970s. Thus, although, in 1970, the seven major oil MNCs owned 61 percent of the crude oil and smaller MNCs owned 33 percent, by 1977, the share of the seven majors decreased to 25 percent and that of other MNCs to 20 percent. During the same period, the producing developing countries increased their share of crude oil ownership to 55 percent.[4] Despite this drastic change in crude oil ownership, oil MNCs still dominate the international oil trade. In 1980, for example, of the total crude oil production outside North America and the socialist countries, 43 percent of the production and purchase were by the seven major MNCs, and 24 percent were by other MNCs.[5]

Even though, during the 1960s and particularly the 1970s, the nature of contractual terms between oil MNCs and oil-producing developing countries had undergone a major change, the relationship between MNCs and the state-owned enterprises in developing countries has remained close. Along with production sharing and purchase arrangements, joint ventures have been formed in several cases. In several other cases, MNCs provide technical assistance, as ARAMCO does in Saudi Arabia and CFP does for the Bombay High program in India or state enterprise in Venezuela. PEMEX in Mexico has several agreements for technology and know-how with foreign suppliers, as have other state enterprises from developing countries.

Despite the dominant role of the major petroleum MNCs in the past, which continues even to the present in marketing, transportation, and refining, technology ownership in the petroleum sector is not confined to these companies alone. Although MNCs in this sector have extensive knowledge and experience, in both the exploratory and secondary stages of oil and gas exploitation, and most of these companies have set up subsidiaries for various technical services, a considerable proportion of technological knowledge is held by specialist companies that concentrate only on certain operations or on particular equipment or in providing specialized engineering services.[6] Thus, certain companies, such as Teledyne, have developed specialized expertise in geological and geophysical surveys and investigations, while others, such as Schlumberger, have developed specialized expertise in logging, reservoir engineering, and other areas. Several companies produce specialized equipment, such as drilling bits manufactured by the Hughes Tool Company, or drill pipes by Smith International, or security and other equipment by Dresser Industries. The specialized engineering companies—such as Kellogg, Lummus, Fluor, Stone and Webster, and Foster Wheeler (U.S.), Lurgi (FRG), Snam Progetti (Italy), Technip (France), and Chiyoda (Japan)—also constitute major sources of technology and services and are extensively utilized in energy installations, refineries, liquefied gas plants, and the like.[7] During the 1970s, following the oil crisis, a number of smaller specialist consultancy firms were also established in specific petroleum activities and have added to the availability of alternative sources of petroleum technology. The extent of the competition in this field has increased considerably, and developing countries have a much greater choice in the selection of foreign investors, partners, or contractors, depending on the nature of the contractual arrangement. Regardless of the growth in the number of suppliers of petroleum technology, it must be emphasized that the risk element and operational control at the stage of petroleum exploration continues to be exercised largely by MNCs.[8] A greater degree of technological application and orientation generally takes place only after a commercial discovery of oil or gas has been made.

The principal emphasis in petroleum agreements between host countries and MNCs has been on commercial and financial provisions and on the sharing of revenue and production of crude oil and gas. Consequently, much greater consideration has been given, in such agreements, to provisions relating to ownership, recovery of exploration costs with discovery and subsequent commercial exploitation, duration of exploration agreements (with phased relinquishment provisions), royalties and taxes, production sharing and pricing arrangements, and the like. In fact, petroleum agreements generally give relatively little emphasis to technology transfer,[9] and this aspect normally does not constitute a central element in such contracts.[10]

The development of indigenous technological capability in the petroleum sector must, however, be considered an important objective in Third World countries with petroleum reserves and potential. This objective extends from development of the capability to formulate and implement petroleum development programs to decision making in geophysical surveys, alternative contractual arrangements for exploration and development, and effective monitoring and participation in various stages of petroleum operations.[11] National capability needs to be developed, not only in negotiating suitable commercial arrangements for development of petroleum resources but also with regard to all aspects of petroleum operations. Such capability should not be confined to individual nationals in these countries but should also be acquired and applied by national institutions, which usually take the form of state petroleum enterprises and national research and consulting engineering organizations.

Certain provisions in petroleum contracts have a direct impact on technology transfer. Thus, most such contracts in recent years specifically provide for employment and training of local people and for the development of local capability. General provisions to this effect are usually accepted by MNCs and foreign partners or contractors, since it is more economical to employ local personnel up to certain levels, even with the added cost of training, which is generally provided on the job. In some agreements, programs of training are defined and stipulated, and provision is also made for scholarships to local individuals for training in specific fields and operations. In an agreement with the government of Trinidad and Tobago in 1974, it was provided that the foreign company would provide $50,000 annually for the first six years and $250,000 for the subsequent ten years for training, scholarships, and the development of local capability.[12] In regard to employment, some agreements provide up to certain percentages of total employment to local people. In Nigeria, for example, the Petroleum Decree (1969) stipulates that foreign companies should employ local persons in 75 percent of the management and supervisory positions and 100 percent of all other jobs.[13] In some contracts, such as the one by PETRONAS in Malaysia, provision has been made to set apart 0.5 percent of profits for research and development.

The provision for reversion of petroleum installations and equipment, once an agreement is terminated, can be of importance in developing local technological capability. Operational capability to use such equipment is acquired by local personnel during the contract period, and the continued use of such equipment can be very useful for technological absorption and future adaptation. Provision is also often made in petroleum contracts for the use of local materials, equipment, and other inputs, as far as possible. This is useful in developing local production capability for parts and components and for various auxiliary products. In some developing countries, such as Brazil, India, and Mexico, a considerable proportion of the equipment and material required is produced internally and is increasingly utilized by companies operating in these countries.

At the institutional level, particularly in state petroleum enterprises in these countries, petroleum technology can be absorbed mainly through varying degrees of monitoring and participation in operations. Contractual provisions to this effect are incorporated in most agreements, although the degree of participation by national enterprises in host countries varies considerably. Foreign operators are required to submit periodic reports regarding their activities. Review and assessment of such reports may even provide considerable technological insight. In many agreements, foreign companies are also required to obtain approval to undertake certain programs and activities. This may also enable host governments to participate effectively in technical operations and to coordinate the implementation of national programs for petroleum development.

The nature of petroleum agreements may also have considerable effect on the extent of the technology transferred. In petroleum concessions, operational responsibilities and decisions primarily rest with the foreign operator, usually an MNC. Although technology is transferred to local nationals in various operations and reversion of installations and equipment can provide the basic physical requirements, the basic elements of petroleum technology are generally not transferred. In the case of production-sharing and service contracts, the scope for technology transfer is usually much greater, though the extent of transfer largely depends, even in these agreements, on the local technological infrastructure and the absorptive capacity of national installations and human resources. In production-sharing and risk-service contracts, investments at the exploration stage are made by the foreign company, and participation by host country institutions during this stage is generally quite limited. Nevertheless, certain state enterprises have been able to participate in these operations also and then gradually to develop knowledge and expertise even in such complex operations as offshore drilling and collection systems. In Algeria, for example, the state-owned enterprise has set up a number of joint ventures with specialist companies in various operations at the exploration stage and has acquired considerable expertise through these arrangements. PERTAMINA in Indonesia has also acquired considerable expertise in monitoring and coordinating the operations of foreign companies in petroleum exploration. Also, in several other developing countries, specific provision is made for participation by state petroleum enterprises during the exploration stage. It is, however, after commercial discovery of oil or gas that a greater degree of participation, and consequently technology transfer and absorption, takes place, because host country institutions and entities tend to be more closely involved at these stages through joint management boards and other arrangements. In many instances, provision is made for joint ventures or other forms of production and revenue participation. This enables different degrees of participation in technological operations and management.

The downstream processing of petroleum and natural gas up to the stage of transportation and refining raises important technological issues. Transportation through long-distance pipelines of liquefied gas poses complex technical problems and requires considerable technological capability, which has been adequately absorbed in certain developing countries. As for refining technology, certain processes, such as vacuum distillation and desulfurization are no longer protected by patents, but technical know-how still must be obtained from foreign companies in most developing countries. These companies may be either oil MNCs participating in refining operations or specialist engineering companies providing engineering and production know-how.

The development of research capability and of consulting engineering capacity in the petroleum sector is of major importance for Third World countries and has been given high priority in several developing countries. The Institute of Petroleum in Mexico and similar bodies in the Arab region and in countries such as Brazil and India have developed considerable research capability in various aspects of petroleum technology. Special emphasis has also been given in some of these countries to the development of consulting engineering capability, and an increasing proportion of detailed engineering work is gradually being performed in these countries, usually through state-owned or state-supported institutions and enterprises.

While oil-producing developing countries have considerably increased their income and other benefits from oil production and have assumed a large degree of control over their operations, oil MNCs continue to retain a critical role in the industry. Apart from their dominant position in distribution and their specialized knowledge of petroleum technology and operations, these corporations are able to mobilize large financial resources for oil exploration. Largely in response to the growing control exercised by producing developing countries and the strong bargaining position of their governments in negotiations, during the 1970s, MNCs decreased oil exploration in developing countries in favor of locating such operations in industrialized countries and in their offshore areas. During the 1975–79 period, for example, "party months" of seismic prospecting in developing countries decreased from 35.5 percent in the early 1970s to 29.7 percent of the world total exploratory efforts.[14] Even though developing countries have access to a number of alternative sources for financing exploration, such as the World Bank, these sources may not be adequate and may retard the development of oil exploration and development in some of these countries in the future.

Mining and Mineral Processing

The mining and mineral processing sector has been a field in which MNCs have traditionally played a dominant role in most developing countries with mineral resources. With the demand for processed minerals largely concentrated in industrialized economies, mining and extraction operations have been largely undertaken by MNCs from these countries. In most areas of mining, especially nonfuel minerals—including iron, bauxite, copper, tin and zinc—a relatively small number of MNCs have dominated mining and processing operations for particular minerals. Considerable literature is available on the historical growth of mining in developing countries and the extent of

MNC concentration in different stages of the processing of various mineral ores.[15] This section will analyze only the effect of changes in the relationships between host developing countries and MNCs on the pattern of technology transfer in this sector. These changes generally reflect the relative bargaining positions of the host country and the MNC concerned. The MNC's strength lies principally in its capacity to mobilize the large capital outlays required for most mining projects and the managerial and technological expertise needed. In many instances, the MNCs concerned also enjoy a high degree of concentration in the particular sector of mining, and considerable vertical integration in various stages of processing. The host country's bargaining capability primarily lies in the advantageous features of the ore deposits, including the scarcity value of the particular ore and its size and accessibility. Apart from the exercise of national sovereignty over its own natural resources, host country objectives include maximization of revenue through taxes, royalties, and dividends, and the utilization of mining operations as a core for overall economic development of the area concerned.[16] In recent years, another important aim has been to determine basic policies and programs in particular mining projects and to participate effectively in the decision-making process in such projects. As in the case of petroleum exploration and development, issues relating to technology transfer do not generally receive undue emphasis and priority in mining agreements with foreign investors or managers, though the need for developing national technological capability in mining operations is increasingly recognized in these countries.

Significant changes have occurred in the ownership structure of the mining sector in the last two decades. Before the 1960s, apart from surface mining and small-scale operations undertaken by local companies and individuals in coal, iron ore, and similar resources, large-scale mining operations in Third World countries were mainly undertaken by MNCs, whose operations were vertically integrated and covered ore extraction, beneficiation, processing, refining, smelting, and semifabrication. Most processing operations were conducted in industrialized countries, and whatever technology was transferred to developing countries related mainly to ore extraction and machinery operations. In the postcolonial period, and particularly during the 1960s and early 1970s, the issue of national sovereignty over natural resources, especially petroleum and minerals, assumed major sociopolitical and socioeconomic significance. Several developing countries increased the extent of national ownership.[17] In some instances, this took the form of outright nationalization, as in Chile, Peru, and Zaire, or the assumption of majority ownership, as in Zambia, Ghana, and Sierra Leone. In other countries, the earlier concession agreements were renegotiated to provide higher returns to host countries, as in Jamaica, Surinam, and the Dominican Republic. At times, these returns came through participation in the ownership of state-owned companies, such as in Papua New Guinea in the Bougainville copper project.

The assumption of full or partial national ownership by host country governments of mining operations often did not lead to effective control over technological operations and management. In many instances, the services of MNCs were retained, through management and technical assistance contracts, for fairly long periods. When new joint mining ventures have been negotiated, the management function has also often been entrusted to the MNC partner, regardless of the extent of holdings. In recent years, the nature of contractual arrangements also has varied considerably in mining agreements with MNCs, determined mostly by the degree of dependence of the host country on foreign MNCs for technological and managerial expertise.[18]

The nature and extent of technology transfer in the mining sector have depended largely on the extent of participation of host country governments and enterprises in mining operations and on the extent of forward linkages in the form of ore beneficiation and refining, smelting, and ore processing. Complex techniques and heavy-duty mining equipment are often required for certain mining operations and in the production of ore concentrates, and a high degree of mine engineering capability may be applied. Considerable mechanization may also be necessary in most mining operations. The complexity of such operations and of the infrastructure and material-handling requirement varies for different nonfuel minerals; the capital costs and technological complexity of various stages of processing may also differ considerably. The varying pattern of technological requirements and experience may be seen in certain nonfuel minerals, such as iron, aluminum, copper, zinc, lead, and tin.

With steel production taking place only in some developing countries, most of these countries with iron ore have been extracting such ores for exports. The major iron ore producer among developing countries is Brazil, with over 15 percent of the global mining capacity.[19] Although steel production in Brazil has increased considerably, it represented only about 2 percent of world steel capacity in the early 1980s.[20] Iron ore exports have, on the other hand, increased steadily. Brazil is followed in iron ore production in developing countries by India and Chile, both of which are also producing sizable quantities of steel, then by several other countries, including Venezuela, Cuba, Peru, Mauritania, Nigeria, Liberia, Angola, and Gabon. Most of the iron ore exports from African countries are to steel plants in Western Europe, while Japan imports large quantities of ore from Brazil and, to a lesser extent, from India.

Technology for iron ore extraction has remained fairly stable, although in some cases, ore extraction has involved complex technological operations and higher mechanization, including transportation through ropeways and conveyors, beneficiation processes, pelletization, slurrying, and mechanical loading facilities at ports. These processes and equipment, once established, have not posed major technological problems at the operational stage and are often undertaken by national, state-owned enterprises that have been set up in ore-producing developing countries. Important Third World companies that are extracting and exporting iron ore include Cia Vale de Rio Doce, which has the highest ore production, Mineracao, Brasileiras Reunides, and Mineracao de Trinidade in Brazil, Cia Acero del Pacifico in Chile, CVG Ferrominera Orinoco in Venezuela, the state-owned National Mineral Development Corporation and the Mineral and Metals Trading Corporation in India, Hierro in Peru, and SNIM in Mauritania.[21]

Technological requirements of steel production are far more complex than those of ore development and pig iron production, and slow absorption of the technology may constitute an important constraint in many developing countries. On the other hand, acquisition of technology by developing country enterprises from steel manufacturers in developed countries and from specialized engineering companies has not restricted the growth of the steel industry so far. In most developing countries, government policies have reserved iron and steel production for domestic companies, and such production has usually been undertaken in the public sector. Thus, for manufacturers in industrialized countries, which are mostly large, domestically oriented companies, licensing of technology and monies from various technical services have provided the principal revenues from steel-producing developing countries. Production of steel in most developing countries is, however, strongly hindered by the large capital requirement of steel production and the limited size of local markets, which, except in a few countries such as Argentina, Brazil, Mexico, India, and the Republic of Korea, prevents the economical production of steel.

Several technological innovations that have taken place in the past decade in steel manufacture have been transferred to developing countries and have been incorporated in recent integrated plants, especially in Brazil and the Republic of Korea, thus enabling these countries to compete in export markets, especially in the United States. In industrialized countries, continuous technological innovations are also taking place, such as high-speed steel casting and rapid solidification and new developments in powder metallurgy; these innovations are likely to have a significant impact on materials technology in the future. Although some of the innovations are incorporated in machinery and equipment, several of these processes are commercialized by engineering companies.

An area of technological development of special interest to developing countries relates to the direct-reduction process, which enables steel production for much smaller capacities. This technology has been utilized in developing countries to a considerable extent in recent years. With a growing requirement for steel in several developing countries, smaller plants using this process or similar processes may adequately meet technological requirements in developing countries. In this context, it is important to point out that, in the development of the basic technology for direct reduction process, the

Mexican company Industria Monterrey has played a pioneer role. The Hylsa process, which has been developed indigenously by this company, has been licensed to several developed and developing country enterprises.

Bauxite is mainly produced in developing countries, which have over 77 percent of the world's bauxite reserves, located largely in Guinea, Brazil, Jamaica, India, and Guyana.[22] Alumina refining and the smelting of aluminum have, however, taken place mostly in industrialized countries. It is only in the last two decades that some additional capacity for alumina refining and aluminum smelting has been established in developing countries, particularly in Brazil and India. Most of the refining and smelting operations are directed by a few MNCs, which have dominated the world industry outside the centrally planned economies.[23] Refining and smelting by these MNCs have been carried out in a large number of operations: ALCAN has twenty smelters, including a joint venture in the Republic of Korea; ALCOA has fifteen smelters, including units in Mexico, Brazil, and Surinam; Alusuisse has thirteen smelters, all of which are located in industrialized countries; Kaiser has eleven smelters, including plants in Ghana, Bahrain, and a minority joint venture in India; and Reynolds has eleven smelters, including a unit in Ghana. With a few exceptions, most of these operations are majority or wholly owned by the parent companies, and the predominant share of the capacity is located in developed countries. In the mid-1970s, for example, although these six MNCs extracted more than half of their bauxite production in developing countries, they processed less than one-third of the alumina in these countries and locally produced less than 10 percent of their aluminum.[24]

Several factors have contributed to the dominant position of these companies over time. Since the major share of the world's bauxite production is processed by these vertically integrated companies, marketing tends to pose considerable difficulties for new entrants. The large capital outlays and the complexity of the technology utilized have acted as further constraints for new producers. While the basic technological processes for extracting alumina from bauxite have remained unchanged for several decades, many improvements that allow processing of different types and grades of raw material have been made. Similarly, in aluminum refining, the basic processes of digestion, precipitation, and calcination have remained stable, but continuing technological improvements have increased the efficiency of the techniques. Most MNCs have also developed proprietary knowledge and techniques in various phases of production (for example, more efficient use of energy), which, though not patented, cannot be obtained from other sources. The small number of manufacturers and international engineering companies in this field has concentrated technological expertise among a few companies.

During the 1970s, the rising costs of new projects and the increasing emphasis on national ownership in developing countries have resulted in major adaptations of the strategy of MNCs.[25] Thus, the large capital outlays required for bauxite mining and processing have led, in several cases, to the formation of consortia among MNCs, as in Guinea and Brazil, so that the size of the investment and risk for individual companies is reduced. In response to developing country requirements, MNCs have accepted minority holdings or technology-supply agreements with nationally owned companies, either state-owned or in the private sector, as in Bahrain, India, Indonesia, and Mexico. In these cases, plant engineering and production technology have been supplied by MNCs. In several cases, MNCs have also provided technological services and marketing and management support. Plant engineering and production know-how have been important instruments for participation and control by MNCs. The substantial costs of engineering, technology, and other services have generally been capitalized by MNCs and have enabled these companies to obtain equity shares in developing country enterprises. Although the basic engineering and production technologies for alumina and aluminum production have not changed significantly during the past decades, the complex process of production generally requires technological assistance, either by international engineering companies or by MNCs with production experience in the field. In Argentina, for example, Montecatini Edison (Italy) provided smelter technology to a local company, Alvar, while Reynolds (U.S.) supplied technology and know-how to Venalum in Venezuela. In several cases, MNCs have functioned as turnkey contractors and have assumed management responsibilities during the initial stages of operation. The Companhia Brasileira de Aluminio in Brazil, for example, received technical assistance initially from Montecatini Edison (Italy) and from Pechiney (France) during its expansion stage.

New entrants in alumina/aluminum production, most of them from developing countries, have largely relied on these MNCs for technological support, except for those projects that have been based on technology and know-how from the Soviet Union (such as the Indian public sector enterprise, Bharat Aluminium) or from Eastern European countries. In the next few years, however, with several plants being operated by nationally owned companies in developing countries, these companies will increasingly be in a position to offer additional sources of technology. As the demand for aluminum increases in the 1980s and 1990s, additional smelting capacity will need to be established. Smelters are increasingly likely to be set up in proximity to raw material availability in developing countries and through nationally owned enterprises in these countries. At the same time, the major MNCs will continue to be important sources for technology and for improvements in technological processes, though they are likely to face greater competition from developing country enterprises in this field.

In the case of copper, a large proportion of the reserves (about 58 percent), are located in developing countries, mainly in Chile, Zaire, Panama,

Peru, Zambia, and Mexico, besides the major deposits located recently in Papua New Guinea, West Iran, Indonesia, and the Philippines.[26] Until the early 1960s, the major share of copper mining was undertaken by seven major MNCs: Kennecott, Anaconda, Phelps Dodge, and Roan-AMC (U.S.), Anglo-American Group (South Africa), Union Miniere (Belgium), and International Nickel (Canada). In the early 1960s, copper production by these seven MNCs accounted for about 60 percent of the world production.[27] Since the 1960s, however, major changes have taken place in the industry. In 1967, in Zaire, Union Miniere was nationalized; during 1969–71, in Chile, the copper industry was nationalized; and in Zambia, foreign companies were taken over in 1970 and ZIMCO was established. By 1979, the three state-owned corporations—Codelco in Chile, Gecamines in Zaire, and ZIMCO in Zambia—had the largest mining capacity, constituting over 24 percent of the world's mining capacity, excluding centrally planned economies.[28] Largely as a result of the newly established companies in several developing countries, by the late 1970s the share of the seven leading MNCs in copper mining had decreased to 25 percent.[29] Unlike the situation in the aluminum industry, there has been a much lower degree of integration of mining and copper smelting capacity, and smelting and fabrication operations have often been undertaken by different companies. Smelting and refining operations, however, are increasingly being located near major deposits.

Copper mining technology, though fairly old and well established, has undergone considerable improvement during the last decade, with a greater degree of mechanization in mining and ore handling and increased chemical processing. Treatment of both oxide and sulphide ores has become fairly standardized over the years, but several technological improvements have been introduced, such as concentration through the process of flotation, copper recovery through chemical precipitation, and the like. Such technological developments have been applied largely by copper MNCs, although they have also been introduced in new projects involving state-owned corporations by specialized engineering companies such as Fluor, Bechtel, and Morrison-Knudsen (U.S.), Krupp Industries (FRG), and Outokumpu Oy (Finland). Besides their involvement in the construction phase in new and expansion projects, MNCs specializing in the copper industry are also in a position to contribute significantly to production techniques and day-to-day operations. Their role has also been critical in mobilizing the major capital cost of the Bougainville project in Papua New Guinea, where Rio Tinto Zinc has majority holding, nearly $480 million in 1971–72.[30] With present-day costs of mining and processing equipment considerably higher, the magnitude of capital costs of copper mining and smelting projects has become very large.[31] The Cerro Colorado project in Panama is expected to cost over $1.6 billion, and the OK Tedi project in Papua New Guinea is also likely to exceed $1 billion.[32]. Financial institutions funding such projects often insist on effective participation of MNCs specializing in this field. Such participation may also be necessary, particularly in new projects, because of the complex technological and managerial expertise required for implementation of large-scale copper projects. The extent of the technological requirements would, of course, depend on the stage of processing to be undertaken. In several developing countries, including the Philippines, Indonesia, Papua New Guinea, and Mexico, and also in Zaire and Peru to a substantial extent, production is limited to concentrates or blister, which is then exported to the United States, Japan, Belgium, and the Federal Republic of Germany. Although the mining and handling requirements up to this stage are highly complex and demand considerable technological and managerial capability, the further stages of refining and smelting require even more ability and expertise. Chile and Zambia refine most of their copper production, and the state-owned undertakings in these countries have been able to achieve adequate technological capabilities and absorption of the processes involved. Additional smelting capacity is being set up or planned in other developing countries, such as Brazil, Mexico, Taiwan, and the Republic of Korea, and technological absorption is not likely to present any major problem in these countries.

Besides iron, bauxite, and copper, important nonfuel minerals include lead, nickel, zinc, and tin. In most of these minerals, MNCs have also played a fairly dominant role. In lead, most of the mining and processing is done in industrialized countries; only about 25 percent is processed in developing countries,[33] mainly in Peru, Mexico, Morocco, Iran, and Namibia, with smaller quantities in several countries in Asia. Some of the major MNCs involved in lead refining are ASARCO, AMAX, St. Joe Minerals, Rio Tinto Zinc, COMINCO, and Industria Mineria, Mexico. There has been no major problem of technological absorption in lead extraction and refining in these countries, although most of the refining capacity is controlled by the MNCs in this field. In the case of nickel, most of the reserves, except for those in Canada, are located in developing countries. The largest producer among these countries is New Caledonia, followed by Cuba, Indonesia, Philippines, Dominican Republic, Guatemala, Brazil, and other smaller producers.[34] The major MNCs involved in these countries, other than in Cuba, are International Nickel, with over 35 percent of production capacity of refined nickel or ferro-nickel, Falconbridge from Canada, and several Japanese companies operating in Southeast Asia. The technological processes for mining, processing, and refining are fairly well established but are closely held by the major MNCs. Since the lateritic ores, which are generally found in developing countries, are difficult to convert into concentrates for shipment abroad, they generally are refined up to the ferro-nickel stage in the producing countries. Most of the production and refining capacity continues to be controlled by MNCs. Most of the production capacity for zinc is in industrialized countries. Among developing countries, the principal producers are Peru and

Mexico. Processing facilities have been developed in these countries, though part of the production is exported as concentrates. Other producers include Iran, Thailand, and Bolivia with no processing facilities, and Brazil, India, the Republic of Korea, Zaire, Zambia, and Algeria with local processing capability. Some of the major MNCs in this field are ASARCO, Noranda, Texasgulf, Rio Tinto Zinc, Centromin Peru, and COMINCO in mining and Societe Generale de Belgique, Mitsui, and other Japanese companies—including Mitsubishi, Sumitomo, and Nippon Mining—Rio Tinto Zinc, and COMINCO in zink processing. Although mining does not present technological problems, zinc processing is fairly technical, and the technology lies mainly with the MNCs in this field. In the case of tin, the situation relating to processing is significantly different in that most such processing is undertaken in the developing countries where most tin reserves are located.[35] The major producing countries are Malaysia and Bolivia, with smaller reserves in the People's Republic of China, Indonesia, Thailand, Brazil, Nigeria, and Zaire. Most tin smelting capacity is located in Malaysia, with smaller capacities in the other developing countries that are designed to process the output of their respective mines. Major MNCs in this field include Patino NY (with smelting capacity in Malaysia, Nigeria, and Brazil), Shell-Billiton (operating in Thailand), Rio Tinto Zinc, COMIBOL (Bolivia), and Gulf Chemicals.[36] An important state-owned undertaking is PT Timah in Indonesia, with large mining and smelting capacity. Technology for mining and smelting has been adequately absorbed in the developing countries where tin is produced and processed.

The foregoing survey of nonfuel mining and mineral processing indicates the important role of MNCs and the major structural and technological changes in this sector. There has been significant change in the ownership pattern and a gradual shift on the part of MNCs to minority holdings and management and service agreements. This has been due largely to the national policies of developing countries, and with the large capital outlays that new mining projects will require in future, this pattern is likely to continue, with direct capital investment by MNCs being gradually reduced. Technology transfer and absorption in developing countries have largely depended on the extent to which refining and processing operations have been undertaken. Mining technology has posed no problems of technological absorption, although the extent to which mine mechanization is necessary, or even appropriate, may need to be considered further in the context of particular countries. As for processing and ore-refining technology, most of the techniques and processes are fairly well established, although technological improvements have been made from time to time. The process of technological absorption of the refining stage has also posed little difficulty in most developing countries where such processing activities have been undertaken. Such technology was initially obtained from MNCs, as a result of MNC investments or through contractual arrangements, but subsequent technological absorption and adaptation have been fairly rapid and adequate in most of these countries.

An aspect of mining in which technological issues would be in the forefront is deep-sea mining of manganese nodules, from which copper, nickel, and cobalt can be recovered. The prolonged negotiations over rights to seabed resources and their exploitation ended with the Convention on the Law of the Sea, adopted by the United Nations. Although this convention has not been signed by the United States, it is likely to spur considerable initiative on deep-sea mining in future years. A critical issue in this regard is the development of technology to enable seabed mining. Several MNCs joined in consortia for research and development activities, and considerable equipment has been developed. Certain developing countries, particularly India, China, and the Republic of Korea, are also initiating programs in this regard. The exploitation of seabed mineral resources would represent a major and significant technological breakthrough in the mining sector.

Processing Industries—Fertilizers

Closely related to exploration and development of petroleum and natural resources are those technological processes that convert these products into industrial raw materials and feedstock for a wide range of industries. In Third World countries, processing industries related to petroleum that are of special priority are fertilizers and chemicals. Most of these projects involve very large capital outlays, besides specialized technological capability and managerial know-how. Production technology in fertilizers, petrochemicals, and other process industries is composed of specialized and complex processes, which tend to be highly capital-intensive.[37] Besides the process knowhow for particular fertilizers or petrochemicals, an essential element of technology is the basic and detailed engineering involved in the design and construction of such plants. Consequently, technology transfer in such process industries necessarily requires not only operational technology once a plant is in production but also the capability to plan, design, and construct such plants. This poses a further problem in that engineering and construction technology, including process know-how in certain cases, is often held by engineering MNCs that may have little or no stake in actual investments in these fields.

Since agriculture continues to be the mainstay of the economy of most developing countries, increased production of urea and other chemical fertilizers is a matter of high priority in these countries. Although large investments have been made in this sector during the last two decades, the production of fertilizers in developing countries continues to be much less than that in industrialized economies and will constitute only about 19.5 percent and 18.3 percent, respectively, of global production of nitrogen and phosphatic fertilizers in 1984–85.[38] Nitrogenous fertilizers are mostly based on ammonia, which in turn, is based mostly on natural gas, somewhat on naphtha. In some instances, coal has also been utilized. Since natural gas is available in several Third World countries, it has served as the principal feedstock for chemical fertilizer production in these countries, including in Mexico, Trinidad and Tobago, Indonesia, India, and a number of oil-producing countries in the Middle East. In the case of phosphatic fertilizers, raw materials in the form of phosphatic rock are available in a number of developing countries, including Morocco, Tunisia, China, Senegal, Jordan, Togo, Navru, and Vietnam, with smaller quantities in Algeria, Egypt, India, and others.

Despite raw material availability, the growth of fertilizer production in Third World countries has tended to be slow. This is largely because of the large capital outlays required and the fact that there has been comparatively limited investment by MNCs in this field. In fact, foreign investment in this sector is mainly confined to a few plants in Trinidad and Tobago, Pakistan, India, the Republic of Korea, Malaysia, and Qatar, with foreign minority holdings in several of these cases. Apart from a marked trend toward majority national ownership of fertilizer production, such production has been undertaken through state-owned enterprises in many Third World countries, including Bangladesh, Brazil, India, Indonesia, Kuwait, and Mexico. This has taken place partly because of limited MNC investments in this sector, but also because of deliberate policies in several countries to take up fertilizer production through state-owned companies or state-controlled organizations because of its importance to agriculture.

An important technological feature in the establishment of large fertilizer projects has been the fact that planning, engineering, and construction have generally been undertaken by the major engineering corporations in this field, which operate on a global basis in technological designs and engineering. In the case of ammonia plants, for example, Kellogg (U.S.) has provided basic designs and engineering and has undertaken plant construction responsibilities for nearly 40 percent of the ammonia plants completed or under construction in 1979–80.[39] Several other engineering firms have also been involved in specialized designs and construction in fertilizer plants—for example, Fluor, Braun, and Foster Wheeler (U.S.); Snam Projetti (Italy); Toyo Engineering, Mitsubishi, and Sumitomo (Japan); Haldor Topsoe (Denmark); Uhde (FRG); and Davey Power Gass (UK). The role of such engineering companies has been particularly pronounced in Third World countries, where several fertilizer plants have been designed and constructed on a turnkey basis.

In terms of technology transfer, operational technology in chemical fertilizer production, including ammonia and various types of nitrogenous and phosphatic fertilizers, has been effectively transferred in developing countries with established plants. Despite initial problems, most of these plants are working fairly satisfactorily and are operated and managed by local personnel. A major gap in technology transfer, however, concerns the limited capability available in these countries, with the exception of one or two of the larger countries, for design, engineering, and construction of such plants. Most Third World countries continue to be dependent on the major engineering companies from the United States, Western Europe, and Japan for designs and engineering and for the supply of machinery and equipment. With the cost of ammonia plants (including infrastructure costs) estimated at over $400 million per 1,000 tonnes per day (1980 estimates), not counting costs for subsequent stages of processing, design engineering and construction responsibilities must necessarily be entrusted to companies with specialized expertise and experience in this field.[40] At the same time, unless national capability in the engineering and construction of such plants is established in developing countries, technology transfer would continue to be limited to plant operations and to the mixing of various types of fertilizers to meet local requirements.

In the case of phosphatic fertilizers, the techniques for the mining of phosphatic rock in developing countries continue to be more labor-intensive than those in industrialized economies, where such operations are highly mechanized. This may be quite desirable, since it not only provides greater flexibility in operations and costs but also provides considerable employment potential. It is, however, with regard to the process technology and associated basic and detailed engineering and construction requirements that a significant technology gap continues to exist. This relates not only to ammonia and urea production but also to the production of nitric acid, phosphoric acid, superphosphates, and various other products that require complex technology. The growth of national capability in design, engineering, and construction of fertilizer plants is limited to a few developing countries. In India, the state-owned Fertiliser Corporation of India has developed considerable capability in the design and engineering of such plants, especially ammonia and urea plants, and most of the detailed engineering is done within the country. A large proportion of the machinery and equipment for fertilizer plants is also presently manufactured in India. In other countries, such as Brazil, Mexico, and the Republic of Korea, a considerable proportion of the equipment can be produced within the countries, and a part of the detailed engineering is done by local consultancy organizations. The pattern of technological growth in these countries indicates, however, that national capability in the basic and detailed engineering of fertilizer projects can be built up only gradually and only after a series of similar projects.

Although most of the fertilizer plants in Third World countries, with the exception of India, have been designed and constructed by foreign engineering companies, the transfer of operational technology has been fairly effective once such plants have been commissioned. In several instances, adjustments and modifications have been necessary in plant designs, depending on the availability of industrial raw materials, the production capacity required, and the nature of the final fertilizer product to be manufactured. Such modifications have, for the most part, been managed by foreign consultancy organizations responsible for design and plant construction. National capability has, however, been built up to varying extents in several developing countries in the mixing of compound fertilizers and in plant installation, operations, and maintenance. As for basic and detailed engineering capability, the progress achieved in India has been very signficant, although foreign consultancy services are still utilized for some of the more complex production processes. Research and development in fertilizers in developing countries have largely concentrated on the analysis of alternative fertilizer use under different soil and climatic conditions, and only limited research has been undertaken, mostly in India, on alternative process design and engineering for fertilizer plants.

The experience of technology transfer in chemical and other process industries in Third World countries has been mostly similar to transfer in the chemical fertilizer industry, with plant design and engineering being largely undertaken by foreign engineering companies. Chemicals and petrochemicals cover a very wide range of products and related technological processes. The product range extends from basic organic chemicals, such as ethylene, propylene, benzene, zylene, and methanol to different plastics, synthetic fibers, synthetic rubber, agrochemicals and pesticides, and various other product groups. Various industrial raw materials can be used in such production, with varying technological implications. While petroleum constitutes the principal feedstock for petrochemicals, other materials that can be used are naphtha (associated with petroleum), coal tar, calcium carbide, and biomass. With the escalation in oil prices in the early 1970s, there was a switch to other hydrocarbons as basic feedstock, including coal, oil shale, tar sands, and biomass. The use of feedstocks other than petroleum or natural gas involves different technologies, some of which are still in the process of development. For the most part, however, major technological innovations in products and processes in the chemical industry took place largely in the 1950s and 1960s, especially with respect to basic and intermediate chemicals. Also, during the last decade, there have been several technological developments. Considerable technological progress has also been made in several other fields, including the size and complexity of naphtha crackers, the steak cracking of ethane, the conversion of propylene to acrilonitrile, the simultaneous production of propylene oxide and styrene, the large-scale use of oxotechnology, and detergent materials based on propylene. Despite these continuing technological developments, however, a fairly high degree of technological maturity has been achieved for most basic chemicals and petrochemicals, and production and process technology is fairly well established.

The production of chemicals, except in recent years, has been largely concentrated in industrialized economies. The leading MNCs in this field include Hoechst, BASF, and Bayer from the Federal Republic of Germany; Du Pont, Union Carbide, Dow Chemical, Monsanto, and Exxon from the United States; Imperial Chemical Industries (ICI) from the United Kingdom; Montedison from Italy; Rhone-Poulenc from France; and Ciba Geigy and Hoffman La Roche from Switzerland. Most of these and other MNCs in this field produce a wide range of chemical products and have developed proprietary technology and know-how in several fields. On the whole, there has been much less licensing of technology in the production of chemicals than in machine building and the engineering industries in general, and most MNCs in this field have developed specific, differentiated products with modifications in the basic technology. Plant engineering and construction of new plants has often been undertaken through large engineering companies such as Linde, Uhde, and Lurgi, and by other engineering companies operating in the fertilizer industry, although some MNCs have also established their own plant engineering units. In general, few new petrochemical plants are presently planned in industrialized economies that are dependent on oil imports, and there is likely to be a growing shift to proprietary and specialty products and increased downstream production by MNCs in these countries. With several plants in the oil-producing countries going on-stream during 1985–86, the structure of the petrochemical industry is likely to undergo considerable change, since oil-producing countries would have great advantage in the availability and pricing of feedstocks.[41] Such change will also be reflected in the pattern of ownership of new plants and enterprises in these countries. In recent years, however, including in petroleum-producing countries, the trend has been increasingly toward either nationally owned enterprises or joint ventures with minority MNC participation in the chemical and petrochemical sector. In several instances, state-owned enterprises have been set up in countries such as Algeria, Argentina, Brazil, Colombia, India, Iran, Iraq, Libya, Saudi Arabia, and Qatar for petrochemical production, and petrochemical plants have been set up, either through turnkey engineering and construction contracts given to major engineering corporations or through joint ventures with MNCs.

Notes

1. These objectives are well documented, for example, in the Report of the Secretary General, *Permanent Sovereignty over Natural Resources* (New York: United Nations Committee on Natural Resources, February 1985).

2. The variety of such arrangements is presented in *Alternative Arrangements for Petroleum Development* (New York: United Nations, 1982).

3. M. Zakariya, "State Petroleum Companies," *Journal of World Trade Law* (November–December 1978): 481.

4. *International Petroleum Encyclopedia* (Tulsa: Pennwell, 1982), 426.

5. Ibid.

6. See, for example, M. Hiegel, "Ownership of Petroleum Technologies," Paper presented at the United Nations Interregional Symposium on State Petroleum Enterprises, Vienna, March 1978.

7. Several examples of this trend are provided in *Energy Supplies for Developing Countries—Issues in Transfer and Development of Technologies* (Geneva: UNCTAD, 1980).

8. A detailed analysis of the risks in exploration is presented in M. Adelman, *The World Petroleum Market* (Baltimore: Johns Hopkins University Press, 1972).

9. M. Zakariya, "Transfer of Technology under Petroleum Development Contracts," *Journal of World Trade Law* 16(May–June 1982): 207–22.

10. This issue is discussed, for instance, in UNCTAD, "Petroleum Exploration Contracts and Agreements and the Transfer of Technology," TD/B/C6/AC 9/5, Paper submitted to the Trade and Development Board, August 1982.

11. For a detailed presentation, see ibid.

12. Government policies on training in the petroleum sector, including several case histories on countries, are presented in *Main Features and Trends in Petroleum and Mining Agreements* (New York: United Nations Centre on Transnational Corporations, 1983), 43.

13. Zakariya, "Transfer of Technology."

14. The term *party months* refers to the number of months' work undertaken by the group of seismic prospectors. See H. Le Leuch and J. Favre, "Oil and Gas Supply in the Developing Countries," Paper presented at the United Nations Conference on Petroleum in the 1980s, New York, December 1981, table 4.

15. Discussion of the mining industry in developing countries is presented, for example, in R. Bosson and B. Varon, *Mining Industry and the Developing Countries* (Oxford: Oxford University Press, 1977). The role of MNCs in the mining sector is reviewed in *Transnational Corporations in World Development* (New York: United Nations Centre on Transnational Corporations, 1983), ch. 5.

16. For an analysis of the relative bargaining strength of the parties, see D.N. Smith and L.T. Wells, *Negotiating Third-World Mineral Agreements* (Cambridge, Mass.: Ballinger, 1975).

17. This objective is elaborated on in *Permanent Sovereignty over Natural Resources* (New York: United Nations, September 1974).

18. There is extensive literature on changing contractual conditions in the mining sector. For a review, see T. Waelde, "Lifting the Veil from Transnational Mineral Contracts: A Review of the Literature," *Natural Resources Forum* 1(April 1977). Also see S.A. Zorn, "New Developments in Third World Mining Agreements," ibid.; and *Main Features and Trends in Petroleum and Mining Agreements* (New York: United Nations Centre on Transnational corporations, 1983).

19. *Mineral Processing in Developing Countries* (Vienna: United Nations Industrial Development Organization, 1979), 31.

20. Estimates are from ibid.

21. For production and share of total world production of major producers, see *Skillings Mining Review,* various issues.

22. For the bauxite reserves of major producer countries, see U.S. Bureau of Mines, *Mineral Commodity Profiles: Aluminum* (Washington, D.C.: U.S. Government Printing Office, May 1978), 9.

23. In the early 1970s, for example, these six MNCs controlled 75.5 percent of the market economies' primary aluminum production capacity. See *Problems and Prospects of the Primary Aluminium Industry* (Paris: OECD, 1973).

24. Data on the extraction of bauxite, the processing of alumina, and the production of aluminum by the six MNCs in developing countries are given in K.P. Sauvant and F.G. Lavipour (eds.), *Controlling Multinational Enterprises* (Boulder, Colo.: Westview Press, 1976).

25. The strategy of MNCs in the bauxite/aluminum industry is analyzed in *Transnational Corporations in the Bauxite/Aluminium Industry* (New York: United Nations Centre on Transnational Corporations, 1981), ch. 3.

26. Reserves, measured in millions of tons, were estimated in 1976. See W. Gluschke, J. Shaw, and B. Varon, *Copper: The Next Fifteen Years* (Dordrecht, Netherlands: D. Reidel, 1979), 56.

27. Data on copper production of the seven leading corporations between 1948 and 1978 are presented in *Transnational Corporations in the Copper Industry* (New York: United Nations Centre on Transnational Corporations, 1981), 30.

28. For the mine capacity of the major copper producers, see *Copper Studies* (Commodities Research Unit, Ltd., 15 December 1978).

29. United Nations Centre on Transnational Corporations, *Transnational Corporations,* 30.

30. For information on the financing of the Bougainville copper projects, see M. Radetzki and S. Zorn, *Financing Mining Projects in Developing Countries: A United Nations Study* (London: Mining Journal Books, 1979).

31. For an analysis of investment costs, see Gluschke, Shaw, and Varon, *Copper,* 79.

32. Capital costs of several other mining projects are given in United Nations Centre on Transnational Corporations, *Transnational Corporations,* 17–19.

33. Although this estimate was made in the late 1970s, current plans and projections suggest no expectations of change until the mid-1980s. See *Mineral Processing in Developing Countries,* Vol. 5 (Vienna: United Nations Industrial Development Organization, December 1979), 43.

34. For data on world nickel reserves and resources, see U.S. Bureau of Mines, *Mineral Commodity Profiles: Nickel* (Washington, D.C.: U.S. Government Printing Office, 1982).

35. In 1981, developing countries produced 85 percent of the world's tin concentrate outside the socialist countries and processed about 90 percent of their production. See *Transnational Corporations and the Distribution of Gains in the Tin Industry of South East Asia* (New York: United Nations Economic and Social Commission for Asia and the Pacific, 1984), table 1.

36. For the role of MNCs in the tin production of developing countries, see *Transnational Corporations and the Distribution of Gains in the Tin Industry of Bolivia and South East Asia* (New York: United Nations Economic Commission for Latin America, January 1983), tables 3, 4.

37. For estimated capital requirements of various fertilizer plants in developing

countries, see W.F. Sheldrick, "Investment and Production Costs for Fertilisers," Paper submitted to the United Nations Food and Agriculture Organization, Commission on Fertilisers, July 1980.

38. Projections are in *Current Situation and Outlook* (New York: United Nations Food and Agriculture Organization, Commission on Fertilisers, May 1980).

39. Based on plant listings in European Chemical News, *Chemscope,* 5 March 1979 and 24 March 1980.

40. Sheldrick, "Investment and Production Costs."

41. For an analysis of such potential changes in the distribution of worldwide capacity in the petrochemical industry, see L. Turner and J. Bedore, "Saudi and Iranian Petrochemicals and Oil Refining: Trade Warfare in the 1980s," *International Affairs* (October 1977), 572–86.

5
Food Processing
and Pharmaceuticals

T he manufacturing activities of MNCs in Third World countries impinge directly on individual consumers in these countries in several fields, ranging from foods and beverages, pharmaceuticals, textiles and shoes, and a variety of household goods to various durable consumer products. Some of the durable goods, including automobiles, are dealt with in subsequent chapters. In this chapter, the impact of MNC investments and technology transfer is examined in two critical sectors, food processing and pharmaceuticals.

Food Processing

The transfer of technology by MNCs in food products and food-processing industries has to be considered, first, in relation to production for internal markets in these countries and, second, in relation to production designed primarily for exports. The first category comprises a large variety of products, including vegetable oils and fats, dairy products, sugar and related items (including confectionery), soft drinks, alcoholic beverages, fish, meat, and vegetables, and canned and packaged food products of various types that are finding a growing market in developing countries. Export-oriented production and processing relates largely to plantation crops such as tea, coffee, cocoa, bananas, and pineapples, and also to other food products packaged in developing countries.

In overall terms, the role of MNCs in the food industries of developing countries has been less dominant than it has been in most other manufacturing sectors. It is estimated that production by foreign subsidiaries in these countries accounts for approximately one-eighth of the total food output.[1] Foreign investments, however, have concentrated predominantly in the export-oriented sector and the area of branded products manufactured for local markets, where the involvement of MNCs in certain developing countries for specific products has been significant. In the early 1980s, 130 of the largest food-producing MNCs from developed countries had about 750 foreign subsidiaries in the food-processing industries of developing countries.[2]

Since the 1950s, MNCs have set up a relatively large network of food-processing subsidiaries in several developing countries to meet local demand. Most of these operations have concentrated in Latin American countries and, apart from Unilever and Nestlé, have been subsidiaries of U.S.-based MNCs. Entry of these subsidiaries was often by takeover of existing local food processors. In the case of U.S. companies in Mexico, for example, during the 1966–73 period, 75 percent of the foreign subsidiaries were established by acquisition of local companies.[3] In Asian and African countries, MNCs from the United Kingdom, especially Unilever, have been most active, with the exception of Nestlé. The extent of involvement of MNCs in food processing for the local market has, however, varied significantly by subsectors of the industry and, depending on the particular subsector, this role has also changed over time.

In vegetable oils and fats, Unilever (UK/Netherlands) has been the principal MNC, with production operations in more than twenty developing countries. Its production activities in many of these countries include margarine, other vegetable oils, soaps, and detergents.[4] The company established production plants and plantations in several countries and expanded palm and soya oil production considerably during the 1970s. Its operations in developing countries include manufacturing activities in India, Pakistan, Malaysia, and other countries in Asia; Kenya, Nigeria, Cameroons, and other African countries; and major operations in Brazil, among others in South America. Other MNCs in this field that have undertaken production operations extensively in developing countries include several U.S. companies, such as Cargil, Foremost McKesson, United Brands, Standard Brands, Continental Grain, Anderson, Clayton, and others such as the French Lesieur. Most of the U.S.-based MNCs have production activities in Latin America, mainly in Brazil and Mexico. In margarine and cooking oils, major MNCs operating in developing countries include Unilever (twenty countries), followed by Corn Products Corporations (U.S.), with production in fourteen developing countries, and Standard Brands, with eight plants, of which six are in Latin America.[5]

In dairy industries, MNC activities in developing countries are largely dominated by Nestlé (Switzerland), with milk processing facilities in twenty-six developing countries in Asia, Africa, and Latin America. Its principal products in most of these countries have been condensed or dried milk and milk-based infant formula. Research facilities have been centralized near Vevey (Switzerland), though a regional research and development center is being set up in Latin America. One of its subsidiaries is responsible for the planning, engineering, and installation of its plants in different countries.

Nestlé has faced considerable criticism and hostility in several countries because of its marketing policy of promoting the Nestlé infant formula in preference to mother's milk. A code of conduct on infant formula has since been prescribed by the World Health Organization, and Nestlé is complying. Other important MNCs operating in this field in developing countries include Foremost McKesson with twelve plants, Carnation with eleven plants, Beatrice (U.S.) with eight plants, Kraft (U.S.) with five plants, and others, including Unilever with five plants and Unigate (U.K.) with two plants.

The sugar industry was initially dominated by MNCs but in recent decades has largely been taken over by state or local industrial groups in most developing countries.[6] Only a few MNCs, such as Tate and Lyle (UK) and some Japanese companies, retain interest in sugar plantations and refining in developing countries. Technology for sugar refining is fairly stable and has been adequately absorbed in most sugar-producing developing countries. Some of these countries are also producing sugar plant equipment, and India is exporting such machinery.

The domination of MNCs is particularly marked in the soft drink industry in developing countries. The leading MNCs in this field are Coca-Cola (U.S.), Pepsico (U.S.), and Cadbury Schweppes (UK), followed by General Foods (U.S.), Norton Simon, and others. Some of these corporations are producing their respective products directly through subsidiary operations, while others, especially Coca-Cola, operate through the sale of concentrates to local bottling plants, which are licensed to sell the resulting product. The technology for bottling is relatively simple, and its rapid absorption has not presented any problem. The technology involved in the basic concentrate, however, is closely held by MNCs in food processing and beverages, is guarded by the MNC concerned, and is not made available to local companies through licensing. This led to the withdrawal of Coca-Cola from India in 1977. The bottling plants in India, which were all locally owned, were able to switch to other concentrates, including "77," a formulation developed by the Indian Food Research Institute, with the name signifying the year of Coca-Cola's demise in the country. The switch by Indian bottlers to concentrates other than Coca-Cola indicates that technological absorption and adaptation does not constitute any major difficulty in the soft drink industry and that the problem primarily lies in consumer preference for internationally known brand names and flavorings.

In the field of alcoholic beverages, MNC activities in developing countries have largely been confined to beer production, although certain linkages have also developed in the production of wines and liquors, mainly between European producers and enterprises in Latin America. Beer manufacture has developed extensively in several developing countries; in many cases, this has taken place through locally owned enterprises, as in a number of Latin American countries and in India. Several beer manufacturers from Western Europe, however, have also set up beer production activities in developing countries; they include Heineken (Netherlands), Guinness (UK), Allied Breweries (UK), Brassiries et Glacier (FR), and others, and these brands enjoy considerable consumer preference. In general, however, the technology for beer manufacture has been absorbed and adapted by local enterprises in a number of developing countries.

MNC subsidiaries have also been active in several other food products and processing operations in developing countries. These include corn milling, animal feed production, breakfast cereals and biscuits, confectionery products, and the like. In corn milling, Corn Products Corporation (U.S.) has milling operations in twenty-one developing countries, including ten in Latin America, while Standard Brands has ten mills in Latin American countries. In Asia and Africa, milling operations are largely done through local companies. The technology is relatively simple and is largely embodied in the equipment. The animal feed industry has developed considerably in the Latin American region, and about forty-eight units, of which Ralston Purina has eleven, have been set up by MNCs. Corn Products Corporation and Unilever have set up some plants in these countries as well. The cracker and biscuit industry has a few MNC subsidiaries operating in developing countries, notably Nabisco and Beatrice Foods (U.S.) in Latin America, and a few units of Associated British Foods (UK) in certain Asian countries. Breakfast cereals are manufactured by MNCs in some developing countries, especially in Latin America, where Nestlé has eight plants and Kellogg and Quaker Oats (U.S.) have seven plants each. In confectionery products, Warner Lambert (U.S.) has ten plants in Latin America, followed by Standard Brands (U.S.), Nestlé, and several others. A few units have also been set up in some Asian and African countries.

Although food production by MNCs for the local market of developing countries usually represents only a small share of the total food production and processing in these countries, even of the particular food-processing segment in which such companies may be engaged, MNCs have played an important role in technology transfer through their subsidiaries and affiliates. In most of these subsectors, however, the nature of production technology is not highly complex and can easily be absorbed by most countries. The production technology used by MNC subsidiaries and affiliates for most food products intended for local consumption has followed the techniques and processes used by parent corporations—although the scale of production generally tends to be much smaller, except in developing countries with large internal markets such as Brazil. Most of the production technology for branded food products tend to be standardized, and the sector has a relatively low level of innovation.[7] Consequently, much of the technology utilized by foreign subsidiaries may be nonproprietary and used extensively in developed countries. There has been little technological adjustment to any special needs of developing countries in this field, although a certain degree of product modification is made to suit local tastes and preferences.

Since most of the MNC involvement in branded food products has taken place through subsidiaries and has utilized rather well-established, standard technologies, the impact on local technological development in these countries has been fairly limited. These activities may be said to have had some catalytic effect in improving production and packaging techniques. This has been achieved, however, at a rather high cost to local consumers and often through displacing locally owned manufacturers.

The special feature that marks the activities of MNCs in food products and beverages is the high degree of product differentiation that is achieved through aggressive marketing and extensive advertising activities. In the case of Mexico and Brazil, for example, it was noted that the advertising/sales ratio of foreign subsidiaries in the food industry was between 2 and 5 percent in Brazil, and about 17 percent for some products in Mexico.[8] Local consumer preference for particular MNC brand names, which has developed over years of advertising and aggressive marketing, gives MNCs an important competitive advantage over local manufacturers in the same field.

Export-Oriented Production

Historically, the involvement of MNCs in the food industry of developing countries originated from their role in export-oriented food processing, and its distribution in this sector continues to be dominated to a large extent by MNCs. Most tea and coffee plantations in the former British colonial regions in Asia and Africa were formerly owned by United Kingdom companies, but a large proportion of these plantations are now owned by local industrial groups or state-owned corporations. In the tea industry, most of the MNCs, such as Brooke Bond, Lipton, Unilever, Finlay, and others, are from the United Kingdom and, though plantations in developing countries are increasingly being acquired by local companies, the marketing of tea, extending from tea auctions and blending to wholesale and retail marketing, is still largely controlled by United Kingdom companies. In Latin America, also, Nestlé has been operating through subsidiaries in three countries. MNCs from the United States have played a limited role in the production and marketing of tea in developing countries, except for the activities of Standard Brands and McCormack in Latin America. In the case of coffee, the two major MNCs are Nestlé and General Foods (U.S.). Nestlé has the most extensive operations by far in this field in twenty-one developing countries. Also, for cocoa products, Nestlé has by far the highest total sales, with production activities in seventeen developing countries. Other MNCs in this field that produce in developing countries include Cadbury Schweppes (UK), operating in five developing countries, Hershey and General Foods (U.S.), and Interfood (Switzerland), with subsidiaries in one or two countries. As indicated earlier, plantation technology was fully absorbed and also adapted to local conditions in these industries. Effective control by MNCs, however, particularly by large corporations such as Nestlé in the areas of coffee and cocoa, has continued to be exercised through processing and marketing functions.

Mention should be made, in this context, of MNC activities with regard to bananas, pineapples, and other fruits. A major proportion of banana exports is handled by three U.S.-based MNCs: United Brands, Castle and Cooke, and DelMonte. These companies have several plantations in Central America and the Philippines and purchasing agencies in Africa and other Latin American countries. Their dominance of banana exports has been reduced by the Union of Banana Exporting countries, but only partially.[9] In the case of pineapples, Castle and Cooke and DelMonte undertook fairly large plantation and marketing operations in Thailand and the Philippines, with DelMonte also operating in Kenya. Fruit and juice production from most other developing countries is increasingly being undertaken by local companies, although MNCs continue to play a critical role in export markets.[10] The implication of technological control by MNCs in this field primarily relates to marketing and distribution and less to production aspects, although major investments are involved in the development of large plantation operations.

The fishery industry, particularly sea fisheries, in developing countries has also received considerable attention from MNCs in recent decades.[11] As demand for fish and seafood rapidly increased, fishery corporations extended their operations to the coastal regions of several developing countries. The operations of MNCs in this field relate largely to tuna and shrimp, for which there is the highest demand. There have been important technological developments in fishing practices and processing—for instance, refrigerated offshore and onshore processing and packaging operations. The latest technological practices are used by most MNCs operating in this field. In the Pacific and Indian Ocean region, the major MNCs include Taiyo Fisheries (Japan), with eleven subsidiaries, and Nippon Suisan Koush (Japan), with eight subsidiaries, followed by Nichiro Gyogo (Japan), Ralston Purina (U.S.), Heinz (U.S.), and Kyokuyo (Japan). Other MNCs operating in this region include Brooke Bond (UK), Peche et Froid (France), Saupignet (France), and Hoko Fishing Company (Japan). In the Latin American region, MNCs from the United States are more dominant, with several companies, such as Borden Zapata, Consolidated Foods, and others, having two or three subsidiaries each. Most subsidiaries (5) in that region, however, are held by Pescanova (Spain), with Japanese companies, such as Taiya and Nippon Swisan Kaisha also expanding their operations in recent years. Most developing countries have left sea fishing to MNC subsidiaries and, during the 1960s and early 1970s, gave MNCs incentives to undertake such activities in order to increase exports. In recent years, however, there has been a greater tendency to set up local companies for fishery operations in their respective coastal regions and to enter into joint ventures with MNCs, both for mobilization of the substantial resources required and for the technology necessary for sea-fishing operations.

In the export-oriented sector, MNC activities have been concentrated largely in plantation industries, where technology has followed a fairly traditional pattern—although plantations and processing operations for sugar, pineapples, and other tropical products have increased significantly in size and volume, especially during the 1950s and 1960s. There have been major technological innovations in certain of these fields, such as freeze-dried coffee, instant tea and coffee, decaffeinated coffee, and the like, the use of which has gradually been extended to developing countries. By and large, however, production technology at the plantation level in most of these fields has tended to be fairly stable and has been transferred to MNC subsidiaries and affiliates in these developing countries. In recent decades, nationalization and pressure to transfer plantation ownership of foreign subsidiaries to local groups in several countries have not resulted in major dislocation of production, since production technology had been adequately absorbed. In some cases, however, as in certain Caribbean countries, plantation industries have encountered problems of additional investment and export marketing without the involvement of MNCs. Although MNC ownership of plantations has been reduced significantly in several developing countries in recent decades, MNCs continue to play an important role in exports. Through their access to worldwide distribution systems and established brand names, they continue to exercise a major role in several export-oriented food sectors. As marketing and distribution from developing countries continues to take place through wholly owned subsidiaries, such skills are not transferred to local industry. The important role of MNCs in export markets for a wide range of export-oriented food products has also tended to distribute the returns from these operations in their favor.

Pharmaceuticals

One of the sectors in which innovative technological development has been most marked in recent decades has been the pharmaceutical industry. Major new products have been developed in several therapeutic branches, and global production of drugs and pharmaceuticals rose to $29.5 billion in 1973 and to $84 billion in 1980, outside of centrally planned economies.[12] Most of the production is concentrated in industrialized countries, with the United

States accounting for almost 30 percent, followed by Japan and Western European nations. Pharmaceutical usage has also largely been concentrated in industrialized market economies, which consume 75 percent of the world production.[13] Production in developing countries increased from about $3.1 billion in 1973 to over $8 billion in 1980 and is mostly concentrated in Argentina, Brazil, Egypt, India, Mexico, and the Republic of Korea.[14] The pharmaceutical needs of most other developing countries have been met largely by imports from industrialized countries. Production capability in developing countries ranges from little or no production to formulation and packaging, as in Colombia, Kenya, and Thailand, and to various stages of processing intermediates and bulk chemicals in some of the countries mentioned.

The major share of drug and pharmaceutical production in market economies has been undertaken by MNCs based in industrialized countries, most of which have a wide network of distribution and production companies located in several countries. Since the pharmaceutical industry comprises a wide range of products, most MNCs have specialized their production in various therapeutic groups, such as antibiotics, antihistamines, tranquilizers, analgesics, and vitamins. Often, such specialization takes the form of a specific branded product that accounts for a dominant market share in a specific therapeutic branch, as in the case of Valium (Roche) among tranquilizers, Indocim (Merck) and Butazolidin (Ciba) among antiarthritics, Darvon (Lilly) and Tylenol (Johnson & Johnson) among analgesics, and Benadryl (Parke-Davis) among antihistamines. Thus, while a relatively large number of pharmeceutical companies are operating in developed countries, the concentration of the major companies on specific product classes has resulted in most subsegments of the industry having a highly concentrated, oligopolistic market structure.[15] Apart from their specialization, however, most of the major pharmaceutical manufacturers have a fairly wide range of products and also have often diversified into other fields outside pharmaceuticals. Thus, several pharmaceutical MNCs are important producers of chemicals and agrochemicals—for instance, Pfizer, Cyanamid, and Upjohn (U.S.), Hoesch and Bayer (FRG), Ciba Geigy and Sandoz (Switzerland), Rhone-Poulenc (France), and Takeda (Japan). Others, such as Bristol Myers, Squibb (U.S.), and Beecham (OK), are manufacturing several consumer products, while Schering-Plough and Eli Lilly are engaged in cosmetics manufacture, and several companies, such as Johnson & Johnson, are increasingly expanding into the health care field.[16]

Unlike resource-based and capital-intensive industries, where mobilization of large capital investments constitutes an important feature of MNC involvement, MNCs in the pharmaceutical sector control their global activities largely through the ownership of proprietary technology and patents and brand names. The marketing of new drugs and pharmaceutical products requires not only large investments in research and product development but also prolonged periods of clinical testing. With increasingly strict regulations adopted for the marketing of new drugs, especially in the United States, several Western European countries, and Japan, the period between the time a drug is developed and the time it can be marketed extends to several years of tests and analyses. Regulatory control is essential because of the high potency of several drugs and the hazards and dangers involved in their use without adeuqate tests and scrutiny. The Thalidomide experience was followed by several instances of new and experimental drugs being found unsafe and necessarily withdrawn from the market in some industrialized countries. There is less-stringent drug control and enforcement in most developing countries, and certain pharmaceutical products that are not marketed in their country of origin are marketed in Third World countries. Clinical testing of new drugs and products is also taking place in these countries to a greater extent.

With the high research intensity of the pharmaceutical industry and the rising costs of research, including testing and regulatory approval, pharmaceutical research has increasingly been undertaken by the larger drug companies. It was estimated, for example, that during the 1966–72 period, the twenty largest U.S. pharmaceutical companies, measured by sales, produced 82 percent of new single entities and nearly half of the new dosage forms, while smaller firms have generally produced new formulations of old drugs whose patents had expired.[17] The costs of R&D for a new drug, including allocated research costs for drugs that are not marketed, were estimated at $24 million in the mid 1970s and have increased further in recent years.[18] The magnitude of such costs leads inevitably to the concentration of pharmaceutical research and innovation among large companies.[19] At the same time, returns from research expenditures generally depend on the patent life of the drug after its use has been approved by regulatory authorities. The process of clearance through regulatory institutions may take considerable time, and the total period of research up to the stage of marketing may take 5 to 10 years.[20] Since a patent is necessarily taken out at a fairly early stage, the effective patent life for the marketing of a particular drug may be much less than the valid period of the patent. Despite this constraint, patent protection has been a key factor in pharmaceutical research. The expiry of patents is generally followed by the rapid entry of competitive manufacturers and the production of generic products. In most cases, this leads to a reduction in the price of the drugs whose patents have expired. At the same time, product differentiation and well-known brand names of established manufacturers, together with their heavy promotional expenditure, have in many cases protected the market share of the original inventor.[21] Consequently, despite the entry of competitive products, including generics, several pharmaceutical products have continued to retain a significant share of the market even after expiration of their patents.

In the pharmaceutical industries of developing countries, MNCs have played an important role. Given the importance of the health system, governments in most developing countries have promoted entry of foreign pharmaceutical subsidiaries to their countries since the earlier phases of import substitution. For MNCs, even relatively small developing country markets have been attractive for some form of MNC involvement, because there has been little competition from domestically owned companies in meeting the basic needs for drugs and pharmaceuticals. Consequently, MNCs that have a dominant position in their home markets and in other developed countries have been operating, through various channels, in most developing countries.[22]

The form and extent of MNC operations in particular developing countries has depended strongly on the size of the local market. Thus, in the largest developing countries, most pharmaceutical MNCs established operations and by the late 1960s had achieved a dominant position in the local market. In 1982 in Brazil, for example, seventy-one foreign subsidiaries were operating, and their sales accounted for about 75 percent of the local market.[23] During the past three decades, their position was consolidated by the takeover of domestically owned companies. Between 1957 and 1979, for example, thirty-five of the largest Brazilian-owned companies were taken over by MNCs.[24] By 1979, foreign direct investments in the pharmaceutical industry were $646 million, compared with $113 million in 1971.[25] Similarly, in Mexico, which is among the ten largest pharmaceutical markets in the world, the thirty-eight largest companies are foreign-owned, and their sales account for 72 percent of the local market.[26] In Argentina, where domestically owned companies had a relatively strong position in the 1960s, the share of foreign-owned subsidiaries has increased significantly, with the market share of the largest twenty-two foreign subsidiaries increasing from 48 to 57 percent by 1973.[27] A similar major foreign presence characterizes smaller Latin American countries. In Colombia, for example, about sixty foreign subsidiaries have been operating, and their market share reached 88 percent by the late 1970s, compared with 75 percent in 1960.[28] As a result of the large number of MNC subsidiaries operating in the major Latin American countries, these operations have often brought a considerable proliferation of branded drugs, exceeding significantly the number of basic drugs used. It was estimated, for example, that in Mexico in the late 1970s, drugs were sold under 80,000 brand names, compared with 20,000 in the United States and 8,500 in France.[29] Among Asian developing countries, foreign subsidiaries have established an important position in India, despite the fact that entry and operations of foreign companies have been subject to strict regulation by the government. In 1980–81, foreign subsidiaries accounted for 42 percent of the locally produced formulations and 27.1 percent of the bulk drugs.[30]

Several factors have accounted for the dominant role of MNC subsidiaries in the largest pharmaceutical markets in developing countries. On the one hand, for pharmaceutical MNCs, these major markets have offered significant opportunities for large sales. On the other hand, their strong competitive position in relation to domestically owned companies has been strengthened by their access to the parent company's technology, which has been protected by patents. But even where the government prohibits patents in the pharmaceutical sector—for instance, Brazil in 1969—foreign subsidiaries could dominate the market by several means. Thus, apart from the patent protection, active ingredients for a wide range of drugs may be specific to a particular MNC, and control over the supply of such ingredients has been an effective method of exercising control over actual or potential domestically owned companies. Another major competitive feature of foreign subsidiaries has been their ability to spend a significant share of their sales revenues on promoting drugs and, thus, creating and maintaining consumer preference for their products.

In most developing countries, the operations of foreign subsidiaries take the form of local formulation and packaging of drugs from imported bulk chemicals.[31] Backward integration in drug manufacture generally requires large investments and fairly large local markets. From the viewpoint of the MNCs, it has been more advantageous to limit operations in most developing countries to formulations only, since this requires low investments in production, on the one hand, and high returns from the supply of bulk, intermediate products, on the other. Consequently, most of the MNC operations in Southeast Asian, African, and smaller Latin American countries are engaged in local formulations. In the largest Latin American countries—Brazil, Mexico, and Argentina—however, where governments have insisted on progressive localization of production, foreign subsidiaries have increased the local manufacture of intermediate inputs and active ingredients. In the late 1970s in Brazil, for example, the estimated share of locally produced intermediate drugs was in the range of 30 to 50 percent, while the balance, mostly the most complex inputs, has continued to be covered through imports.[32] In Mexico, which at present locally manufactures most of its drug requirement, the share of locally produced ingredients is significantly lower, and only about half of the foreign subsidiaries are engaged in the local manufacture of ingredients. Operations of foreign subsidiaries, however, have been very different in India, where manufacture by these companies has reached a very high level of local integration. Among all developing countries, with the possible exception of the Republic of China, the industry has reached the highest level of vertical integration.[33] This has largely resulted from a deliberate government policy of achieving a high level of import substitution through rigorous import controls. Besides the general industrial policies that regulate all imports, particular attention has been given to the achievement of self-sufficiency in essential drugs. In 1975, the Hathi Committee Report identified 117 of such essential items. In pursuit of this objective, in 1978–79, the National Drug Policy was issued, requiring foreign-owned firms to reduce their equity share to 40 percent if they are engaged only in formulations. Only manufacturers of bulk drugs are permitted to retain a foreign equity share up to 74 percent.

Although, in most developing countries production by foreign subsidiaries accounts for the major share of the market, there are several developing countries where the extent of MNC involvement has been much less or absent. Among these, the People's Republic of China stands out, since the local industry has largely been developed indigenously. Also, in Egypt, where in 1962–63 most of the drug and pharmaceutical companies were nationalized, about 70 percent of the local production is provided by nine public sector companies, while the balance is covered by imports and MNC affiliates operating in joint ventures with local companies.[34] Another developing country where pharmaceutical production by locally owned companies has grown rapidly is the Republic of Korea. Most of the country's production (over 82 percent) is undertaken by about 300 domestic companies. In 1981, there were only 4 MNCs operating in the country in joint ventures with domestic companies, mostly on a 50-50 equity-share basis.[35] The local market is dominated by locally owned companies, and out of the twenty largest manufacturers, only three are joint ventures.[36] The country is also exporting substantial quantities of drugs, the value of which rose to $65 million in 1980.[37] Development of the locally owned industry was promoted by the prevailing patent system, which allows patenting only for processes in the pharmaceutical industry and in which the use of foreign trademarks is permitted only in conjunction with foreign investments or licensing agreements.

Except for the least developed countries, such as several countries in Africa, which continue to cover most of their needs through import of finished products, a large number of locally owned companies coexist with foreign subsidiaries in most developing countries. Often, these companies are relatively small and manufacture drugs based on indigenous technology. In several of the Southeast Asian countries, for example, an important share of the local demand is supplied by these domestically owned companies. In some countries, such as India, there are also several large domestically owned companies that compete effectively with foreign subsidiaries in several subsegments of the pharmaceutical market. Of the ten largest companies in India, for example, five are domestically owned, and produce drugs mostly with locally developed technology.[38]

Technology licensing by MNCs to unaffiliated companies in developing countries has been relatively rare. Since most of the pharmaceutical MNCs have set up subsidiaries in most developing countries, particularly in the largest markets, they have not licensed their technology to domestic companies. Technology licensing has taken place mostly in a few countries where operations of MNC subsidiaries were severely restricted by the governments and where revenues from licensing agreements and associated sales represented the only revenues from such markets. In Korea, for example, where foreign direct investments in the pharmaceutical field are limited, several major MNCs have licensed their technology to major domestically owned companies.[39]

Technology transfer in the pharmaceutical industries of developing countries has been shaped by two major factors. One relates to the high degree of foreign ownership in this sector in most developing countries and the implication that most of the transfer has taken place within the corporations, between parent companies and their wholly owned and majority-owned subsidiaries. While these subsidiaries could rely on the centralized research of their parent companies, local R&D by these subsidiaries has been undertaken only in a relatively few cases. Examples of local R&D efforts would be Ciba Geigy's efforts in India and those of some subsidiaries in Brazil, which have been directed to develop drugs for diseases that are specific to the country. The second major feature of technology transfer is its partial nature, which results from the relatively low level of production integration in most countries by both subsidiaries and licensees. Effective technology transfer in the pharmaceutical sector, however, can take place primarily in situations in which technological capabilities for the production of bulk chemicals and intermediate products are created. Consequently, in countries where MNC subsidiaries and local licensees of MNCs are engaged in local formulations, the extent of technology transfer is very limited. These subsidiaries and licensees continue to depend entirely on the parent companies for the provision of the necessary formulas and also, in most cases, for the supply of intermediates. Apart from the continuous payments for technology, sourcing of intermediate inputs tends to place a significant burden on these countries, because overpricing of intermediate products through transfer pricing has been cited as an important feature of the industry.[40] Since transactions are generally between parent corporations and their wholly owned or controlled subsidiaries, transfer pricing of intermediate products is extremely difficult for local agencies to control.[41] It is only in the relatively few countries where MNCs have undertaken production of intermediate products, such as India, that such backward integration has reached a very high level, although rather significant levels have been reached in Brazil and Argentina and lower levels in Mexico.

It can be seen from the foregoing discussion that the pattern of technology transfer in the manufacture of drugs and pharmaceuticals has varied considerably, depending on the level of integration and production of bulk intermediates on the one hand and the dominance of MNC subsidiaries on the other. In developing countries where MNCs do not play any major part, as in the People's Republic of China, in Cuba, and in Egypt, pharmaceutical production has been based on indigenously developed technology. These countries may not have had access to the latest technological developments in this field, but the basic needs of the population have been served. In fact, China has exported large quantities of drugs to several Asian countries. In some developing countries, such as India and the Republic of Korea, a large market share is held by locally owned companies that have achieved high levels of integration and, in the case of Korea, significant export capability. Technology transfer and development have been very pronounced in these countries. Production through state-owned enterprises has also increased in certain developing countries—for example, in Egypt, India, and Malaysia and in the state laboratories of the CEME in Brazil—and significant indigenous technological development has taken place through these units. At the same time, MNCs continue to dominate global production of various categories and groups of pharmaceutical products, principally because of their research capability and the development of new products. Once these products have been developed and marketed in the MNC's country of origin, they are protected by patents and proprietary rights for some years, and their global manufacture takes place through subsidiaries with varying levels of integration and a high transfer price for bulk intermediate products.

National policies in developing countries have generally concentrated on the pricing of essential drugs and their internal distribution, but technological aspects of pharmaceutical manufacture are receiving greater attention. Apart from production of intermediate products, the question of drug patents is being reviewed in certain countries, and compulsory licensing provisions after a certain period are being considered. The extent of transfer pricing in drugs and intermediates is also causing concern, and regulatory measures in this regard may also be introduced in several countries.

Notes

1. Data as estimated in *Transnational Corporations in Food and Beverage Processing* (New York: United Nations Centre on Transnational Corporations, 1981), 14.

2. Investments in these subsidiaries accounted for about 85 to 95 percent of all foreign investments in this sector. See ibid., 18.

3. J.M. Connor, *The Market Power of Multinationals* (New York: Praeger, 1977).

4. For Unilever's involvement in vegetable oil and related products in developing countries since the early 1900s, see D.K. Fieldhouse, *Unilever Overseas: The Anatomy of a Multinational* (London: Croom Helm, 1978); and C. Wilson, *The History of Unilever* (London: Cassel, 1968).

5. Annual reports for various companies.

6. For information on the growing local control of sugar production in developing countries, see G. Hagelberg, *Structural and Institutional Aspects of the Sugar*

Industry in Developing Countries, Research Report No. 5, (Berlin: Institute fur Zuckerindustrie, 1976).

7. For an analysis of the relatively low technological dynamism of the food processing industry, see W.S. Grieg, *The Changing Technological Base in Food Processing* (Westport, Conn.: AVI, 1971). It has also been shown that most of the innovations in processing tend to originate from other industries. See *Impact of Multinational Enterprises on National Scientific and Technical Capacities: Food Industry* (Paris: OECD, August 1979).

8. The advertising/sales ratio of foreign subsidiaries in selected subsectors of the food and beverage industry in Mexico and Brazil is presented in Connor, *The Market Power,* table C.1.

9. For the role of MNCs in the banana production and trade of developing countries, see *Review of the Economic Aspects of Production, Trade and Distribution of Bananas* (Rome: United Nations Food and Agriculture Organization, Committee on Commodity Problems, 1978).

10. The export problems of domestically owned companies in tropical foods is discussed in *Transnational Corporations and the International Commercialization of Pineapple Canned in Thailand* (Bangkok: United Nations ESCAP/CTC, August 1979).

11. The role of MNCs in the fisheries industry is discussed in J.L. Trioel, *Les Strategies des Groupes Internationaux dans le Secteur de la Mer et de l'Agriculture* (Nantes Institut Nacional de la Recherche Agronomique, 1978).

12. *The Growth of the Pharmaceutical Industry in Developing Countries: Problems and Prospects* (New York: United Nations Industrial Development Organization, 1978), 4; and *Global Study of the Pharmaceutical Industry* (New York: United Nations, 1980), 11.

13. United Nations, *Global Study of the Pharmaceutical Industry,* 11.

14. For a review of the production of pharmaceuticals in developing countries, see United Nations Industrial Development Organization, *The Growth of the Pharmaceutical Industry.*

15. The concentration of the pharmaceutical industry in various developed countries and the changes in market structure in these countries over time are analyzed, for example, in S. Lall, "The International Pharmaceutical Industry and Less-developed Countries," *Oxford Bulletin of Economics and Statistics* 56(August 1974): 143–72.

16. For the diversification pattern of major pharmaceutical MNCs, see B.G. James, *The Future of the Multinational Pharmaceutical Industry to 1990* (New York: Halsted Press, 1977), 39–51.

17. D. Schwartzman, *Innovation in the Pharmaceutical Industry* (Baltimore: Johns Hopkins University Press, 1976).

18. Ibid., ch. 2.

19. The concentration of innovation in the U.S. ethical drug industry for the 1957–71 period is analyzed in H.G. Grabowski and J.M. Vernon, "Structural Effects of Regulation on Innovation in the Ethical Drug Industry," in *Essays on Industrial Organization in Honor of Joe S. Bain,* ed. R.T. Masson and D.P. Qualls (Cambridge, Mass.: Ballinger), 181–205, table 10–1.

20. This period is estimated to be five to seven years in H.A. Clymer, "The

Economic and Regulatory Climate: United States and Overseas Trends," in *Drug Development and Marketing,* ed. R.B. Helms (Washington, D.C.: American Enterprise Institute for Public Policy Research, 1975), 137–54.

21. It was estimated, for example, that in the late 1970s, U.S. drug companies spent about 20 percent of their sales revenues for promotion. In 1978, the promotion expenditure by U.S. companies was estimated at $1.9 billion. See *Annual Survey Report: Ethical Pharmaceutical Industry Operations, 1977–1978* (Washington, D.C.: Pharmaceutical Manufacturers Association, 1978), 111, table 1.

22. The relationship between the market structure of the pharmaceutical industry in developed countries and its market structure in developing countries is discussed in Lall, "The International Pharmaceutical Industry," 176–86.

23. For the share of foreign-owned companies between 1975 and 1979, see *Perfil de la Industria Farmaceutical Brasileira* (Rio de Janeiro: Abifarma, 25 January 1980), 13.

24. For a list of Brazilian pharmaceutical companies that were taken over by MNCs, see ibid., 33.

25. *Visao,* various issues.

26. *Transnational Corporations in the Pharmaceutical Industry of Developing Countries* (New York: United Nations Centre on Transnational Corporations, 1984), 111.

27. PJB Publications, Richmond, Surrey, United Kingdom, *SCRIP,* no. 723, 30 August 1982, p. 9.

28. *Datos y Apreciaciones sobre Algunos Aspectos de la Industria Farmaceutica en Colombia* (Bogota: Departamento Nacional de Planeacion, March 1972) and *Politica de Precios de los Medicamentos* (Bogota: Departamento Nacional de Planeacion, 23 May 1980).

29. P. O'Brien, *Trademarks, the International Pharmaceutical Industry and the Developing Countries,* Occasional Papers No. 63 (The Hague: Institute of Social Studies, 1977), 2.

30. United Nations Centre on Transnational Corporations, *Transnational Corporations in the Pharmaceutical Industry,* 100.

31. Operations of pharmaceutical subsidiaries are analyzed, for example, in Lall, "The International Pharmaceutical Industry," 176–86.

32. Estimates of the share of imported raw materials vary according to published sources. Abifarma, *Perfil de la Industria Farmaceutical,* estimates it at 60 percent. The share is estimated at about 50 percent in *Brazil, A Industria Farmaceutica: Sua Evoluçao no Quinquenio 1974–1978* (Rio de Janeiro: Pesguira Economica, March 1980): 20.

33. For a review of the Indian pharmaceutical industry, see United Nations Centre on Transnational Corporations, *Transnational Corporations in the Pharmaceutical Industry,* 99–104.

34. Development of the Egyptian pharmaceutical industry is discussed in *Development of the Drug Industry in Egypt* (New York: United Nations Industrial Development Organization, 1979).

35. *SCRIP,* no. 671, 1 March 1982, p. 12.

36. *SCRIP,* no. 663, 1 February 1982, p. 13.

37. United Nations Centre on Transnational Corporations, *Transnational Corporations in the Pharmaceutical Industry,* 203, table K.5.

38. *SCRIP,* no. 648, 2 December 1981, p. 12.

39. In 1980, there were thirty-seven licensing agreements with twenty-seven foreign pharmaceutical companies. See United Nations Centre on Transnational Corporations, *Transnational Corporations in the Pharmaceutical Industry,* 109.

40. A study of the transfer pricing practices of pharmaceutical subsidiaries in Colombia during the 1966–70 period showed that, for the selected eleven items, overpricing ranged from 33 to 300 percent. See C.F. Vaitsos, *Inter-Country Income Distribution and Transnational Corporations* (Oxford: Clarendon Press, 1974). In Brazil, during the 1971–75 period, a comparison of the cost structure of Brazilian-owned companies and foreign subsidiaries showed that the costs of materials of foreign subsidaries were 54 percent higher than those of local companies, indicating the potentially high transfer prices incurred by foreign subsidiaries. See J. Frenkel et al., *Technologia e Competiçao na Industria Farmaceutica Brasileira* (Rio de Janeiro: Financiadora de Estudos e Projectos (FINEP), Centro de Estudos e Pesquisas, 1978), 158–73, table VI.14.

41. For the issues involved in transfer pricing, see S. Lall, "Transfer-pricing and LDCs: Some Problems of Investigation," in S. Lall *The Multinational Corporation* (London: Macmillan, 1980), ch. 6.

6
Capital Goods Manufacture

The capital goods sector, comprising the production of electrical, mechanical, and transport equipment, constitutes a critical area of industrial and technological growth for Third World developing countries. With the rapid expansion of internal demand for a very wide range of machinery and equipment in these countries, foreign exchange requirements for machinery imports have posed, and continue to pose, a major constraint. Efforts for import substitution in this field have yielded useful results in certain countries, but, as discussed in an earlier chapter, the growth of capital goods production and technological absorption has been slow, and most developing countries still depend heavily on equipment imports from industrialized economies. Increased manufacturing capability in this sector is, however, of crucial importance, both for diversification of industrial production and for the accelerated growth of a variety of technological skills and capabilities, including production of complex castings and forgings, welding, precision machining, heat treatment, testing, and the like.

In this chapter, the state of production in critical machinery subsectors, the impact on technological development in developing countries, and future trends will be analyzed, together with the role of MNC subsidiaries and affiliates in this regard. The subsectors covered are electrical power machinery, machine tools, tractors, and automobiles.

Electrical Power Equipment

The rapid increase in the demand for electricity to sustain industrial and agricultural growth in developing countries has necessitated the implementation of major programs for electrical power generation and distribution in most of these countries during the past two to three decades. The establishment of large thermal and hydroelectric power stations and, in some instances, nuclear power generation plants in these countries has led to growing demand for electrical power equipment—generators and turbines, circuit breakers and switchgear, transformers, power boilers, electric motors, and transmission line and power-distribution equipment. Most such equipment in developing economies, except for a few countries, is imported from a small group of MNCs in the United States, Western Europe, and Japan. Although production of electrical goods has expanded rapidly in a number of developing countries, the items manufactured are primarily electrical consumer goods, such as heaters, light bulbs, and switches, and simple standard industrial products, such as fans and refrigerators. Only in a few developing countries has the manufacture of electrical power equipment been undertaken. The range of such manufacture and the varying pattern of technology acquisition and transfer to enterprises manufacturing such equipment in developing countries is of considerable interest, since the production and sale of electrical power equipment has remained largely dominated by a few MNCs.

A considerable proportion of the global production of such equipment is accounted for by about ten companies, operating through a large number of subsidiaries and affiliates in different countries. The largest MNCs in this field are General Electric (U.S.); Siemens (FRG); Westinghouse (U.S); the Schneider Group, including Merlin Gerin and Alsthom Atlantique (France); Brown Boveri (Switzerland); Hitachi, Toshiba, and Mitsubishi (Japan); ASEA (Sweden); and General Electric Company and Northern Engineering Industries (UK). Most of these corporations manufacture a full line of heavy electrical equipment and a wide range of mechanical equipment.

Production and technological trends in heavy electrical equipment manufacture indicate a rapid shift to higher ranges and capacities. Since the 1950s sizes of turbine generators have increased from 200MW to 1,000–1,300MW, while sizes of hydraulic turbines rose to 500MW.[1] Electric motors are being manufactured with capacities of up to 45MW in AC motors and 12MW in DC motors. Power transformers often have capacities up to 500MVA–800kV. SF-type circuit breakers are being manufactured for capacities up to 500kV. Transmission lines also carry much heavier loads of above 756kV and are integrated with grid systems, often extending beyond national boundaries. The technological developments embodied in the increased capacities of electrical power equipment have mainly resulted from extensive research by major MNCs, with research expenditures of over $1 billion annually by some corporations, such as General Electric (U.S.), constituting 5 to 10 percent of sales earnings of several MNCs in this field. A great deal of technology licensing and cross-licensing has also taken place among these corporations, which has enabled the MNCs to share the benefits of costly technological research to a considerable extent. There are, for example, licensing arrangements for turbine generators between General Electric (U.S.) and several companies, including Toshiba and Hitachi, between Westinghouse and Siemens, Mitsubishi, and Marelly, and between Brown Boveri and ASEA, Alsthom, Mitsubishi, and others. Similar arrangements exist with respect to power circuit breakers, power transformers, and other heavy equipment for power system design and engineering.[2]

The manufacture of electrical equipment requires large capital outlays, in heavy mechanical equipment, machine tools, foundries and forge shops, and specialized testing facilities. With the higher capacities and ranges of equipment required, increasingly complex production and testing facilities are needed. In the case of the large MNCs in this field, the production facilities have been operating for several decades and the upgrading and retooling of those plants have been a gradual process. Since heavy electrical equipment is generally custom-made to suit particular conditions and requirements, production plants for such equipment are primarily in the form of large engineering and metal-processing facilities, which are capable of adjustment to meet production requirements for specific equipment orders. At the same time, with the high investment costs of such production facilities, scale economies assume considerable significance. It has been estimated, on the basis of Western European costs, that efficient production of turbine generators of 200–300MW requires annual orders of at least ten to fifteen units, and for those in the 1,000–1,300MW range, eight to ten units.[3] Since the early 1970s, however, electricity consumption in industrialized countries has increased at a relatively slow rate. At the same time, as major electrification programs have been undertaken in most developing countries, the demand for power equipment has increased rapidly, and these countries have become important export markets for MNCs in this field.[4]

Installation of large power-generation units and the modest growth rate in electricity consumption in industrialized countries had contributed to significant overcapacities by the early 1970s in most producer countries. In the case of Western European manufacturers, this was further intensified by a decline in exports resulting from the entry of Japanese manufacturers in world export markets. Consequently, in Western Europe, manufacturers tried to rationalize their operations through mergers. This was particularly pronounced in the United Kingdom, France, and Italy, where, by the late 1970s, concentration of the industry increased rapidly.[5] Several other manufacturers diversified their production to a wider range of activities, such as telecommunications and electronics, mining machinery, railway equipment, cranes, and other mechanical equipment.

An important feature of power-equipment manufacture is its close linkage with the planning and implementation of major electrical power projects and systems. Most of the major equipment manufacturers possess the necessary engineering ability to plan and execute power projects on a turnkey basis. With the increasing size and capacity of thermal, hydropower, and nuclear-power plants for utilities, the design and construction of power systems have become important factors in the choice of the particular equipment and the technology embodied in such equipment. For some of the large power-generation projects, MNCs have also set up consortia to divide the various aspects of design, construction, and equipment supply among their members.[6]

The highly concentrated nature of the power-equipment sector has ensured a very strong market position for MNCs in this field. This was strengthened by the extensive licensing and cross-licensing relationships among several of the major manufacturers. The extent of control over the industry by these MNCs was further intensified by cartel arrangements, which were established even before World War II and were reportedly renewed, with some interruptions, in the 1960s and 1970s. The organization through which such arrangements were reportedly effected was the International Electrical Association, headquartered in Switzerland, which, in 1977, reportedly included fifty-five manufacturers in European and Japanese companies. The arrangements related to a wide range of electrical products and were said to include provisions on pricing, tenders, and export market allocation among members.[7]

It is against this background of MNC operations in the power-equipment field that technology transfer to developing countries should be viewed. As electricity generation and distribution increased in these countries, new markets emerged and production activities were undertaken for consumer electrical products and also for fractional-horsepower motors, insulated wires and switches, distribution transformers, low-voltage transmission lines, and distribution equipment. Most of this production was undertaken by subsidiaries of MNCs, particularly in Latin America and certain countries of Asia and Africa. The manufacture of electrical power equipment, especially in the middle and higher ranges, however, was confined to a few countries, mostly in response to pressure by host governments for local assembly and production. While the small market size in most developing countries has militated against extensive local manufacture of power equipment, the growing domestic demand in several Latin American and Asian countries has provided an adequate market base. As a result of import-substitution policies and the high degree of protection given to locally manufactured products in these countries, several MNCs have set up production facilities, which were initially based on assembly operations, with a gradual increase of local content. In some of these countries, locally owned companies have also undertaken power-equipment manufacture, mostly covering the lower ranges and capacities of switchgear, transformers, motors, transmission towers, and various ancillary equipment. By the early 1960s, considerable production was taking place by local manufacturers in Brazil and India and, to a lesser extent, in Argentina, Mexico, and some Southeast Asian countries. An important development took place in India during the 1960s, when state-owned enterprises were established for the manufacture of power equipment; they were subsequently merged in Bharat Heavy Electricals Ltd. (BHEL).

During the same period, state-owned production of electrical equipment was also undertaken in Egypt. The technology transfer arrangements between MNCs and their subsidiaries in developing countries, on the one hand, and the acquisition of technology by the state-owned BHEL, on the other, provide an interesting contrast. Varying levels of technological absorption have been achieved in these countries, as measured in terms of local content, export performance, and design and engineering capability.

Several MNCs have set up production and assembly facilities in developing countries.[8] General Electric (U.S.) has production operations in Brazil, Argentina, Colombia, and Mexico and joint ventures in the Philippines and Taiwan, besides plants in other developing countries. Siemens has manufacturing activities in Brazil, Argentina, Mexico, Colombia, Venezuela, India, Pakistan, and Indonesia, with joint ventures in Iran and Egypt and licensing arrangements with BHEL in India. Brown Boveri has subsidiaries in Brazil, Argentina, Mexico, Venezuela, and Peru, joint ventures in India and the Philippines, and licensing arrangements in South Korea. Westinghouse has a subsidiary in Brazil and a joint venture in Mexico. ASEA has a major production facility in Brazil and a small plant in Kenya. General Electric Company (UK) and Alsthom have plants in Brazil and Alsthom has a joint venture in India. Japanese MNCs have major production operations in Southeast Asian countries, besides plants in Brazil and Mexico and licensing arrangements in India and some other countries.

The nature and extent of production operations vary considerably in these countries, depending largely on local market demand, production and technological infrastructure, and host country policies. In some instances, production activities in developing countries are little more than assembly operations, with equipment imported from the parent corporation in completely knocked-down or semi–knocked-down condition. In such cases, the extent of technology transfer is obviously very limited and the subsidiary company's operations are primarily intended to meet host country requirements for machinery imports through partial local assembly rather than through direct imports from external sources. In most developing countries, however, local content requirements are prescribed, ensuring that the extent of local integration in manufacture is gradually increased up to levels of 40 to 50 percent, or more, of value. Up to these levels, local production activities are generally conducted at the subsidiary's plant and there is relatively little horizontal integration with other plants in the country. It is only when local content levels are substantially higher and in countries where the production and technological infrastructure has developed adequately, including the production of precision castings and forgings, that effective horizontal integration is achieved in this sector.

In terms of overall production capability and local content, the highest levels achieved have been in Brazil and India, followed by Argentina, Mexico, and South Korea, and at a much lower level of production in other countries such as Algeria, Colombia, Egypt, Peru, Pakistan, and Turkey. The large internal markets in Brazil and India (as a result of major electrical power development programs) have brought very rapid growth of power-equipment production, but the pattern of growth in terms of ownership of the industry has been significantly different. In most other developing countries, except in South Korea, MNC subsidiaries have played a dominant role.

In Brazil, most major MNCs in this field have established large subsidiary operations. With the strong technological infrastructure available in the country, the emphasis in Brazilian policies for maximizing local content has resulted in very high levels of manufacturing integration in the production of most categories and ranges of power equipment. The great expansion in electrical power generation—a growth rate of 11 percent during 1973–78 and a generating capacity anticipated to increase from 19,578MW (of which 85 percent is hydropower) to over 82,000MW in 1990—has necessitated, and will continue to require, power equipment in high ranges and capacities in very large quantities.[9] Government policies, which strongly encouraged foreign direct investments during the 1960s, attracted several major power equipment manufacturers, and sixteen such MNCs set up manufacturing subsidiaries while others established joint ventures and licensing arrangements with Brazilian enterprises. It must be emphasized, however, that Brazilian enterprises were already fairly well developed in power equipment manufacture even prior to the major surge of MNC subsidiary operations in the 1960s and 1970s, and, in several instances, they were taken over by the major MNC subsidiaries.[10] This, in fact, constituted a serious setback for Brazilian-owned industry. The companies that survived were able to grow rapidly—for example, Industria Villares, which manufactures a wide range of mechanical and electrical equipment; Industrie de Transformadores, producing power and distribution transformers; Bardella Borrielo Electro Mecanica SA, manufacturing electric motors; and several others. Nevertheless, the major share of electrical power equipment production in Brazil is presently controlled by MNC subsidiaries. This has undoubtedly resulted in a high level of production capability and local integration. At the same time, since technological decisions are made primarily from the viewpoint of MNC operations, the development of local design and engineering capability has not been as great as could be expected from the very large production capability set up in the country. Although, in the latter half of the 1970s, Brazilian manufacturers of power equipment met over 65 percent of internal demand, imports have continued to be fairly heavy, especially with regard to equipment for large thermal and nuclear-power stations, and this pattern is likely to continue during the present decade.[11] It is difficult now to judge the technological impact of a different growth pattern that would have concentrated on greater incentives and support to Brazilian-owned industrial enterprises against the establishment of large foreign-owned subsidiaries that did take over most of this sector. The level of development of Brazilian-owned enterprises in this field by the early 1960s undoubtedly constituted a strong production and technological base that could have been built upon. Although the pace of growth of the industry may have been slower and foreign technology through joint ventures and licensing undoubtedly would have been necessary, Brazilian-owned industry would have expanded rapidly and could have achieved high technological capability in most fields of power-equipment production, as some of the locally owned enterprises were able to do.

The growth of power-equipment manufacture followed a different pattern in India, with the establishment of major production capacity in the higher ranges by state-owned units, supported by a large number of private sector manufacturers, including affiliates of several MNCs. Power-generation capacity in India increased from 2,300MW in 1950 to about 30,000MW in 1980, and additional generation capacity during 1980–90 is expected to be over 43,000MW.[12] Most of India's power-equipment requirements are met by local production, which expanded at a very rapid pace during 1960–80. The major state-owned corporation, BHEL, has four large manufacturing plants for turbine generators, thermal and hydro projects, and nuclear units, besides power transformers, switchgear, boilers, and other heavy electrical equipment. Although BHEL's initial production capacity was set up with Soviet and Czech collaboration, with one plant in Bhopal being built with technological support and assistance from UK manufacturers, BHEL presently has a number of technology license agreements with several MNCs, including Siemens, ASEA, Combustion Engineering, Nuovo Pignone, and others; these arrangements have enabled the corporation to divesify its production to a considerable extent and also to undertake extensive R&D activities and programs for technological adaptation. Besides BHEL, there are thirty-two transformer manufacturers in the large and medium sectors, twenty producers of circuit breakers of various types, and more than thirty-five manufacturers of electric motors, including seven companies producing at various high ranges. Most other requirements of power-equipment production, including capacitors, insulators, transmission and distribution equipment, and others, are met by local manufacturers. Since public utilities in India are state-owned, with only one or two exceptions, and since overall power generation and distribution is controlled by state-owned electricity boards, the country has sought to link the planning of new generation capacity with equipment production capacity. This has led to major power shortages from time to time but has enabled a high degree of technological self-reliance in power-equipment manufacture. The regulatory policies toward foreign investment and technology have also ensured that Indian-owned enterprises achieve technological absorption and design capability in various aspects of such manufacture. In terms of local content, the Indian power-equipment industry has achieved very high levels, and there is very little import of components and materials at present. It has also demonstrated considerable export capability, with BHEL exports of power boilers and exports of transformers, switchgear, motors, and transmissions by several Indian manufacturers—though exports of power equipment have tended to lag because of heavy internal demand for most such equipment. Although production and technological capability in India has not achieved the highest ranges and capacities presently common in industrialized economies, the close linkage between planning for power generation and local production and technological capacity has ensured a substantial degree of technological self-reliance in this critical field of capital goods manufacture.[13]

Power-equipment production also proceeded at a fast pace in the Republic of Korea, especially in the 1970s. With a presently installed capacity of 9,400MW projected to increase to 27,400MW by 1991, demand for power equipment is rising rapidly.[14] Production capacity in medium and high equipment ranges is mostly with approximately fifteen major Korean manufacturers that have joint ventures or licensing arrangements with MNCs. With the technological infrastructure available in South Korea, the expansion in production has been very rapid. Major manufacturers such as Hyundai are producing through licensing arrangements with Siemens and Westinghouse, Dae Woo with Brown Boveri and Deutsche Babcock, Korea Heavy Industrial Company with Alsthom and Babcock and Wilcox (U.S.), Lee Chun with Tokyo Shibaura, Shin Yeong with Mitsubishi, Gold Star with Fuji Electric Corporation, and several others with technology licenses from various sources, mostly Japanese. An important feature of Korean power equipment manufacture has been its export orientation. Exports of transformers alone came to over $55 million in 1980, comprising 15 percent of production.[15] Although the country continues to import power-generation equipment, it has developed considerable technological capability and self-reliance in power transmission and distribution equipment.

Considerable production of power equipment has been undertaken in Argentina and Mexico, mostly of tranformers, switchgear, and motors. Most of the production, as in other Latin American countries such as Venezuela, Colombia, and Peru, is by MNC subsidiaries, which also manufacture various electrical consumer goods for local markets. Some locally owned companies, such as the Alpha group in Mexico, have set up joint ventures, while others have licensing agreements with MNCs. In other developing countries, including Turkey, Pakistan, Kenya, and the Philippines, MNC subsidiaries have been established that are producing power equipment in the lower ranges and capacities. The prevailing trend for new plants has been the establishment of joint ventures, as in the case of the General Electric (U.S.) minority participation with the Private Development Corporation of the Philippines, the participation of the CGE-Alsthom (52 percent of equity) with

P.T. UNINDO in Indonesia, and Siemens' participation (31 percent of equity) in switchgear manufacture with EGEMAC in Egypt.

The development of the power-equipment industry in developing countries is undoubtedly hindered by several factors. There is considerable production overcapacity in industrialized countries, but technology for the production of higher ranges of equipment is available only from a few sources in these countries. Furthermore, the capital outlay on new plants is high, while gestation periods are fairly long and technological capabilities can only be absorbed and developed over several years. Internal markets in most developing countries are also relatively small, except during periods when major expansion of electricity generation capacity is undertaken. Generation and distribution systems are often linked to particular standards and specifications, which are usually those of a major MNC that has supplied the equipment to the country over several years. With the increasing size and range of power-generation equipment, equipment designs not only need constant modifications and development but also have to be integrated with existing power systems, in which the major MNCs have the most extensive experience and capability. Despite these major constraints, however, with expanding markets and improved technological infrastructure in several developing countries, there is considerable scope for establishment and growth of power-equipment manufacture in these countries. The response of MNCs to joint ventures and licensing arrangements is also likely to be positive, especially for products with technology that is mature, well established, and available from alternative sources. Although the manufacture of large turbine generators may not be feasible, except in a few countries such as Brazil and India where there is large internal demand, there is undoubtedly a wide range of electrical machinery, including boilers, transformers, switchgear, motors and transmission equipment, that can be produced at economic and internationally competitive levels in a number of countries. The growing exports of transformers and motors from South Korea and of power boilers and other electrical equipment from India indicate the considerable potential of such production for both internal and external markets. Production technology for a wide range of such equipment is available from one or another MNC or equipment manufacturer and can be acquired through licensing agreements or through joint venture arrangements. It is only at the level of very heavy and high-capacity power equipment that production technology and know-how may be difficult to obtain through such means. The role of governments in developing countries will undoubtedly be very critical if local power-equipment manufacture is to be fostered. Since public utilities are the principal consumers and, for certain equipment, the only purchasers, it is necessary that sizes and standards prescribed by such agencies be consistent and in accordance with local production capability. Since public utilities in these countries are usually state-owned, this should generally be possible. In the matter of costs and the extent of preference to be given to locally manufactured equipment, however, there can be considerable difference of opinion between public utilities and local manufacturers. Initial production costs of locally manufactured equipment would undoubtedly be higher and would require protective tariffs or import restrictions. At the same time, the extent of such a cost differential may have an unduly adverse impact on the cost of electrical power generation.

It is necessary to achieve an effective balance between protecting local manufacture and ensuring that the level of protection does not lead to unduly high costs of power generation. It may also be necessary to provide financial resources to public utilities and other purchasers of electrical equipment at similar or comparable levels to those provided by foreign manufacturers through "tied" aid arrangements. Governmental support may also be required for financial participation, in the form of various incentives, including subsidies for testing facilities and equipment, to encourage local production and technological absorption and adaptation. It is also essential that adequate research capability be developed, both in specialized research institutions and at an enterprise level in these countries. This would also necessitate governmental assistance and support. There are undoubtedly considerable difficulties and limitations in the development of competitive production capability for power-equipment manufacture. However, experience in Brazil, India, and the Republic of Korea has amply demonstrated that it is not only practicable but may be necessary for technological development and self-reliance, even though the range of manufacture would differ from country to country, depending on market size and other factors.

Mechanical Equipment

Mechanical equipment comprises several groups and categories of machinery, which, in turn, vary considerably in their functions and complexity. Such equipment ranges from simple pumps, cranes, and diesel engines to complex and sophisticated machine tools, machining centers, and specialized equipment for various industrial branches. With expanding activities in construction, mining, and industrial production in most developing countries, the demand for such machinery has increased rapidly. Most of this demand is met through imports. Although production of machinery has increased, albeit from a low base, during the 1970s, the range of production and the level of technological development have remained fairly low, with the exception of a few countries where capital goods production has received special emphasis and priority.

As in the case of electrical power equipment, a major cause for the slow growth of machinery production in most developing countries has been the relatively small size of internal markets and the limited industrial infrastructure by way of foundries and forge shops. Acquisition of production technology and know-how had to be from foreign sources, especially during initial stages of manufacture. The major equipment manufacturers from industrialized countries have had the necessary production capacity to meet the machinery needs of developing countries; in fact, developing countries have emerged as major markets for various types of machinery and equipment. Besides the fact that MNCs treated these countries as export markets, they have generally been reluctant to make the substantial investments necessary to undertake local manufacture in these countries. Nevertheless, production of such equipment has increased considerably, particularly in recent years. One major factor has been the emphasis on import substitution, which resulted in foreign equipment manufacturers setting up local production operations in these countries, principally to protect their markets. These policies have also led local entrepreneurs and industrial groups to enter this field, mostly through joint ventures with foreign manufacturers. In certain countries, particularly Egypt, India, and later Algeria, a deliberate policy was initiated to undertake such production through state-owned companies, which obtained foreign technology through licensing arrangements. State enterprises in capital goods production have also been set up in several other developing countries, partly because private industry has not been forthcoming in investing in this sector, partly because of the large capital outlays and long gestation periods and partly because certain governments have considered machinery production to be of such priority as to merit direct investment by national authorities.

Machine Tools

Since the subject of mechanical equipment covers a very wide range, this chapter will illustrate the major production and technological trends in developing countries only for the manufacture of machine tools, which constitute a critical component in the capital stock of any country. The nature of machine tools utilized determines, to a large extent, the technological processes of user industries and their final products. Furthermore, since machine tools are key producer goods, the technological development in the machinery sector has direct impact on the productivity of various industrial branches. Machine tool manufacture covers a very wide range, with different levels of technological complexity. Production capability in this field in developing countries varies considerably and is limited to relatively few countries. Nevertheless, the experience of machine tool manufacture provides valuable indicators regarding the nature and extent of technology transfer and development in the mechanical equipment sector as a whole.

The production of machine tools constitutes an essential element of industrial infrastructure. Most production activities in the metal industry require the use of some type of metal-cutting, metal-forming, and metal-processing machine tools, and with an expanding demand for such equipment, there is growing need and potential for domestic manufacture of certain machine tools in most countries. This requires a strong foundry industry and precision forging facilities, which are necessary for other capital goods production as well. Technological skills must also be developed in modernized foundry operations, in precision machining, and in the use of various tool material and designs, apart from the acquisition of production technology and know-how.

Machine tool production in industrialized countries has undergone major technological development in recent years. Specialized machine tools with complex designs and production capability have been developed for particular industries such as aerospace, armaments, and aircraft.[16] Operational techniques have also become highly sophisticated with machining centers controlled by computerized numerical control (CNC) or direct numerical control (DNC), tool chargers, transfer lines, and flexible computer-aided manufacturing (CAM) systems, with a high degree of automation.[17] Important technological developments have also taken place in materials for cutting tools, such as ceramic tools, special materials for tool changers, and high-precision diamond tips. With rapid growth in microelectronics, machine tool control systems have become increasingly complex and automated. Most of these developments are related to the need for higher degrees of precision, which can be achieved through microprocessors and computerized operations. Machine tools are being constructed on a modular basis to provide for a rapid shift in machining facilities for various items. Measurement techniques have also become increasingly complex and accurate, and there is a trend toward remote sensing, using lasers and other new techniques. Apart from these major technological developments, there has also been a gradual improvement in the design of standard equipment that makes older designs obsolete in international markets.

The structure of the machine tool industry in industrialized countries differs from that of most other capital goods industries. With the exception of Japanese companies, a large number of relatively small firms (often held privately) operate in this field, which covers a large range of products. Machine tool companies generally specialize either in certain metal-cutting or metal-forming machinery but most of them also manufacture universal machine tools, for which there is the highest demand. As a result of the substantial degree of specialization among manufacturers of machine tools, the machine tool industry has shown a high degree of export propensity. In the late 1970s, for example, about 40 percent of machine tool production was exported, compared with one-third during the 1960s.[18] There has been intense competition, particularly in the area of standard, universal machine tools, which are produced by a number of companies in all industrialized countries. In export markets, high-quality models, incorporating the latest technological developments, have played an important role in the competitive position of the companies.

Although, in most developed countries, the machine tool industry has been characterized by a relatively large number of producers, the degree of concentration has increased in recent decades. In several instances, manufacturers have acquired competitive firms or companies with complementary product lines. In other cases, large producers in the metal-working and processing industries have acquired machine tool companies to diversify their activities. More recently, manufacturers of automobiles have also started to produce certain types of machine tools and robots, largely to meet their own requirements. At the same time, strong competition from Japanese companies has also resulted in the closing of several plants in other industrialized countries and the abandonment of machine tool production by several companies.

The machine tool industry in developing countries is confined to a few countries and is operating at a relatively lower level of technological sophistication than it does in industrialized economies. The major share of production is concentrated in Argentina, Brazil, India, Mexico, the Republic of Korea, Singapore, and Taiwan.[19] While MNCs have played an important role in most of these countries in the development of local machine tool manufacture, the channel of technology transfer has tended to be different from what it is in most other industrial sectors. As production of machine tools was undertaken in these countries, at the lower levels of technological sophistication, foreign subsidiaries played a more limited role, and most of such production was implemented by joint ventures and licensing arrangements. One important exception in this regard was Brazil, where several machine tool manufacturers, mostly from the Federal Republic of Germany, set up production facilities during the 1960s and early 1970s. By the 1980s, there were eighteen foreign subsidiaries operating in this field in Brazil, including subsidiaries of leading German manufacturers such as Gildemeister and Schuler, Burkhards, MWM Motoren Diesel, and Muller. Most of the companies were foreign-owned, and their entry was motivated by the expanding internal market and the various government incentives enjoyed by local manufacturers of machinery in Brazil, including protection from imports. At the time of entry of these subsidiaries, Brazil already had a fairly well-developed machine tool industry that covered the manufacture of a wide range of standard equipment. Foreign subsidiaries, for the most part, have avoided active competition with locally owned industry and have concentrated on machine tools with a higher degree of complexity than most of the local companies. These subsidiaries have played an important role in the

Brazilian machine tool industry; their production reached $380 million by 1980[20] and covered 79 percent of local demand.[21] More recently, foreign subsidiaries have also increased exports of machine tools, mostly to other Latin American countries.[22] Brazilian-owned machine tool companies, including the largest manufacturer in the country, Industria Romi SA, have relied heavily on foreign sources of technology through licensing arrangements and, in most cases, have obtained exclusive rights to manufacture certain types and models of equipment for the local market and for exports in Latin America.[23]

In the Republic of Korea and in India, although machine tool production has been undertaken mainly by locally owned companies, MNCs in this field have been the major sources of technology. In Korea, major growth in machine tool production took place only in the 1970s, and production reached $130 million by 1980. This, however, covered only about 23 percent of the local demand, and the country relies heavily on imports.[24] Most of the manufacture is based on technology licensed from Japanese manufacturers and covers standard, universal machinery. Apart from foreign sources of technology, major efforts have also been made to develop indigenous technology, particularly in those areas where acquisition through licensing has proved to be difficult, and an important role has been played by the Precision Machinery and Technology Centre of the Korean Advanced Institute of Science and Technology (KAIST). Designs and production technology for numerically controlled lathes were developed in this institution and subsequently licensed to domestically owned companies. The growth of the machine tool industry in India has been fairly rapid since the 1960s, and a large number of locally owned companies are engaged in production of a wide variety of machine tools. Most of these companies have licensing arrangements with U.S. and European manufacturers. There are also several joint ventures with minority foreign participation.

The Indian machine tool industry, however, is dominated by Hindustan Machine Tools (HMT), a public sector enterprise that has a major share of production of complex and sophisticated machine tools. Most of the technology utilized by HMT has been acquired through licenses from several MNCs. HMT is now producing a considerable range of machine tools, including numerical control (NC) and computerized numerical control (CNC) turning and vertical machining centers. Manufacturers in the private sector are producing various machines of relatively simple design, based largely on foreign technology. The industry has also been supported by the Central Machine Tool Institute and several of the designs developed by this research institute are utilized by local industry.

Substantial production of machine tools also takes place in Singapore and Taiwan where several domestically owned companies produce simple, standard equipment, based on foreign technology and obtained through joint ventures or licensing. Most of such production is exported. One major U.S. manufacturer has also set up a wholly owned subsidiary in Singapore for machine tool exports from this country.

In other Third World countries, production of machine tools is fairly limited. In Latin America, except for Brazil and despite the large internal market in countries such as Argentina and Mexico, local production has only covered a very small share of domestic demand.[25] Considerable emphasis was given to the establishment of machine tool plants in Mexico during the 1970s, and there has been increased production of lathes and milling machines, although the rate of growth has been fairly slow. In other developing countries, such as Egypt and Pakistan, certain ranges of machine tools are being locally produced, mostly in state-owned enterprises.

Technology transfer in machine tool production in developing countries has largely comprised transfer of designs and production technology for machine tools that are gradually being phased out in industrialized countries. Except in Brazil, South Korea, and India, and to some extent in the export-oriented production in Singapore and Taiwan, most of the ranges and types of machine tools produced in other developing countries are in the lower end of the technology spectrum. Since most machine tool manufacturers in industrialized countries have been relatively medium-size enterprises, they have had little propensity to invest abroad. Their interest has primarily been in extending their operations to foreign markets through exports or by way of licensing technology, rather than undertaking foreign production. Apart from licensing agreements in Brazil, Korea, and India, most of the licenses cover technology for the manufacture of standard machine tools produced by a large number of companies worldwide. Also, in many cases, the licensing agreements provide for the initial transfer of designs and production know-how, but subsequent improvements by the licensor have often not been transferred in order to protect the export markets of licensors. Since the international market for standard and universal machine tools is very competitive and production technology for such items is available from several manufacturers, revenue from licensing can often be the only income from these markets in developing countries.

In the few developing countries in which MNCs have undertaken local production—either by wholly owned subsidiaries, as in Brazil or Singapore, or through joint ventures, as in India, South Korea, Argentina, and Mexico—MNC subsidiaries and affiliates have depended to a large extent on the technical support of their parent company and have made only limited local R&D efforts. In Brazil, for example, most of the R&D expenditure in this industry has been undertaken by locally owned companies, although they have also relied heavily on foreign technology.[26] Similarly, comparative data on a sample of machine tool manufacturers in India show that while domestically owned companies spent 6.9 percent of their sales on R&D,[27] for joint ventures, this only amounted to 1.3 percent.[28] Furthermore, in most of these countries, while locally owned companies have worked in close cooperation with domestic research institutions and universities to adapt their technology and develop local designs, foreign subsidiaries have made little use of such facilities.[29] The acquisition of technology through licensing arrangements, however, has undoubtedly led to several limitations in machine tool production in developing countries. On the one hand, in many of these countries, the technological capability of locally owned industry is very limited and is often unable to utilize and absorb foreign technology, even for the manufacture of standard machine tools and upgrading of such production. In several instances, simple tools are produced locally by reverse engineering and by copying imported equipment. The manufacture of more complex machinery, even with foreign designs and production know-how, is often far more difficult because of the limited absorptive capacity. This is further compounded by the lack of supplier industries, which can be a major restraint, even for the most advanced developing countries in this field.[30] At the same time, where local production and technological capabilities have achieved a relatively high level, as in India, Brazil, and South Korea, the main problem in the future will be to ensure that technological developments in machine tool design and production keep pace with those in industrialized countries. This can be achieved either through much greater research efforts at institutional and enterprise levels in these countries or through continued inflow of technology. Relying on continued inflow, however, may pose difficulties, since, as in other manufacturing sectors, producers of specialized machine tools may not be inclined to transfer technology in such specialized fields to unaffiliated companies until these technologies have been fully exploited in industrialized economies. With the growing trend to design, manufacture, and use computerized machine tools in industrialized countries, the technological gap between developed and developing countries may increase further in this field. This may, in turn, influence not only the productivity of user industries but also the export potential of these countries where products with the latest technological developments compete.

Tractors

With agriculture continuing to be the mainstay of the economy of most developing countries, the local production of agricultural machinery and implements has constituted an important aspect of developmental planning. Agricultural equipment is necessary for a large variety of farm operations ranging from irrigation, ploughing, reaping, cutting, and threshing to drying and storage and transport to markets. The requirements for such equipment range from hand-operated or animal-driven items, which generally involve relatively simple technology, to agricultural machinery such as large, power-operated pumps, power tillers, tractors and combines, and specialized machinery for dairy, fishery, and forest operations, which involve fairly complex production processes. The manufacture of agricultural implements such as ploughs and harrows, for example, has been undertaken in most developing countries. Differences in the nature and quality of such implements have mostly been related to various local soil conditions and agricultural production techniques. The production of these items is mostly based on indigenous technology and is generally undertaken by small-scale industrial units, although, in several countries, large companies have also been engaged in producing these items. The manufacture of tractors in various ranges, power tillers, and power-driven attachments to this equipment requires production technology that is available only from a relatively few large companies, most of which operate on a multinational scale. The issues of technology transfer discussed here relate largely to tractors and power tillers and may be less relevant for equipment for irrigation and for dairies, fisheries, and forestry operations.

As with most other engineering goods, the production of tractors and power tillers is largely concentrated in industrialized countries, both market and planned economies, which in the early 1980s accounted for about 85 percent of world production.[31] In market economies, most of the production has been undertaken by a few large companies that have maintained a dominant market share, not only in their respective home markets but in world export markets as well. It was estimated, for example, that in the late 1970s, eight MNCs accounted for 55 percent of worldwide sales of agricultural machinery,[32] and sales of the ten largest MNCs accounted for 75 to 80 percent of world exports of agricultural equipment.[33]

The manufacture of tractors in developed countries is highly capital-intensive; consequently, economies of scale assume considerable significance. In the late 1960s, for example, a study of the sensitivity of production costs to output indicated that, in North America, unit costs of tractor production decreased by 18 percent as annual output increased from 20,000 to 90,000 units, and a further 5 percent decrease was realized as output reached 120,000 units.[34] Such economies of scale became even more pronounced as the product mix shifted toward the manufacture of higher horsepower units. In industrialized regions in North America, Western Europe, and Japan, the industry is highly concentrated in a few companies, such as Deere and Company (U.S.), International Harvester (U.S.), Massey Ferguson (Canada), Fiat (Italy), Ford (U.S.) Kubota (Japan), Renault (France), and Klockner-Humboldt-Deutz (FRG). Most of these companies produce a full line of products, including tractors, combines, and other machinery and implements. These major companies were the early founders of the industry in their respective countries, and their position became consolidated by the acquisition of smaller companies. Apart from the capital intensity of manufacture, significant capital outlay is also required for establishing the distribution and service networks that have acted as deterrents for new entrants to the market. In the late 1970s and early 1980s, the relatively low growth rate of demand for tractors in the major industrialized countries and the large excess capacity of most producers have led to further concentration in this industry. In some countries, however, there are smaller manufacturers that produce specialized machinery of this type but do not compete directly with the major producers.

The technological features of tractor production have not undergone major changes during the past two decades. Technological improvements were directed toward providing greater comfort and convenience to tractor operators and increasing fuel efficiency. Tractor designs and manufacturing processes have been based on agricultural conditions and requirements in North American and Western European countries. In the case of power tillers, the technological characteristics and product functions have primarily met the soil, climate, and usage conditions prevailing in Japan. The range of tractor manufacture extends to various horsepower capacities, and the smaller capacities are usually adequate and more suitable for developing country conditions in which most of the farm holdings are very small compared to those of Western economies. The techniques of tractor manufacture, comprising the assembly line production of the final product and the manufacture of hundreds of components and parts by supplier industries, are the same in both industrialized and developing countries.

The production of tractors in developing countries accounted for about 15 percent of the world output in 1980.[35] Most of this production has been concentrated in a few countries, including Argentina, Brazil, China, India, the Republic of Korea, Peru, and Venezuela, excluding certain other countries where local production largely comprises assembly activities.[36] Manufacture in developing countries covers mostly the lower horsepower ranges. Compared with several other industries, the production of tractors by MNCs in developing countries has remained relatively limited. For MNCs, the preferred method to serve developing country markets has remained exports, which have allowed these companies to utilize existing production facilities in their home countries and in major subsidiaries located in other industrialized countries. Major MNC foreign production facilities have been established only in a few developed countries where local government import-substitution policies and a relatively large local market made such investments attractive. Thus, in Brazil, where, in the early 1980s, annual tractor production was around 55,000 to 60,000 units,[37] ten foreign subsidiaries were operating, but most of the market has been dominated by the subsidiaries of Massey Ferguson and Ford from the United States and Valmet from Finland. In Mexico, local tractor production was undertaken by Massey Ferguson, Deere,

International Harvester, Ford, and Tenneco, and total production reached approximately 16,000 units by 1980.[38] The ownership structure of foreign subsidiaries has varied among the countries. Thus, in Brazil and Argentina, most of the operations are majority or wholly foreign owned, while in Mexico, in response to foreign direct investment regulations, most majority-owned subsidiaries have reduced their equity share to below 50 percent, even though effective control has remained with the MNCs concerned. The more recently established operations of Volvo and Massey Ferguson in Peru and Deere in Venezuela are joint ventures with local partners. Thus, although in countries such as Brazil, where joint venture requirements have not been demanded by the government, MNCs have preferred to operate through majority or wholly owned subsidiaries, in other Latin American countries, they have been responsive to local government requirements and operate in joint ventures with local partners, often on a minority equity basis. This has been partly because all the foreign operations in developing countries produce only part of the final product, and the dependency of the foreign affiliate on the parent company, not only on technology but also on critical parts and components, has allowed the MNC to effectively control local operations in these countries.

Despite host government pressure in countries where MNCs produce tractors, the local content of production has remained relatively low in most countries, with the exception of Brazil. In Mexico, for example, local content is around 50 to 60 percent, even though most of the subsidiaries have been operating in the country for two decades.[39] In Brazil, where the output of each of the major manufacturers exceeds total Mexican production, local content has reached almost 80 percent, but the most critical parts and components are still imported, and transfer of technology has consequently remained partial.[40] An exception to this pattern has been the case of Velmet, a manufacturer from Finland, which has relied heavily on local suppliers for the manufacture of parts and components and has also established an R&D facility.

MNCs have produced tractors and related equipment in several Asian countries through semiassembly operations. Ford, International Harvester, and Massey Ferguson have such operations in Turkey; International Harvester assembles tractors in the Philippines; Allis Chalmers, Deere, and Massey Ferguson had production operations in Iran; Massey Ferguson has assembly operations in Pakistan and in the Republic of Korea, where it manufactures diesel engines. In the Southeast Asian region, Kubota has production activities in Malaysia, Indonesia, the Philippines, and Thailand, while Yanmar has set up semiassembly operations in Indonesia. In many of these instances, the MNCs concerned are operating through joint ventures with local partners, but production and technological activities are largely controlled by the MNCs. Technology transfer has often been limited to assembly activities, and the level of integration has largely depended on the extent to which other manufacturers in these countries have been able to produce diesel engines and components to the specifications set up by the tractor manufacturers.

During the 1970s, MNCs started several assembly operations in African countries—for instance, Ford and Klockner-Humboldt in Egypt and Fiat in Nigeria. Joint ventures with minority foreign holdings have been established by Massey Ferguson in Egypt, Sudan, Morocco, and Libya; in Kenya, Massey Ferguson has a licensing arrangement with a local foreign subsidiary, Burns and Blane. Most of these enterprises are tractor assembly operations, with low levels of local content and, consequently, limited technology transfer.

In India, where tractor production—over 65,000 units annually by 1981[41]—is the highest among developing countries, the development of the industry has shown a different pattern from that of tractor production operations in other developing countries. Although, with the exception of Punjab Tractors, all the manufacturers initially used foreign technology, the technology was secured either through licensing agreements or through joint ventures with minority foreign participation. Consequently, all eleven major tractor manufacturers either are wholly Indian-owned or are Indian-majority companies. Most of the licensing arrangements are with MNCs, as in the case of Escorts with Ford, Tractors and Farm Equipment with Massey Ferguson (UK), Mahindra and Mahindra with International Harvester, and Eicher with Eicher Tractoren (FRG), but management and control have been primarily with the Indian partners in all these cases. One plant of Hindustan Machine Tools, is based on technology supplied by Czechoslovakia. The two important features of Indian tractor manufacture are, first, that manufacturing integration is almost 100 percent, with hardly any foreign component imports, and second, that production is quite competitive by international standards. The high local content of production is largely the result of the advanced production capability for diesel engines and components in the country, which has enabled a high degree of horizontal integration of production and has kept production costs competitive in the industry. At the same time, the low volume of production of domestic companies indicates that economies of scale can be reached in tractor production at a much lower output level, provided that component manufacture is well developed by supplier companies and that the tractor manufacturers produce only a limited number of models.

Although the production of tractors in developing countries has been based mostly on foreign technology, it is interesting to note that there have been exceptions in which tractor technology was developed indigenously to a large extent. In the Republic of China, for example, tractor design was initially based on imported models, but these were subsequently adapted to a large extent to meet local conditions.[42] The local models were made much simpler, which not only reduced the capital investment needed for manufacture but also decreased unit production costs and facilitated servicing. They were also designed to be more versatile in use than the more specialized units produced by MNCs and thus more suitable for rural conditions. An example of a completely indigenously designed model in developing countries is the tractors made by Punjab Tractors in India. These tractors were designed by the National Engineering Research Laboratory and included tractor models between 19hp and 55hp, which were wholly based on locally available inputs and were adjusted to local soil and usage conditions. Punjab Tractors, which started manufacture of these indigenous models in the mid-1970s, has been competing effectively with several other local companies that produce tractors with foreign technology, including joint ventures with major MNCs.

The experience of the production of tractors and power tillers in developing countries shows that in countries where this industry has developed, MNCs have played an important role in transferring basic technology. MNCs, however, have established major production facilities only in a few developing countries whose large internal markets and import substitution policies allowed adequate returns on investments and income from associated imports of parts and components. In these countries, the growth of local technological capability in this field has largely depended on the degree of horizontal integration of manufacture, which has varied among countries and has been significant only in Brazil and India. Two major factors have mitigated against increasing the local content of production: the techno-economic characteristics of production by MNCs and the global interests of these companies. Thus, since production of tractors with the technology in use by MNCs requires large-scale production, most developing country markets are too small for such manufacture. At the same time, MNCs have sought to utilize production facilities in their home countries, an activity that has become increasingly important with stagnating sales in their major markets since the 1970s. MNCs have made only limited efforts to undertake R&D for the design of products or production techniques that would be more suitable to developing country conditions. Instead, MNC subsidiaries have primarily utilized models and blueprints that have been used for production in industrialized economies. Consequently, high production costs and prices of equipment have inevitably limited the extent of sales and use in developing countries. The experience of India must be emphasized in this context, since it indicates that even at an annual production of fewer than 7,000 tractors, production costs can be competitive—provided that the number of models and power ratings are limited and parts and components, particularly engines, can be obtained at prices that are internationally competitive.

MNCs have, however, responded favorably to requests from developing country governments to operate on a joint venture basis rather than through the traditional pattern of wholly owned subsidiaries, and they have also licensed standard technology to unaffiliated companies. This is reflected in the large number of licensing agreements entered into by MNCs with local enterprises in India and also in the arrangements operating in Algeria and the Republic of Korea. This suggests that production technology can also be transferred through licensing arrangements and that MNC involvement as a majority partner is not essential. The nature of production technology is not unduly complex and has remained relatively stable, enabling fairly rapid technological absorption in countries in which there has been substantial growth of engineering goods manufacture. It is important to emphasize, however, that the strong market position of MNCs in the tractor industry of most developing countries is not only the result of their ownership of technology but also, to a large extent, the result of their ability to provide after-sales services and financing arrangements. In most developing countries, local companies do not have adequate means to finance such operations, and their growth and ability to compete with foreign subsidiaries largely depend on provisions of institutional financing by governmental agencies.

Automobiles

The automotive sector, comprising the production of passenger automobiles and commercial vehicles, is perhaps the largest manufacturing industry and has major impact, both direct and indirect, on employment and on the growth of a wide range of ancillary and related industries.[43] This sector, which involves large capital outlays on initial investments and tooling costs, continues to be dominated by MNCs from the United States, Western Europe, and Japan. Manufacturing capacity is largely concentrated in these countries, which are also the principal markets.

Following the petroleum crisis in the early 1970s, the automobile industry underwent considerable changes. The major shift to the use of smaller cars was accompanied by highly competitive exports from Japan, and Japanese companies increased their share of world exports very rapidly, achieving 39.4 percent by 1980.[44] In more recent years, however, Japanese manufacturers have exercised restraints on automobile exports to the United States and several Western European countries; these restraints largely continue to be in effect in 1985.

The intense competition in this sector has led to significant technological developments in design and performance capabilities and also in the manufacturing process. While the basic technology for automobile and commercial vehicle production has remained relatively stable, several improvements have been made to reduce fuel consumption and to meet emission standards prescribed in some countries. The use of microprocessors, electronic controls, and improved safety mechanisms has also increased considerably. With greater competition, improved designs and higher quality performance standards have been established. Important developments have also taken place in the production process, and a high degree of automation has been introduced in various production functions. Thus, the use of robotics and automation has extended to body welding, painting, and various assemblyline operations of several major manufacturers.[45]

As in other assembly industries, the production of automobiles and commercial vehicles requires the integration of various parts and components that are produced by other manufacturers. The growth of the automotive industry in a particular country has, to a substantial extent, reflected the expansion in production and increased technological capability in the manufacture of components. The production of parts and components is generally related to the size of assembly operations at a national level, but, in many instances, the magnitude of such production activities extends beyond national boundaries. Similarly, manufacturing activities of several MNCs, are spread over a number of countries, with major parts and subassemblies being manufactured in some countries for integration and final assembly in others.

Organization of global production has varied among MNCs. Ford, for example, has pursued a greater degree of specialization among its various foreign subsidiaries, mostly located in North America and Western Europe, for the production of specific models, parts, and components. Other MNCs have established close production linkages with manufacturers in other countries, such as Chrysler with Peugeot-Citroen and Renault with American Motors Corporation. In recent years, joint ventures and production linkages have increasingly been established with Japanese manufacturers—for example, between General Motors and Toyota, Ford and Mazda, and Honda and Austin Rover.[46] Foreign competition and increasing R&D and production costs have led to a surge of joint ventures among Western European manufacturers as well. By the early 1980s, there were more than seventy such joint ventures, covering arrangements for development and production of engines and specific parts and components among various manufacturers.[47]

The largest manufacturers in this sector in terms of global production are General Motors (U.S.), Ford (U.S.), and Toyota-Daihatsu (Japan), followed by Nissan Fuji (Japan), Volkswagen-Audi (FRG), Peugeot-Citroen (France), Renault (France), Fiat (Italy), Toyo Kogyo (Japan), and Chrysler (U.S.). Other major manufacturers operating on a worldwide scale are Honda (Japan), Daimler Benz (FRG), British Leyland (Great Britain), and Volvo (Sweden). Automobile production in 1984 ranged from 6.3 million cars by General Motors and 3.6 million by Ford to 1.27 million and 1.02 million by Chrysler and Honda, respectively.[48] The share of foreign production is highest for Ford, with 34 percent, followed by General Motors with 29 percent, Volkswagen with 13 percent, Peugeot-Citroen with 5.5 percent, and Fiat with 3.3 percent.[49] Most of the foreign production of Ford and General Motors has been in Western Europe, although a large number of subsidiaries are also operating in developing countries, particularly in Latin America.

The production of automobiles and commercial vehicles in Third World countries constitutes a small proportion of global production and ranged between 2 million and 2.5 million during 1980–82, or 5–6 percent of world production.[50] With the growing demand for vehicles in Argentina, Brazil, and Mexico, production operations were established in these countries by MNCs in the 1950s and early 1960s. Most of the investments in these countries at that time were undertaken by U.S. manufacturers, often in the form of used equipment supplied from U.S. plants. Initial production operations in these countries followed a similar pattern, comprising assembly operations to meet internal demand. With gradual local manufacture of parts and components, the extent of domestic integration or local value-added increased, although the extent has varied considerably and has depended, to a large extent, on national policies. Production in these countries has expanded quite rapidly, with the manufacture of more than 800,000 vehicles in Brazil, 650,000 vehicles in Mexico, and 180,000 vehicles in Argentina by the early 1980s.[51] MNCs also set up assembly operations in other South American countries during the 1960s—for example, Chile, Venezuela, Colombia, Peru, and Uruguay. During the 1960s and early 1970s, the foreign network of MNCs expanded to several Asian and African countries, largely in the form of assembly operations with limited local content—for instance, in Indonesia, Malaysia, Thailand, the Philippines, Kenya, Morocco, and Nigeria.[52]

Thus, since the 1950s and throughout the 1960s and 1970s, MNCs have established a relatively large network of foreign subsidiaries in developing countries. Because of the low local content of production in most of these countries, these subsidiaries have been effectively integrated within the MNC system, and they have relied heavily on the parent company not only for their technology but, more important, for the supply of major parts and components. Although the automobile industry in developing countries is predominantly owned and controlled by MNCs, there are exceptions in which MNCs are willing to supply technology to unaffiliated foreign companies. Thus, in India, manufacture of automobiles has been undertaken by nationally owned companies, which obtained technology from foreign manufacturers without foreign equity participation. These agreements, however, have generally provided only for the initial transfer of technology and have not included provisions for the transfer of subsequent improvements by the licensor. Also, the government's rigorous policy toward imports forced local companies to manufacture parts and components locally, rather than relying on the licensor for supply. Consequently, by the late 1970s, Indian companies manufactured over 90 percent of the units locally and achieved a high level of technological and production self-reliance in their manufacture.[53] The pattern of production by nationally owned companies in India has consequently varied significantly from that of foreign subsidiaries operating in other developing countries. In India, where production was around 113,000 units in the early 1980s,[54] manufacture has been almost entirely locally sourced in the case of the older, established companies, such as Hindustan Motors and Premier Motors. During 1984–85, however, an agreement was finalized by an Indian company with Suzuki of Japan for production of automobiles. This may involve substantial importing of components in early stages. Other agreements are also being negotiated by Indian manufacturers with Japanese and Western European manufacturers. Production levels in India, however, continue to be in strong contrast to the operation of MNC subsidiaries in other countries, which, even at output levels that exceed that of India several times, continue to integrate the operations of their subsidiaries internationally rather than nationally.

Similar to the situation in India, most of the automobile production in South Korea is undertaken by a locally owned company, the Hyundai group. For the acquisition of the necessary technology, Hyundai turned to several foreign manufacturers for various elements and components. Thus, the basic design was licensed from Fiat, an MNC manufacturer that in contrast to most others, has shown a willingness to license its technology to unaffiliated foreign companies.[55] Engine technology was licensed from Mitsubishi, and there were several agreements with other manufacturers covering the production of various parts and components. The locally manufactured product, called "Pony," is based on various foreign technologies, but Hyundai has succeeded in integrating the various elements to produce over 90 percent of the value of the final product locally.[56] This model has also been competing effectively in the local market. Other foreign manufacturers are also reviewing the potential for automobile manufacture in South Korea, mainly for exports, and a joint venture is being undertaken by General Motors with the Daewoo group in Korea.

The extent of technology transfer to developing countries in this sector and its impact on local technological capabilities are reflected in the pattern of production in different countries. The extent of technology transfer and absorption can be assessed, first, by the level of national integration achieved; second, by the competitive capacity in international markets; and third, by the capacity to design and produce new makes and models. These constitute broad indicators of overall technological capability, but a certain degree of technology transfer is also achieved at lower levels of manufacturing integration, as it is in assembly manufacture or in limited production designed primarily to meet internal market requirements.

The level of national manufacturing integration is of particular importance in the production of automobiles and commercial vehicles, since these industrial enterprises manufacture various related products, ranging from tires and batteries to carburetors, pistons, radiators, and a wide range of parts and components. A national program in this sector thus involves the establishment and development of a large number of production units, besides the principal subassembly and assembly plants. Most governments in developing countries have accordingly prescribed national content requirements and have sought to increase local content in manufacture as far as possible. There are, however, obvious constraints in this regard. First, significant economies of scale can impose serious limitations on the production of components and bought-out items for this industry.[57] Second, an increase in the local content of production can lead to high unit costs, since both the main assembly operation and the production of major components are at significantly lower output levels than they would be in industrialized countries. Third, the extent to which production activities are wholly controlled by MNCs may also be an important determinant of the degree of integration in a particular economy. Since production by subsidiaires is controlled by parent MNCs, the extent of local content and the pricing of subassemblies and components supplied from plants of parent MNCs or from their subsidiaries are determined by the global strategy of the MNC, which may not necessarily be consistent with the interests of companies producing in developing countries.[58] Finally, the level of integration also depends on the interests of manufacturers of parts and bought-out components, which may differ from those of automobile manufacturers.

Despite these constraints, national policies to achieve greater local content in manufacture in several developing countries have been successful. In Brazil, fairly high levels of domestic content had been reached by the early 1970s; nevertheless, the import of parts and components by vehicle manufacturers imposed a heavy burden on the country's balance of trade.[59] A similar situation prevailed in Argentina[60] and, to a greater extent, in Mexico, where the level of integration remained much lower. In India, on the other hand, the development of the automobile industry was planned on the basis of much closer linkages with local manufacture of parts and components. This resulted in a very high level of local content, despite the fact that the volume of production has been significantly below that of Brazil and Mexico. In some other countries, the small size of the national market was to be compensated by regional collaboration efforts, as it is in the Andean group countries.[61]

By the late 1970s, the burden of maintenance imports of automobile parts and components on the national balance of trade has resulted in the adoption of a series of policy measures by several governments. Requirements to increase local content have been accompanied by pressure to develop exports of automobiles or components and thus to compensate for the foreign exchange outflow for imports. Such measures were rigorously pursued by the governments of Brazil and Mexico. In terms of local content requirements, certain MNCs, such as Volkswagen, have reached a very high level of local integration in Brazil and Mexico, while other MNCs, mainly from the United States claim to have achieved suitable levels in the context of their global operations and economies of local manufacture. With respect to export requirements, however, response of MNCs has been quite favorable. Largely also induced by the various financial incentives of the governments, exports and planned exports from these countries have increased rapidly. In Brazil, for example, exports of vehicles and parts increased to $1,039 million by 1980 from $25 million in 1971, and in Mexico, such exports increased from $59 million to $404 million during the same period.[62] Several MNCs have developed their Brazilian and Mexican subidiaries to manufacture either particular types of automobiles, such as Volkswagen, for the global market or certain parts, such as engines, for the United States or for other plants located in different countries. These export efforts have had a favorable impact on the manufacturing capabilities of these countries and have contributed to the implementation of national economic objectives. Other countries that have developed export markets for automobiles, trucks, or components are the Republic of Korea and India, although their exports are much lower than those of Brazil or Mexico.

The development of automobile research and design capability in developing countries has been very limited so far, mainly because, in most of these countries, production is handled by MNC subsidiaries and affiliates. It is only in the Republic of Korea, where the indigenous Pony has been developed, and in India, where earlier licensing arrangements with MNCs have expired or where new license agreements have been entered into, such as the Maruti Company's agreement with Suzuki (Japan), that efforts toward indigenous design and production capability are being developed to any extent. It is essential, however, that research and design efforts be intensified in these countries so that automobiles and commercial vehicles that are more appropriate for use in these countries can be developed.

With rapid technological development in materials and electronic components used in automobiles, and with increased automation in automobile manufacture, the nature of automobile production is undergoing major changes. This will become more pronounced in the next few years, as global competition between Japanese, U.S., and Western European manufacturers intensifies still further. In this context, the production of automobiles and commercial vehicles in developing countries may have to be developed with greater consideration of local and regional markets and of local factor advantages in particular countries. Although it is difficult to project the future global pattern of the automobile industry, the development of national capabilities in production, technological design, and engineering will undoubtedly constitute a critical prerequisite for developing countries in this manufacturing sector.

Notes

1. The trend of technological development of various types of power equipment is discussed in B. Epstein, *Politics of Trade in Power Plants* (London: Trade Policy Research Centre, 1971).

2. A historical review of the licensing and cross-licensing agreements in the power-equipment industry is presented in R. Newfarmer, "Multinational Conglomerates and the Economics of Dependent Development: A Case Study of the International Electrical Oligopoly and Brazil's Electrical Industry," Unpublished doctoral dissertation, University of Wisconsin, 1977.

3. A.J. Surrey, *World Market for Electric Power Equipment—Rationalization and Technical Change* (Sussex: University of Sussex, Science Policy Research Unit, 1973), 29.

4. By the late 1970s, for example, developing countries accounted for approximately one-third to one-half of world imports for various power-equipment categories, based on information in *Statistical Yearbook* (New York: United Nations, 1982.

5. By the early 1970s, for example, the four Italian transformer manufacturers, A.L.C.E., Breda, Ocrean, and part of A.S.G.E.N., were merged into Ital-Trafo.

6. In most cases, in forming consortia, manufacturers from Western Europe tend to join together and U.S. companies usually join with the Japanese.

7. For a detailed description of the IEA, see B. Epstein and R. Newfarmer, "International Electrical Association: A Continuing Cartel," Report prepared for the U.S. House of Representatives, Committee on Interstate and Foreign Commerce and Subcommittee on Oversight and Investigation (Washington, D.C.: U.S. Government Printing Office, 1980).

8. The role of MNCs in the power-equipment industry in developing countries is presented in *Transnational Corporations in the Power Equipment Industry* (New York: United Nations Centre on Transnational Corporations, 1982).

9. *Brazil,* Staff Appraisal Report (Washington, D.C.: World Bank, 1981).

10. This phenomenon is discussed in R.S. Newfarmer, "International Oligopoly in the Electrical Industry," in *International Oligopoly and Development,* ed. R.S. Newfarmer (Notre Dame, Ind.: University of Notre Dame Press, 1984).

11. U.S. Department of Commerce, *Electrical Energy Systems, Brazil* (Washington, D.C.: U.S. Government Printing Office, 1977), 14.

12. *Sixth Five-Year Plan, 1980–1985* (New Delhi: Government of India, Planning Commission, 1981).

13. In power generators, for example, generators up to 500MW are built in India, whereas major manufacturers in industrialized countries manufacture generators in excess of 1,300MW.

14. *Electric Power in Korea* (Seoul: Korea Electric Company, 1981), 12.

15. U.S. Department of Commerce, *Electrical Energy Systems, Korea* (Washington, D.C.: U.S. Government Printing Office, 1981), 14.

16. Recent development in the machine tool industry is discussed in S.M. Patil, *Technological Perspectives in the Machine Tool Industry and Their Implications for Developing Countries* (Vienna: United Nations Industrial Development Organization, July 1982).

17. Between 1970 and 1977, for instance, the share of numerically controlled (NC) machine tools from total machine tool shipments nearly doubled in the United States and the United Kingdom and more than tripled in Japan. See *The Capital Goods Sector in Developing Countries: Technology Issues for Further Research* (Geneva: United Nations Conference on Trade and Development, 1980), 31.

18. Trends in machine tool exports are presented in A.H. Amsden, "The Foreign Involvement of the Machine Tool Industry" (New York: Barnard College, Department of Economics, 1981, mimeographed), ch. 4.

19. The manufacture of machine tools in selected developing countries is analyzed in *Technology Transfer through Transnational Corporations in Capital Goods Manufacture in Selected Developing Countries,* Vol. III (New York: United Nations Centre on Transnational Corporations, 1982).

20. *Economic Handbook of the Machine Tools Industry* (McLean, Va.: National Machine Tool Builders' Association, 1981), 165.

21. *Problems and Issues Concerning the Transfer, Application and Development of Technology in the Capital Goods and Industrial Machinery Sector* (Geneva: United Nations Conference on Trade and Development, 1982), 51.

22. In 1980, the total exports of machine tools from Brazil were $46 million. Ibid., 13, table 1.3.

23. Contractual terms and conditions of a sample of machine tool manufacturers in Brazil, both foreign and domestic, are analyzed in ibid., 73–82.

24. Ibid., 51.

25. In 1980, for example, local production of machine tools in Mexico amounted to approximately $15.5 million, while imports were about $130 million. See United Nations Centre on Transnational Corporations, *Technology Transfer,* Vol. III.

26. United Nations Conference on Trade and Development, *Problems and Issues,* 82.

27. Ibid., 78.

28. Ibid.

29. Ibid., 82.

30. These issues are analyzed for Taiwan in A.H. Amsden, "The Division of Labour Is Limited by the Type of Market: The Case of the Taiwanese Machine Tool Industry," *World Development* 5(1977): 226–27.

31. *Yearbook of Industrial Statistics, 1980,* Vol. II (New York: United Nations, 1981).

32. *Transnational Corporations in the Agricultural Machinery and Equipment Industry* (New York: United Nations, 1981), 22.

33. *Worldwide Study of the Agricultural Machinery Industry* (Vienna: United Nations Industrial Development Organization, International Centre for Industrial Studies, 1979).

34. Canadian Royal Commission on Farm Machinery, *Special Report on Prices* (Ottawa: Queen's Printer, 1969).

35. United Nations, *Yearbook, 1980,* Vol. II.

36. For a review of tractor production, see United Nations, *Transnational Corporations,* Appendix.

37. United Nations, *Yearbook, 1980,* Vol. I.

38. Ibid.

39. Development of local manufacture of agricultural machines in Mexico, including the role of MNCs in the industry, is discussed in United Nations Centre on Transnational Corporations, *Technology Transfer,* Vol. III.

40. For an analysis of the Brazilian experience, see ibid.

41. Information provided by the Ministry of Industry, Government of India.

42. China's first tractor plant in Loyang, established with Soviet aid, started prouction in 1959. The adaptation of foreign technology and its diffusion within the country are analyzed in H. Heymann, *Acquisition and Diffusion of Technology in China: A Reassessment of the Economy* (Washington, D.C.: U.S. Congress, Joint Economic Committee, July 1975).

43. In automobile manufacture in industrialized countries, component manufacturers account for 40 to 60 percent of the value of the final product. See G. Maxcy, *The Multinational Motor Industry* (London: Croom Helm, 1981), 199.

44. *Motor Vehicle Facts and Figures* (Detroit: Motor Vehicle Manufacturers' Association (MVMA), 1982), 69.

45. General Motors, for example, reported that by 1990 it will use 14,000 robots, most to be manufactured internally.

46. The ownership linkages among major automobile manufactures in the early 1980s are presented in *Transnational Corporations in the Internationl Auto Industry* (New York: United Nations Centre on Transnational Corporations, 1983).

47. Ibid., 57.

48. This information is from the 1984 annual reports of General Motors and Ford.

49. These data were calculated from MVMA, *Motor Vehicle Facts,* 69.

50. *World Motor Vehicle Data,* Detroit: MVMA, 1981), 9–13.

51. Ibid., 9–12.

52. For a detailed description of MNC activities in the automobile industry in Latin America, Asia, and Africa, see United Nations Centre on Transnational Corporations, *Technology Transfer,* ch. V, VI.

53. Information provided by the Ministry of Industry, Government of India.

54. MVMA, *World Motor Vehicle Data,* 10.

55. The technology acquisition process followed by Hyundai is discussed in Maxcy, *The Multinational Motor Industry,* 209.

56. United Nations Centre on Transnational Corporations, *Technology Transfer,* Vol. III., 135.

57. Detailed descriptions of economies of scale in plants and firms are presented, for example, in D.G. Rhys, "Economies of Scale in the Motor Industry," *Bulletin of Economic Research* (November 1972). See also D.G. Rhys, "European Mass-Producing Car Makers and Minimum Efficient Scale: A Note," *Journal of Industrial Economics* (June 1977).

58. Issues related to transfer pricing of parts and components are discussed in S. Lall, "Developing Countries and Transfer Pricing: Some Problems of Investigation," *World Development* (January 1979): 59–72.

59. The balance-of-payments effects of automobile manufacture during the early 1970s are discussed in F. De Oliveira and M.A. Travolo Popoutchi, "El Complejo Automotor en Brazil," *ILET/Nuova Imagen* (1979).

60. This is analyzed, for instance in S. MacDonell and M. Lascano, *La Industria*

Automotriz: Prospectos Economicos y Fiscales (Buenos Aires: Departamento de Estudios Division Planes, Direccion General Impositive, 1974).

61. The regional allocation of components among member countries is presented in R.N. Gwynne, "The Andean Group Automobile Programme: An Interim Assessment," *Bank of London and South America Review* (August 1980).

62. See United Nations Centre on Transnational Corporations, *Technology Transfer,* Vol. III, tables 30, 31, for a listing of auto industry exports for Brazil, 1971–80, and for Mexico, 1967–80.

7
Microelectronics and Computers

One of the high-technology areas that is likely to be of critical importance to Third World countries is microelectronics and computer applications.[1] The far-reaching innovations in computer use and in the application of semiconductors are bringing about a new technological revolution in data and information processing, telecommunications, and several other production and service sectors. The rapid growth of electronic data processing systems and their integration with manufacturing processes through computer-aided design (CAD) and computer-aided manufacture (CAM), including highly automated operations, are having considerable effect on competitive manufacturing capability in fields extending from clothing and garments to complex machining operations. The increasingly close linkages between dataprocessing and telecommunications and the processing, storage, and retrieval of a wide variety of information on an international scale are also ushering in a new era of global communications, which will inevitably have a major impact on corporate relationships and technological linkages among enterprises in different countries.

The computer industry has undergone rapid growth as well as radical technological change in the last two decades in industrialized economies, particularly in the United States. The industry continues to be dominated by IBM, with nearly 60 percent of the world market and annual revenues of over $45 billion in 1984.[2] Other major U.S. manufacturers, such as Honeywell, Univac, Burroughs, CDC, and NCR accounted for about one-to-seven percent of the world market in the late 1970s. The Japanese manufacturers, including Fujitsu, Hitachi, NEC, Oki Electric, Mitsubishi, and Toshiba, have been relative late-comers to the international market, and their sales in the late 1970s accounted for about 6 percent of world sales.[3] By the late 1980s, however, Japanese manufacturers are expected to close the technological gap with U.S. companies and, with several major innovations, are only a few months behind developments made by IBM. Three major factors have played a critical role in the rapid technological development of

Japanese manufacturers. The most important factor has been the extensive licensing of technology from U.S. companies. Besides technology agreements made with IBM, a wide range of patents and know-how was acquired by various Japanese manufacturers — by Hitachi from RCA, by Mitsubishi from TRW, by NEC from Honeywell, by Oki from Sperry Rand, and by Toshiba from General Electric. Second, although basic computer technology was mainly obtained through licensing, considerable R&D efforts were made by Japanese corporations. It was estimated that in 1979 alone, the six manufacturers of general-purpose computers spent Y60 billion to Y80 billion on R&D.[4] Third, as early as the late 1950s, the Japanese government actively subsidized R&D through various forms of financial assistance and incentives.[5] Western European corporations in computer manufacture include Nixdorf (FRG), ICL (UK), which also has licensing arrangements with Fujitsu, and Olivetti (Italy).

Technological developments in the 1970s were rapid, with the lead taken by IBM in developing new mainframe computers and peripherals, extending through the IBM 370/135 to the IBM 3081-K. Several firms followed IBM's technological developments through compatible equipment, peripherals, and software that could be utilized in conjunction with IBM equipment. Major technological innovations have been made in terms of performance capability, measured in millions of instructions per second, and in capacity for storage and retrieval. The size and weight of mainframe computers have also been reduced considerably in recent years. The major manufacturer of very large supercomputers in the United States is Control Data Corporation, while IBM dominates the middle and large range of general-purpose computers. Research and development costs in this field have escalated considerably. In a court case in the United States in 1982, IBM indicated that it employed as many as 3,500 people in its mainframe development laboratories at Poughkeepsie, New York, and that it introduces a new mainframe about every three or four years at a cost of $1.2 billion.[6] To provide for research expenditure of this order is difficult for most computer manufacturers other the IBM. It is, in Japan, however — where there are several mainframe manufacturers — that alternative non-IBM mainframe development may be expected for the next generation of such computers.

Technological development in computer applications has been significantly transformed through the increased and diversified application of semiconductors and innovations in chip technology. The small and medium-size computers of companies as Digital Equipment Corporation (DEC), Hewlett Packard, and Data General provide a viable alternative to mainframe computers for a wide range of information processing. IBM's PC and AT computers also perform similar functions. Several other manufacturers have entered the market for the relatively small, desk-top computer that is based on microprocessors of increasing capability and versatility. Microprocessor technology has come a long way during the last decade, and semiconductors constitute one of the fastest-growing industries at present. Intel Corporation (U.S.), which introduced microprocessors in 1971, and its licensees have the largest share of the 16-bit micro-processor market, although three other U.S. manufacturers—National Semi-Conductor, Texas Instruments, and Motorola—are providing considerable competition. The incorporation of advanced semiconductor technology in computer usage, which is represented in microprocessors, is undoubtedly going to be followed by more advanced "computer-on-a-chip" concepts and applications in the next few years. The demand for microprocessors is expected to increase very rapidly in the principal markets and to rise to over $5 billion in 1985. In 1983, the United States accounted for 55 percent of the world market of 1.7 billion,[7] but the fastest growth (44 percent annually) is likely to be in Japan.[8] Besides their use in computers, other end uses of semiconductors have increased rapidly; they include telecommunications, industrial applications, consumer electronics, and military and automotive applications.[9]

Technological developments in microprocessors center partially on the 32-bit model, which can handle data similarly to a mainframe computer at over one million instructions per second. Considerable competition is likely to develop at this level, not only among U.S. companies but also with INMOS (UK) and with NEC (Japan), which is likely to play an increasingly important role with the rapid expansion of semiconductor use in Japan. The enormous range of usage of 32-bit chips and the need for the development of equivalent software may slow the growth of the market, but with the expansion in the scope and potential of robotics and artificial intelligence, the 32-bit chip is likely to constitute the base of the new generation of microprocessors and other micro applications in the future.

In the case of semiconductors, there are several manufacturers engaged in captive production. The largest by far is IBM, followed by Western Electric, Hewlett Packard, Honeywell, and others. The principal sellers of integrated circuits have been U.S. firms, particularly Texas Instruments, with the highest production, Motorola, National, and Fairchild in the 1960s, followed by National Semi-Conductor, INTEL, Mostek, Advanced Micro Devices, and others. Several of these firms have concentrated on meeting specialized needs. Although the basic technology for semiconductors was mostly developed by U.S. companies, with Texas Instruments, IBM, and Motorola in the lead in terms of production, Japanese production increased greatly during the 1970s. By 1979, when the 64K RAM was introduced, nearly half of its sales were by Japanese companies. Four of these firms are full-line producers—for example, NEC, Hitachi, Toshiba, and Mitsubishi. Technology was acquired through licensing from U.S. companies, starting with Fairchild's license to NEC in the 1960s and a joint venture between Texas Instruments and SONY.[10] Several Japanese companies also obtained licenses from AT & T.[11] Technological developments center on very large scale integration (VLSI), with major manufacturers developing their own system designs and production. Innovations are continuing in computer-aided design and in lithographic applications of wafer processing, which may broaden the market significantly, since several circuit designs can be etched on a single wafer.

It is against this brief background of the global computer and semiconductor industry that trends in this field in developing countries should be viewed. It is evident that technological development in these high-technology fields has been almost entirely concentrated in the industrialized economies, and Third World countries are lagging far behind. In fact, the rapid pace of technological innovations in microprocessors and in computers and telecommunications and the enormous variety of soft-ware programs and facilities are resulting in greatly increased technological disparity. This disparity is not only pronounced in the technological and production capabilities of these products but also in their application. The application of microelectronics in developing countries is very limited. According to 1981 estimates, for example, the value of computerized systems installed in developing countries was only 4 percent of global installations, and even this was largely concentrated in a few developing countries.[12] Furthermore, in these countries, industrial application for production and process control has been confined to only a relatively few companies.[13] Yet, although the technology gap in these fields is growing, this growth is very uneven, in respect to both products and countries in the Third World. Thus, except for pure assembly operations by certain MNCs, mainframe computers are not produced in developing countries.[14] At the same time, considerable assembly and electronic-component production facilities have been established by MNCs in certain developing countries to take advantage of cheap labor. MNCs have concentrated these operations in certain parts of the Third World, mainly in Southeast Asia.

Manufacturing operations in electronics, especially microelectronic components, has taken two forms in developing countries. First, by far the most common form has been through the establishment of offshore production and assembly of components by MNC subsidiaries. Second, in some countries, efforts have been made by MNC affiliates and domestically owned companies to achieve a higher level of local integration of production. In terms of technology transfer, the two approaches pose significantly different technological requirements, and their implications differ considerably.

Offshore production of electronic components, especially in the export processing zones of Southeast Asian countries, expanded very rapidly during the 1970s, because several MNCs, mostly from the United States, set up manufacturing facilities to take advantage of the relatively low wages in these countries. Fairchild, for example—the first company to start offshore sourcing of components—started operating in Hong Kong in 1962 and in the Republic of Korea in 1966; it followed with a series of offshore units in Singapore, Indonesia, the Philippines, Brazil, and Mexico, and included testing facilities in some of these units. National Semi-Conductor has nine factories in Southeast Asia, including Hong Kong, Singapore, Indonesia, Malaysia, the Philippines, and Thailand, most of which produce discrete semiconductor components; several of them manufacture digital watch modules and electronic calculators. Motorola established plants in Hong Kong, Republic of Korea, Malaysia, Mexico, and the Philippines and has reached a fairly high level of domestic integration in communication equipment. Texas Instruments has plants in Singapore (including testing facilities), Taiwan, Malaysia, and the Philippines. INTEL operates offshore assembly units in Malaysia, Barbados, and Puerto Rico. Mostek has such facilities in Malaysia, while Signetics has been operating in Taiwan, the Republic of Korea, and Thailand. RCA has assembly units in Malaysia and Brazil, where a joint venture was entered into with Ford (Brazil) for producing solid-state devices; AMI has offshore units in the Republic of Korea and the Philippines and a joint venture with the Gold Star Group in the Republic of Korea.

Although virtually all U.S. manufacturers of electronic products and components have a rather large number of operations in Southeast Asia, Japanese and Western European companies have made relatively less use of offshore operations, even though most of these manufacturers also maintain such operations and rely on these units for the supply of certain parts and components for their final product. Thus, the Southeast Asian region also attracted several Japanese semiconductor manufacturers during the 1970s, with Oki Electric setting up plants in Taiwan and the Philippines, Hitachi in Hong Kong, Matsushita in Singapore, and New Japan Radio in Hong Kong and Malaysia. Investments in semiconductors were made mostly in South Korea, and consumer electronics were largely concentrated in Taiwan. Along with these export-oriented offshore units, several Japanese manufacturers established assembly units in Latin America (for instance, Toshiba's project in Mexico and NCR and Sanyo in Brazil) that were mainly designed to meet internal demand in these countries.

Most Western European manufacturers also have offshore operations in Southeast Asia, but their network is far more limited than that of U.S. producers. Siemens, for example, operates in Singapore and Malaysia, AEG-Telefunken has a joint venture in the Philippines, and Philips (Netherlands) is producing power transistors, diodes, and hybrids, as well as consumer electronics, in Taiwan, Hong Kong, Singapore, and the Philippines. Philips also has subsidiaries in Argentina, Brazil, and Mexico that are producing consumer electronics and semiconductors. SGS-Ates (Italy) also has an assembly and test facility in Singapore that is highly automated and is intended to develop into an integrated production centre. Plessey (UK) has production facilities in Malta, Portugal, and Malaysia, with a significant level of semiconductor assembly operations.

By late 1982, it was estimated that MNCs had about 120 offshore assembly and component manufacture operations in the semiconductor field in about twenty developing countries.[15] The predominant share of these operations were owned by MNCs from the United States, which owned about 70 percent of the subsidiaries, and the balance was distributed among Japanese and Western European companies.[16] A survey of the expansion of thirty-seven major MNCs during the 1970s shows that most of these operations were concentrated, however, in the relatively few countries that MNCs in this field have preferred. Thus, while in the early 1970s most of these offshore operations were located in the Republic of Korea and Singapore, by the mid-1970s, Taiwan and Malaysia, and subsequently the Philippines, attracted most of the foreign investments.[17] This shift in the attractiveness of certain countries has largely been related to the rising wage level in the countries once several MNCs have established operations, which made it more attractive to move to other developing countries with similar labor force skills and availability but much lower wages. Government policies offering various incentives have also contributed to the attractiveness of particular host countries. Despite the existence of a very large number of offshore assembly and component manufacturing units, offshore sourcing of MNCs has been concentrated in only a few developing countries. As of 1980, for example, the three largest semiconductor component manufacturers—that is, Malaysia, Singapore, and the Philippines—exported $2.7 billion or 70 percent of all developing country exports.[18] Over two-thirds of these exports were directed to the United States.[19]

The location of offshore semiconductor component manufacture in the Southeast Asian region and, to a much lesser extent, in the Caribbean, has primarily been motivated by the desire of MNCs to supply components and subassemblies to industrialized countries and to take advantage of the low wage rate and availability of semiskilled labor that could be trained rapidly in routine tasks. Consequently, the volume of imports into OECD countries of integrated circuits, transistors, thermionic valves and tubes, and other components from developing countries rose from $157 million in 1970 to $3.738 billion in 1980.[20] In some developing countries, however, such as Argentina, Brazil, and Mexico, and in certain Asian countries, such as Singapore and the Republic of Korea, components have also been manufactured to meet the growing demand of the domestic consumer electronics industry.

The technological impact of offshore component manufacture, in terms of the growth of technological capability, has generally been limited to operational skills in dealing with one or another stage of repetitive production activity. With little or no backward integration in most MNC offshore units, there has been hardly any technological absorption and development of capability in design engineering or production operations, other than the narrow area of specific component manufacture and assembly. Although operational training and skills in factory operations were developed in these plants, they were of a very limited nature and have not resulted in the growth of mobile technical work groups that can shift or adapt to other avenues of employment. Furthermore, since manufacture of semiconductors can be disaggregated into several discrete stages, and offshore operations generally perform only a few of these stages, even the transfer of the operational know-how is partial, encompassing only a particular stage of production or assembly. Also, as MNCs increasingly turn to automation of their assembly process in which the technology is largely embodied in the machinery, the skill level of the labor will tend to be even more limited, even though there may be an increase in requirements for qualified technicians in machinery maintenance.

It is only in some developing countries that offshore component manufacture has provided the base for varying levels of backward integration and increased transfer of manufacturing technology beyond the limited manufacture of certain components. Singapore has increasingly emerged as a testing center for advanced circuits produced in the region; by 1981, testing of high-reliability military circuits and 16K RAM accounted for half of the total value produced in the country. Also, several offshore operations in Singapore have produced higher value items, often with considerable assistance and support from the government. Various technology-intensive projects have been undertaken; these included wafer manufacture and production of computer systems and peripherals. The case of the Republic of Korea is interesting, not only for the rapid development of its consumer electronics industry but also for the manufacture of wafers by domestically owned companies. The domestically owned company Samsung Electron Devices is the largest wafer producer in developing countries, with a daily production of 1,000 CMOS wafers per day in 1980.[21] Technology for wafer production was acquired from its joint venture partner, Integrated Circuits International from the United States, but Samsung subsequently acquired the equity of the licensor. Similarly, wafers are produced by Gold Star in joint venture with AMU from the United States. The large nationally owned group, Hyundai, has started to establish production capabilities for 64K RAM memory chips through licensing agreement without equity participation. The efforts of these companies have been strongly supported by the government through the establishment of the Korean Institute of Electronics Technology (KIET). KIET has agreements with several MNCs from the United States, Western Europe, and Japan for training in hardware and software designs and in production and design testing. The models developed by KIET are provided to local manufacturers at a fee.

The case of South Korea is interesting because it indicates that several MNCs have been willing to transfer rather advanced technologies to joint ventures and even to entirely locally owned companies, such as Hyundai. A large number of technical assistance agreements have also been entered into with the government-supported KIET, including those for design of circuits and software. It is important to note, however, that the technologies thus acquired by Korean manufacturers and KIET have mostly related to the comparatively lower end of technological sophistication in semiconductor manufacture and cover relatively mature products. Also, the major local manufacturers of semiconductors are captive producers, and wafers manufactured by them are not planned to be exported in the near future.

Apart from these countries, manufacture of semiconductors among developing countries in Southeast Asia has advanced relatively rapidly in Hong Kong and Taiwan. In Hong Kong, for example, some of the assembly subcontractors of MNCs, which are locally owned, plan to produce wafers. In Taiwan, also, local firms have played a major part in the development of the electronics industry, including component manufacture. Since the local industry produces fairly sophisticated components in large quantities and at internationally competitive costs, local manufacturers of consumer electronics products have had considerable advantages. Several firms have also undertaken wafer fabrication. Research support has been provided through the Electronics Research Service Organisation of Taiwan. Industrial park facilities have also been provided, and several products, such as minicomputers, laser components, silicon ingots and wafers, and other high-technology items, are being produced through MNC affiliates and through joint ventures.

In most other offshore assembly operations in Southeast Asia—for example, in Malaysia, in the Philippines, and to a lesser extent in Thailand and Indonesia—production is largely limited to components for re-export, with little local integration. In Mexico, several foreign subsidiaries manufacture electronic components, most of them located along the U.S.-Mexican border, especially in the Tijuana area. The consumer electronics industry in Mexico has also increased considerably in recent years, and several computer manufacturers, including IBM and Hewlett Packard, assemble computers. Although offshore assembly operations in developing countries have generally followed a fairly uniform pattern, with varying degrees of backward integration in the form of testing facilities, wafer fabrication, and the like, being undertaken only in a few Southeast Asian countries, two countries—Brazil and India—have sought to implement more comprehensive policies on local technological development in computers and microelectronics.

The growth of the data processing industry in Brazil has been very rapid in recent years. Burroughs has a large share of the market for small computers, and IBM, with several subsidiaries (led by IBM do Brazil), dominates the market for large computers, with an overall share of 53.8 percent of the national computer market. Moreover, government policy in Brazil has had a major effect in stimulating local industry and in developing national technological capability in the data processing and telecommunication sectors.[23] A coordination committee (CAPRE) has been set up, and all imports of computers require its approval. A national informatics policy was announced in July 1976 that classified the branches of computers and electronics products reserved for nationally owned companies. Largely as a result of these regulatory controls, the share of nationally owned companies in the production of computers and components rose to 35 percent in 1981.[24] Out of the thirty computer models produced in Brazil, twenty-five are manufactured by nationally owned companies that maintain licensing agreements with foreign producers. The Cobra 530 model has been designed locally and is produced by a locally owned company. The share of production of locally owned companies in modems, terminals, and peripherals has also grown rapidly. The software market is also largely controlled by local producers. Some of the public sector organizations involved in data procurement services have also expanded their operations during the past decade. The high degree of protection provided to local producers has enabled a large number of Brazilian-owned companies to enter and expand rapidly in the domestic market for computers and related products. Further policy measures announced in 1984 indicate that although existing manufacturers of mainframe computers, including IBM, may continue to operate, new foreign investments in this field will need to be channeled toward exports, since the national market for mini- and microcomputers would be reserved for Brazilian companies for at least eight years. An Informatics and Automation Council is being set up to prescribe further policies in this regard, and a special fund has been created composed of 0.8 percent of tax revenue, to support national technological development in this field. Although the growth of national owned Brazilian companies has been very fast in recent years, costs of locally produced computers tend to be considerably higher than those of imported units. Nevertheless, through its regulatory policy, Brazil has undoubtedly achieved rapid expansion of nationally owned industry in computers and related products. This was largely possible because of the relatively large internal market in the country, which enabled effective integration of the country's semiconductor industry with its overall electronics sector, including consumer electronics, telecommunications, and other electronics applications.

Another developing country where electronics development, including computer applications and microelectronics, has been largely undertaken through nationally owned companies is India. During the 1970s, when the Indian electronics industry was in its early stages, IBM terminated its operations in India because of differences with the Indian government regarding its 100 percent ownership of its Indian operations and the limited production programs planned for India. Since then, joint ventures have been set up in India with International Computers Limited (ICL) and some other MNCs, but by and large, the electronics industry has developed mostly through Indian-owned companies, including state enterprises. A small but growing computer and data processing industry has developed, with production of 1,000 to 1,500 machines per year, ranging from small data entry machines to medium-size mainframe computers. The production of computers and calculators in 1982, however, was only around $29 million.[25] Several local companies are also manufacturing peripherals, data entry terminals, keyboards, and the like, as well as systems and interfaces based on microprocessors. Major emphasis has been given to the production of electronic switching systems and of LSI/VLSI circuits. A technology agreement has also been entered into with Rockwell for the manufacture of 6502 microprocessors and peripheral chips. Production of middle-sized to large mainframe computers has also been undertaken apart from working mask plats. A National Information Centre has also been set up, with two major computer networks. Software skills have grown considerably and software exports reached $11 million by 1980.

Although technological capabilities of national owned companies in the field of computers and microelectronics have developed to a significant extent in Brazil and to a lesser extent in India, it is difficult to assess the long-term technological impact of government measures that have facilitated this trend. Since the pace of technological innovations in these fields is extremely rapid, and since such innovations have taken place only in industrialized countries so far, it may be necessary to arrange technological linkages with foreign companies that are developing new technologies in these fields. The example of Japan, where much of the initial technology was acquired by Japanese companies through licensing arrangements with U.S. corporations, may be useful to emulate. The establishment of nationally owned corporations in data processing, telecommunications, and microelectronics may, in itself, be of great value, since this provides the national corporate counterpart institutions with technological linkages through licensing and joint ventures. Such linkages may be of crucial importance in the present stage of technological development in these countries, since otherwise there may be a danger that the insulated national markets, large as they are, may not be able to avail themselves of latest technical developments in these fields. Although microelectronics have played a key role in technological development in computers and communications, future developments are likely to concentrate more on software engineering and very large scale integrated circuits, together with computer-aided design and manufacture. Countries such as Brazil and India, with large pools of skilled human resources, can develop competitive capabilities in sophisticated software engineering, but other fields of technological innovations, including fifth-generation computers and developments in artificial intelligence and robotics, may require close technical links with corporate technological leaders from industrialized economies.

Future trends and developments in computers and microelectronics in developing countries present a mixed picture. In some Southeast Asian countries, rapid technical developments are undoubtedly taking place through greater technological absorption and increased backward integration by

MNC subsidiaries and affiliates. The production of a wide range of components for the semiconductor industry has enabled countries such as the Republic of Korea, Singapore, and Taiwan to develop considerable technological and entrepreneurial capability among local enterprises. The alternative of regulatory controls and a high degree of protection for local manufacturers, as in Brazil and India, is an approach open to developing countries with large, internal markets but it may need to be tempered with adequate inflow of innovative foreign technologies through licensing and joint venture arrangements.

Notes

1. For a recent review of potential applications of microelectronics in developing countries, see F.S. Erber, *ATAS Bulletin II: Microelectronics-based Automation Technologies and Development* (New York: United Nations Centre for Science and Technology for Development, May 1985).

2. Data refer to 1977. For the world market share of U.S., Japanese, and Western European computer manufacturers, see *EDP Industry Report* (International Data Corporation, 1978).

3. Ibid.

4. Estimates are in *Nihon Kigro no Sekai Senryaky* (Multinational strategies of Japanese enterprises) (Tokyo: Nomura Research Institute, 1981).

5. For the various government support programs from 1950 through 1979, see A.T. Pugel, R. Kimura, and R. Hawkins, "Semiconductors and Computers: Emerging Competitive Battlegrounds in the Asia-Pacific Region," *Research in International Business and Finance* 4, pt. B: 231–86.

6. K. Cahill, "Workhorse's Obituary Was a Big Mistake," *Sunday Times* (London), 29 July 1984.

7. *Electronics,* 13 January 1982.

8. *Transnational Corporations in the International Semiconductor Industry* (New York: United Nations Centre on Transnational Corporations, 1983), 16.

9. In the United States in the late 1970s, for instance, the percentage breakdown of end-user markets for integrated circuits was 10 percent military, 37.5 percent computer, 37.5 percent industry, and 15 percent consumer markets. See Pugel, Kimura, and Hawkins, "Semiconductors and Computers," 237, table 3. For projections for the mid-1980s, see *Rosen Electronics Letter,* 26 September 1980.

10. For a detailed analysis of the major semiconductor manufacturers, see United Nations Centre on Transnational Corporations, *Transnational Corporations,* ch. 5.

11. During the 1966–75 period, for example, it is estimated that Japanese companies paid royalties of $260 million to U.S. companies. See Sterling Hobe Corporation, "International Transfer of Semiconductor Technology," Paper prepared for the U.S. Department of Labor, Bureau of International Labor Affairs, October 1978.

12. For information on the worldwide distribution of computerized systems, see M. Delapierre and J.B. Zimmerman, "Le Tiers Monde et l'Informatique," *Amerique Latine* (January-March 1983).

13. *Report of the APO Symposium on Computer Application Technology* (Tokyo: Asian Productivity Organisation, February 1981).

14. There are several assembly operations for mainframe computers in Brazil and Mexico (through wholly owned subsidiaries) and in India (through joint ventures).

15. United Nations Centre on Transnational Corporations, *Transnational Corporations*, 307.

16. Of the offshore units, 17.5 percent were owned by Japanese MNCs and 12.5 percent by Western European MNCs. Ibid., 307.

17. J.L. Truel, "Les Nouvelles Strategies de Localisation Internationale: Le Case des Semi-Conducteurs," *Revue d'Economie Industrielle,* no. 14(4e trimestre 1980): 12.

18. Trend data for 1970–80 are presented in United Nations Centre on Transnational Corporations, *Transnational Corporations,* 298, table VII.I.

19. Ibid., 298.

20. *Statistics of Foreign Trade: Trade by Commodities* (Paris: OECD, various issues).

21. *Electronics Industry in Korea, 1982* (Seoul: Electronics Industries Association of Korea, 1983).

22. S. Wajmberg, "A Industria Electronica Brasileira — Situaco em 1982," *Suplemento Tecnico Telebrasil,* no. 1 (1982).

23. For a review of Brazilian government policies in the computer and semiconductor industries, see Erber, *ATAS Bulletin II,* 182–97.

24. S. Wajnberg, Section on Brazil in *The Electronics Industry* (Vienna: United Nations Industrial Development Organization, September 1981).

25. *1983–4 Annual Report* (New Delhi: Government of India, Department of Electronics, 1985).

26. Ibid.

Part III
National Policies in
Developing Countries

8
Policies on Foreign Investment and Technology

I n recent decades, the role and function of governments in promoting technological development have assumed great significance in most countries. The growing technological complexity and sophistication in most production sectors, together with the large financial outlays required for research and development, have necessitated various policy measures and governmental support, both direct and indirect, for national programs designed to achieve greater technological development and capability. Since technology is used by industrial enterprises, relationships among enterprises in different countries are of particular importance. At the same time, the role of national governments is assuming much greater importance for the activities of MNC subsidiaries and affiliates and also for technology licensing, which is emerging as a major channel of transfer of industrial technology. In the industrialized, free-market economies, governmental support for technological development has ranged from direct governmental financing of certain research programs to large subsidies and major incentives for technical research and application. However, technological decisions at the enterprise level (including research and development) and the terms and conditions under which various technologies are acquired and applied are determined entirely by the firms concerned. In a number of developing countries, the patterns have differed considerably. On the one hand, there has been considerable emphasis on the development of institutional research capability, which is mostly government financed. On the other hand, varying degrees of regulatory control are exercised in a number of developing countries regarding the arrangements, terms, and conditions for the acquisition of foreign technology by local enterprises. Such regulatory control has a direct impact not only on the nature of technology transactions, and on the terms and conditions in particular cases, but also on the overall industrial and economic environment in which technological decisions are made.

Decisions on the choice of technology are made by private companies in developing market economies, but as is the case in industrialized countries, government policies can influence the decision-making process very significantly because such policies and procedures can create an environment that either promotes or hinders certain types of decisions. Regulatory measures often prohibit certain conditions and provisions in technology agreements between foreign technology suppliers and local enterprises. Such measures can, for example, prohibit the import of parts and intermediate products except in accordance with an approved pattern, or the employment of foreign personnel, or the inclusion of certain restrictive provisions in agreements for foreign direct investment or technology. In some cases, the use of domestic technology is specifically promoted, either through special incentives or through restrictions on foreign technology in the same field. The overall policy toward foreign direct investment itself has a direct impact on technological development to the extent that such investments are accompanied by the inflow of modern technology and managerial expertise.

Besides the policy measures that directly relate to technological decisions, industrial and economic policies with broader scope can also significantly affect the development of technological capability at the national level or in particular enterprises. Technological development generally tends to be directed by the flow of investment in different production sectors, since the implementation of new or expanded production activities initiates the need for new technologies. Consequently, the sectoral direction of technological development is largely subject to the structure and composition of the industrial development within a country. This is particularly true in the manufacturing sector, although it is also applicable in other production branches. In most developing countries, the extent to which foreign technology and know-how have been utilized in particular sectors has often depended on the extent of foreign investment and MNC activities through their subsidiaries and affiliates. In several of these countries, however, domestic industrial groups and state-owned enterprises are also increasingly acquiring foreign technology through licensing or through contracts for technical services. Another important factor in technological development, particularly in the manufacturing sector, concerns the local content or domestic integration, particularly in assembly-oriented industries. In several industries, such as the manufacture of durable consumer goods and of machinery and equipment, unless there is a gradual increase in the local content of production, the technological skills that are locally developed may remain at a fairly low level. A related aspect of technological choice is the extent to which technology is used for import substitution in the domestic market, as opposed to production technologies that are primarily oriented toward exports. In all these aspects, governmental policies and measures can have considerable impact.

Trends in Foreign Investment Policies

The impact of various industrial strategies on technological development was discussed in part I of this book. It was shown that regardless of whether national industrial strategy has been geared toward import substitution or toward the development of exports, policies on foreign direct investments have had a major impact on technological development and the pattern of technology inflow and transfer in most developing countries. The close linkage between foreign investment and foreign technology has already been stressed. The impact of national policies in host developing countries, however, has brought about substantial changes in the nature of foreign investments and the structure of ownership of MNC subsidiaries and affiliates, and this, in turn, has had a considerable effect on the pattern of foreign technology transfer to these countries. National economic and industrial policies can affect the activities of MNC subsidiaries in a variety of ways and at various stages of operations. The impact on the application and use of foreign technology has primarily been at the stage of initial entry of such investments or at the time when the structure of ownership of a foreign subsidiary or affiliate is significantly altered. At initial entry, the sectoral allocations of foreign investment has determined the nature of the technology that will accompany such investments, while the degree of foreign ownership and control has been an important determinant of the extent and pattern of transfer. Major changes in the structure of ownership, particularly when foreign MNC holdings are either fully nationalized or are reduced to a minority, have resulted in changes in the technological relationship between the foreign and local companies and a shift to an arrangement that would be governed more by contractual terms and conditions than by technical requirements. In both these aspects, national policies toward foreign investments and MNCs have constituted important determining factors.

Until the late 1960s and early 1970s, developing countries with market economies imposed relatively few restrictions on the entry or operations of foreign subsidiaries, except in India and some other countries. In most developing countries, foreign investments were encouraged and promoted, directly or indirectly, through various measures. Where the emphasis was on import substitution, foreign subsidiaries were given a high degree of protection in internal markets and often enjoyed a monopolistic position because of the absence of local competition. In several instances, the entry of foreign companies was on condition that no other production facilities would be permitted by the host government in those specific fields of manufacture. Where local production was primarily for exports, a variety of special facilities and incentives was provided.

The entry and growth of foreign subsidiaries were also actively promoted through various fiscal and financial measures. Several tax concessions were provided, and tax holidays for several years were common in many developing countries in the 1960s and most of the 1970s. The entry of foreign subsidiaries was also encouraged through duty-free imports of various capital goods, including used machinery and equipment, the costs of which were capitalized. Few restrictions were placed on the operations of subsidiaries, and they enjoyed considerable freedom in determining the extent of vertical integration and local production in relation to imports of various intermediate products and inputs.

With experience and a greater awareness of the operations of MNCs, both as investors and as technology licensors, host government policies and guidelines of developing countries paid greater attention to areas of divergence between MNCs and national development objectives. As a result, several developing countries prescribed regulatory measures for foreign investments and technology during the 1970s.[1] The aim of these measures has been to regulate the operation of MNCs in such a manner that their activities are more consistent with identified national objectives. Initial efforts have been directed toward channeling the inflow of foreign investments and technology in sectors that have been considered to be of priority by the government. In most of these countries, certain fields of activities have also been closed to foreign investors.[2]

In a number of developing countries during the 1970s, policies toward foreign investments were modified considerably on these lines. Although entry of MNC subsidiaries continued to be encouraged, certain qualifications were prescribed, together with requirements for obtaining the host government's approval for foreign investment proposals in a number of countries. Broad norms and guidelines also prescribed the fields in which foreign investments were considered necessary, and those invariably included areas of complex industrial technology and know-how. Foreign investment policy announcements also defined the sectors in which such investments were either not permitted, such as utilities or transportation, or were restricted in some manner, such as mining and certain subsectors of manufacture. In some developing countries, certain fields of activity were closed to foreign subsidiaries when it was considered that domestic companies already had sufficient production capacity and that additional investments were not required in these fields. In some countries, specific industrial activities have been reserved for domestic companies. In certain countries, industrial branches in which investment participation by MNCs was particularly welcome were identified and various incentives were provided for such investments. These generally included industrial operations that required high initial capital investment or that involved technology and know-how not available locally. During the past decade, MNC subsidiaries continued to be viewed primarily as a source of capital investment in the developing countries that continue to be in relatively early stages of industrialization, but the activities of MNCs were considered from a different perspective in countries in which significant industrial development had taken place and a diversified industrial structure had been created. In these countries, the approach to foreign investments has become increasingly selective, and such investments have been encouraged mostly in sectors where their technological contribution was considered essential or where financial capital investments by MNCs were considered necessary, as in major resource-based projects. The degree of selectivity and regulatory control exercised by countries has varied, however, not only across countries but also within the same country, over time.

Along with the exercise of greater selectivity in the entry and operations of foreign subsidiaries, there has also been growing emphasis on increased participation of domestic enterprises in various sectors of industry in which foreign subsidiaries have commanded a dominant market position. There has been much greater preference on the part of host governments for joint ventures between local and foreign companies, and this pattern has been encouraged through various government incentives. Increased local participation through the establishment of joint ventures has been considered important, because joint ventures limit the outflow of profits and lead to greater participation by local managerial and other personnel as well as increased use of local technical services and local materials and inputs. This results in greater integration of the enterprise into the local economy. With greater local participation in decision making, it has been expected that the operations of MNC affiliates would be less governed by the global interests of the parent MNCs and that local interests and objectives would be adequately taken into account. These interests and aims can cover various aspects of activities of the company, including the range of production, the size and nature of investments, the use of local inputs, and subcontracting. Joint ventures between foreign and domestic companies are also expected to contribute to the technological development of local companies and the formation of managerial and other skills.

In countries such as India, where the operations of foreign affiliates have been largely restricted to joint ventures, exceptions have been made in certain industrial sectors and subsectors. Wholly or majority foreign-owned companies have generally been permitted in high-technology areas, where because of the specialized nature of technology, its transfer would be feasible only through subsidiaries or foreign-majority affiliates. Exceptions have also been made for largely export-oriented production, when most of the production of the local foreign subsidiary has been sold within a firm or exported to global markets, and the contributions of such companies have been primarily evaluated as the generation of foreign exchange revenue and the creation of employment.

The impact on technological development of national policies on foreign investments is particularly marked with respect to, first, the form of foreign investment entry and the structure of ownership of the proposed company; second, the program of local manufacture and the conditions of supply of technological inputs; and, third, the proposed activities for adaptation and R&D at the enterprise level. Since the entry of MNCs through takeovers of existing local companies can have undesirable effects on local entrepreneurial development, such takeovers, which were fairly common in the 1970s, are not permitted in several developing countries except under special circumstances. Negotiations on the extent of foreign capital ownership and the period over which foreign majority holdings would be reduced to below 50 percent have also assumed greater importance, since it is considered that if the MNC continues to be in effective control through majority holdings, the supply of technology and know-how will be limited to the local company's immediate requirements, as it is with MNC subsidiaries in general. Much greater emphasis has also been given by regulatory bodies to increased local content in the manufacturing activities of MNCs, because such manufacture, confined to assembly operations or to certain stages of production only, may not be suitable or appropriate from the viewpoint of domestic technological development. Increased emphasis has also been given by regulatory agencies to the implementation of R&D activities and adjustments to local factor conditions. These and other related issues are increasingly the subject of negotiations between host governments and prospective foreign investors at the stage of review of foreign investment proposals, since the basic purpose of such review has been to ensure that essential developmental objectives are adequately served.

The technological impact of divestment of foreign holdings is somewhat different. In these cases, the foreign subsidiary becomes converted to a joint venture or wholly domestically owned enterprise and the MNC ceases to have effective control. The continuing responsibilities for supply of technology and know-how are then generally determined in considerable detail through contractual arrangements, which are also subject to approval by regulatory bodies in several developing countries.

To some extent, the close relationship between foreign investments by MNCs and foreign technology inflow in developing countries is also reflected in the fact that policies on such investments in several of these countries are generally oriented toward greater national control and a higher degree of domestic technological self-reliance. Although these policies are intended to regulate investments and related activities of foreign companies, which continue to be the principal sources of industrial technology, the regulatory measures of host developing countries have sought primarily to channel the investments and the technological expertise of MNCs so that the growth of domestic companies is not adversely affected and they can acquire and develop the necessary industrial and technological capability to the maximum extent. At the same time, national policies in these countries have also sought to identify and encourage MNC investments in sectors in which their contribution would be most significant from the viewpoint of the industrial and technological development of the host economy.

Trends in Foreign Technology Policies

Although the importance of technology planning and the planned development of technological capability is fully recognized in most developing countries, the explicit government policies thus far adopted have only concentrated on certain aspects of planning. Emphasis has been given to technical
manpower planning in several countries, and a large number of technical
education institutions have been established. Training programs, including
foreign training, have also been undertaken in most countries. In several
countries, state-financed research institutions have been established for both
basic and adaptive research. These institutions, such as the Korean Institute
on Science and Technology, the chain of national research institutes and
laboratories in India, and the large number of research institutions established in Latin America and in some African countries, not only have undertaken basic research but also have concentrated on the upgrading of existing
technologies in the country, in agriculture and in various branches of industry. The linkage between such research institutions and the technological
requirements for industry has tended to be weak, however, and there has
been continued dependence on foreign technology in most of these countries.[3]
At the same time, there has been growing concern about the nature, implications, and suitability of foreign technology and the terms and conditions
under which such technology is acquired and transferred. It is this selectivity
and a closer scrutiny and evaluation of the terms and conditions of technology-supply arrangements that have resulted in varying degrees of institutional
regulation of foreign technology in a number of developing countries. With
the wide differences in the level of development and in overall industrial policies, the approach to this question has differed from country to country, and
there are still many countries where there is no regulatory control over foreign technology. Yet there is a growing trend for greater selectivity in technological choice and for some degree of regulatory control over the terms and
conditions under which foreign technology is acquired in developing countries.

The pattern of technological development in most developing countries
indicates that in the absence of regulatory measures, the nature of such development takes on certain specific characteristics. Because of weak domestic
technological infrastructure and capability, most of the technological needs
of local industry tend to be met by acquisition from abroad and are mostly
transmitted in conjunction with foreign direct investments. The direction of
technological development has also tended to be closely related to that of foreign direct investment and the extent to which local integration of production
is undertaken by foreign subsidiaries and affiliates. In countries where foreign

investments have been channeled by the government to sectors of national priority, the accompanying technology inflow has tended to be more consistent with national requirements. In other countries, where few or no restrictions have been placed on the activities of foreign companies and on acquisition of foreign technology, the nature of technology transfer has been largely determined by foreign investors and foreign technology suppliers.

The need for regulation of foreign technology in certain developing countries has stemmed from several factors and has been a gradual process in most of these countries. Most of these factors have been related to the industrial growth pattern and the impact of foreign technology at the early and intermediate levels of industrialization in these countries. The unrestricted inflow of foreign technology has tended to perpetuate the technological dependence of these countries on MNCs and foreign technology suppliers and to stultify the growth of local innovative skills and capability. Just as MNC affiliates that have technology licensing arrangements with parent companies are inherently dependent on these parent companies, developing country licensees tend to depend to an undue extent on their foreign licensors for assistance, even on simple technical issues. Increased efforts toward technological absorption and adaptation have been made only when the period of agreement is drawing to a close. The use of foreign technology, foreign brand names, and more sophisticated marketing techniques, which often accompany such technology, adds significantly to the attractiveness of new industrial projects and enterprises, and there is little incentive for local companies to use similar technology developed locally.[4]

Another factor is the use of foreign technology in developing countries, which is often limited to certain stages of processing or manufacture, with the other stages being completed in industrialized countries. In mineral-based industries, only the early stages of ore processing are undertaken in developing countries; until recently, this was also true in petroleum-based industries. In the engineering-goods sector, which generally comprises assembly-type production, foreign technology has often been confined to the final stages of finishing and assembly, with subassemblies, parts, and components being supplied by the licensor for indefinite periods.

In other cases, the terms and conditions imposed in technology agreements were often unduly in favor of the foreign partner or licensor and militated against the legitimate interests of licensees from these countries. Contractual provisions were often imposed that would not be legally enforceable in the home countries of the licensors. Inadequate knowledge of licensing practices and of alternative sources of technology placed licensee enterprises at a considerable disadvantage.

Perhaps most important, certain types of foreign technology could be unsuitable and inappropriate when applied to factor conditions in developing countries. Such unsuitability could be related to the capital intensity of cer-

tain technologies or to the scale of operations or the requirements for specialized skills and other factors, all of which could apply differently in different
developing countries.

Most of these issues are particularly relevant at the earlier stages of industrialization. Thus, while the "trickle-down" effect of MNC operations on
local technological capability may be extremely slow, it will inevitably have
impact over the long term. The process can, however, be greatly hastened by
governmental policies for more selective use of foreign technology and for
limiting it to only the periods required for effective absorption. The insistence
on the maximum use of local inputs and on a greater degree of local integration in manufacture over a period of time has also had a major impact on the
development of technological skills and capability in ancillary and feeder
industries in many of these countries.

Until the early 1970s, in most developing countries except India, foreign
technology was imported by local industrial enterprises, including MNC subsidiaries and affiliates, without any restrictions. In many instances, there
were no formal technology agreements between parent MNCs and their affiliates, although certain royalty and lump-sum payments were made toward
centralized R&D and the supply of technological assistance. The remittance
of payments of royalties and technology fees, however, was generally subject
to foreign exchange regulations, either by the central bank or the finance
ministry. In some countries, it was also necessary to file a copy of the agreement containing the payment conditions with the tax authorities, which
established maximum levels of royalties for permissible deductions. Such
institutions, however, seldom analyzed the substantive elements of the technology agreements and focused mainly on the payment conditions and the
foreign exchange remittance involved. In some countries, maximum permissible royalty rates were prescribed, either for all sectors or at varying rates for
different sectors. In others, royalties were approved on a case-by-case basis.
Since these measures aimed at controlling the outflow of foreign exchange
and reducing the evasion of local taxes, any examination of the agreement for
supply of technology and services that took place related primarily to the
financial and fiscal aspects, and other contractual and technical provisions of
the agreement were seldom examined or reviewed. The institutions concerned—the central bank or the tax authorities—did not even have the necessary technical personnel to analyze the legal and technological provisions in
these agreements, particularly in respect to the technological aspects. Even in
the 1980s, a large number of developing countries have not adopted explicit
measures for the regulation of foreign technology; in most of these countries,
the only control is related to payment conditions and is exercised by the foreign exchange control system.

During the 1970s, the issues and implications of foreign technology
received considerable attention in several developing countries—particularly

in Latin America during the first half of the 1970s and in several countries of Asia and some in Africa during the latter part. There was growing awareness that local technological development constituted an essential prerequisite for industrialization and that the technological gap with industrialized countries was increasing, instead of being narrowed down. There was also considerable disenchantment with the activities of MNCs, which was reflected in the large number of nationalizations and the varying measures of control over foreign investments. Because of the close links between foreign investments and technology in many of these countries, greater attention began to be paid to the nature and conditions of foreign technology transfer to MNC subsidiaries and affiliates. It was also increasingly apparent that the impact of technology transfer extended considerably beyond the foreign exchange costs of such arrangements. These issues related to the nature of the technology transferred, the extent to which such transfer was effectively absorbed by domestic industry, and the impact on the operations of licensees and recipients of technology in these countries. These issues assumed even greater significance with the growing trend toward joint ventures and licensing agreements without foreign equity holdings. The experience in several developing countries indicated that a large number of such agreements contained restrictive conditions that not only limited the development of technological capability but also placed undue restrictions on production and sales. They also prescribed several tie-in conditions that significantly increased the costs of technology acquisition and affected the production of licensee enterprises.[5]

The objectives of foreign technology regulation in developing countries should be considered within the framework of national technological objectives and the pursuit of self-reliance.[6] Foreign technology is viewed as an essential requirement in all countries today. What developing countries generally have sought to achieve through regulation is the flow of technology to the sectors of particular priority in each country, either in conjunction with foreign investment or through licensing. Regulatory institutions also try to assess whether technological choice has been suitably exercised in relation to local conditions and circumstances and whether selection of a particular technology has been made only after consideration of alternatives. An important aim in certain countries is to ensure that foreign technology complements and does not supplant indigenous technology and that the imported technology is absorbed and adapted as soon as possible. A further essential objective is to ensure that the terms and conditions under which foreign technology is being acquired are fair and equitable and are not unduly weighted in favor of the licensor. The overall objective of regulation is to increase the technological capability of domestic enterprises and to enable them to achieve self-reliance as rapidly as possible. The regulation and screening of such agreements are also intended to improve the bargaining position of local enterprises in acquiring suitable technology on reasonable terms and conditions.[7]

In most developing countries, technology agreements are increasingly emerging as the principal contractual arrangement between foreign companies and domestic enterprises, regardless of whether the local enterprises are foreign subsidiaries, affiliates, or wholly domestically owned companies. Consequently, this is of considerable importance to governments in directing industrial and technological development in accordance with the various policy criteria prescribed. The specificity of such criteria has varied widely among countries, ranging from broad functions and categories to sectoral and subsectoral identification of fields where foreign technology is considered particularly necessary. In most of these countries, the regulatory guidelines prescribe the elements and conditions that must form part of the agreements and the conditions that are prohibited. Besides improving the bargaining position of domestically owned companies in acquiring foreign technology, such regulation has enabled varying degrees of institutional control over the operations of MNC subsidiaries and affiliates in these countries, and it has emerged as a critical instrument of technology policy.

It is important to emphasize that the forerunner in the regulation of foreign investment and technology was Japan. Since the late 1950s, applications for the import of foreign technology to Japan for sums exceeding a certain figure had to be approved by the Ministry of Industry and Trade. The importation of technology was regulated through this procedure, but what this administration actually accomplished was to enable Japanese industry to import a very wide range of foreign technologies and processes.[8] At the same time, regulation also enabled Japanese authorities to monitor the technologies imported by various Japanese enterprises and the absorption and adaptation of such technologies over a period of time. The Japanese experience in technology regulation provides an excellent illustration of the manner in which regulatory policy can be effectively dovetailed with the accelerated flow of new foreign technologies and processes.

Some developing countries, especially India, undertook the regulation of technology in the mid-1950s. This was, however, an integral part of the process of evaluating proposals for foreign investment. A major factor in the evaluation of such proposals at that time was their impact on the country's scarce foreign exchange resources. In 1969, fairly detailed guidelines for foreign technology acquisition were prescribed by the Indian Government. These guidelines were based on the need to develop indigenous technology as far as possible, and they laid down the policy parameters for foreign technology contracts. Consequently, three lists were prescribed, one of industrial fields where foreign technology would not be permitted at all, one of fields in which foreign technology would be permitted without any related foreign equity holdings, and one of fields in which foreign technology would be permitted together with foreign equity holdings, usually minority holdings. These aspects and their implications are discussed in the next chapter, but it should be mentioned here that the 1969 guidelines issued by the Indian authorities were among the earliest policy announcements on foreign technology acquisition in developing countries. The 1969 guidelines were followed, in 1973, by the Foreign Exchange Regulation Act (FERA), which prescribed the requirements for divestment of foreign holdings and covered various other aspects of the operations of foreign companies.

During the early 1970s, policy announcements and legislative and administrative measures relating to foreign technology were introduced in several countries of Latin America, where there was considerable outcry against MNCs and against technological *dependencia* during this period. The countries involved included the Andean Group (Bolivia, Colombia, Chile— which later withdrew—Ecuador, Peru, and subsequently Venezuela), which formulated Decision 24 for regional regulation of foreign investments and Decisions 84 and 85 for foreign technology acquisition;[9] Argentina (Law N19231 in 1971, modified in 1974 and 1981); Brazil (Normative Act 015/INPI); and Mexico (Law on Technology in 1972, amended in 1982). Over the past decade, specific national policies in these countries have undergone some changes, but the policy approach basically has been to have the relevant government institutions review and scrutinized foreign technology agreements. Similar policies were introduced in several other developing countries, particularly in Southeast Asia—including the Republic of Korea, Malaysia, and the Philippines—and in Europe—Portugal and Yugoslavia. In some cases, such policies have been closely linked with those on foreign direct investment, while in other countries, these policies have been more closely related to indigenous technological development. In these guidelines, emphasis was primarily given to the improvement of the terms and conditions of technology agreements. The initial objective of regulatory institutions was mostly to ensure that the bargaining position of local enterprises improved and that foreign technology suppliers did not impose unduly onerous and restrictive provisions in technology contracts. As institutional capability and experience has increased in these countries, greater attention has been given to the nature of the technology proposed and its impact on local technological development.

Despite the differences in technological development in these countries, a common pattern is discernible in the regulatory measures and guidelines and the institutional mechanisms adopted for their implementation. This common pattern primarily includes the various contractual provisions in agreements for foreign technology acquisition and, in some countries, the relationship between foreign direct investments and payments for technology to MNCs. In most of these countries, policy guidelines on most contractual provisions tend to be similar, although there may be differences in the approach to particular contract provisions. Beyond guidelines for contractual terms and conditions, technology agreements between MNCs and developing country enterprises are increasingly emerging as the principal instrument for defining the conditions of operations of particular companies and the performance required in terms of local integration, technology, absorption, and adaptation and development of export capability. This is so not only in the case of MNC subsidiaries but also in the case of joint ventures in which MNCs have minority holdings—or even in cases where the foreign company is acting only as a licensor of technology, without any foreign equity participation. Since foreign technology agreements become effective only after approval by the regulatory institution designated for this purpose, that institution is in a position to prescribe the terms and conditions for the foreign partner or licensor that would significantly influence the operations of the local enterprise over a considerable period of time.

In countries where regulatory measures toward foreign technology have been introduced, they have taken different forms and have been implemented by different institutions. In a number of countries, such as Argentina, Mexico, and Nigeria, specific laws for technology acquisition have been enacted that require registration and approval of all technology agreements. In other countries, such as the Republic of Korea and Turkey, foreign technology has been covered by legislation on foreign investment. In Brazil, the regulatory enactment was promulgated by the institution that deals with industrial properties. In India, there is no specific legislation on foreign technology acquisition, and regulatory measures are administered through guidelines directed at local entrepreneurs and executed within the industrial licensing system.

The institutional mechanism for the implementation of regulatory measures has also taken different forms. In most countries, centralized technology registries or technology evaluation agencies were established to screen evaluate, and register technology contracts. The position of such institutions, however, varies in different government systems. In Argentina, for example, the respective regulatory agency for foreign technology is the National Institute for Industrial Technology (INTI), under the direction of the Ministry of Industry; in Brazil, it forms part of the National Institute for Industrial Property; and in Nigeria, technology agreements must be registered with the National Office of Industrial Property. In Mexico, the National Registry of Technology Transfer was created and, until 1977, functioned as an independent department of the Ministry of Industry and Trade. Recently, it was merged with the Ministry of National Patrimony and the Commission on Foreign Investments. In India, the Republic of Korea, and Turkey, the same government institution that deals with foreign investment is also charged with the screening, evaluation, and registration of foreign technology agreements and works in close coordination with various other government departments. In some countries, foreign technology and foreign investment proposals are processed separately, although they may finally be assessed together. In the Philippines, foreign technology agreements are reviewed by the Technology Transfer Board, while the Board of Investment deals directly with proposals for foreign investments. In Malaysia, technology agreements are processed by the Ministry of Trade and Industry and foreign direct investments are reviewed by the Malaysian Industrial Development Authority. In most countries, the remittance of payments for royalties and fees has also remained subject to the approval of the central bank. The extent of coordination between the central bank and the technology regulation agency also varies in different countries.[10]

There has also been considerable difference among countries in the role and authority given to the foreign technology regulatory agency. The variations in approach may be seen in the role and participation of the regulatory institution in the negotiations and decisions between the licensor and licensee and in the discretionary power vested in such institutions to make exceptions from the general provisions of the law or guidelines. In most countries, the various contractual provisions in technology agreements are negotiated by the parties to the agreement, and the role of the regulatory institution is confined to a review of whether the terms of the contract are in compliance with the provisions of the law or prescribed guidelines. In some countries, however, the regulatory agency may actively participate in the negotiation process with the technology licensor and the local licensee. This generally takes place when license agreement between parent MNCs and their local subsidiaries and affiliates are involved, but it can extend to other situations to ensure that the socioeconomic costs and benefits are not widely divergent. The participation of regulatory institutions in negotiations is primarily intended to improve the bargaining position of local licensee enterprises, although in some cases there may be differences in approach between the narrower interests of the licensee and broader national policy considerations represented by the regulatory body. Besides reviewing specific technology agreements, regulatory institutions in some developing countries have also performed advisory functions to local industry, especially in the area of technological alternatives. With the growing experience and negotiating ability of domestic companies, including state-owned enterprises, in most of these countries, regulatory institutions are increasingly performing review functions and are less often involved in negotiations.

The discretionary power exercised by technology regulation agencies depends partly on how the relevant law is construed. In some countries, such as Brazil, the legal provisions are fairly specific and detailed, and exceptions have not generally been provided for in most provisions. In India, there is also relatively limited flexibility in interpreting the administrative guidelines. In some countries, such as Mexico, particularly since the 1982 amendment of the technology legislation, the registry has considerable discretionary power to approve contracts that are considered to be in the national interest, even if they contain provisions relating to restrictive business practices that are generally prohibited. In most countries, provisions for exceptions have been made in the legislation and in the administrative guidelines for contractual terms relating to technology and know-how considered to be of special importance to the country.

Regardless of the legal or administrative form that such regulation may take, the regulatory measures generally provide for certain common elements. First, these regulations require the compulsory registration of all agreements for the acquisition of foreign technology and know-how through the licensing of patents and trademarks or the provision of technical services. In some countries, such as Argentina and Mexico, technology agreements in force at the time of the passage of legislation relating to foreign technology have had to be renegotiated to comply with the provisions of the legislation within a defined period of time. Second, the terms and conditions of such agreements must be approved by the government agency prescribed for this purpose before any payments can be made to the foreign partner or licensor. The agreements are not considered legally binding until such approval is granted. Third, detailed administrative procedures have been laid down for registering applications and for processing and approving technology agreements within specific periods, with such modifications as the regulatory institution considers necessary. Fourth, specific guidelines have been prescribed for several important provisions that are generally included in technology agreements. Since these provisions are usually applicable to agreements for technology and know-how and technological services in all sectors, it would be useful to examine the nature of these terms and conditions as they are applied in most developing countries in which foreign technology agreements are subjected to government review.

Major Issues in Technology Agreements

Before the 1960s, the detailed terms and conditions of technology agreements, except payment provisions, were mainly determined by technology suppliers or licensors and related primarily to the responsibilities of licensee enterprises. This was partly because the market for industrial technology was more a seller's market and partly because most technology agreements were between firms in industrialized economies and usually related to patent licensing—although a large number of agreements also dealt with unpatented proprietary know-how. Apart from payment terms, which were a matter of negotiations between the licensor and licensee, the terms of technology license agreements generally spelled out the duration, terms of payment, restrictions on licensees, and various responsibilities of licensees regarding reporting, confidentiality, quality control, and the like. The licensor permitted the use of patents and proprietary technology and provided the necessary technical know-how. Certain general conditions were prescribed for grant-backs, governing law, settlement of disputes, and the like, which tended to favor the licensor. Since technology agreements were, for the most part, between firms in industrialized countries that functioned in a similar technological environment and since they generally related to proprietary technology or trade secrets covered by industrial property rights, licensors were usually in an advantageous position. In the case of MNC subsidiaries and affiliates using the parent company's technology, formal technology agreements may not have been necessary and were often not entered into. Where such agreements were contracted with subsidiaries, they were intended to provide funds for centralized R&D or were formalized for tax purposes, often in both the home and host countries.

With the gradual industrialization of several developing countries in the 1960s and 1970s and an increasing trend toward joint ventures and technology licensing without foreign equity participation, technology agreements assumed a growing importance. Since the nature of technology transfer was much greater in scope and content for most projects using foreign technology, the coverage of technology agreements also tended to expand. With the implementation of economic planning programs and policies for greater import substitution, increased exports, and greater conservation of foreign exchange in many of these countries, there was much greater involvement by government authorities in industrial programs and projects. Policies toward foreign direct investment received much greater attention, and by the early 1970s, the focus shifted to the implications of foreign technology and the development of indigenous technological capability. This, in turn, led to a closer look at contracts relating to foreign technology and technological services, and the regulatory review of such agreements began being utilized as a policy instrument for the implementation of performance requirements by MNC subsidiaries and affiliates and for increased use of domestically produced inputs. These inputs included intermediate products and parts and components produced by local manufacturers and technological services, including various consulting-engineering services provided by local consultants and contractors. At the same time, greater attention was paid to specific contractual conditions in technology agreements; in several countries, mandatory requirements and guidelines were prescribed for this purpose. Some of the important contractual provisions for which fairly similar regulatory measures have been adopted in several developing countries will be discussed later.

An essential aspect of regulatory policies in several countries concerns the selection of the most appropriate technology. Although this goal may be stated, the task of selection is generally left to the prospective licensee enterprise. Regulatory institutions may, however, investigate to see whether various technological alternatives have been considered, because with certain exceptions, production technology and know-how for most products and techniques can usually be acquired from more than one source. In selecting the source, national guidelines may require that the recipient enterprise determine the relationship of the technology with locally available or potentially available inputs and determine the relationship of the technology with market demand. It may also be necessary to define the nature and type of technology required in terms of capital resources and to link the use of foreign technology, so far as possible, with available raw materials and local skills. This is particularly stressed in certain countries, including Brazil, India, and Mexico, so that the supply of foreign technology is not unduly associated with substantial and continuing imports of components or processed materials from the technology licensor or other foreign sources. The regulatory agency may well suggest that where alternative technology is available that would utilize domestic materials more fully, the use of such technology should be preferred, provided that comparable production efficiency can be achieved. The relationship with potential growth of local skills may also be an important aspect, from the viewpoint of both generating and maximizing local employment and for effective absorption and adaptation of imported know-how. In certain countries, the review of technology selection includes the extent of employment that can be generated without affecting efficiency significantly, especially in countries where employment generation is a major goal of industrial policy. To the extent that more labor-intensive technologies are available, and provided that cost efficiency is maintained, the regulatory agency may suggest its selection by the prospective licensee, since this may be advantageous in terms of costs and local employment. The most advanced technology in a particular manufacturing sector may not be the most appropriate, and regulatory agencies often try to assess the various alternative techniques that can be adopted in terms of their impact on the imports required for maintenance, the effects on employment, and the growth of local skills and talents, although the final choice of technology rests with the prospective licensee enterprise.

Regulatory measures may focus not only on the consideration of technological alternatives for the selection of the most appropriate technology but also on the selection of the most appropriate licensor or supplier of technology. This may be of little relevance to MNC subsidiaries and affiliates, which would normally use the technology and know-how available from the parent corporation. In the case of joint ventures and licensing without equity participation, the guidelines may require that prospective licensee enterprises evaluate alternative technologies and search for suitable licensors from those in possession of a particular technology. This would require adequate information on both technological alternatives and the activities of possible licensors. The selection of suitable licensors is ultimately left to the licensee enterprise, but guidelines may require that the choice of a partner or licensor be made after consideration of possible alternatives and justification of the proposed selection.

Most regulatory measures give considerable emphasis to a comprehensive formulation of the scope and coverage of technology agreements. It is considered important to provide a fairly detailed description of the nature and characteristics of the foreign technology supplied.[11] Regulatory guidelines in several countries provide that the license agreement must clearly define the product to be covered, the production processes involved — with specific reference to relevant production capacities — and the production of necessary related documentation — blueprints, manufacturing drawings, and other items. The various technological aspects of the production of the goods and of intermediate products, parts, and components that are to be locally manufactured over a period of time generally must be covered. Technological services also need to be specifically defined, so that the scope of technical assistance is clearly determined by the licensor and licensee from the start. Technological assistance can often include services that a licensor would not normally be expected to provide in a developed country but that would be essential for a licensee in a developing economy. The guidelines also often require that agreements between MNC parents and their subsidiaries and affiliates define the nature and details of the technology and technical services to be provided, so that these aspects can be reviewed by the technology regulatory agency.

Payment Conditions

The bill for technology imports, including technology fees and royalties besides maintenance imports from the use of particular foreign technology, tends to increase rapidly with increased industrialization. Since industrial technologies are frequently protected by patents and industrial property rights and in several high-technology areas are owned or controlled by a few companies, considerable payments for the acquisition of foreign technology may be required. The composite nature of the foreign technology package, comprising production know-how and technical services required by enterprises in developing countries, and inadequate experience in negotiating such agreements often places licensees from developing countries at considerable disadvantage, particularly in the terms of payment. The regulatory function is often designed to ensure that foreign technology payments by local companies are reasonable and equitable.

Since the inception of foreign technology regulation in developing countries, payments for such technologies have received considerable attention by regulatory agencies. Since such payments involve remittance of foreign exchange and affect the tax liability of licensee enterprises, more than one government institution might be dealing with payments. Although keeping records of technology payments is not a problem, the determination of the appropriate amount of payment is a highly complex issue and its evaluation presents considerable difficulty. In the absence of a well-organized technology market, there is no set price for any given technology, and the lack of clarity in the conditions of technology commercialization makes it difficult to assess the particular figure at which the owner of proprietary technology should transfer technology to various users. Although technology suppliers seek to optimize their returns from the commercialization of technology, the price of technology is considerably influenced by the degree of competition from similar technologies. In the case of developing countries, it may also depend on the extent to which technology owners may wish to enter particular markets, since this may be the only form of entry in certain countries. Also, since most developing countries acquire technology in composite form, often including various elements of know-how and technical assistance besides the use of trademarks, the cost of technology is more difficult to assess and compare with patent licensing to firms in industrialized countries. The nature of the technology package often varies from one case to another, which also makes comparison of costs very difficult.

Payments for technology are usually in the form of a lump-sum fee, a royalty on sales, or a combination of the two. Lump-sum payments are generally made for technologies that are transferred on a one-time basis. These can be either fairly simple production processes or highly complex technologies that are bought on the basis of a single-stage transfer. A more common form of payment is a royalty on sales by the licensee.[12] Payments for specific technical services depend on the extent and nature of the services to be provided, such as the length of a visit by technical personnel of the licensor and the extent of the training imparted.

Earlier attempts to regulate the amounts of technology payments sought to set ceilings on the permissible percentage of royalties on the sales of the licensee. This was the practice in India and later in Brazil, Mexico, and some other countries, although exceptions were made in a number of cases in these countries. Maximum rates generally varied for different sectors of industry.[13] This method of regulation can be implemented through control of foreign exchange remittances, and it is still being utilized in some countries. The maximum rates prescribed have generally been about a 5 percent royalty on net sales, with a lower percentage figure for relatively simple technologies in certain sectors. This approach is no longer applied in most countries that have adopted more comprehensive technology regulation policies. Instead, the permissible payments are differentiated according to the variations in the nature of the technology, market conditions, and the country's need for a specific technology. With the approach, which is more common at present, it is generally considered that maturity and standardized technologies can be acquired at rates substantially below the maximum set as part of the foreign exchange control mechanism. At the same time, it is recognized that, in the case of advanced and high-technology fields involving oligopolistic market conditions, technologies may only be available at higher royalty rates. This approach is more flexible and has allowed for variations in benefits accruing to the local licensee and to the national economy from the use of particular technologies. Although the parties in technology contracts initially negotiate the payment conditions, they are subject to approval by the regulatory body. The legislative or administrative norms for payments generally state that payments have to be reasonable and commensurate with the value of the technology to the economy. In the Mexican law, for example, it is stated that contracts will not be approved if payments do not stay in proportion to the technology acquired or if they constitute an unjustified or excessive burden on the national economy. Similar formulation can also be found in the legislation of the Andean Pact countries. In some countries, such as India, Malaysia, and the Philippines, the regulatory agency uses internal guidelines that set maximum permissible levels for various sectors.[14] Considerable flexibility is exercised, however, and the specific nature of industrial technology and its importance to the national economy are taken into account.[15] In some countries, such as India, regulatory agencies have permitted higher royalty rates in the case of technology that is utilized for export-oriented projects. The extent to which higher rates have been allowed has depended on the export commitment of the licensee.

The ultimate decision on the rate of royalty payment depends on the technology supplier and the licensee enterprise, but regulatory agencies, by establishing certain ranges of permissible payment, have played a critical role. In a number of cases, the regulatory body has also intervened directly in the establishment of specific payment conditions.[16]

The actual payment for technology is significantly affected by the base price used to calculate the royalties. During earlier stages of regulation, royalties were generally calculated on the total sales of the licensee. Presently, in most countries in which foreign technology acquisition is regulated, the base price is defined as the net sales price, which is calculated by deducting the price of imported components from the licensor. In India, the price of standard bought-out components is also deducted from the base price in calculating royalties.

In the regulatory measures of certain countries, determination of the permissible rate of royalty for technology includes the extent of foreign equity ownership. In Brazil and India, for example, technology payments are not permitted by MNC subsidiaries to their parent corporations. In some other countries, it is generally considered that royalty payments by MNC subsidiaries and affiliates to the parent company should be at a lower rate than those in technology agreements with unaffiliated companies. This variation in permissible payments is argued on the grounds that parent companies are compensated by the profitability of their affiliates and that the benefits derived from technology usage are part of such profit. In most countries, however, the regulatory body does not differentiate between permissible technology payments on the basis of affiliation between the partners.

In some countries, specific provisions have been prescribed concerning payments for the use of industrial property rights. In India, for example, if a technical collaboration agreement involves the supply of technical know-how that is based on patented information, payments in licensing agreements also include remuneration for patent rights, and no separate payments can be charged for such rights. In Brazil, if a technology agreement involves use of a patent, then apart from the right to patent usage, the technology payment covers this supply of all necessary know-how to the licensee that would enable effective use of the patent, including research activities related to the patent. Payments for the use of foreign trademark rights have also undergone increased scrutiny by some regulatory agencies. In some countries, such payments are prohibited between MNC subsidiaries and their parent companies, although in most others, it is usually limited to around 1 percent of net sales.

In view of the close relationship between foreign investments and technology, an important issue to be considered initially is the capitalization of technology and know-how costs. Until the introduction of regulatory measures, foreign affiliates often had been created through capitalization of payments for foreign technology and services. This was common in the past, but in recent years, there has been a trend in certain developing countries either to disallow such capitalization or to limit the conversion of technology and know-how costs to a certain percentage of the equity. This has partly been due to the difficulties in assessing overall technology costs, particularly where royalty payments are involved, and partly because it is considered that capitalization of such costs may involve much larger payments over a long period. With the limitations imposed on such capitalization by regulatory bodies, these countries require that the equity of foreign subsidiaries be either in the form of tangible assets, such as cash or capital equipment, or by way of reinvested earnings. Such provisions are contained in the regulations of most Latin American countries, including the members of the Andean Pact, Brazil, and Mexico. An exception is Argentina, which, since the amendment of its technology legislation in 1977, permits capitalization of technical know-how. In India, all equity shares of foreign companies have to be bought in the form of foreign exchange. In cases where the transfer of foreign technology involves a lump-sum initial payment, however, it can be converted to foreign equity holdings, subject to the approval of the regulatory body. Despite restrictions on the capitalization of technology costs in certain countries, it is still fairly common, particularly where lump-sum payments are involved. It is often felt that equity participation by the technology supplier ensures a long-term commitment for full and effective transfer of technology and also provides the local company with future improvements. This may also be unavoidable for the acquisition of advanced technologies, which may be difficult to obtain under arms-length transactions.

Duration of Agreements

Foreign technology payments in the form of royalties also depend, to a considerable extent, on the duration of the technology agreement, since such payments are made throughout the period of the agreement. In the case of royalty agreements, licensors prefer as long a contract period as possible. In many cases, licensee enterprises in developing countries have given relatively little importance for continuing technological dependence on the foreign licensor. Consequently, before the introduction of regulatory measures, technology agreements with developing country enterprises were often made for indefinite periods.[17] It was also a common practice to renew agreements automatically, unless one of the parties had objections to the renewal. Despite the long periods of the agreements, they frequently did not provide for the transfer of improvements following the initial transfer and continuing royalty payments were often made for the use of a technology, not for new developments. Technology suppliers also often included a provision that on termination of the agreement, the licensee would be prohibited from the use of any knowledge transferred by the licensor, and it was often required that the licensee return all the documentation supplied during the term of the agreement.

An important aspect of regulatory measures has been that the permissible maximum length of contract duration is usually prescribed. This is done mainly to limit the period for which royalty payments have to be made by the licensee and also to accelerate the process of technological absorption. Technology agreements have also increasingly been considered as purchase agreements stating that, during the contract period, the licensor is obliged to transfer all the elements of technology and know-how required by the licensee to undertake independent production after the expiration of the contract. Restrictions on the duration of agreements are also intended to limit foreign payments for technology that is fully absorbed and to reduce continuing dependence on foreign licensors.

The maximum duration of technology agreements, as prescribed by regulatory measures, varies among countries; in most cases, it ranges between five years, as in Brazil, India, and the Philippines, and ten years, as in Mexico and the Republic of Korea. Differences also exist in the flexibility and authority of regulatory bodies to make exceptions and to approve agreements for longer periods. In some countries, such as Brazil, with the exception of patent and license agreements, the maximum permissible duration is generally adhered to. In others, such as the Republic of Korea, with the recent softening of foreign technology regulations measures, much greater flexibility has been allowed. In most countries, however, it is believed that for agreements involving complex technologies, it is in the interest of local licensee enterprises to permit a longer duration, if necessary, to absorb the technology effectively, even if the legal duration period is exceeded.

The actual duration of technology agreements has also depended on regulatory policies for renewals and extensions of agreements. Although, prior to regulatory measures, renewals took place fairly automatically, proposals for renewals and extensions are generally scrutinized fairly closely by regulatory bodies. In some countries, including Brazil and India, extensions are approved only if the technology in question is based on a patent that is still in force or if the renewal provides for transfer of significant technological improvements. In some countries, regulatory agencies have also followed a practice of setting royalty payments in renewed agreements at a lower rate than in the original agreement.

Access to Improvements

In several developing countries, legal provisions or guidelines require the inclusion of a clause that provides for the transfer of improvements achieved by the licensor during the valid period of the contract. Such provision is required, for example, by the regulatory bodies of Brazil, India, the Republic of Korea, Mexico, and the Philippines. National regulatory bodies have, however, encountered difficulties in monitoring the implementation of this requirement, and it has generally been left to licensee enterprises to ensure that improvements are, in fact, transferred. In many instances, the implementation of this requirement is also limited by the manner in which the regulation is defined. In most cases, the relevant provisions of the law or guidelines state that improvements have to be transferred, but they do not define the term, *improvements* very concisely. This has usually enabled licensors to interpret the term as excluding major innovations in products or technical processes, since these are considered to be new developments rather than improvements of the technology in question. Nevertheless, the emphasis on transfer of improvements to licensee enterprises is an important factor for regulatory bodies in granting extensions and in approving agreements with durations exceeding the prescribed maximum period.

Restrictive Business Provisions

Until the introduction of regulatory measures, a large portion of technology agreements contained provisions that limited the freedom of action of licensee companies.[18] One of the major reasons for introducing such regulation was to eliminate these practices, which were considered to be undesirable and unduly restrictive for licensee enterprises. Restrictive measures are generally imposed by MNCs and technology licensors for two main reasons. The first relates to the objective of optimizing earnings from licensing arrangements; the second involved retaining control over the use of proprietary technology. Although the two motives are closely interrelated, in that control over the technology ultimately contributes to the maintenance of profitability from a company's technological assets, some restrictions are more closely related to immediate profitability considerations, whereas others are oriented primarily toward control over the diffusion of technology. For licensee enterprises, these restrictions not only indicate the indirect costs of technology acquisition but also frequently limit the selection, adaptation, and effective absorption of foreign technology. Examples of such restrictions are the various tie-in arrangements that require the licensee to purchase imported inputs, such as capital goods, raw materials, and intermediate goods from the licensor. For the licensor, such provisions ensure a ready export market in which prices are determined solely by the licensor; for the licensee, however, the inability to purchase inputs from potentially lower-priced alternative suppliers can substantially increase the total costs of the technology. Although developing country licensee often might require the assistance of its licensor for the supply of intermediates and components, the pricing of such components and intermediate products may often present difficulties. Even where a program of domestic integration is defined, the problem of pricing of imported components and materials still remains. In some countries, regulatory guidelines suggest that for intermediate product bought and supplied by licensors, the price charged should be the cost to the licensor plus any handling or other charges that may be involved, while intermediate products manufactured by the licensor should be priced as if for arms-length transactions. In any event, regulatory measures generally prescribe that local licensees should be free to obtain intermediate products and inputs from any source and that if the licensor supplies these products and components, they should be supplied at internationally competitive prices. Several countries also have regulations providing for the employment of personnel designated by the licensor and for other tie-in conditions.

An important regulatory provision often imposed on licensees concerns sales territory, and most countries have given considerable emphasis to this issue. A technology license is usually exclusive for a country and may be exclusive for a region. When sales rights, however, are restricted to a particular country or region, it can place major restraints on potential exports by licensees and on the growth of export capability. Technology licensors, on the other hand, often have licensing arrangements in several countries, particularly when these licensors are MNCs operating through a large number of subsidiaries and affiliates and exporting a substantial share of inputs from the parent's plant. In some cases, the licensor may be legally precluded from giving export rights to certain areas, because these rights may have been given to other licensee. Even where nonexclusive territorial rights have been granted as part of the license agreement, the licensee enterprise may, and often does, emerge as a competitor over a period of time. From the host country viewpoint, significant restrictions constitute a grave handicap in license agreements. Consequently, in most regulatory guidelines, unreasonable sales restrictions are prohibited. In some countries, such as Mexico, the law itself prohibits such restrictions, and justification has to be made whenever certain restrictions are accepted by the regulatory body. The general trend in regulatory measures on this issue appears to be primarily to ensure that sales rights granted to local licensees by foreign licensors are not unduly restrictive.[19]

Licensors have sought to control diffusion of their technology in several ways. Contractual provisions, for example, prohibit the licensee from making use of the technology after the expiration of the agreement, from using the technology for purposes other than those defined in the contract, or from sublicensing the technology to other local suppliers or subcontractors. Some of these restrictions have hindered the development of technological capabilities of licensee enterprises and also of other ancillary and feeder industries.

With increasing scrutiny of licensing agreements in several developing countries, the negative impact of several types of restrictions incorporated in these agreements has become much more evident. These restrictions may often result in a substantial increase in foreign technology costs, considerably beyond the direct payments for such technology and related services. Many of these provisions also limit the effective absorption of technology by domestic companies and licensees and delay the development of indigenous technological capabilities. Also, since several developing countries consider increased exports of nontraditional manufactured goods an important objective, the restrictions imposed on exports rights in technology licensing agreements often constitute an important constraint.

Industrial Property Rights

The right to use the licensor's patent and proprietary rights is the only subject of many technology agreements. Even in the composite technology packages to developing countries, the use of industrial property rights by licensees constitutes an important issue, and this issue has received considerable attention in the regulations of several countries. These regulations generally require that the various patents involved in any technology transfer agreement be listed and defined. It also must be stipulated that the licensee has user rights over all patents. The life of relevant patents is also very important in negotiating technology agreements. Provisions in some countries require that user rights to patented know-how be granted for the entire life of the patents in question. Where the lifespan of patents extends beyond the duration of the agreement, the arrangements for continued use of the patents should be made at the initial stage. In some countries, the license agreement is also required to state that if any patents related to the licensed technology are registered by the licensor during the period of the agreement, the licensee will be kept informed and will acquire user rights to those patents as well. An important provision in some countries, such as Brazil, concerns the infringement of third-party patent rights; it is often stipulated that in the event of any alleged or actual infringement of third-party patents by the use of the licensed technology, responsibility is primarily with the technology supplier.

A related issue is that of foreign trademarks and brand names, which, because of the consumer preference attached to them, are often viewed as important by licensees in developing countries. Regulatory measures in some countries, particularly India and Mexico, emphasize the need for local licensees to develop their own brand names over a period of time. This has often resulted in increased use of foreign brand names in conjunction with local names. This practice is still relative infrequent, however. In Mexico, for example, where this kind of legislation was enacted in 1975, implementation was postponed for several years.

Besides the regulatory measures on these issues—largely intended to modify and reduce the impact of contractual conditions usually imposed by suppliers and licensors or foreign technology—national regulatory norms also stipulate that certain other conditions be incorporated in technology agreements. These rules may range from the overall pattern of domestic integration over a period of time to the incorporation of certain specific provisions on the governing law and language.

In most developing countries, considerable emphasis is being given to the domestic content of manufacture in proposals involving foreign technology. Regulatory guidelines in India, Mexico, and some other countries stipulate that a phased program of domestic integration be specified in the technology agreement, so that the regulatory agency is able to appraise the proposal. Licensors tend to supply technology and know-how for increased domestic content only in gradual stages, so that an assured market for their inputs can continue for a longer period. For the regulatory body, the objective of increasing local content subject to techno-economic and market considerations can be a critical aspect of particular proposals.

Mention has been made of provisions that require access to the technological improvements of the licensor during the period of agreement. Although provisions for "grant-backs" of free transfer of any improvements effected by the licensee are prohibited in several countries, regulatory norms stipulate that free access to improvements be made by the licensor. However, since the coverage of the term *improvement* is often difficult to define, major and significant developments are generally not transferred by foreign licensors, except when the technology licensor has an important stake in the licensee's production or when information on such developments has become generally known.

Other Provisions

Another important point often included in regulatory measures concerns the guarantee or warranty for the technology and know-how supplied. This may take the form of a warranty to achieve a specified level of production in a process industry or a level of production and degree of integration over a period of time in assembly-type manufacture. Guidelines may require, in any event, that the technology supplied be full and complete for the purpose defined in the agreement.

There is also growing emphasis on a detailed program for training and technological absorption to be provided by the licensor. From a host country's viewpoint, and also that of local licensees, provision for the adequate training of domestic personnel is a very critical issue. General provisions for visits of some of the licensee's personnel to the licensor's plant for short, defined periods are often found to be inadequate. It is necessary to ensure that the number of such personnel and the time period specified for training, both in the licensor's plant and in the licensee enterprise, are really adequate for absorption of the technological processes and techniques involved. An important element, particularly in contracts for the production of machinery and engineering goods, relates to training in design, which can prove to be of crucial importance to local licensees for future adaptations and innovations. Regulatory measures on training requirements have been prescribed in several countries, although they are more detailed in certain countries, particularly Brazil and India. Detailed training provisions are important elements in the evaluation of contracts by regulatory agencies in these countries, and there is a growing trend for more detailed stipulations in this regard. In some developing countries, however, even though regulatory measures have been implemented for over a decade, most technology contracts, including recent one, refer to training in a broad and vague manner, generally allowing that training be provided by the licensor whenever it is considered necessary.

Another important stipulation in most regulatory measures concerns the use of foreign technology after the expiration of the contracts. If the technology is covered by valid patents or other industrial property rights, the user rights have to be acquired by the licensee; otherwise, most regulatory measures provide that unpatented know-how can be used by local licensees after the expiration of the agreement. Consequently, any contractual provisions that restrict the use of transferred, unpatented information and know-how after the period of agreement may be disallowed by the regulatory body.

In some countries, regulatory measures provide that if arbitrations becomes necessary, it should take place in the country of the licensee and it should be handled by a group of three persons, two of whom would be appointed by the respective parties and the third by mutual agreement. In some cases, the place of arbitration may be outside the host country, but in general, the country of the licensor is not accepted by most host country government. As for governing law, regulatory measures in most developing countries prescribe that it be the law of the country of the licensee.

Regulatory measures may also relate to other contractual aspects, such as assignability, confidentiality, sublicensing, language, currency of payment, inspection and reporting, *force majeure,* and the like, although these provisions do not normally present undue difficulty in the course of negotiations, and they can generally be satisfactorily resolved.

It may be seen, therefore, that regulatory measures and guidelines cover most important provisions in technology agreements. Technology regulation agencies in most developing countries view the licensing function from a national perspective, and there are several situations in which the approach of local licensee enterprises and that of the regulatory institutions may differ considerably. This may take place on issues such as the need for importing technology for a particular product, the appropriateness of a specific foreign technology, or the costs of technology or on other contractual conditions, such as the phasing of local integration, the duration of agreements, and the like. A national approach may often be adopted on many of these matters, and it may not coincide with the views of local licensee enterprises.

In most developing countries, however, experience has shown that unless regulatory measures are administered with considerable flexibility, the flow of essential foreign technology may be adversely affected. In several cases, tie-in arrangements with the foreign licensor may be unavoidable. It may also be necessary to accept certain restrictions on export rights, particularly when the licensor has other legal commitments that have to be observed. In any event, a licensing agreement depends to a considerable extent on the goodwill and sound business relations between the contracting parties, and the terms and conditions finally incorporated must be acceptable to the licensor as well as to the licensee and the regulatory agency concerned. Consequently, considerable flexibility has been exercised in most developing countries in implementing the provisions of technology legislation and of the regulatory guidelines prescribed. In some countries, major changes have occurred in technological needs, which has also led to greater flexibility. As technological requirements gradually shift to more advanced and complex technologies, the range of alternatives tends to be reduced, and this factor has been reflected in the approach toward technology agreements.

The degree of flexibility has varied according to various provisions covered by national regulatory norms. For certain provisions, however, regulatory agencies have made relatively few exceptions, particularly in recent years. For example, just as restrictions on the use of foreign technology after the expiration of the agreement are generally not permitted, so, too, restrictions on the volume of production, on the use of complementary technologies, on sales and pricing in the domestic market, and on R&D limitations have generally not been approved. In several countries, the imposition of grant-back provisions on the licensee are not accepted, although in some cases, the stipulation that improvements made by both partners during the period of contract are freely exchanged may be approved. Several countries, however, have allowed contractual provisions stating that the licensor has the right to patent relevant inventions made by the licensee worldwide except in the home country of the licensee. In many countries, regulatory agencies have also approved technology agreements even though the licensor has not accepted liability, financial or legal, for the infringement of patents of third parties by the licensee or for other damages resulting from the use of the licensed technology. In Brazil, contracts define the liability of the licensor for the licensed technology. In several developing countries, regulatory agencies have also made exceptions to the provision that the settlement of dispute be subject to local law, and contracts have been approved that call for international arbitration through either the International Chamber of Commerce or other international conciliatory bodies.

Besides the liberal treatment of various contractual provisions in technology agreements, several regulatory bodies have also given considerable freedom and latitude to contracting parties to determine the level and terms of technology payments, intervening only if the payment has been excessively above that charged for similar technologies. The norms in most countries prescribe the basis of royalty calculation usually defined as the ex-factory value of sales, minus the landed costs of components imported from the licensor. Also, minimum royalty payments have been prohibited in most countries. Although internal guidelines have been established for maximum royalties in certain countries, exceptions have been made, usually in the case of complex technology and know-how. It has also been recognized that if guidelines for maximum royalties are viewed inflexibly, the technology licensor will tend to increase the initial lump-sum payment or will not be willing to make the technology available. In a few countries, however, such as Brazil, guidelines relating to royalty rates have been treated with much less flexibility than they have in other developing countries.

The acquisition of foreign technology and its use for domestic technological development has also been affected by changes and modifications in legislation regarding patents and other industrial property rights in a number of countries. Although the details of provisions differ among countries, a common trend is emerging. In several developing countries, patent laws have been amended with a view to achieving more rapid technological development in priority sectors. These measures are intended to increase the utilization of essential technologies and to promote greater local adaptation and innovation. In some countries, the definition of inventions eligible for patent has been narrowed, and only manufacturing processes can be registered. Certain fields that are considered to be of socioeconomic priority, such as pharmaceuticals and food products, either are not covered by patents or have been accorded a reduced patent life. The duration of patent validity, in general, has also been reduced — for example, in Mexico to ten years, in the Republic of Korea to twelve years, and in Chile to five to fifteen years, depending on the type of invention. In certain countries, the patent law provides for the government's right to expropriate patents if this is necessary for national purposes. Compulsory licensing provisions have also been introduced in some developing countries, such as Mexico, the Philippines, India, and Brazil. These measures are indicative of a broader trend. In addition to national efforts, protracted negotiations relating to the revision of the Paris Convention are continuing through the World Intellectual Property Organization.

In several countries in which regulatory measures on foreign technology were introduced in the early 1970s, significant changes took place in the latter half of the 1970s and the early 1980s. Although initial regulatory efforts were directed largely at improving conditions for the acquisition of foreign technology, the policies adopted subsequently have become more comprehensive and differentiated. Thus, while regulatory measures continue, the inflow of foreign investments and technology have also been promoted through various incentives and concessions. Several factors have contributed to such policy developments. In a number of countries, as sophistication in sectoral industrial planning increase, the specific technological needs of various industrial branches are being assessed in much greater detail, enabling the regulatory body to identify the areas in which foreign technology is particularly necessary. Also, with progress in industrialization, sectoral development plans have included more advanced industrial branches in which the availability of technology is limited to a few suppliers, calling for greater flexibility by regulatory agencies. It is also recognized that effective technological absorption often requires a period exceeding the generally prescribed duration and that payments for complex technologies may be significantly higher than the maximum rates applicable to the manufacturing sector as a whole. Certain export restrictions may also have to be permitted to enable licensors to meet their legal obligations toward other licensees. The slowdown in economic growth has also had considerable impact on foreign technology flow to different countries, particularly to Third World economies. This has induced several countries to promote the inflow of foreign technology by making exceptions to the provisions of their national legislation and guidelines.

Changes and modifications in policies have been implemented either within the framework of existing regulations or through changes in laws or administrative guidelines. In several countries, such as Brazil, Mexico, the Andean Group members, India, Pakistan, and Nigeria, although the laws and guidelines have not been modified significantly, a certain softening has taken place in their implementation. Regulatory bodies have made more use of their authority to make exceptions from the general provisions of the law or guidelines in a large number of cases. In the Republic of Korea, however, since 1978, significant liberalization of foreign technology regulation has taken place and new guidelines have been issued incorporating the liberalized provisions. In a number of countries, selective promotion of foreign investments and technology is taking place as a result of changes in government and in economic policies. Such changes have been particularly significant, for example, in the case of Egypt since 1974, in Sri Lanka since 1977, in Bangladesh since 1975, and in Jamaica since 1980.

Diversity in National Policies

It must be emphasized that, despite policy trends toward regulatory control, there continues to be a great deal of diversity in national policies toward foreign direct investment and technology inflow in Third World countries. National policies on foreign investments continue to range from unrestricted inflow, supported by various incentives and concessions for investments from abroad, to stringent regulations restricting foreign investments to certain sectors and levels of ownership. As for foreign technology, despite the implementation of regulations and guidelines in some developing countries discussed previously, there is no control over foreign technology in other Third World countries, and such inflow is considered an integral and vital aspect of foreign investments and MNC operations in these countries.

Several developing countries, especially those in Southeast Asia, North and West Africa, Latin America, and the Caribbean, permit fairly unrestricted entry of foreign investments. These countries are at various stages of economic and industrial development and extend from industrialized economies such as Brazil, Singapore, and Taiwan to semi-industrialized countries such as Pakistan, Turkey, and Nigeria, as well as to countries in which there has been very little industrial growth and limited foreign investments, as in parts of Africa. In some countries—for example, Brazil and Thailand— governmental approval becomes necessary only when specific incentives and financial and other concessions are sought. In certain countries, although foreign investments in new projects are permitted without restriction, the takeover of existing locally owned companies requires government approval. In certain countries, such as Indonesia and the Philippines, foreign investments are actively encouraged, especially in defined priority sectors, but foreign ownership of local enterprises is expected to be reduced to minority holdings over a period of time. In Egypt, although foreign investments have been actively promoted since 1974, governmental policies favor the formation of joint ventures with foreign holdings up to 50 percent. In joint ventures with state-owned enterprises, foreign investors are permitted to own up to 25 percent of equity and up to 40 percent in exceptional cases. Although foreign capital inflow is unrestricted and welcomed in some countries, such investments must be registered with the government or require some form of approval. Thus, in Kenya, the Foreign Investment Protection Act (1964) guarantees freedom to transfer profits and foreign loans for registered investments. This legislation was amended in 1978, however, and a ceiling of 10 percent was prescribed for dividend repatriation. A "certificate of approved enterprise" is required for day-to-day operations of foreign companies, such approval being accorded by the interdepartmental New Projects Committee. The contribution of the proposed investment to national technological development is one of the major criteria for evaluating new investment proposals, including the suitability of the technology in relation to local conditions and the training of Kenyans at various levels of management and operations. It is only in a few developing countries that foreign direct investments are generally restricted to minority holdings. In these countries governmental pressure has been exerted to reduce foreign holdings to minority levels. Countries in this category include Mexico and Nigeria. Among free-market developing countries, restrictions on foreign ownership are imposed to the maximum extent in India, where foreign equity, if permitted at all, is generally restricted to 40 percent of total equity.

Apart from the issue of foreign ownership, the intent of governmental policies in most countries in which some degree of regulation has been imposed is to channel foreign investments to particular sectors of priority. Thus, the Board of Investments in the Philippines, which administers financial and other incentives, also identifies specific industrial sectors and projects within a framework of priorities, besides encouraging foreign investments in most fields. In Indonesia, since the promulgation of the Foreign Capital Investment Law in 1967, priority areas for foreign investment have been defined periodically. The list of such sectors is published annually, along with their level of importance and priority status. In Malaysia, the Malaysian Industrial Development Authority (MIDA) plays an important role in promoting foreign investment and participation in sectors of special priority. The definition of priority sectors in which foreign investments are particularly welcomed is a policy feature of several Third World countries, including India and Mexico. Although priority criteria differ from country to country, the inflow of specialized technology and know-how and the development of export capability in the selected sectors are generally considered the critical elements.

This regulation of foreign technology has been undertaken in relatively few Third World countries; in most developing economies, technology inflow is not restricted or controlled. However, in several countries, varying degrees of control are being exercised, some of them directly applicable to contracts dealing with foreign technology and others related to proposals involving foreign direct investment and technology. It is possible to categorize developing countries into three broad groups on the basis of their overall approach to foreign technology and domestic technological development. First, there is the large majority of countries in which there is no regulation of foreign technology and in which no restrictions are exercised on remittances of fees and royalties for technology. These include countries in Southeast Asia, such as Hong Kong, Singapore, Taiwan, and Thailand, which have registered a rapid rate of industrial growth, and most countries in Africa as well as some countries in Latin America and the Caribbean. In some countries, such as Sri Lanka, Chile, and Egypt, major policy changes in the 1970s led to a more open-door approach to foreign investment and technology. A similar policy has been followed in several countries of Africa, including most countries in northern Africa. Technological development in various industrial sectors in these countries has been largely influenced by MNCs and by the commercialization of their technology through various forms of participation. A second group comprises those countries in which a certain degree of selectivity regarding the entry and operations of foreign companies is exercised without, however, the adoption of explicit regulatory measures toward foreign technology. These include Bangladesh, Indonesia, Pakistan, Kenya, Ghana, and others in which foreign investment proposals require the approval of governmental agencies but no specific approval is necessary for contracts relating to foreign technology and services. The third group of countries comprises those in which foreign technology agreements are reviewed by a governmental agency, usually one specifically set up for this purpose. In most of these countries, similar screening and varying degrees of selectivity are also exercised for foreign investment proposals. The countries that fall in this category include the Andean Pact countries, India, Malaysia, Mexico, Nigeria, the Philippines, the Republic of Korea, Turkey, and Yugoslavia. In these countries, the specific policies adopted have differed considerably from country to country and over time, and major changes have occurred in some of these countries in recent years. Brazil, for example, has followed a policy of encouraging foreign investments without restrictions on ownership but has fairly rigid regulatory measures for foreign technology and service agreements. In contrast, India has been restrictive in allowing foreign investments, particularly majority holdings, but has recently adopted a more flexible approach toward technology agreements, especially in high-technology areas. In the Republic of Korea, foreign investments were encouraged in the 1960s but are much less encouraged at present, although a very flexible attitude toward foreign technology agreements has lately been adopted. In Mexico, since 1973 restrictions have been imposed on foreign majority holdings in most cases, and fairly comprehensive legislation was enacted on foreign technology agreements, but its implementation has been rather flexible.

In other developing countries—those in which foreign technology inflow remains largely unregulated—limited control is exercised through the foreign-exchange control system, which covers remittances of fees and royalties. In some other countries, the examination of foreign investment proposals also takes account of certain aspects of the technology supply arrangements. Thus, in Egypt, although there are no legislative or administrative guidelines on the acquisition of foreign technology, technology agreements that involve remittance of foreign exchange are subject to the approval of the General Organization for Industrialization (GOFI), operating under the Minister of Industry. For the screening and evaluation of technology contracts, GOFI applies internal guidelines requiring that the technology transfer be complete and detailed documentation of the product or process be provided. Contracts are permitted for a duration of five or ten years, depending on the nature of technology. Agreements can be renewed for further periods of one year, subject to the approval of GOFI. The guidelines do not prescribe maximum permissible payments, and in practice, considerable flexibility is exercised in this regard. Several contracts involving lump-sum payments have been approved, and the royalty rates have been in the range of 2 to 5 percent of an agreed, fixed unit price for the products manufactured. In joint ventures between foreign investors and public sector companies, royalties have been generally between 1 to 4 percent of the base price, although higher royalties have also been approved in certain cases.

In Indonesia, Repelita III, which covers the five-year period beginning April 1, 1979, restates the role of foreign direct investments and technology in selected areas. It is emphasized that capital-intensive foreign technologies need to be adapted to labor-intensive processes. Concern is also expressed about the high concentration of foreign technology from Japan and the need to diversify the sources of foreign technology acquisition to European and U.S. suppliers. This intent has not, however, been reflected so far in specific policy measures. In 1977, the Indonesian Capital Investment Co-ordinating Board (BKPM) was established to centralize decision making related to foreign direct investments. In the screening and evaluation of investment proposals in priority sectors, BKPM applies several criteria, including the need for absorbing new technology and know-how as well as increasing exports, utilizing local raw materials and products, and increasing local integration and added value.

In Kenya, foreign technology agreements are not subject to registration, but under the provisions of the Exchange Control Act of 1962 and its amendment in 1965, remittances of technology fees and payments are subject to the approval of the Central Bank. According to the provisions of the Exchange Control Act, foreign exchange remittances for technology payments have to be evaluated by the Capital Issue Committee in the Ministry of Finance. Although the committee has not published specific guidelines for evaluation, its major criterion relates to the examination of the financial implications of the contract from the viewpoint of foreign exchange inflow and outflow. There are no maximum permissible royalty rates, but in practice, the generally applied royalty rates have been between 2.5 percent and 5 percent of net sales for management contracts and 1 percent to 2.5 percent for technology contracts. Besides the royalty rate, the committee takes the export potential of the licensee company into account, but the imposition of restrictive clauses, including export market restrictions, has not been prohibited. Applications to the committee have to include estimated company sales, which provides the basis for the calculation of the royalty or management fee. Approval of the agreement by the committee, however, does not guarantee a blanket permission for the remittance of royalties. Each year, a new application has to be filed, and permission is subject to the foreign exchange situation at the time.

In Thailand, foreign technology contracts have only to be filed with the Central Bank for permission to remit technology payments. The Central Bank has not prescribed guidelines for the evaluation of such contracts and primarily reviews remittance proposals in relation to payment provisions in these contracts. The importance of foreign technology has, however, been expressed in the role expected from foreign investors. At the end of 1979, the Bank of Thailand held only about 300 technology agreements, most of which related to the manufacture of drugs, cosmetics, and other branded products. When a company, whether foreign or domestically owned, receives incentives from the Thai Board of Investment, this body also investigates the technology element as part of the overall investment proposal, but has not prescribed guidelines or criteria for the evaluation of technology agreements. In other countries, such as Bangladesh, Pakistan, and Turkey, some degree of control is exercised on technology issues as part of the analysis of foreign investment proposals, but no specific guidelines have been prescribed for technology contracts.

The issue of governmental regulation of foreign technology agreements has been under increased consideration in several developing countries. With the growing emphasis on technological development as an essential prerequisite for industrialization, various issues and aspects of foreign technology acquisition will inevitably receive greater attention in these countries. However, regardless of whether or not foreign technology is regulated by government agencies, these issues and their contractual implications will undoubtedly be taken into account by licensee enterprises in these countries and will become important elements in the negotiations for foreign technology acquisition and transfer.

In the following chapters, the role of foreign technology in industrial development, and the national policies in this regard will be examined in greater detail for four developing countries: Brazil, India, the Republic of Korea, and Mexico. In all of these countries, significant industrial development has taken place in recent decades and foreign investments and technology have played a major role within the framework of fairly comprehensive and well-defined government policies in this regard. In these countries, the major channel for foreign technology inflow has been through foreign direct investments, although there is a growing trend toward technology licensing without foreign investments in the countries in which substantial domestic industrial capability has been developed. Government policies on foreign direct investment and technology in these countries have had considerable impact on the pattern of industrial and technological development. These policies have generally been regulatory in nature, although major incentives have been given to attract foreign investments, technology, and expertise in most of these countries. The broad impact of these policies on technological development of the industry will be analyzed, as will the policy changes that took place with increasing industrialization.

The pace of industrialization has been faster in some other developing countries, especially Singapore, Hong Kong, and Taiwan, which have developed as major export-oriented island economies with few or no controls on foreign investments and technology. Certain other countries, such as Malaysia, Nigeria, and Pakistan, which have comparable policies, have also achieved significant economic and industrial growth. The selection of the countries to be analyzed must therefore be considered illustrative. In these countries, industrial growth and diversification in recent decades has been among the most rapid. Also, these countries, along with the Andean Group and Argentina, have been among the earliest to regulate the inflow of foreign technology, and the experience with such measures in these countries extends to about two decades.

Notes

1. Regulation of the operation of foreign subsidiaries and affiliates was introduced in India, for example, through the "Guidelines and Procedures Concerning Foreign Collaboration Agreements," January 1969; in Mexico, through the Law on the Promotion of Mexican Investment and Regulation of Foreign Investment, May 8, 1973; and in the Andean Group, through Decision No. 23 of the Commission of the Cartagena Agreement.

2. In India, for instance, the guidelines specify the industries in which foreign investments are permitted, the industries in which foreign technology but not foreign investments are permitted, and those in which neither foreign investment nor foreign technology are allowed. In Mexico, the law reserved certain activities for domestic companies and does not allow foreign-controlled enterprises in activities in which they might displace domestic companies. A detailed analysis of foreign investment regulation is presented in *Handbook on the Acquisition of Technology by Developing Countries* (New York: United Nations, 1978).

3. The weak linkages among the scientific, technological, and production systems in developing countries are analyzed in O.A. El-Kholy, "The Structure and Functioning of Technology Systems in Developing Countries," Paper presented at the United Nations Industrial Development Organization Export Group Meeting on Technology Development and Self-Reliance in Developing Countries, Vienna, 1979, mimeographed.

4. Several case studies of this phenomena in Kenya are discussed in F. Stewart, *Technology and Underdevelopment* (London: Macmillan, 1977).

5. The frequent occurrence of restrictive business clauses in licensing agreements has been studied extensively by various United Nations agencies. Findings from the early 1970s, when most countries had no regulatory acts, are presented in "Restrictive Business Practices in Relation to the Trade and Development of Developing Countries," Report by the Ad Hoc Group of Experts to the United Nations, 1974.

6. See the 24th Pugwash Symposium, "Self-Reliance and Alternative Development Strategies," Dar-es-Salaam, June 1976; and the Jamaica Symposium, *Mobilizing Technology for World Development* (Washington, D.C.: International Institute for Environment and Development, March 1979). For the Andean Group, see "Policies on Technology of the Andean Pact: Their Foundations" (Cartagena, Colombia: Junta del Acuerdo de Cartagena, 6 December 1971, mimeographed).

7. Major features of technology regulatory policies and, more specifically, of licensing agreements that can improve the bargaining position of developing country companies have been the subject of various United Nations publications, including *Guidelines for the Acquisition of Foreign Technologies in Developing Countries, with Special Reference to Technology License Agreements,* No. E.73.11.B (Vienna: United Nations Industrial Development Organization, 1973) and *Licensing Guide for Developing Countries* (Geneva: United Nations World Intellectual Property Organization, 1977).

8. In Japan, for example, between 1950 and 1970, about 14,000 licensing agreements were entered into; of these, about 60 percent were with licensors from the United States. License agreements must be submitted to the Fair Trade Commission,

which has been set up under the antimonopoly legislation and which prohibits the imposition of certain restrictions in technology agreements. These restrictions include export limits, tie-in clauses, and limits on the acquisition of competitive technologies. See *National Approaches to the Acquisition of Technology* (New York: United Nations Industrial Development Organization, 1977).

9. The formulation of the regulatory policies toward foreign direct investments and technology in the Andean Group is analyzed in L.K. Mytelka, "Regulating Direct Foreign Investment and Technology Transfer in the Andean Group," *Journal of Peace Research* 14 (1977): 155–84.

10. A comprehensive review of technology transfer registries is presented in United Nations Industrial Development Organization "A Comparative Study of the Technology Transfer Registries of Selected Countries," Paper presented for the fifth meeting of the Heads of Technology Transfer Registries, Buenos Aires, September 1980.

11. It is also argued that the bargaining power of developing country technology is weakened by the "information paradox"—that is, the insufficient information the buyer has on the value of the technology and its specific nature, since sellers generally do not disclose such information in enough detail to permit effective evaluation. See C.V. Vaitsos, "Commercialization of Technology in the Andean Pact, in *International Firms and Imperialism,* ed. H. Radice (Harmondsworth, England: Penguin, 1975).

12. In the sample of U.S. companies surveyed by Contractor in the late 1970s, over 80 percent of the contracts involved payment of royalties. See F. Contractor, *International Technology Licensing* (Lexington, Mass.: Lexington Books, 1981). In the late 1970s in four Asian countries (Thailand, the Republic of Korea, Sri Lanka, and Malaysia), between 40 and 60 percent of the sampled firms had running royalties for payment. See *Cost and Conditions of Technology Transfer through Transnational Corporations,* ESCAP/UNCTC Publication Series B, No. 3 (New York: United Nations Centre on Transnational Corporations, April 1984).

13. In many countries, regulatory bodies have applied ranges of permissible royalties according to industrial sectors. General norms for selected industrial sectors were the following: pharmaceuticals, 10 to 15 percent; data processing, 3 to 5 percent; chemicals, 2 to 3 percent; consumer industries, 2 percent. See United Nations Centre on Transnational Corporation, *Costs and Conditions,* 63, 65, 69.

14. In most of the countries in which regulatory measures had been introduced by the end of the 1970s, royalty rates were between 1 and 5 percent of sales. See *The Implementation of Transfer of Technology Regulations: A Preliminary Analysis of the Experience of Latin America, India and the Philippines* (Geneva: UNCTAD, 28 August 1980).

15. For example, since 1979 in the Republic of Korea, the liberalization of technology regulations for the manufacture of various machinery, equipment, and other products involving complex technology royalty rates in excess of 10 percent of sales was quite common.

16. There is empirical evidence that fee reductions were achieved in a great number of contracts following negotiating efforts on the part of the technology import-control agency. See UNCTAD, *The Implementation of Transfer of Technology Regulations.*

17. In the Philippines, for example, 68 percent of the existing agreements in

1970 were of indefinite duration. Such contracts were also common in most other countries. See *Restrictions on Exports in Foreign Collaboration Agreements in the Republic of the Philippines* (New York: United Nations, 1972).

18. In 1970, before the regulation of foreign technology acquisition, studies showed that almost 50 percent of the sample agreements analyzed contained restrictive business clauses. Ibid.

19. Although the frequency of restrictive business clauses has decreased in most countries following the adoption of regulatory measures, such restrictions still exist. A study of selected Asian countries (including the Republic of Korea, the Philippines, Thailand, Malaysia, and Sri Lanka) in the late 1970s showed, for example, that various export restrictions were imposed in 20 to 30 percent of the contracts entered into in these countries. Although, in most cases, these restrictions were not related to an outright prohibition of all exports, they contained various limitations on the licensee, such as the need for prior permission by the licensor, or major restrictions on the territory covered. The tie-in purchase of raw materials or equipment was among the most frequent restrictions imposed. See United Nations Centre on Transnational Corporations, *Costs and Conditions.*

9
Brazil

Although Brazil faces a great many economic difficulties in the 1980s, largely because of its massive foreign debts, the pace of industrialization over the past three decades has been extremely rapid. The contribution of the industrial sector to GDP rose from 24 percent at factor costs in 1960 to 35 percent by 1980.[1] In this period, a substantial transformation took place in Brazil's economy, which was converted from a base that was primarily agricultural and oriented toward commodity exports to a highly diversified industrial structure, with rapid growth of production and technological capability in most manufacturing and service sectors. With an annual increase of about 11 percent in GDP during the period 1965–74, the country's economic and industrial development proceeded at a very fast pace. The increase in oil prices since 1973, combined with the impact of recession and the growing burden of international debt, however, has had a very adverse impact on Brazil's economy during the early 1980s. Nevertheless, with a strong and diversified industrial base, the country has increased its exports substantially during this period, and the economic situation is gradually improving.

Foreign capital and technology have played a dominant role in Brazil's industrialization from the earliest stage of its development. Between 1860 and 1889, for example, 113 foreign companies, mostly from Great Britain, were established in the country; they built up the railroad system and developed several resource-based industries.[2] Since World War I, MNCs from the United States have constituted the major source of foreign capital and technology and have established many manufacturing industries. Since the mid-1950s, however, the industrial growth rate accelerated rapidly after the government adopted a number of policies initially geared toward import substitution and, more recently, toward exports of manufactured products, with foreign capital and technology playing a major role.[3] The entry of foreign companies was considered necessary to provide both capital and the required technology, and this was promoted through a program of incentives that included an effective protection system for local manufacture. Although the "law of similars," which prohibited imports of products that were manufactured locally, was enacted as early as 1890, it was not effectively enforced until the mid–1950s and was implemented strictly only in the 1960s and 1970s. Abolished in 1979, it was replaced by progressive import duties. Another major incentive was the issue of SUMOC Instruction 113, which provided for the duty-free import of machinery and equipment by foreign investors if the value of the machinery was converted to cruzeiro equity in a local company. Other incentives included tax concessions and various fiscal benefits.

Foreign companies were attracted to Brazil by both the various incentives and the large internal market, which expanded rapidly with the implementation of major economic development programs. During the 1960s, several MNCs, particularly from the United States, utilized the provisions of SUMOC Instruction 113 and often imported used machinery and equipment from their home countries. This was particularly prevalent in the automobile industry. Foreign companies gradually expanded their initial investments in various sectors, including consumer durables, such as electrical appliances and transport equipment; various intermediate products, such as chemicals, rubber, and plastics; and the local manufacture of various types of industrial machinery and equipment. Foreign direct investments averaged $100 million annually during the 1955–61 period but rose more rapidly during the 1960s. By 1976, such investments amounted to over $9 billion.[4] The entry of MNCs in Brazil often took place through takeovers of Brazilian-owned companies. One notable example in this regard was the electrical equipment industry, in which several Brazilian companies were absorbed in the operations of MNC subsidiaries, leading to a significant increase in foreign ownership in this sector.[5] Although the takeover of locally owned companies resulted in major expansion of existing production facilities, it hindered the growth of domestic technological capability in this and other industrial branches in which considerable production capacity had been established prior to such takeovers.

Industrial investments by domestically owned companies also expanded considerably during the 1960–80 period. These included state-owned enterprises in key sectors of the economy that also provided an important industrial base for the rapid growth of local industry.[6] In the early 1930s, the establishment of an integrated steel mill through the state-owned Companhia Siderurgica Nacional facilitated the development of local engineering goods production. In 1943, the state-owned Fabrica Nacional de Motores was set up; it manufactured various types of motors and other machinery products and functioned as a public sector enterprise until 1968, when it was sold to the private sector.

Since World War II, the public sector has grown rapidly and the government's policy has been to engage in production activities in which private investments have not been adequate to meet development objectives (except for basic industries such as mining and petroleum). In 1953, PETROBRAS was created for petroleum exploration and refining, and in the 1960s and 1970s, the activities of PETROBRAS expanded to the production of a wide range of petrochemicals through several subsidiaries. Many of these subsidiaries were set up as joint ventures between PETROBRAS, private Brazilian-owned companies, and foreign partners, which supplied the technology and generally kept minority equity participation.[7] In the 1970s, joint ventures between public sector companies and foreign companies with minority equity participation have also included various branches of the metallurgical industry, besides steel, telecommunications equipment, automobile components, and several other industries. The role of the state in industry has also increased significantly with the creation, in 1954, of the Banco Nacional de Desenvolvimento Economico (National Bank for Economic Development), which has subsidized the financing of infrastructure and major industrial projects and has also participated in the equity holdings of a large number of Brazilian companies. Since public sector companies have a virtual monopoly in utilities, including energy generation and distribution, communications, and petroleum refining, and play a major role in mining and the manufacture of steel and petrochemicals, these enterprises include the largest companies in the country. In 1982, of the 200 largest companies in Brazil, ranked by sale, 46 were owned by the government.[8]

Investments by Brazilian-owned companies in the private sector have largely been concentrated in consumer goods manufacture but have also played an important role in the production of intermediates and of machinery and equipment. Apart from agro industries and food-processing plants, Brazilian companies have a substantial share in the production of textiles, cement, paper, and several other industries, including capital goods manufacture. In capital goods manufacture, several Brazilian companies are competing effectively with MNC subsidiaries, in both Brazilian and export markets. In machine tool production, for example, a field in which several foreign subsidiaries are engaged in Brazil, the largest manufacturer is Industrias Romi, a Brazilian-owned enterprise; other locally owned machine tool producers include Industria Nardini and Industria Emanuel Rocco. Agrale SA Tractores e Motores and Fabrica de Motores Tiete SA are two Brazilian-owned firms engaged in the production of diesel engines, besides four MNC subsidiaries in the same field. Equipamentos Villares SA, a Brazilian company, produces a wide range of mechanical equipment, including mobile cranes and excavators, mill cranes, and the like. Another local manufacturer of heavy duty cranes is Torque SA. An important Brazilian company manufacturing equipment for the sugar industry is Mausa SA Equipamentos Industrialies. Most of these manufacturers have licensing arrangements with foreign manufacturers, but they have also developed significant design and adaptation capability. In electrical equipment manufacture, where a large number of MNC subsidiaries are operating, some Brazilian-owned companies continue to play an important role. These include Industria de Transformadores, producing power and distribution transformers; Bardella Boriello Electro Mecanica SA, manufacturing special motors; Spig SA, with majority Brazilian holdings, engaged in the design and erection of electrical plants and installations; and Industria Villares, producing a large range of mechanical and electrical equipment. Most of these companies are licensees of foreign companies that have not set up manufacturing subsidiaries in Brazil. The high degree of competition in this subsector, mostly from local subsidiaries of several MNCs, has made it necessary for Brazilian companies to develop considerable capability for technological absorption and adaptation in order to survive and compete.

The rapid pace of industrialization in Brazil since the mid–1950s has ensured a high degree of import substitution within a relatively short period. By the early 1960s, domestic production accounted for 95 percent of domestic supplies for consumer durables, 90 percent for intermediate products, and about 80 percent for machinery and equipment.[9] This was partly due to import restrictions, but it was also largely the result of substantial industrial investments in Brazil, including those by foreign companies. Over the past two decades, the pattern of industrial growth has become increasingly diversified. By 1980, Brazil's production of capital goods had reached $17.6 billion.[10] Domestic production of machinery and equipment covered 73 percent of the country's fast-growing demand for investment goods.[11] Exports of capital goods also increased rapidly; by 1980, they amounted to $2.4 billion, constituting 15 percent of total exports.[12]

An important feature of industrial development in Brazil has been the substantial increase in the local content of domestic manufacture. In various industrial sectors, the proportion of foreign inputs has been considerably reduced, largely as a result of government policies and pressure. In the automobile industry, which is entirely foreign-owned, a nationalization index was set up in the 1970s, and production in this sector achieved over 95 percent local content in the early 1980s. Local content requirements have also been set for various other sectors, including railway equipment, electrical and mechanical equipment, and other assembly-type industries. The growth of local content has considerable technological implications, since it has accompanied the acquisition and application of industrial technology for a large number of parts, components, and intermediate products in various industrial branches. Although most of the technology has been acquired from foreign sources, rapid absorption and adaptation by local enterprises, including MNC subsidiaries, has resulted in the assimilation of foreign technology, not only by equipment manufacturers but also by a broad spectrum of supplier industries. The government's insistence on a high degree of local content in most industrial sectors has also resulted in significant growth in design and engineering capabilities.

Foreign Investment Policies

Until the late 1970s, the entry of foreign investments was encouraged and promoted by various incentives, and very few restrictions were imposed on such inflow. With few exceptions, all sectors of manufacturing industry were open to foreign investments through wholly foreign-owned subsidiaries. This policy is reflected in the basic law governing investments. Law 4131 (1964) states: "Foreign capital to be invested in Brazil will be given legal treatment identical to that granted to local capital, under equal conditions; any discrimination whatsoever not provided in this law being prohibited."[13] Foreign investments, however, have to be registered with the Central Bank in order to obtain permission for the remittance of profits and other foreign exchange payments. This mandatory registration is primarily for administrative purposes, and no substantive evaluation is made of foreign investment proposals, unless the foreign investor wishes to be availed of incentives and promotion privileges that are granted in certain priority sectors by the Conselho de Desenvolvimento Industrial (CDI), the investment promotion body.

Policies toward foreign direct investments remained relatively stable during the 1960s and 1970s. In the Second Development Plan (1975–79), however, some concern was expressed about the large and unregulated inflow of foreign investments. By 1973, in the 1,000 largest Brazilian companies, about 22 percent of the assets ($4.98 billion) were foreign-owned and 37 percent of sales ($11 billion) were generated by foreign subsidiaries.[14] Therefore, the Second Development Plan emphasized the need to define the role of foreign companies in national development strategy and to implement this role through appropriate policy measures and instruments. The plan also expressed the need for selective encouragement of foreign investments in several areas, including fields where foreign companies had been expected to diversify and to increase Brazil's exports in manufactured goods. Foreign subsidiaries were also expected to promote the technological development of the country by local R&D activity and to increase the local absorption and dissemination of foreign technology and the development of local management capabilities. Despite these objectives, the basic legislation and policies toward foreign investments remained largely unchanged during the 1970s. Restrictions on the operation of wholly owned subsidiaries were introduced, however, in certain industrial subsectors, such as the manufacture of data processing equipment,[15] locomotives,[16] and cement.[17] These measures aimed at ensuring greater participation and control by national enterprises in these fields, and specialized agencies were established for the implementation of these programs.[18]

Although there continue to be relatively few restrictions on the entry and ownership of foreign companies, the government has significantly reduced the incentives for which wholly owned subsidiaries are eligible. Thus, since the late 1970s, majority-owned foreign companies have been eligible for government incentives only if the CDI, the government's investment promotion agency, considers the investment high priority. If it does, the incentives granted to the company include exemption from duties and excise taxes for imported machinery, equipment, and parts, as well as access to local financing from government sources, accelerated depreciation of fixed assets acquired in Brazil, and tariff protection from competitive imports. In the mid–1970s, it was estimated that these incentives could reduce the costs of fixed assets by almost 50 percent.[19] In 1977, the CDI also issued guidelines for purchases by the public sector, which has been a major purchaser of machinery and equipment. Provisions in the guidelines required that preference be given in tenders to consortia led by locally owned companies. Since 1980, permissible local borrowing by foreign companies has been further limited. Greater scrutiny is also being exercised regarding takeover of domestically owned companies by foreign subsidiaries and, generally, takeovers have been permitted only if the foreign company transfers new and advanced technology considered of special importance for the country.

Despite these measures, which have restricted the access of foreign subsidiaries to government incentives in favor of domestically owned companies, the existing policies still provide considerable freedom for the entry of foreign companies. Foreign investments increased considerably during the period 1976–83, from $9 billion to $22.3 billion.[20] In 1983, reinvested earnings alone amounted to $6.7 billion, since reinvestment is encouraged by regulations restricting profit remittances beyond a certain level.[21] The major foreign investors in Brazil continued to be MNCs from the United States. During the 1970s, however, the share of foreign investments from the United States decreased, and investments from Western Europe, particularly from the Federal Republic of Germany and Switzerland, and from Japan have increased substantially. Presently, MNCs from the United States have approximately one-third of the total investments, followed by companies based in the Federal Republic of Germany, which have approximately 14 percent of the foreign investment stock.[22]

In 1983, total foreign direct investments in manufacturing industries in Brazil amounted to $17 billion, the highest among developing countries.[23] The largest share of such investments (about one-fifth) was in the transport equipment sector, which is entirely foreign-owned. Other major sectors with high foreign capital participation are chemicals and the manufacture of mechanical equipment. Significant foreign investments have also been made in the manufacture of electrical and communication equipment, metal and metallurgical products, pharmaceuticals, and food products. Most of these investments have been by a relatively few large foreign subsidiaries, which have often dominated specific sectors of local industry.[24] In 1983, for example, foreign subsidiaries accounted for over 99 percent of the sales of the automobile industry, for 90 percent of the sales of electrical and communication equipment, 85 percent of pharmaceuticals, 80 percent of tractors and earth-moving machinery, 80 percent of chemicals and petrochemicals, 71 percent of rubber, and 61 percent of nonferrous metals.[25]

The dominant role of foreign subsidiaries and affiliates in several industrial sectors has had considerable impact on technological development in Brazil. Although there has been significant inflow of foreign technology, it has generally been limited to the immediate requirements of MNC subsidiaries and affiliates. At the same time, the policies of government toward local content and exports have resulted in substantial technological absorption and adaptation by several MNC subsidiaries and affiliates operating in Brazil. The contribution of foreign subsidiaries to the country's industrialization and the high degree of self-sufficiency in a large number of industries, including the most advanced sectors, have, however, also resulted in foreign subsidiaries playing a a dominant role in several of the most dynamic sectors of the economy. The more recent efforts of the government to strengthen the position of domestically owned companies may be effective in limiting the further growth of foreign penetration in certain sectors. These measures have been quite successful, for example, in the case of minicomputers, which have been reserved for domestically owned companies. The intent of the legislation introduced in 1984 to confine future growth of the local computer industry to Brazilian-owned firms is similar. Although reservation of such advanced industrial sectors may not necessarily eliminate the dependency of national firms on foreign technology, these are important measures for increasing the participation of domestic companies in the most dynamic and technologically advanced sectors of the economy. At the same time, these measures may make it difficult for Brazilian companies to acquire the latest technologies in these fields. Unless local R&D efforts are greatly intensified, it may be difficult to keep pace with technological developments and innovations in these areas.

Foreign Technology Regulation

Although Brazil has imposed relatively few restrictions on foreign investment and ownership by foreign companies, the regulation of foreign technology and services, which was introduced in the early 1970s, is one of the most restrictive among developing countries, both as the law is formulated and as it is implemented by the regulatory body. Regulation of foreign technology was initiated in 1958, when the Ministry of Finance issued Portaria No. 436, which established ceilings for royalty payments in various industrial sectors for the purpose of permissible tax deductions.[26] These ranged between 1 and 5 percent of net sales, depending on the sector. A maximum of 5 percent was defined, for example for the manufacture of oil equipment, urban railway systems, communications, transportation equipment, and heavy metallurgical products; 4 percent for food-processing, pharmaceutical, and textile industries; 3 percent for electrical equipment and home appliances; 2 percent for rubber, plastics, and soap; and 1 percent for most other products. Although these ceilings were primarily prescribed for tax deduction purposes, they became the maximum permissible government payments.[27] It is also interesting to note, that during the past twenty-five years since the introduction of this act, the maximum permissible rate of 5 percent has been applied consistently, even though other aspects of the regulatory measures have been modified considerably.

In 1963, Law 4131, which regulated foreign investments also made provision for the compulsory registration of all technology agreements between foreign and domestic companies, and remittance of technology payments was made subject to the registration of the agreement with the Central Bank. The law also authorized the Ministry of Finance to verify, whenever considered necessary, that the technology defined in the agreement had been effectively transferred. It also provided for the differential treatment of technology payments, depending on the relationship between the licensor and the licensee company. Thus, Article 14 prohibits royalty payments between parent and subsidiary companies for the use of industrial property rights, including patents and trademarks.[28] The rationale for this provision was that in a parent-subsidiary relationship, the benefits resulting from the transfer of technology to the subsidiary accrue to the parent company in the form of profits, and consequently, no separate remuneration for the use of technology is justified.[29] Article 12 of the law states the maximum permissible duration of contracts to be five years, with the possibility of extending it for a further five-year period if the necessity for extension can be demonstrated. On maximum permissible royalty payments, the law restates the relevant provisions of Portaria 435, which established the ceiling of 5 percent.

Foreign technology acquisition was also made subject to the provisions of Law 4137, which regulates competition. According to Article 2 of this law, it is considered abuse of economic power to dominate local markets or to eliminate competition totally or partially by creating difficulties to the establishment, the working, or the development of a company. On the basis of this provision, technology licensors were prohibited from imposing restrictions on the freedom of action of licensees, for example, to restrict production, marketing, and exports, or to use competitive technologies.

Until 1970, the Central Bank, in its evaluation, scrutinized the proposed technology agreement to determine whether it violated the relevant provisions of the legislation on foreign investments and competition. Most of these provisions, however, related to economic and legal issues of the technology agreement, and relatively little consideration was given to the technological aspects of such contracts. Partly because of the experience of the Central

Bank in processing technology agreements, it became increasingly evident that the acquisition of foreign technology had a broad economic and social impact and that the evaluation of such contracts required a more comprehensive approach. Consequently, on December 11, 1970, Law 5648 was promulgated, empowering the National Institute of Industrial Property (INPI) to apply the rules regulating industrial property rights, taking into account their social, economic, legal, and technical impact. The INPI was also made responsible for adopting the measures necessary for the regulation and acceleration of technology transfer and for the establishment of improved conditions for the negotiation and use of patents.

Although the mandate given to INPI was to both promote and regulate the inflow of foreign technology, its initial action was primarily regulatory. Thus, in December of 1970, it issued Law 5772, also known as the Industrial Property Code (CPI), which incorporated the provisions of Laws 4131 and 4137 relating to the acquisition of foreign technology and the relevant provisions of the Industrial Property Law. Article 29 states that remuneration should be in accordance with the legislation in force and the instructions issued by the authorities responsible for finance and exchange. The same article also prohibits the imposition of marketing and export restrictions on the licensee and limit the importation of raw materials. In a general sense, these provisions are also contained in the law on unfair competition, and the CPI only elaborated the specifically prohibited practices. Article 30 refers to the Industrial Property Law, which states that licensing agreements involving patented technology are not valid unless the patent is duly registered in Brazil. Besides restating the existing regulatory norms, the CPI also introduced several new provisions. These included the obligation of the parties to formulate all aspects of the agreement in due legal form, the prohibition of grant-back arrangements and the mandatory inclusion of a provision stating that during the period of the agreement, the licensee had the right to obtain all improvements on the licensed technology.

In 1975, the INPI issued Normative Act 015, which comprises and enunciates the rules and regulations relating to the flow of foreign technology to Brazil, and its use in the country for exports.[30] Although Normative Act 015 may not be viewed as a formal enactment by the government, it is intended as a regulatory measure to guide the parties to the contract on the policies of the INPI and the relevant laws and regulations on foreign technology acquisition. Thus, Normative Act 015 is supplemental to the Industrial Property Code (Law 5772/71), the Foreign Capital Law (Law 4131/62), and the Anti-Trust Law (Law 4137/62). It was intended, through such a comprehensive regulatory measure, to achieve both short-term and long-term objectives. It was hoped that exercising selectivity in the acquisition of foreign technology would reduce the country's dependence on foreign technology and promote the development of domestic technological capability. By reducing the costs of foreign technology acquisition, the regulations also aimed at conserving funds for the generation and development of indigenous technology and controlling foreign exchange remittances. The intention was also to enhance the country's export capability for manufactured goods based on foreign technology.

Normative Act 015 established a classification system consisting of five types of technology supply arrangements. The classification of an agreement into one of the five categories is based on the nature of the technology transferred, which can be one of the following: patent license (part 2), trademark license (part 3), industrial technology supply contract (part 4), or technical services contract (part 6). A major criterion for differentiation of the various categories is whether the subject of the agreement is proprietary technology. According to the classification of agreements, the permissible contractual provisions may vary. Thus, consistent with Article 14 of Law 4131, payments for license of patents or trademarks between parent and subsidiaries are forbidden. In the case of contracts involving nonproprietary technology, such payments may be permitted. A major provision of the act, which has created considerable controversy among licensors to Brazilian companies, is the mandatory requirement for patent license agreements to provide the licensee with all the information, technical data, formulas, specifications, and so on, related to the use of the patent and the performance of R&D on the licensed process or product. Training must also be imparted, so that after the expiration of the agreement, the licensee is able to produce independently of the licensor. Such requirements for a patent license agreement are at variance with generally accepted practices. Although patent specifications should be sufficiently complete to enable the licensee to use the patented technology, in most cases, the licensee requires supplemental information to apply the patent effectively. In other developing countries, a technical know-how agreement with additional remuneration is generally made for this purpose. According to Act 015, however, technical know-how agreements are prohibited in the case of patent license agreements, since such information is required under the licensing agreement at no extra cost for the technical know-how. It would appear from this provision that the Brazilian government considers that the transfer of ownership should be a license, rather than the right to use the patent, as it is commonly conceived of in most other countries, particularly by technology licensors. The desideratum of a licensing operation, from the viewpoint of the INPI, is that once a license contract expires, the licensee should be able to continue production and research to improve the process or product without assistance from the licensor.

In exceptional cases, the INPI has allowed technical service agreements to accompany patent agreements. Approval, however, has been subject to detailed scrutiny by the INPI, and the permissible payments for such services have differed from the generally accepted practices in other countries. According to the act, the remuneration in technical service agreements has to be based on an exact calculation of the costs, with detailed specification of the man-hours and personnel involved in the implementation of the defined task. These costs would, in most cases, be substantially less than the market value of company-specific, proprietary technology.

For the regulation of patent license agreements, the act also provides that although a pending Brazilian application for patent may be the subject of a patent license agreement, no royalties can be paid by the licensee until the patent has been approved. Although similar provisions exist in several other countries, the implications in Brazil can differ considerably. Generally, in other countries, the common practice in these cases has been to enter into a supplementary know-how agreement that provides for the licensor's remuneration until the patent is approved. Since such know-how agreements are prohibited in Brazil, however, the licensor may not be reimbursed until the patent becomes valid. Because of the relatively slow approval procedure for patent applications, this may take several years.

The act's provisions relating to confidentiality issues of the technology transferred are among the most rigorous among developing countries. Agreement provisions that require confidentiality of the transferred information after the expiration of the agreement are prohibited. This relates not only to information transferred at the time the agreement is signed, but also to all improvements transferred during the valid period of the contract. This lack of protection has raised considerable concern among licensors to Brazilian companies, and frequent objections have been made to the INPI. The INPI's views in this regard appear to be that during the last years of a contract, major improvements are rarely imparted to the licensee, especially if the improvements are not patented. In the case of breakthrough improvements by the licensor that are not patented, a new agreement might be approved if the INPI finds this justified and advantageous for the licensee. The INPI has, however, made some exceptions on the confidentiality question. In the petrochemical sector, for example, it decided that if the information were not kept confidential beyond the expiration date of the agreement, the continuous flow of information on improvements would be hindered. Consequently, in this sector, the INPI has generally approved agreements that provide for confidentiality for five years subsequent to the disclosure of the last information.

Act 015 has not modified the INPI's policies on permissible payments. Remuneration in the form of lump-sum payments is strongly discouraged and is approved only rarely. The range of royalties approved has been between 1 and 5 percent of net sales, and the ceiling of 5 percent has been maintained. In approving payments, the INPI evaluates the technology and the rights and advantages enjoyed by the licensee. Although payments between parent companies and subsidiares for the use of proprietary technology are generally prohibited, in cases where the licensor has an equity participation of less than 50 percent in the licensed enterprise, payments have been permitted. The approved payments have, however, been generally below those considered justified among unaffiliated companies. In the evaluation of payment conditions and other provisions, the initial emphasis on legal and economic considerations has increasingly been broadened by the consideration of the technology itself. In the late 1970s, besides calling on its own staff, the INPI consulted with several outside technical organizations for technical assessment of agreements. In 1980, technical advice was obtained from outside institutions for the evaluation of 536 contracts, compared to 19 contracts two years earlier.[31] Outside institutions most often contributing technical advice include the Brazilian Association of Engineering and Industrial Construction (ABEMI) and the Brazilian Association of Engineering Consultants (ABCE).

The duration of technology agreements approved by the INPI has depended on the type of contract. For patent license agreements, the duration of the agreement cannot extend beyond the validity of the patent, which, according to Brazilian patent law, is fifteen years. For trademark agreements, the duration may not exceed the duration of the technology agreement to which the trademark is related. Agreements for the supply of industrial technology are treated by the INPI as temporary, and their duration must be based on the time necessary for the licensee to absorb the specific technology. This must be justified by a detailed schedule of the time required for the absorption of technology and for relevant training programs. In the case of technical-industrial cooperation agreements, the maximum permissible duration is five years from the effective commencement of production, although it can be extended under special circumstances. For the supply of specialized technical services, the act does not define a permissible duration, and approval is based on the evaluation of the detailed specifications of the project and the time schedule.

In prohibiting the imposition of restrictive business practices, the act refers to the respective provisions of the Industrial Property Code (Law No. 5.772./71) and the antitrust law governing unfair competitive acts resulting from the abuse of economic power (Law No. 4.137/62). These acts prohibit the imposition of any limitations on the freedom of action of the licensee. Under patent license agreements, for example, the act states that provisions are prohibited if they impose limitations on production, sales, pricing, or export of the product. Export restrictions are permitted only when they are required by specific legislation of the licensor's country or by an international agreement to which Brazil is a signatory. Similarly, tie-in agreements, both for inputs and for employment of personnel, are prohibited. Clauses that prevent free use of data and information handed over during the agreement after lapse of relevant patents are also prohibited. (Some exceptions have been made in this regard, as in the petrochemical industry, which has been mentioned.) The act also places great emphasis on the liability to be borne by the licensor of the technology. Thus, contracts are prohibited if they contain provisions preventing the licensee from challenging the industrial property rights in the country claimed by the licensor. Prohibited also are specifications that exempt the licensor from liability in the event of any action brought by third parties and arising from faults or defects inherent in the content or the subject of the license to which the contract pertains.

Despite the rather rigorous formulation of technology regulation and its implementation, technology contracts entered into between foreign technology suppliers and local companies have increased significantly, from 1,117 contracts entered into in 1972 to 1,761 in 1980.[32] Agreements for specialized technical services alone numbered 2,839 during the three years 1979–81.[33] Most of these contracts related to the metallurgical and mineral sectors and were for project consulting. During the 1979–81 period, approximately one-third of the total contracts were entered into by domestically owned private companies, and about one-fourth were entered into by state-owned companies. About 18 percent of all agreements were between parent companies and their local subsidiaries, while about 10 percent were accounted for by foreign subsidiaries and unaffiliated foreign licensors. The balance related to foreign-minority joint ventures.[34]

During the 1970s, technology payments also increased, and authorized payments rose from $221 million in 1972 to $373 million in 1978.[35] Increased technology payments have coincided with the deteriorating foreign trade position of the country and its constraints in foreign exchange. It is against this background that, in January 1978, the INPI issued Normative Act 30, which imposed several restrictions on technology payments and technology transfer transactions that qualify for registration. The main target of the act was the automobile industry, which, by the late 1970s, accounted for about 40 percent of total technology payment remittances. According to the act, the INPI no longer approves technology agreements in the automobile industry. Exception can be made only in the case of specialized technical services if they are not available in Brazil. It also prohibits payments for agreements already in force if they cover the development of new models or manufacturing techniques that are undertaken abroad. Excluded from this provision are projects for the manufacture of engines and mechanical components if such capabilities are not adequately developed in Brazil. Payments are also prohibited if they result from the allocation of a proportionate share of the parent company's R&D expenditure. Furthermore, salaries and travel expenses of foreign officials cannot be charged against technology payments if the officials are at a managerial level or if their visit is not directly related to a specific and temporary service. Besides the saving in foreign exchange, the intent of Act 30 has been to make greater use of the country's indigenous technical capability, particularly its technical personnel, at various levels. In

the case of the automobile industry, it was considered that the local technological capability was sufficient for self-sustained technological development.
The measure also reflects the government's concern about continuing technological dependence and its aim to reduce this dependency and the associated
costs. This concern is also reflected in Normative Act 31, issued in May
1982, which requires compulsory prior examination of technology agreements, with only agreements relating to certain technical services exempted.
Such prior examination is aimed at improving the process of scrutiny and
expediting approval. Apart from this, it is also expected that as a result of the
advanced knowledge of negotiation before the agreement is actually executed, there will be larger scope in which to utilize local inputs.

Impact of Policies

There can be little doubt that regulatory policies relating to foreign technology have been prescribed and implemented in Brazil in much greater detail
than in other countries, especially since Normative Act 015 came into force.
This was primarily reaction against foreign technological dependence, but it
largely took the form of regulatory control that aimed, first, at reducing foreign technology costs and, second, at improving contractual conditions in
technology agreements in favor of Brazilian licensee enterprises. Since payments to foreign technology suppliers rose rapidly in the early 1970s and
were continuing to increase, they were constituting an important item of foreign exchange outflow, even though such payments were a relatively small
percentage of Brazil's export earnings. The restrictive conditions imposed on
Brazilian licensee enterprises in a large number of technology agreements
were also affecting the operations, particularly the export potential, of local
licensees adversely. The INPI regulatory measures, which have been effectively enforced, were quite comprehensive on most of the contractual provisions incorporated in different types of agreements of technology, know-
how, and technical services. At the same time, the INPI procedures have had
little impact on technological choice and on the use of technologies that may
be more suitable to Brazilian conditions.

The experience of foreign technology regulation in Brazil is of special
interest because the implementation of the INPI regulation has led to fairly
stringent terms for the acquisition of foreign technology while, at the same
time, a very liberal policy has continued to be followed toward foreign direct
investments. In most other developing countries in which foreign technology
inflow has been regulated and screened by a government agency—such as
India, Mexico, the Republic of Korea, and the Philippines—policies toward
foreign investments and technology have tended to follow a similar pattern,
with foreign investment proposals often undergoing greater scrutiny. The

opposite has been the case in Brazil. The INPI's provisions have been strictly construed and implemented, and not only have technology payments been severely restricted but a very selective approach has been taken on agreements covering only technical know-how, and these have generally been restricted to five years. In technical service agreements, very detailed information has to be furnished on the services to be provided, and payments are calculated and approved on that basis. Royalty payments have been limited to 5 percent of net sales. Restrictive conditions on Brazilian licensees have usually been prohibited, particularly when they relate to exports. In general, the measures of the INPI have been implemented in a fairly rigid manner, without the exercise of much flexibility.

The implementation of the regulatory provisions of Normative Act 015 have had considerable impact on the nature of technology transactions. In the case of MNC subsidiaries, payments for technology and know-how are no longer permissible to parent companies, and payments can be made only for specific technical services. This has undoubtedly resulted in significant foreign exchange savings without having an unduly adverse impact on the supply of technology and know-how. In view of their large investments in Brazil, parent MNCs have continued to provide this technology. The pressure on MNC subsidiaries to increase exports has also necessitated continuing technology supply by parent companies. In some cases, considerable R&D activities are also being undertaken locally by MNC subsidiaries, because of governmental pressure and because no payments for R&D can be made to parent companies. Most foreign subsidiaries are, however, mostly engaged in technological adaptation, rather than in full-scale R&D activity. Thus, although there has been a high degree of technological absorption in MNC subsidiaries in Brazil, these companies have continued to rely on the supply of basic production and design know-how by their parent corporations.

The impact of foreign technology regulation on Brazilian-owned companies has differed considerably. In the case of Brazilian private sector enterprises, the payment conditions and other contractual provisions that are approved by the INPI constitute a significant improvement in the terms of foreign technology transactions. At the same time, the INPI norms on payments and certain contractual provisions can make it difficult for such companies to acquire certain foreign technology, particularly in high-technology areas. Since these companies have to compete with Brazilian MNC subsidiaries, which have access to designs and know-how from their parent corporations, this can place them at a disadvantage. Despite the regulatory guidelines, however, the number of licensing agreements has continued to increase, indicating that local companies are able to obtain the foreign technology in several sectors within the framework of the INPI measures. Brazilian-owned enterprises have also undertaken far more R&D activities than MNC subsidiaries have, and the extent of technological adaptation and innovation has been much greater in their case.

During the past two decades, private sector companies have relied heavily on foreign sources of technology and have often entered into joint ventures with foreign licensors to secure access to technology. Similarly, in several areas, public sector companies have resorted extensively to foreign suppliers of technology. In 1980, for example, almost one-fourth of the technology agreements approved were between state-owned enterprises and foreign licensors. In the case of public sector companies, acquisition of technology through minority-owned foreign joint ventures has been a relatively recent trend, particularly prevelant in the petrochemical industry. Through the equity participation of foreign technology suppliers, public sector companies can often obtain the most recent technologies for their production activities while maintaining control over basic production sectors. Although the regulatory measures of the INPI are, in principle, applicable to licensing agreements as well, the approval procedures are largely handled by the respective government departments. State enterprises have also invested significantly in R&D activity, which, in most cases, has enabled relatively rapid absorption of foreign technology and has also led to significant technological self-sufficiency in selected production sectors.

The experience of foreign technology regulation in Brazil appears to be quite favorable from the viewpoint of domestic technological development. The regulatory measures, by their nature and application, have provided greater impetus to companies operating in Brazil to become more self-sufficient in their technological requirement and to avail themselves of local technological inputs and services to a larger extent. At the same time, since technological demand has become more complex and certain types of sophisticated foreign technology and know-how cannot be obtained within the framework of the INPI measures, the regulations may pose certain difficulties, particularly for export-oriented production, that will be of crucial importance to Brazil in the next few years. The pattern of foreign technology regulation in India and the Republic of Korea has undergone considerable modification in the direction of greater flexibility, particularly in the case of Korea. It may also be necessary for the Brazilian authorities to consider whether a greater degree of flexibility should be introduced to promote the inflow of foreign technology to Brazilian enterprises in certain selected and priority sectors, particularly those that have significant export potential. At the same time, much greater investment in R&D and the development of design and engineering capability appears to be necessary in several sectors.

The present economic conditions in Brazil pose serious problems for the country's future program of industrialization and technological development. With inflation at over 200 percent, and with a staggering external debt burden of $100 billion, the country is likely to face a period of considerable austerity and economic uncertainty. Yet the industrial and technological foundations of the economy are strong, and the increase in export earnings during

1983–84 suggests that industrial recovery and growth may be fairly rapid and self-sustained.

Notes

1. Based on national accounts in *Statistical Yearbook* (New York: United Nations, various issues).
2. For a review of foreign capital inflow to Brazil in the nineteenth century, see G.H. Smith, *Japanese Technology Transfer to Brazil* (Ann Arbor: University of Michigan Research Press, 1980).
3. The flow of foreign direct investments between 1947 and 1961 is presented in W. Baer, *Industrialization and Economic Development in Brazil* (Homewood, Ill.: Irwin, 1965), 107.
4. Central Bank of Brazil, *Boletim Mensal,* 17 October 1981.
5. Foreign penetration in the Brazilian electrical industry is discussed in R. Newfarmer, "Multinational Conglomerates and the Economics of Dependent Development—A Case Study of International Electrical Oligopoly and Brazil's Electrical Industry," Unpublished doctoral dissertation, University of Wisconsin, 1977.
6. For the role of public sector enterprises in the Brazilian economy, see W. Baer, I. Kerstenetzky, and A.V. Villela, "The Changing Role of the State in the Brazilian Economy," *World Development* 1 (November 1973).
7. J. Tavares de Araujo, E.A. Guimares, and P.S. Malan, "New Forms of Foreign Investment in Developing Countries: The Case of Brazil," Paper presented at the meeting, Changing International Investment Strategies: The "New Forms" of Investment in Developing Countries, OECD Development Centre, Paris, March 1982.
8. *Investment, Licensing and Trading—Brazil* (New York: Business International Corporation, 1985), 6.
9. Industrialization in the 1960s is discussed in R. Farley, *The Economics of Latin America* (New York: Harper & Row, 1972).
10. *Problems and Issues Concerning the Transfer, Application and Development of Technology in the Capital Goods and Industrial Machinery Sector* (Geneva: United Nations Conference on Trade and Development, 1982), 12.
11. Ibid., 13.
12. Ibid., 12.
13. Issued in September 1962, amended in August 1964 by Law 4390, and complemented by decrees: Law 1109/70, Law 1060/69, Resolution 139/70 of the Central Bank, Decree 62252/68, Decree/Law 862/69, Decree 55762/65, and Law 5331 of October 1967.
14. "Quem e Quem na Economia Brasileira," *Visão,* August 1974.
15. Resolution No. 5 of CDE of January 1972.
16. Resolution No. 76075 of July 1975.
17. Resolution No. 7 of CDE of March 1977 and Portaria No. 4/71 of CDI.
18. Coordinating Committee on EDP Activities, CDI, and Coordinating Committee for Acquisition of Locomotives Policy.
19. S.K. Fung and J.E. Cassiolato, *The International Transfer of Technology to*

Brazil through Technology Agreements (Cambridge, Mass.: MIT Center for Policy Alternatives, May 1976).

20. Central Bank of Brazil, *Boletim Mensal,* 17 October 1981.

21. Business International Corporation, *Investment, Licensing and Training,* 3.

22. Ibid., 4.

23. Calculations based on ibid.

24. In 1980, for example, of the 200 largest corporations in Brazil, 29 were foreign subsidiaries. See "Quem a Quem na Economia Brasileira." For 1981 sales, of the fifty largest companies in Latin America, eight were MNC subsidiaries operating in Brazil. See "How Latin America's Leading Firms Performed in '81," *Business Latin America* (9 March 1983).

25. Business International Corporation, *Investment, Licensing and Training,* 4.

26. Portaria No. 436 of the Ministry of Finance of December 1958, amended by Portaria No. 113 of May 1959, Portaria No. 303 of November 1959, and Portaria No. GB-314 of November 1970.

27. F.A.L. Barbosa, *Propriedade e Quasi Propriedade no Comercio de Tecnologia* (Rio de Janeiro: CNP, 1978), 125.

28. This measure was subsequently adopted by Colombia and extended to all know-how agreements. Similar provisions were also introduced in Decision 24 of the Andean Group, which provides that royalty payments shall not be permitted in such cases and that no deduction may be made on that account for tax purposes.

29. The parent-subsidiary relationship was defined as one in which the parent company owns at least 50 percent interest in the company's equity.

30. *Revista da Propriedade Industrial,* Ato Normitivo No. 015 (Rio de Janeiro: Ministerio de Industria e do Comercio, 1975).

31. *Relatorio de Actividades 1980, Plano General de Trevalho* (Rio de Janeiro: Instituto Nacional de Propriedade Industrial, 1981), 12.

32. For 1972 payments, see Fung and Cassiolato, *The International Transfer of Technology.* For 1980 payments, see INPI, *Relatorio,* 1981.

33. INPI, *Relatorio,* 1981.

34. INPI, *Relatorio de Actividades,* various issues.

35. For 1972, see Fung and Cassiolato, *The International Transfer of Technology,* 21. For 1978, see *Revista de Propriedade Industrial,* No. 428, (Rio de Janeiro: INPI, 2 January 1979).

10
India

Since India's independence in 1947, the pace of industrial growth has been fairly steady and broadly based, with government policies focusing on rapid industrialization as one of their basic objectives. Through its successive five-year plans, the government has played a critical role in channeling industrial investments in key sectors. Production targets were set for most important branches during each plan period, and these targets were periodically reviewed in the light of changes in demand and production actually achieved. Government policy was initially geared toward import substitution in most industrial sectors, mainly because of severe foreign exchange constraints faced by the country in the 1950s and 1960s. During the 1970s, however, following fairly rapid and sustained growth in the manufacturing sector, national policies placed greater emphasis on the promotion of exports and the development of export capability. The government has also given high priority to domestic technological developments in various production and service sectors, and fairly well-defined policies have been prescribed and implemented for the acquisition of foreign technology and know-how.

Although a major share of industrial production takes place through private sector companies, considerable regulatory control has been exercised on industrial investments and production. This has been achieved partly through a comprehensive industrial licensing system and partly through controls over foreign exchange and imports and regulatory measures relating to foreign investments and technology. The licensing system requires government permission to establish industrial undertakings and also prescribes the production capacity of individual enterprises.[1] In recent years, the licensing provisions have been liberalized to a considerable extent, although the liberal provisions are not applicable to foreign companies and some large industrial groups that are subject to legislation on monopolies and restrictive trade practices.[2] Controls over foreign exchange and imports have also been a feature of Indian policy over the past three decades, and although there has been some relaxation of import controls in recent years, import restrictions have been utilized as important policy instruments. Although the major objective has been to conserve foreign exchange, import controls have provided a high degree of protection to local manufacturers. They have also been used to achieve prescribed levels of domestic integration in manufacturing. Considerable regulatory control has also been applied for foreign direct investments and technology, and fairly detailed guidelines and procedures have been adopted for this purpose.

An important feature of Indian industrial policy, which has also had a strong impact on technological development, has been the establishment of state-owned enterprises in several priority sectors.[3] Three major factors have contributed to the growth of state-owned companies. First, it was the deliberate policy of the Indian government to exercise control over key sectors of the economy as an integral aspect of achieving greater self-sufficiency in these fields. Second, it was believed that the growth of essential technological and industrial capabilities would be greatly accelerated through the establishment of basic industries. Third, it was believed that unless state-owned industries were established in these fields, major production and technological gaps would continue, since private industry would not be willing to undertake industrial activities that involved large capital outlays and long gestation periods. The government's industrial policy statement of 1956 defined the role of the public and private sectors, and seventeen basic and core industries were reserved for state-owned enterprises, while twelve other industrial sectors in which such enterprises would increasingly play a role were identified.

The establishment of state-owned enterprises for the production of steel, heavy mechanical equipment, heavy electrical machinery, and drugs and pharmaceuticals, as well as for petroleum exploration and development, was a deliberate policy to ensure that state-owned, public sector enterprises should achieve a commanding lead in basic and priority sectors. Public sector enterprises were also intended to develop production capability in those priority sectors in which private investments were not adequately forthcoming. This was particularly the case for machinery manufacture, in which production capacity existed only in the lower product ranges. Thus, state-owned enterprises were set up for the manufacture of higher ranges of machinery products, such as machine tools, heavy mechanical equipment, turbines, generators, and other heavy electrical machinery. Through the industrial licensing system, it was also possible to distribute the various categories and ranges of products between state-owned enterprises and private companies. Since 1969, with the nationalization of the country's fourteen major commercial banks, the role of the state in industrialization has increased still further, since the allocation of credit power was utilized to channel investments in accordance with national priorities. In 1970, the scope of activity of public sector enterprises expanded from basic and heavy industries to the consumer goods sector. Since then, investments in the public sector have increased rapidly. In 1983, total investments in state-owned enterprises amounted to about Rs 300 billion (approximately $28 billion) in 209 public sector enterprises.[4]

Although public sector companies have played an important role in India's economy, special measures were also undertaken for the development of small-scale industries. The small-scale industries program was designed to broaden the industrial and entrepreneurial base so that, over the years, a large number of such enterprises would be established in different parts of the country. Apart from the various financial incentives and concessions that were given to such units, a large number of industrial branches were reserved for production through the small-scale sector only. Although this policy had certain adverse impact on scale economies and production costs in several fields, it did result in very rapid growth of small-scale industries, which extended to almost 40 percent of industrial production by the early 1980s.

National policies also placed considerable restrictions on some of the major Indian industrial groups, such as Birlas, Tatas, and J.K. These groups, which have often been characterized in India as "monopoly houses," are large conglomerates that have extended from traditional industries, such as textiles and jute, to various consumer and intermediate products and engineering goods. During the 1960s, the government believed that the rapid expansion of these groups, twenty of which were identified at the time, had led to undue concentration of economic power in the hands of a few families. In 1964, a comprehensive report on the industrial licensing system by a government-appointed committee highlighted the fact that some of the major Indian-owned industrial groups — particularly the Birla Group, which was the largest in the country — had used the licensing system to expand very rapidly, leading to substantial concentration of economic power in these groups.[5] These and other developments led to the enactment of the Monopolies and Restrictive Practices Act, which was aimed mostly at the large Indian-owned industrial groups and at foreign subsidiaries and affiliates. During the early 1970s, the industrial licensing regulations also restricted the growth of companies controlled by such industrial groups, and new investments and major expansions by such companies were largely limited to certain "core" and priority sectors and to export-oriented projects.

There can be little doubt that government policies have had a major impact on industrial and technological development in India. With a fairly limited industrial base in 1947, much of it controlled by MNC subsidiaries, the country has built up considerable production capacity in most industrial sectors, including capital goods manufacture, fertilizers, and chemicals. The share of mining, manufacturing, and construction in GDP rose from 14.9 percent in 1950–51 to 22.5 percent in 1978–79 and the share of services from 22.3 percent in 1950–51 to 28.5 percent in 1978–79.[6] Infrastructure facilities were expanded substantially, and electrical power generation increased from about 2,300MW in 1950 to 30,000 in 1980.[7] In 1980, 87.1

percent of the local demand for capital goods was met from local production, which, after China, was the highest among developing countries.[8]

As investments in various infrastructure and industrial sectors were channeled in accordance with planned targets, certain broad goals and priorities of the government could be met. Even when there was substantial shortfall in planned targets in certain sectors, or when resources had to be directed to more urgent needs, the overall priorities were fulfilled over a period of time.[9] The process of industrial planning in India is particularly interesting because it set investment and production targets for private industry that it sought to achieve through the industrial licensing system. The role of the private sector, both foreign and Indian-owned, was recognized as being of major significance; Indian entrepreneurial groups, in particular, displayed considerable initiative and the ability to adjust to industrial licensing and to use the system to great advantage.

Foreign Investment Policies

The basic economic philosophy of the government—to ensure national control over key sectors—was also reflected in the policies toward foreign direct investments. Ever since the country's independence, policies on the entry of foreign companies have tended to be fairly selective. As far back as 1949, Prime Minister Nehru perceived the role of foreign direct investments as supplementing domestic capital and as important to those sectors of the economy in which they resulted in the inflow of scientific and technical knowledge required for the country's industrialization.[10] Consequently, while the government has exercised a high degree of selectivity regarding the entry of foreign companies, it has recognized that certain advanced technologies can be acquired only if the technology supplier is permitted to own part of the equity of the licensee enterprise. The government has also considered that foreign equity ownership may be important in some industries to ensure the long-term commitment of the technology supplier and the rapid absorption of the technology by the domestic company. The Industrial Policy Resolution of 1956 and subsequent resolutions have identified sectors in which foreign direct investment and technology have not been considered important and thus, have been closed to foreign investors and technology suppliers as well as those in which such participation would be permitted. The list of such industries has been changed and modified over time, reflecting current priorities and the development of domestic technological capabilities.

Besides the selectivity applied at the stage of entry of foreign investments and technology, there have also been regulatory measures on the permissible equity share to be held by foreign companies. The field of manufacture and the extent of production in various fields have also been prescribed for each company through the system of industrial licensing, which was also utilized to regulate the production and expansion activities of MNCs operating in India.

Policies on foreign investments were significantly modified with the promulgation of the Foreign Exchange Regulation Act (FERA) in 1973, which provided the regulatory framework for companies in which foreign ownership exceeded 40 percent. These companies required the prior permission of the Reserve Bank of India for trading or commercial transactions, for acting as technical or management advisers, or for permitting the use of trademarks for any direct or indirect consideration. The legislation also provided that foreign companies operating in India as of January 1, 1974, could carry on their activities only after obtaining the approval of the Reserve Bank of India. Depending on the nature of the activities, the guidelines provided for three levels of permissible foreign equity: 74 percent, 51 percent, and 40 percent. Companies that were allowed to retain foreign majority holdings were primarily those that were operating in certain industrial sectors defined as core industries, those that were exporting more than 40 percent of their production, or those whose production activities involved complex and sophisticated technology. Other foreign-majority companies engaged in nonpriority fields or operating in trade, commercial, or service activities were required to reduce their foreign equity holding to 40 percent. Because of the importance of tea in India's foreign exchange earnings, an exception was made in the case of tea plantation companies, which were allowed to retain foreign equity up to 74 percent. The FERA guidelines applied to all companies with foreign holdings exceeding 40 percent. The extent of permissible foreign ownership for new foreign investments had to be reduced. The methods generally applied were the issuance of additional equity to Indian nationals when the company required capital for approved expansion or diversification, the sales of a portion of the existing foreign equity, or a combination of the two.

Except in the case of wholly export-oriented companies, new foreign investments are permitted only if they result in inflow of complex and advanced technology and know-how. Normally, such investments are permitted up to 40 percent of equity of a company, except in the core sectors or export-oriented manufacture. The share of permitted foreign-majority holdings usually depends on the nature of the advanced or high technology involved or on the extent of exports undertaken by a company.

In the years following the enactment of the FERA, the number of foreign branches gradually decreased, and by 1981 only 300 were operating.[11] In most cases, their foreign holdings were around 40 percent. By 1981, there were only 111 foreign subsidiaries (over 50 percent foreign equity share) compared with 188 in 1974.[12] Divestment of foreign holdings generally was made at the time of expansion and increase in equity capital and through the sale of shares in the market, with sales to individual shareholders being limited. This enabled parent MNCs to retain effective control over investment and production operations, despite minority holdings.

Another important trend in the 1970s was the diversification of activities by several MNC subsidiaries and affiliates. This was largely due to regulatory policies that required foreign-majority companies to undertake major new investments and expansions in the core or priority industries or in export-oriented enterprises. Some foreign-controlled companies diversified extensively into new areas. For example, India Tobacco (formerly Imperial Tobacco Company) moved into the hotel industry and gradually built up a chain of hotels in various cities; Hindustan Lever, a subsidiary of Unilever, diversified in several areas of the agro and food industries; Union Carbide expanded its production activities to new chemical products; and several MNC affiliates engaged in the manufacture of machinery and engineering goods. For example, Guest, Keen and William, Hindustan Brown Boveri, General Electric, Siemens, and others, expanded their operations to cover new and more complex products. In most of these cases, the sources of technology continued to be the parent MNC, although some affiliates also entered into licensing arrangements with other foreign companies.

The growth of joint ventures, usually with minority foreign holdings, has represented an important trend in industrial development in India, particularly since the early 1960s. Since wholly foreign-owned subsidiaries were not viewed favorably by the government, except in very special circumstances, the policy of import substitution was largely implemented through joint ventures. Even before the enactment of the FERA in 1973, government policy did not generally encourage foreign holdings above 40 percent in new companies. Consequently, a large number of joint ventures emerged in which the foreign partners had holdings of 26 and 50 percent of equity distributed to the public or held by a financing institution. The principal motivation for inviting foreign partners into such joint ventures was to obtain foreign technology and expertise, besides covering the foreign exchange costs of imported equipment through foreign capital participation. During the period 1960–69, 414 new companies were formed with foreign capital participation, mostly in the engineering goods sector. In the 1970s, the pattern remained similar, and during the 1970–79, 388 new companies were formed with foreign partners.[13]

In the early 1980s, foreign investments increased rapidly over previous levels. In 1982, for example, new foreign investments reached $66 million, which was more than the total of the previous nine years, although nearly $30 million of this amount was accounted for by the investment of Suzuki (Japan) in automobile manufacture.[14] At the end of 1982, total cumulative foreign direct investments were about Rs25 billion (approximately $2.2 billion)[15] Thus, largely as a result of the government's selective policy toward foreign direct investment inflow and the rather rigorous regulatory measures applied to such companies, the role of foreign subsidiaries has remained far more limited in India than in other developing countries with similar industrial growth. In Brazil, for example, foreign investments are more than ten times higher, and in Mexico, with a much smaller economy, they are about five times higher. Also, in India, the sectoral distribution of foreign investments has been considerably different from that of the aforementioned countries. Partly because of the major role that state-owned companies play in the manufacturing sector, and partly because of various policy measures relating to foreign investment and those designed to limit the concentration of industrial production, foreign subsidiaries have not been dominant in the most dynamic sectors of the Indian economy.

Foreign Technology Regulation

Rapid technological development has been viewed as a major policy objective since India's independence in 1947. Since the 1950s, a chain of R&D laboratories was set up to promote scientific and technological development in various fields. At the same time, the government sought to regulate the acquisition of foreign technology in order to improve the terms of technology acquisition by Indian enterprises and also to stimulate domestic technological development. Together with foreign investments, proposals for acquisition of foreign technology have also required the administrative approval of government authorities. Thus, India was the first among developing countries to control the inflow of foreign technology and has the most experience with such measures.

Although India has no specific law governing the transfer of foreign technology and services, in practice, considerable regulatory control has been exercised in this regard since the 1950s, and three main phases can be distinguished. During the first phase—up to 1968—foreign technology agreements were approved through administrative procedures based on the country's overall industrial policy and foreign exchange rules.[16] The scrutinization of such agreements during the second stage (1969–78), was according to rather detailed norms and guidelines. The guidelines prescribed three lists; one covering industries in which foreign technology would be permitted, with foreign equity up to certain limits; a second by which foreign technology would be permitted without foreign equity participation; and a third list of industries and subsectors in which no foreign technology would be allowed. Detailed economic and technological evaluation of such agreements was undertaken, particularly after 1974, when a Technical Evaluation Committee was created.[17] In the third stage, after 1978, a more flexible policy toward foreign technology was adopted by replacing the three lists with only one list of industries in which no foreign collaboration, financial or technical, was considered necessary. The new guidelines recognized that with constant technological advancements and changes, it would be necessary to update production technology. Consequently, technology imports were permitted, even in the prohibited fields, indigenous technology for these items was too closely held by local industry and was not available to other entrepreneurs on competitive terms or if updating of existing technology was essential, or when technology imports were accompanied by substantial export commitments backed by buy-back guarantees.[18] There was further streamlining and liberalization in May 1981 by delegating to the government departments concerned the powers of approval of technical collaboration agreements for items outside the banned list if total payments did not exceed Rs5 million for a period of ten years.[19]

Detailed norms and guidelines for the import of foreign technology and services in India prescribe that local companies fully explore possible alternative sources of technology, evaluating them from a techno-economic point of view, and state the reasons for preferring a particular source of technology. Agreements for the supply of technology and know-how are generally allowed for a period of five years, although a longer duration is permitted in the case of complex technologies that may take longer to absorb. Generally, renewals are not granted unless new technology or processes are transferred during the extension. In the agreements, no restrictions can be placed by the licensor on the licensee regarding procurement of capital goods, components, spare parts, or raw materials; pricing policy; selling arrangements; and the like. Export restrictions must also not be imposed on the Indian licensee without valid reason and justification, and the Indian licensee must generally be free to export to any country unless the foreign licensor has a licensing arrangement in that country. The use of foreign brand names on products for domestic sale is often not permitted, although they may be used for exported products. It is also prescribed that an Indian firm must be the main technical consultant for the execution of any industrial project. If foreign consultants are also needed, the Indian firm selected must still be the prime consultant. Technology agreements are required to provide adequately for the training of Indians in production and management. For payments, the guidelines do not favor royalty agreements, which provide only for the right to exploit a patent and do not bring continuing access to technical know-how and new R&D results. The guidelines also dicourage imports of duplicate or similar technology by requiring sublicensing clauses, particularly for less sophisticated technologies.

These guidelines stipulate certain percentages of royalty as the maximum royalty permissible in various industrial sectors. For food, drugs, or medicines, for which compulsory licensing can be imposed, the 1970 Patents Act allows a legal maximum of 4 percent of sales as royalty. Other agreements generally set a ceiling for royalties and fees that ranges up to

5 percent, depending on the product. A guaranteed minimum payment is prohibited. A royalty of up to 5 percent for five years plus lump-sum fee and payments for technical services are common for a wide range of products. If no technical assistance is involved in the manufacture of consumer goods, the royalty is usually limited to 2.5 percent. A royalty higher than 5 percent is, however, permissible for exports. Royalty and fee payments are normally lower for a firm that has a significant ownership interest in an Indian company than for companies with no domestic holdings. The royalty base is the ex-factory selling price less the value of imported components and various materials and components acquired from Indian sources.

The inflow of foreign technology to India during the past three decades reflects, on the one hand, the country's industrialization objectives and on the other hand, the prevailing guidelines at a particular period. Thus, during the Second and Third Five-Year Plans, covering the period 1956–66, there was significant inflow of foreign technology for various basic industries. This was facilitated by a rather liberal approval procedure at the time. Between 1961 and 1964 alone, 1,402 agreements were approved.[20] Since 1968, with the imposition of a wide range of restrictions on permissible agreements and the closing of several industrial sectors in which domestic technological capabilities were considered to be adequate for foreign technology, the inflow of foreign technology declined to an annual average of about 270 agreements. During the 1969–79 period, the Foreign Investment Board, the regulatory agency, approved 2,833 agreements.[21] In the early 1980s, with the greater liberalization of foreign technology inflow, the number of technology agreements entered into among domestic and foreign companies has increased rapidly, reaching 526 agreements in 1980 and 673 agreements in 1983.[22] By 1983–84, technology payments reached about $400 million, from about $150 million in 1980–81.[23]

The sectoral distribution of the 7,211 agreements that were registered by the regulatory agency up to 1984 indicates that the largest share, 41 percent of the agreements, related to the manufacture of mechanical, electrical, and transport equipment.[24] The balance covered a diversified range of technologies, including office machinery, medical appliances, industrial instruments, pharmaceuticals, textiles, pulp and paper, food processing, rubber and leather products, ceramics, and other miscellaneous branches. In the service sector, thirty-two agreements for consulting and engineering know-how were approved. This sectoral pattern of foreign technology inflow continues in the mid–1980s, with continuing emphasis on the manufacture of machinery and equipment to meet the growing internal demand.

Of the total agreements entered into during the 1970s, only about 15 percent related to companies with foreign equity participation.[25] This indicates that, since the early 1970s, the trend has increasingly been toward technology licensing without foreign equity participation, with foreign equity being permitted only in exceptional cases. This reflects partly the Indian government's policy toward foreign direct investments and partly the fact that Indian companies are increasingly in a position to obtain and absorb foreign technology without foreign equity partners. The fields in which foreign investments and technology have been obtained also indicates the growing trend toward more complex technology, particularly for machinery manufacture.

Technological Impact

The ownership structure of Indian industry has strongly influenced the nature and pattern of technological development. The impact of regulatory policies on the acquisition and absorption of foreign technology by both private and public sector companies has also been very significant. Private companies can be broadly considered under three categories: MNC subsidiaries with foreign holdings over 50 percent, joint ventures with minority foreign holdings, and technology license agreements without foreign equity participation.

In the case of majority-owned MNC subsidiaries, 188 of which were operating when the FERA was enacted in 1973, the supply of technology and know-how has generally been limited to the specific activity that the subsidiary was required to perform. In the consumer goods industries, in which several MNC subsidiaries were operating, the technology and know-how supplied by the parent company related to the production and operational requirements of the local subsidiary, but design and R&D functions were entirely dealt with by the parent MNCs. Often, MNC subsidiaries were required to contribute to centralized R&D of the parent company by way of annual payments. During the 1960s, when government regulations regarding payments to parent MNCs became more stringent, several subsidiaries entered into formal technology agreements with their parent companies. These agreements were examined and approved by the government, often after prolonged negotiations. Local operations were effectively controlled by parent MNCs, although local Indian directors and senior management personnel played important roles in several MNC subsidiaries and affiliates.

Private companies in India have tended, by and large, to be very dependent on foreign technology. This has been partly due to the extensive diversification in Indian industry during the 1960s and early 1970s, when a large number of new medium-sized companies were established, most of them based on foreign technology and with minority foreign holdings in several cases. It also has been partly the result of local consumer preferences for the foreign brand names that accompany foreign technology and know-how and partly because joint ventures with foreign partners have been popular with Indian shareholders. In most instances, however, the Indian partners in joint ventures have been active participants in these companies, and foreign minority partners generally have played a limited role in day-to-day management.

The nature of technology supply arrangements of state-owned enterprises has tended to be different, and this factors has had considerable impact on technological absorption and development in the fields in which such enterprises have been set up. First, the sources of technology became much more diversified for state-owned enterprises. While private industry entered into technology agreements and joint ventures mainly with MNCs from Western industrialized economies, several Indian public sector enterprises depended initially on technology and know-how from the Soviet Union and from Eastern European countries. Thus, technology and know-how, together with supply of equipment and parts, was obtained from the Soviet Union for steel production in Bhilai and Bokaro; for heavy mechanical equipment production in the Heavy Engineering Corporation at Ranchi; for heavy electrical equipment in the BHEL plant in Hardwar; for oil-drilling technology through the Oil and Natural Gas Commision; and for certain pharmaceutical products, precision instruments, and several other machinery products. Similarly, technology and equipment for heavy machine tools, heavy castings and forgings, power boilers, and tractors were obtained from Czechoslovakia. At the same time, several state-owned companies also acquired technology on commercial terms from Western countries, including technology for machine tools of various types and ranges, pumps and compressors, heavy plant vessels, and other capital goods items. Over the years, however, the sources of foreign technology of several of these enterprises have become much more diversified and have included technology licensors from different countries for various products and processes.[26]

In addition, technology supply to these enterprises was governed primarily by contractual arrangements, since no foreign equity was permitted in these cases. Consequently, a considerable body of experience and knowledge was developed in these enterprises in the intricacies of technology licensing and in absorption and adaptation. Since technology agreements were for a specified period of time, recipient enterprises were motivated to take necessary measures to absorb the technology as rapidly as possible. This posed major difficulties in some of the machinery manufacturing plants, and the gestation period for acquiring necessary skills extended over several years in some enterprises, such as the Heavy Engineering Corporation and the Mining and Allied Machinery Corporation. Furthermore, in these enterprises and state-owned consulting engineering bodies, considerable capability was developed in design and engineering skills. Consulting organizations were set up, for example, by the Fertiliser Corporation of India for petrochemicals, by Hindustan Steel for steel plants, and by the National Industrial Development Corporation for several industrial sectors. Public sector enterprises were also established to undertake construction and turnkey projects in other countries. By 1982–83, revenues from such projects increased to Rs518 million from Rs10 million in 1974–75.[27]

Having grown rapidly, public sector manufacturing enterprises in India have often faced strong criticism because of unduly large investments and bad planning and projections in some cases and because of shortcomings in management and operations. Several of these undertakings have suffered heavy financial losses for several years of their initial operations. At the same time, however, they have gradually built up considerable technological capability and have achieved a large degree of self-reliance in complex fields of manufacture. By the latter part of the 1970s and particularly in the early 1980s, however, public sector enterprises as a whole began to generate substantial profits, although several of these enterprises, including the Steel Authority of India, have continued to operate at a loss.[28]

The wide range of government policies affecting foreign investments and technology in India have been geared primarily toward achieving greater indigenous technological development. This has been achieved to a large extent, particularly in the manufacture of machinery, equipment, and related components. It has also been achieved in several other production sectors considered basic for the Indian economy, such as electrical power generation, transportation, steel, aluminum, cement, pulp and paper, petroleum, chemicals and fertilizers, and the like, besides technological services, including basic and detailed plant and process engineering. In all these fields, considerable production capacity has been built up and the rate of domestic integration has been very high, with technological capability extending to the production of most complex parts and components. Most of the country's demand for heavy machinery and transport and electrical equipment is currently met by domestic production, either in the public or the private sector. The level of technological absorption and development is illustrated by the rapid growth of export capability in machinery and equipment, in engineering goods, and in consumer products, such as textiles, shoes, and the like. By 1979–80, exports of machinery and equipment reached Rs25 billion, including a fairly broad range of machinery products.[29] In the early 1980s, capital goods accounted for 38 percent of the country's exports, compared with 12 percent in the mid-1950s.[30]

The development of technological capability and the high level of domestic integration for most products have brought about a great degree of technological self-reliance. Most of the industrial technology was initially acquired from foreign sources. Over the years, however, as the durations of technology contracts and the validity of related patents have expired, Indian enterprises have been able to continue production and have often made significant adaptations and changes to suit local conditions. In several cases, new product names have been introduced, as in the case of Tata trucks (formerly Mercedes Benz) and Bajaj scooters (formerly Vespa), which have since developed significant export markets. Exports of machinery through state-owned enterprises such as Bharat Heavy Electricals, Hindustan Machine Tools, and a large number of private-sector companies have been facilitated through export promotion measures and government incentives. The rapid growth of Indian consulting engineering capability has been combined with local machinery manufacture to export complete industrial plants for cement, sugar, textiles, and other industries, along with integrated steel plants and power generation projects. In a number of fields, Indian industry is increasingly in a position to compete in international markets.

At the same time, the fairly detailed planning and extensive regulatory control in India have also posed several problems for and constraints on technological development and efficiency. The system of industrial licensing has curbed domestic competition and has resulted in monopolies and oligopolistic markets in several industrial sectors. This has been particularly pronounced in state-owned enterprises, which face little competition from either internal or external sources. The insistence on high levels of domestic integration has led to high-cost manufacture of several components and intermediate products, often because of an inefficient scale of operation but also because of lack of competition. The degree of protection provided by strict import controls before 1980, when there was greater liberalization, also gave little or no impetus to local manufacturers to improve their efficiency and to reduce costs.[31] While the reservation of a large number of industrial branches for production only in the small-scale sector has accelerated the growth of these units, it has also resulted in high-cost production for several products because scales of manufacture are inadequate.

The impact of the regulatory measures on foreign technology has primarily been to improve the terms and conditions of technology agreements. The guidelines issued for this purpose are rather detailed, and foreign technology suppliers, by and large, have to accept fairly standardized contractual provisions relating to duration, royalty computation, restrictive areas, patents and trademarks, training, sublicensing, governing law, and dispute settlement. Often, negotiations are largely confined to payment conditions, including lump-sum payments, sales rights, and performance requirements, particularly in the case of MNC affiliates. Greater flexibility in the application of the guidelines during the 1980s has, however, resulted in a significant increase in technology agreements, and this trend is likely to continue with an increased demand for more complex technologies by Indian industrial enterprises. This may be particularly important for updating and improving the technological levels of products, designs, and processes. The regulatory system, combined with industrial licensing, has often tended to freeze the level of industrial technology usage at the stage at which the technology was initially acquired, with only marginal improvements. In a period of rapid innovation in global technological development, it may be necessary for Indian enterprises to acquire the latest technological innovations and improvements through licensing, to develop them internally at the institutional or enterprise level, or to use a combination of the two approaches. This may require much greater initiative on the part of Indian companies and much more flexibility by the regulatory authorities. In certain fields, the technological lag is already large, particularly in the field of electronics and semiconductors, for which the country has relied largely on locally developed technology. As a result, there has been an adverse impact on production and technological developments in electronics equipment and products and on electronics applications in various other branches, especially capital goods manufacture, where, with its large pool of cheap skilled and semiskilled labor, India could have built up major export capability.

The limitations imposed on foreign investments in India have undoubtedly enabled state-owned companies and locally owned private industry to expand rapidly. In this respect, the Indian government's policy is comparable to that of Japan in the 1960s and that of the Republic of Korea in the 1980s. A conscious effort was made to ensure that ownership of industry, particularly of new industrial companies, was held by local groups and shareholders as far as possible. As for existing foreign subsidiaries and affiliates, the guidelines for gradual divestment have enabled most of these affiliates to divest only at the time of substantial expansion, when additional equity capital was required, and, in most cases, without significantly effecting control over the local company.[32]

During the past three decades, India's industry has largely become diversified, and technological skills and capability have increased significantly in most industrial sectors. A rather strong industrial base has been built up in the country, but it may now be necessary to achieve accelerated technological development if Indian enterprises are not to lag behind the international technological standard. It may be necessary for state-owned enterprises, which are operating mostly in high-technology areas, to adopt a more flexible attitude toward foreign capital participation in joint ventures in new fields, such as genetic engineering and materials technology, and in various applications of microprocessors. It would also be necessary for such enterprises to acquire the latest techniques and processes in order to compete in export markets more effectively. Similarly, private sector companies may also need to exercise greater dynamism and initiative through the acquisition of new technologies and a greater enterprise-level R&D. This will become all the more necessary as India liberalizes its import policies and Indian companies have to face greater foreign competition. Greater inflow of foreign technology may also be necessary at higher levels of complexity and sophistication, and this may require much greater flexibility on the part of regulatory agencies, especially in payment conditions and performance requirements. Although the requirements of the internal market can perhaps be met adequately by existing regulatory guidelines and procedures, greater flexibility and dynamism may be necessary if Indian enterprises are to compete effectively in global markets.

Notes

1. The industrial licensing system was initially established by the Industries (Development and Regulation) Act in 1951. For details, see *First Five-Year Plan* (New Dehli: Government of India, Planning Commission, 1953).

2. Licenses are not required for industrial production involving capital investments of Rs300 or those requiring foreign exchange inputs up to 15 percent of annual turnover or Rs5 million, whichever is less.

3. This policy was formulated in the Industrial Policy Resolution, 6 April 1948.

4. *Investment, Licensing, and Trading—India* (New York: Business International Corporation, July 1984), 6.

5. *Report of the Licensing Inquiry Committee on Industrial Development* (New Dehli: Government of India, 1979).

6. *Sixth Five-Year Plan* (New Dehli: Government of India, Planning Commission, 1981).

7. Ibid.

8. *Problems and Issues Concerning the Transfer, Application and Development of Technology in the Capital Goods and Industrial Machinery Sector* (Geneva: United Nations Conference on Trade and Development, May 1982), table 1.3.

9. A detailed analysis of the targets and performances of successive Five-Year Plans until 1977 is presented in F.R. Frankel, *India's Political Economy, 1947–1977: The Gradual Revolution* (Princeton, N.J.: Princeton University Press, 1978).

10. J. Nehru, Statement to the Indian Constituent Assembly, 6 April 1949.

11. Business International Corporation, *Investment, Licensing and Trading,* 11.

12. Ibid.

13. *Foreign Investment Policy in India* (New Dehli: Government of India, Indian Investment Centre, 1980), 6.

14. Information provided by the Government of India, Ministry of Industry, 1983.

15. Business International Corporation, *Investment, Licensing and Trading,* 4.

16. During this period, agreements were reviewed by the Foreign Agreements Committee.

17. For details of the guidelines, see *Foreign Investment and Collaborations: Guidelines* (New Dehli: Government of India, Indian Investment Centre, 1968).

18. A detailed description of these measures is presented in *Selected Legislation, Policies and Practices on the Transfer of Technology* (Geneva: United Nations Industrial Development Organization, 1979).

19. Press Announcement No. 9 (19)/80-FC(1), issued by the Ministry of Industry, Government of India, 25 May 1981.

20. *Foreign Collaboration in India,* Second Survey Report (Bombay: Reserve Bank of India, 1974).

21. *Foreign Collaboration in India* (New Dehli: Government of India, Indian Investment Centre, March 1981), 17, table 2.

22. Business International Corporation, *Investment, Licensing and Training,* 4.

23. S.K. Palhan, *Technology Policy and India's Experience in Technology*

Transfer (New Dehli: Government of India, Ministry of Industry, October 1985), annex, fig. 7

24. Ibid., annex, fig. 5.

25. Indian Investment Centre, *Foreign Investment,* 17, table 2.

26. This process of gradual diversification of foreign technology sources and product lines in the case of Hindustan Machine Tools is detailed in R.S. Mascarenhas, *Technology Transfer and Development: India's Hindustan Machine Tool Company* (Boulder, Colo.: Westview Press, 1982).

27. Indian Investment Centre, *Monthly Newsletter* 20(25 December, 1980): 90.

28. In 1982–83, for example, the net profit of all public sector enterprises amounted to Rs6.18 billion. See Business International Corporation, *Investment, Licensing and Training,* 6.

29. *Monthly Statistics of the Foreign Trade of India* (November 1980): 8, 58.

30. Ibid., various issues.

31. The impact of government policies during the 1960s on the design deficiencies of Indian companies in the engineering goods sector—including the manufacture of electric motors and transformers, motor vehicles, machine tools, and cotton textile machinery—is discused in H. Frankena, "The Industrial and Trade Control Regime and Product Designs in India," *Economic Development and Cultural Change* 22(January 1974): 249–65.

32. The much-publicized cases of IBM and Coca-Cola, which withdrew from operation in India during the 1970s, appear to have been based largely on unsatisfactory negotiating positions, rather than on fundamental policy disagreements.

11
Republic of Korea

A country that has experienced fairly spectacular industrial and technological growth during the last two decades is the Republic of Korea. Following the ravages and economic disruption of the Korean War, industrial development and the growth of technological capability in several production sectors have been quite rapid and dynamic since the mid-1960s. There was a period of economic and political upheaval in 1979–80 and recessionary trends during 1982–83, but the South Korean economy has, on the whole, presented an impressive record of achievement, in terms of both a high rate of industrial growth and the development of significant export capability for a wide and diversified range of manufactured goods and technical services.

In 1955, following the partition of the country and the Korean War, manufacturing accounted for only 8 percent of the GNP and exports for about 1.4 percent.[1] At that time, the government adopted import-substitution policies, especially in the nondurable consumer goods sector. This also contributed to the rapid development of several supporting industries and the manufacture of engineering goods through small and medium-sized companies in the ancillary and feeder industries. Because of the relatively small size of the local market and the country's poor natural resource endowments, national economic and industrial policies were increasingly geared, even as early as the early 1960s, toward export-oriented industrialization rather than a broad-based import-substitution strategy. Since the mid-1960s, several policy measures have been introduced that have reflected this objective and that have been principally designed to increase exports of manufactured products.

The pace of industrialization accelerated rapidly, and during the 1970–78 period, production of manufactured goods increased by 17.5 percent annually.[2] Priority was given to shipbuilding and to the consumer goods sector during the 1960s, while during the Third and Fourth Plan periods in the 1970s, machinery manufacture and the chemical and petrochemical industries were given much greater emphasis. During the 1970s, production of capital goods increased fifteen-fold, and Korea has become one of the leading capital goods producers in developing countries.[3] By the late 1970s, 52 percent of the country's rapidly increasing demand for machinery and equipment was provided by local production.[4]

The share of manufactured exports in the country's total exports increased rapidly, from 14 percent in 1960 to 82 percent by the mid–1970s.[5] Products initially exported from Korea were mainly light industrial products such as textiles, garments, and wood products. Korean exports, however, have increasingly diversified, and during the 1970s, the country became an important exporter of various engineering goods, such as electrical appliances and machinery and various metal products. By the early 1980s, industrial growth had reached a high level of diversification; the advanced level of technological capability and absorption has been indicated by the rapid expansion of the exports of manufactured goods, which rose from $33 million in 1960 to $19 billion in 1980.[6]

Foreign Investment Policies

National policies and a wide range of governmental measures have played critical roles in the rapid industrial and technological development of Korea. During the 1960s, when major emphasis was being given to the flow of foreign capital and technology, the purpose of the Capital Inducement Act (Law No. 1802) was "to effectively induce and protect foreign capital conducive to the self-sustainment of the national economy and its sound development and to the improvement of the balance of payments, and to properly utilize and manage the foreign capital thus introduced.[7] Besides investments, loans, capital goods, raw materials, and intermediate goods, the act also considers that the transfer of foreign technology constitutes foreign capital and is thus subject to its rules.

To assess the impact of the Capital Inducement Act, several factors have to be considered; they include the implementation of this legislation in the context of the rapid growth of local industrial groups and the domestic entrepreneurial and technological capability. Thus, as the name of the law implied, its provisions mainly covered various incentives for foreign capital, although the flow of foreign investments was not very large until recently. At the same time, faced with shortage of local capital, the country has maintained a program of rapid industrialization that has relied heavily on foreign capital for financing investments. Most of the foreign capital, however, until the early 1970s, came in the form of commercial loans and supplier credits. Until the late 1960s, for example, the total stock of foreign direct investment in the country was below $100 million, at current prices, which accounted for less than 4 percent of the total foreign capital inflow.[8] A high degree of selectivity was also exercised on the entry of foreign companies; this was partly because of the relatively weak local industrial base during the 1960s and the fear of foreign domination in a country that emerged from colonial status after World War II and was again devastated by the Korean War in the 1950s. Consequently, during the 1960s, the major channel of technology acquisition was through turnkey arrangements, which were also usually associated with foreign supplier loans and credits. Most of the basic industries that were established in the 1960s—such as oil refining, and production of cement, fertilizers, and petrochemicals, together with infrastructure projects for power generation and transportation—were established on such a basis. Turnkey agreements were, however, also often used for plant construction for light industrial projects, particularly those that manufactured mainly for export markets. These agreements generally provided for short-term specialized services by foreign engineering or consulting companies.[9]

Foreign direct investments were subject not only to the Capital Inducement Act but also to the guidelines and case-by-case evaluation and approval of the Economic Board. Until 1981, in accordance with these guidelines, foreign investments were permitted in sectors with high capital intensity and in those that utilize sophisticated technologies or manufacture for export. Although the Foreign Capital Inducement Act does not contain restrictions regarding permissible ownership by foreign investors, the Economic Planning Board, in approving investment proposals, generally discouraged the formation of wholly foreign-owned subsidiaries, instead favoring joint ventures with shares exceeding 50 percent of equity owned by Korean nationals. Until July 1981, even in exceptional cases in which foreign investments were considered critical, the share by Korean nationals was required to reach 50 percent within five years of the company's operations. The Economic Planning Board and the Foreign Capital Inducement Deliberation Committee, however, had the authority to make exceptions to this regualtion. Thus, wholly owned subsidiaries were permitted to operate in entirely export-oriented projects if they did not compete with domestic enterprises. This was considered unavoidable in view of the strong competition from other East Asian nations to attract major U.S. and Western European MNCs, particularly for wholly export-oriented projects in the electronic fields.

Besides regulating the field of operations and the ownership structure of foreign companies through the guidelines of the Economic Planning Board, the Korean authorities have also often prescribed fairly well-defined performance criteria for foreign investors in joint ventures with local companies. They generally cover a wide range of obligations of the foreign partners, with special emphasis on their technological contribution.[10] The conditions required may provide that the foreign partner disclose its designs and know-how to its Korean employees; that Korean engineers be trained in the use of the foreign partner's latest technology, including process design, detailed

engineering, operation, and maintenance; and that Korean engineers participate in all aspects of production and design work and replace foreign employees as soon as possible. In most cases, it is also expected that the foreign partner will furnish information on technological improvements and that the
enterprise will complain to the government if it believes that the foreign partner is not achieving rapid or adequate transfer of technology. In several cases,
the extent to which production will be exported has also been stipulated.

In the late 1970s, starting from a relatively low base, the inflow of foreign direct investments in South Korea accelerated considerably. By 1983,
foreign investments in the manufacturing industry amounted to $1.12 billion
in 794 projects.[11] The sectoral distribution of foreign direct investments
largely followed the priorities laid down in the successive five-year development plans. Since the mid-1970s, these priorities have included development
of the chemical and machinery industries, export-oriented manufacture, and
most of the foreign direct investments were undertaken in these sectors.
Thus, during 1962–83, over one-third of the foreign investments related to
the manufacture of chemicals and about one-fifth to the production of electrical and electronics products, with the machine-building sector next in rank.[12]

Because of government selectivity in approving foreign direct investments, the South Korean authorities succeeded not only in channeling such
investments into priority sectors but also in ensuring effective participation
by domestic companies in local MNC operations. In 1980, over 70 percent of
the foreign investments were on a joint-venture basis, and only 125 projects
were wholly owned by foreign investors, a large share of them relating to
export-oriented production.[13] Foreign subsidiaries have, in fact, played an
important role in the development of export capability in high-technology
products. In 1980, for example, exports of electronics products and components by foreign subsidiaries exceeded $1 billion and accounted for over half
of the country's exports in this industry.[14]

In 1981 (following the liberalization of technology regulation measures),
the Economic Planning Board adopted measures to promote the flow of foreign direct investments into selected priority sectors. An important objective
of these measures was to accelerate the inflow of advanced technologies that,
in certain sectors, would be difficult to obtain without substantial equity participation by their owners. In the current Fifth Plan, several industrial subsectors that have been accorded priority are based on advanced and complex
technologies, the proprietary rights of which are concentrated in a few foreign companies that enjoy a strong bargaining position in commercializing
their technology. Also, in a number of these sectors, it was recognized that
technology may be available only to foreign-controlled affiliates, not to independent domestic licensees. In some sectors, foreign participation was also
considered necessary to ensure the commitment of technology licensors to
transfer their technology effectively and to allow its absorption by local licen-

see enterprises within reasonable periods. It was also believed that foreign holdings would create more favorable conditions for obtaining technological improvements and innovations, which were rapidly taking place in several sectors, by licensee enterprises. With rapid increase in demand for foreign technology and with market imperfections arising out of the oligopolistic nature of the global technology market, particularly for complex and high technologies, major policy changes were considered necessary.

The industrial fields in which foreign investments are presently being encouraged are those that primarily use advanced technologies (such as the machinery and metal-processing industries) and operations that are undertaken entirely for exports and do not compete with existing local companies. Foreign investment inflow has also been encouraged by elimination of the minimum investment requirement of $200,000 for a project, and regulations for capital repatriation have also been eased. Various incentives and tax concessions have also been provided to foreign investors in priority sectors. Therefore, full tax exemptions may be granted to high-technology industries such as electronics, machinery, and metallurgy, while lesser incentives have been provided for lower priority sectors.

In 1982, revised guidelines were prescribed for foreign investments, and up to 100 percent foreign holdings were permitted in sixty-five fields, including high-technology industries and projects requiring large capital outlay. A limit of 50 percent foreign holding was prescribed for 456 other fields covering a wide area of manufacture. In subsequent years, partly because of the rather modest increase in foreign investment inflows in the manufacturing sectors, the government has continued to liberalize its policies toward such investments. In line with this objective, in 1984, the Foreign Capital Inducement Act was modified; it now opens all sectors to foreign investors except those identified on a "negative list." However, in the mid–1980s, the "negative list" covers about half of all Korean industries.[15] Also, there seems to be no change in the government's policy toward the ownership pattern of foreign subsidiaries. It continues to encourage formation of joint ventures with domestic majority holdings, and in the approval of foreign investment proposals, protection of the market position of domestically owned companies remains a critical consideration.

Foreign Technology Regulation

In addition to the regulation of foreign direct investments, the Korean authorities have also regulated the acquisition of foreign technology and reviewed foreign technology agreements. Policies that have been adopted for this purpose and those that aim at promoting domestic technological development are incorporated in several legislative enactments and administrative measures.[16] To a considerable extent, they have been related to policies on foreign direct investment, and one of the major objectives of the Foreign Capital Inducement Law was to promote greater inflow of necessary foreign technology. The various criteria and priorities for the acquisition of foreign technology have been prescribed in guidelines, which have been modified from time to time, and in the administrative procedures for approval of foreign technology agreements. Technology Development Promotion Law, which provided for various incentives and fiscal and other concessions, was enacted in 1967 and amended in 1972 for the promotion of indigenous technology and adaptation of foreign technology and innovations. A Technology Transfer Centre was established to assist in the examination and review of foreign technology agreements and to provide technological information to local industry. The Centre has operated within the framework of fairly detailed guidelines governing various contractual conditions that were approved by the Economic Planning Board.

By the mid-1970s, the policy toward foreign technology was primarily aimed at improving the bargaining position of local companies in joint ventures and licensing agreements. Consequently, policy guidelines were adopted that were fairly similar to those established in several Latin American countries and in India. For the evaluation and review of technology agreements, specific criteria were prescribed to examine the suitability and terms of acquisition of the foreign technology proposed. These covered legal, economic, and technical aspects of the proposed agreements, together with the necessity for the particular technology, the nature of the technology, costs, contract duration, and impact on indigenous technological development and on existing enterprises. Also, an assessment was made of the contribution of a particular technology to the country's exports and of the advantage of importing the technology as compared to developing it domestically. Guidelines also specified restrictive business clauses that are generally prohibited in agreements and certain provisions that must be incorporated in all agreements. Thus, agreements could be rejected when the purpose of the contract was primarily to acquire raw materials, intermediate goods, or brand names, or if major restrictions had been imposed on the export of goods manufactured with the imported technology. The technology licensor was also required to guarantee the quality of the products manufactured with the licensed technology and to transfer all improvements in the licensed technology during the period of agreement. The guidelines also stipulate the responsibility of the licensor for the licensed technology, with the Korean licensee having the right to sue the licensor for damages, financial or legal, that might result from the application of the licensed technology, including the infringement of patents of third parties. The guidelines did not provide for a maximum duration of technology agreements. Until 1978, however, agreements exceeding three years were generally discouraged, and agreements up to six years' validity were approved only in exceptional cases. The permissible maximum royalties were generally set at 10 percent of net sales of the product or products manufactured with the imported technology.

Until the late 1970s, the evaluation and approval or rejection of foreign technology agreements was done in consultation with the other government agencies concerned. Thus, the Ministry of Commerce and Industry examined the general features of the proposal and the contractual conditions and, in consultation with the Ministry of Science and Technology and other relevant agencies, provided an overall evaluation of the proposal to the Economic Planning Board. For contracts of a duration in excess of three years or payments above 3 percent royalty, the Economic Planning Board could obtain the approval of the Foreign Capital Inducement Deliberation Committee, which is a cabinet-level committee including several ministries and financial institutions. Frequently, the process of evaluating the appropriateness of the proposed technology was quite long and was complicated by differences between various ministries and other government agencies involved in the technical and economic evaluation of such proposals.

In the 1960s, the number of foreign technology agreements was rather limited, and during 1962–72, only about 320 agreements were made, with payments during this period of about $10 million.[17] With the development of the chemical and machinery industries during the Third and Fourth Plans in the 1970s, however, local companies turned increasingly to foreign technology suppliers in these sectors, and there was considerable growth in the number of technology agreements during the 1970s. In 1978 alone, 297 agreements were approved and payments rose rapidly, from $11.5 million in 1973 to $85 million in 1978.[18] The inflow of foreign technology has tended to follow the sectoral priorities and targets of the various plan periods. From 1962–77, out of 842 agreements covering industrial technology, 255 dealt with production of machinery, 175 related to electrical equipment and electronics items, and 166 covered petroleum and chemical products.[19] In terms of origin of technology, there has been a heavy concentration on Japanese technology suppliers. Until the late 1970s, more than 70 percent of the agreements were with Japanese companies.[20] The geographic proximity of Japan and past political and socioeconomic ties have played an important role in the heavy dependence on Japanese technology. Japanese companies also availed themselves of the relatively cheap labor in Korea and supplied technology to Korean manufacturers for the production of certain labor-intensive products, most often parts and components for export to Japan.[21]

Liberalization of Foreign Technology Acquisition

In the Fourth Development Plan, covering the period 1976–81, the government again gave priority to the development of heavy industries, particularly machine building and chemicals, which were also designed as priority sectors

during the preceding plan. With the progressive inclusion of more sophisticated product lines for local manufacture, which needed to meet the standards of international export markets in terms of quality and price, there was
much greater demand for a wide range of foreign technologies. The various
government agencies dealing with technological development and planning
concluded that the prevailing regulation on the acquisition of foreign technology would hinder the rapid acquisition of modern, sophisticated technologies
required by Korean industry. Since the prevalent guidelines and evaluation
procedures of the Economic Planning Board generally provided for a duration of three years and royalties averaging only 3 percent, it was considered
that such a limited period would not be sufficient to fully absorb more complex technologies and that the restriction on royalties would be a disincentive
to licensors of sophisticated techniques and processes. This would be particularly applicable to the latest advanced technologies that have higher market
prices than more standardized processes.

Experience with foreign technology licensing in several subsectors of
industry indicated that within the existing permissible terms and conditions,
the foreign technology that had been acquired often tended to be outdated in
terms of international standards and covered only a part of the required
know-how for a specific product. This situation not only extended the dependence of domestic enterprises on foreign technology sources but also required
high maintenance imports for parts and components for which the technology had not been transferred. Also, the experience of the Machinery Promotion Law of 1967 showed that, in many branches, the existing regulatory policies toward foreign technology may have hindered the inflow of required
production know-how. Trends in the electronics industry for example,
demonstrated these concerns. In the mid-1970s, this industry alone
accounted for 20 percent of all technology agreements, and practically all
Korean manufacturers in this sector were manufacturing under foreign licensing agreements—particularly with Japanese companies, which accounted for
84 percent of the agreements in this sector.[22] Most of these agreements
related to the manufacture of consumer electronics rather than to industrial
applications. An important provision in several of the contracts was the purchase of parts and components from the Japanese licensor firms. Because of
the high import content in these cases, the acquisition of foreign technology
often proved to be very limited in scope and did not cover the transfer of
know-how for local manufacture of high-value components and parts. The
technologies required in several fields were also often found to be behind the
latest technological developments in these branches of industry. Some of this
was attributed to the inadequate knowledge and capability of Korean licensees to assess and evaluate foreign technology. In several sectors other than
electronics, it became evident that foreign technology was often being supplied only to a limited extent. In the case of foreign subsidiaries and affiliates,

technology transfer was often partial and related primarily to the labor-intensive elements of the final products, while most high-value inputs were imported from parent companies. Often, the technology supplied to Korean enterprises related only to a relatively small, specialized part of the production process. It was estimated, in the 1970s, that the domestic value-added was generally between 15 percent and 20 percent of the value of the final products and, in the case of electronics components, was often as low as 13 percent.[23]

There was also some concern about the relatively slow approval system for foreign technology agreements. While the final decision-making authority rested with the Economic Planning Board, several other institutions and committees were involved in the evaluation and assessment of the proposed technology. Since the approval procedure involved several stages of processing by various bodies, this had not only resulted in delays in processing agreements but it had also led to disagreements among the various institutions, which further slowed the approval procedure. These delays and disagreements hindered domestic companies from acquiring needed technology rapidly and also often acted as a deterrent to the foreign technology licensors, which had to go through a lengthy approval procedure.

A major situation leading to the significant relaxation of regulatory measures, however, was the fast-expanding role of domestically owned enterprises and industrial groups, particularly in the machinery and engineering goods industries. During the 1960s, when technology regulations were initially introduced, these measures significantly improved the bargaining position of local enterprises and industrial groups with foreign technology licensors. By the late 1970s, however, the activities of these companies had expanded considerably and covered a broad range of operations, particularly in advanced sectors of industry, such as shipbuilding and the manufacture of transport equipment and various other engineering products. Since most of these sectors were among the priority industries, these companies also received various incentives from the government, including loans at subsidized rates, protection from competing imports, and major fiscal concessions. With the rapid growth and diversification of these large domestically owned companies, there was also a significant change in the pattern of foreign technology acquisition during the 1970s, and there was a substantial increase in both technology licensing without foreign equity participation and the establishment of joint ventures with minority foreign holdings. This was particularly marked in the machine-building industry, which made major progress during the 1975–80 period. A number of Korean companies specialized in particular branches of manufacture. For example, Daewoo Heavy Industries became the major producers of mining and construction equipment, besides their extensive interests in light engineering goods and in foreign construction activities. The Hyundai Group also undertook several foreign construction projects, while, for the domestic market, they became the major producers of transport and specialized plant equipment. Recently, the Hyundai Group has entered the electronics field and is likely to emerge as a major producer of microelectronics products. The Korean Shipbuilding and Engineering Group is not only a major shipbuilding company; it also manufactures a wide range of heavy machinery. Samsung Heavy Industries is the largest producer of heavy chemical equipment, and the Samsung Group is the second largest exporter in the country after Daewoo. Samsung Electronics is among the major producers of electronics and electrical products, together with Gold Star, which has also undertaken manufacture of color television sets in the United States.

The twenty major industrial groups in the country control a substantial share of industrial production and foreign trade. Commercial banks, which are state-owned, have been supportive of domestic industrial groups and have enabled bank finance to be channeled to production sectors that have been identified by the government as priority industries. Consequently, these companies have played a major role in implementing the industrial development plans of the government and in meeting established sectoral production targets. Their large size, their access to capital at subsidized rates, and their growing technological capability allowed these companies to acquire and absorb a wide range of foreign technologies. By the late 1970s, these groups and conglomerates had also gained considerable experience and knowledge in foreign licensing and were able to negotiate suitable contractual terms without relying heavily on support provided by regulatory norms and measures.

It is against this background and the desire of the government to facilitate the rapid development of machine-building capabilities and the buildup of other high-technology industries during the Fifth Plan (covering up to 1986) that the government made major revisions in its policies on foreign technology and adopted a series of measures that signficantly liberalized the acquisition of foreign technology and know-how. This was of particular importance in those sectors that were planned to expand rapidly into export markets and were required to undertake manufacture based on the latest technological developments. The new policies were introduced in 1978, but their scope and coverage expanded considerably in 1979. Within the framework of these measures, the government approval system for technology agreements was greatly simplified, and larger latitude was given to the parties in defining the terms and conditions of the contract. In 1979, in order to streamline the approval system, which had caused considerable administrative delays in processing agreements, an automatic approval system was introduced. According to the guidelines issued by the Economic Planning Board in 1978, automatic approval meant that technology agreements would be evaluated, approved, and registered by the ministry dealing with the usage of the proposed technology, making the approval and registration of most technology agreements a one-step process. It became the responsibility of the respective ministries and departments to ensure that the proposed technology was not outdated, had not been reserved for domestic technological development, and was not already available in the country, and that the agreement did not contain restrictive provisions prohibited by the guidelines. This decentralization of decision making replaced the previous system, which had centralized the authority for approval with the Economic Planning Board.

In 1979, the first stage of the automatic approval system was implemented for agreements in heavy industries (except atomic power, computers, and defense) and for contracts with a duration of less than three years and initial payments of less than $30,000 and running royalties of less than 3 percent. The same procedure was also applicable to agreements involving the payment of fixed sums below $100,000. In 1980, the application of the automatic approval system was further broadened. The only agreements that were not under the automatic approval system were those relating to technologies for atomic power and defense-related industries, or those providing for a duration of more than ten years or involving royalty payments above 10 percent and a down payment of $500,000, or—in the case of the outright purchase of technologies—those exceeding $1 million. The new guidelines do not provide for a maximum period of duration and state only that contracts exceeding ten years are not eligible for automatic approval and have to be evaluated and approved by the Economic Planning Board. Similarly, no maximum permissible payments are defined, but if the proposed contract provides for payments above the level processed under the automatic approval system, they have to be evaluated by the Economic Planning Board, which takes into account whether the payment conditions are commensurate with the value of the technology to the economy. Agreements with indefinite duration have also been permitted in priority sectors in which technological changes occur rapidly and in which the continuous access of the licensee to the improvements of the licensor is considered essential to the maintenance of technological eminence in a particular industry. In similar situations, such agreements are also allowed for joint ventures between the foreign technology licensor and domestic partners.

Following this liberalization of regulatory measures, the inflow of foreign technology has grown rapidly. Recently concluded agreements have included technologies licensed from leading foreign manufacturers in their respective field of production and have included the most recent production techniques. There has also been a shift from the previous concentration of Japanese licensor companies in favor of U.S. and Western European manufacturers. Several of the agreements entered into by large Korean manufacturers have included technologies that their licensors have rarely transfered without equity participation. At the same time, experience with the newly adopted measures has posed certain problems to various government agencies. An analysis of agreements during 1979–82, for example, showed that repetitive acquisition of technologies had increased significantly over previous years.[24] This has taken place mainly because of the new decentralization in the evaluation and approval of agreements. In the absence of a centralized approval system and effective coordination among various ministries and departments, similar technologies often have been imported under varying terms and conditions. For Korean companies, mostly those in the medium-scale sector, the increased inflow of fairly standardized foreign technologies has also been motivated by the acquisition of trademarks and brand names of foreign licensors, rather than of the technology itself. Concern has also been expressed that as a result of the automatic approval procedures, less consideration has been given to the technical evaluation of agreements and that this had resulted in increased inflow of outdated technologies, especially in the case of medium-sized companies, which have less experience in technology licensing and often lack adequate information on foreign technological alternatives. It also appears that a higher share of agreements contain unfavorable terms and conditions for the licensee than there were in the period prior to the liberalization measures. Provisions that avoid the licensor's responsibilities for the performance of the licensed technology and the licensor's obligations in the case of infringement of third-party industrial property rights have often been included in recent agreements.

Although regulatory measures for the acquisition of foreign technology and foreign direct investments in selected sectors have been relaxed significantly, an Antimonopoly and Fair Trade Law came into effect in South Korea after April 1981, and it may also have an impact on foreign technology transfer. Article 23 of this law defines contractual provisions that constitute restraints on trade. These include tie-in conditions for supply of inputs by licensors; territorial restrictions on sales; restrictions on production, sales, and the use of sales agents; restrictions on the use of competitive technology and grant-backs; and restrictions on the use of technology after the expiry of agreement. Certain similar contractual conditions in joint venture agreements would also be deemed restraints on trade and will have to be avoided in joint venture agreements.

There can be little doubt that government policies relating to foreign investments and technology have had a considerable impact on industrial and technological development in Korea. These policies have also undergone several modifications in the light of changing situations. While policies toward foreign direct investments have become more selective, though fairly flexible for certain priority production fields, policies for foreign technology acquisition have become far more relaxed. Partly as a result of the trend toward liberalization, the number of technology agreements rose to 222 in 1980 and to 432 in 1984.[26] Following the liberalization, there has been a sharp increase in technology payments; in 1978, such payments were $58 million and by 1980 they had reached $107 million.[27] This increase was due partly to the larger number of agreements entered into in the years following the liberalization and partly to the nature of technologies, which have increasingly been more advanced and sophisticated. At the same time, there is some evidence that following liberalization, royalty rates also increased for more standardized technologies. Similarly, there has been an increase in the lump-sum payments provided in more recent agreements.[28]

An important feature of foreign technology transfer to Korea has been the relatively low local content in several industrial sectors. The emphasis on export-oriented production often led to the acceptance of a high production of imported inputs for intermediate products, parts, and components. In recent years, greater attention is being given to increased local-content requirements, particularly in the manufacture of machinery and equipment. Targets for higher local content have been set for a large number of industries, mostly in machinery and equipment subsectors. It is planned that by 1986, 100 percent local content will be achieved in transport equipment, including automobiles, shipbuilding, and aircraft, heavy construction equipment, and large diesel engines, and 70 to 80 percent for locomotives and specialized industrial machinery and equipment. With greater emphasis on local content, the technological requirements will also increase significantly in several sectors and may necessitate greater inflow of foreign know-how.

In the implementation of the Fifth Plan (1982–86), the major Korean conglomerates are likely to grow and expand considerably in new and diversified fields of manufacture. At the same time, the government may encourage greater decentralization of industry and reduce the dominance of the major domestically owned conglomerates in various sectors. This may well lead to greater technological diffusion, but the experience of the 1970s indicates that these industrial groups have played a major role in technological absorption and development so far. The technological sophistication of companies in several sectors and their financial resources is also indicated by the growing trend of foreign direct investments undertaken by these companies. By mid-1982, such investments were about $210 million in more than 300 projects.[29] A substantial share of these investments has been in mining (22 percent) and forest-based industries (15.4 percent), in which local technology had been adequately developed and has proved quite competitive. Participation by these companies in various natural resource projects has facilitated access to these resources.

To promote indigenous technological development, the government has supported institutional R&D through a number of government-owned and government assisted organizations. Among the largest are the Korean Institute of Science and Technology (KIST) and the Korean Advanced Institute of Science and Technology (KAIST). In the late 1970s, the institutional R&D

system was reorganized according to the new priorities of Korean industry, and several institutions were merged along functional lines. Their activity was also expanded to meet the requirements of private industry, and increased efforts are being undertaken to advance in several high-technology areas such as microelectronics. Partly because of the experience with Japan, measures were also introduced to improve the linkage between the government-operated R&D system and private industry, and thus to improve the diffusion and assimilation of research findings by the private sector.

Notes

1. L.E. Westphal, *Korea's Experience with Export-Led Industrial Development,* Staff Working Paper No. 249 (Washington, D.C.: World Bank, February 1977).

2. *Korea Machinery Industry* (Seoul: Korean Society for the Advancement of the Machinery Industry, 1981), 6.

3. Ibid., table 1 (computation of the rate of growth includes ISIC 38). A historical review of the Korean machine-building industry is presented in *Development and Perspectives of the Korean Machinery Industry Industry—with Special Reference to Machine Tool, Electrical Machinery, and Plant Equipment Manufacturing* (Berlin: German Development Institute, 1978).

4. *Problems and Issues Concerning the Transfer, Application and Development of Technology in the Capital Goods and Industrial Machinery Sector—The Capital Goods and Machinery Sector in Developing Countries: Issues in the Transfer and Development of Technology* (Geneva: United Nations Conference on Trade and Development, 1982), 51.

5. *Korea Machinery Industry,* 10.

6. For 1960, Westphal, *Korea's Experience;* for 1980, *Korea Machinery Industry.*

7. *The Foreign Capital Inducement Act* (Seoul: Government of the Republic of Korea, Economic Planning Board, n.d.) 1, Article 1.

8. Westphal, *Korea's Experience.*

9. Since 1973, these agreements (up to one year in duration) have been governed by the Engineering Service Promotion Law and have been evaluated and registered by the Ministry of Science and Technology in cooperation with the Ministry of Finance and other relevant agencies.

10. Examples of these performance criteria in four case studies are presented in W.H. Park, "Absorption and Diffusion of Imported Technology: A Case Study of the Republic of Korea," in *Proceedings of the Workshop on Absorption and Diffusion of Imported Technology,* Singapore, January 1981 (Ottawa: International Development Research Centre, 1983).

11. *Investment, Licensing and Trading—Korea* (New York: Business International Corporation, 1984), 4.

12. Foreign investments in the chemical sector were $326 million; in the electric and electronic sectors, $262 million; and in machinery, $95 million. See ibid.

13. *Costs and Conditions of Technology Transfer through Transnational Corporations* (Bangkok: United Nations, ESCAP/UNCTC Joint Unit, 1984), 54.

14. Ibid., 59.

15. The Korean Standard Industrial Classification List contains 1,048 industries.

16. A detailed review of the earlier phase of foreign technology regulation is presented in W.W. Pack, *A Study on the Transfer of Technology—Korean Case* (Seoul: Korean Institute of Science and Technology, Technology Transfer Centre, 1977).

17. *The Comparative Studies of National Experience in Technology Policies—The Case of the Republic of Korea* (Seoul: Korean Institute of Science and Technology, Technology Transfer Centre, 1981) appendix, table 5.

18. Ibid.

19. Ibid., appendix, table 4.

20. Ibid.

21. K.M. Chung, "Commercial Transfer of Technology in the Korean Electronics Industry" (Seoul: Korean Science and Technology Instrument Project, 1975, mimeographed).

22. Ibid, 21.

23. Ibid.

24. "The Pattern of Contractual Arrangements and the Cost of Technology after Liberalization of Technology Imports in the Republic of Korea: An Analysis of Agreements Made during 1979–1982," in the United Nations, ESCAP/UNCTC, *Costs and Conditions,* 66–91.

25. Ibid., 70.

26. L. Young-Hoi, *Korea's Experience in Technology Transfer* (Seoul: Ministry of Finance, Economic Cooperation Bureau, October 1985), 3.

27. United Nations, ESCAP/UNCTC, *Costs and Conditions,* 70.

28. Ibid. This United Nations study, covering Korea for the period 1979–82, analyzed 200 contracts entered into after the liberalization of technology agreements, comparing them with agreements signed before liberalization, and arrived at the following conclusion: "Analysis of the data indicates that the scale and pattern of payments has changed radically since 1978. In the absence of any information to the contrary, it may be concluded that there is a direct relationship between the relaxation of technology import restrictions in 1978 and the increasingly unfavorable contract terms for businessmen in the Republic of Korea wishing to import technology since that date" (p. 73). The data on which these findings are based are summarized in table 18 (for royalties) and table 19 (for lump-sum payments).

29. Information provided by the Government of Korea, Economic Planning Board, Seoul.

12
Mexico

T he difficult economic situation faced by Mexico during the early 1960s—grave international indebtedness, a high level of inflation, and continuing industrial recession—is in sharp contrast to the buoyant and flourishing picture of the Mexican economy during the two decades from 1955 to 1975, when a rapid rate of industrial and technological growth was achieved. The production of manufactured goods increased annually at 8.8 percent during the 1960s and at 7 percent during the 1970s. By 1980, the manufacturing sector was contributing 23.2 percent of GDP. In Mexico's Industrial Development Plan, prepared in 1979, it was estimated that the share of the manufacturing sector would increase to 25.1 percent by 1990.[1] With the present economic difficulties faced by the country, however, this target may need to be revised.

The high rate of industrial growth during the 1950s and 1960s was achieved by a combination of factors. With the growing demand for a variety of consumption goods and intermediate products, the government followed a policy of import substitution, and foreign and domestic companies, were given many incentives, including duty-free import of machinery, permission to import used equipment, tax concessions, and a high level of protection through tariffs and quantitative import restrictions. The law for the establishment of new and necessary industries was broad in its scope and application, encouraging inflow of foreign capital in most sectors of the economy. A large number of MNCs, mostly from the United States but also from the United Kingdom and other Western European countries, set up subsidiaries to manufacture various consumer goods, including consumer durables and intermediate products. The automobile industry, which assembled more than twenty models of cars in Mexico in the 1960s, with limited local content in most cases, was typical of the pattern of foreign investments at that time. The manufacture of mechanical and electrical equipment by foreign subsidiaries was relatively limited during this period, and although MNCs such as General Electric and Westinghouse had manufacturing subsidiaries in Mexico, their production was mainly concentrated in consumer electrical goods.

Domestically owned industrial enterprises also developed rapidly during this period, and the Alpha group in Monterey, Industria del Hierro, the Ika group, and several others took up production of certain types of machinery and equipment, besides the establishment of cement plants, paper and pulp units, breweries, agro-processing plants, and other manufacturing enterprises.

In the public sector, major expansion of electricity generation and distribution was undertaken by the Comision Federal de Electricidad (CFE), and by 1980, 14,600MW of generation capacity had been installed. In the petroleum sector, Petroleos Mexicanos (PEMEX), which was founded after the nationalization of foreign oil companies in 1938, expanded substantially during the 1960s, in the areas of both petroleum development and petrochemical production. A much greater expansion of PEMEX's activities took place in the 1970s, when major petroleum fields in southern Mexico were exploited and when petroleum exports emerged as a critical factor in Mexico's balance of payments.

Besides CFE and PEMEX, several other major state-owned enterprises are operating in various sectors of the economy, including steel, mining, chemicals, paper, mechanical and electrical machinery, and transport equipment. By 1975, public sector enterprises were contributing about 11.2 percent of GDP, and investments through these firms represented nearly half of the total investments in the country.[2] During the 1970s, financial institutions such as Nacional Financiera and SOMEX also made substantial investments in the manufacturing sector. In several instances, joint ventures were set up between Mexican financing institutions, local companies, and foreign corporations, generally with minority foreign ownership. Since 1982, with the nationalization of the banking sector and state control over the lending policy of banks, the role of government in industrial development has become more pronounced, and industrial investments are increasingly being channeled in accordance with national priorities. In 1984, there were 743 enterprises with financial participation by state-owned bodies, of which 486 enterprises had majority state ownership.[3]

By the late 1960s and early 1970s, the earlier policy of unrestricted inflow of foreign capital and technology began to be seriously questioned. Although the activities of MNC subsidiaries in several industrial sectors had raised industrial production considerably, the large increase in imported equipment and intermediate goods and components resulted in major deficits in the balance of trade, which became of growing concern to the government. A significant share of the manufacturing sector, particularly in technologically advanced fields, was held by foreign-majority subsidiaries. In the early 1970s, it was estimated, for example, that the share of production of such companies amounted to 97 percent for tobacco production, 69 percent for electrical equipment, 65 percent for transport equipment, and 64 percent for pharmaceuticals.[4] Similarly, a major share of the production of consumer electrical products, basic metals, construction and mining equipment, chemicals, and standard industrial products was held by foreign companies. A large proportion of the new entries by foreign companies during the late 1960s and early 1970s was through takeover of Mexican-owned companies, which found it increasingly difficult to compete with foreign subsidiaries.[5] Although these foreign-controlled companies progressively increased local production of technologically simple items, particularly nondurable and durable consumer goods, the manufacture of technologically complex and sophisticated products generally remained at the assembly level, with a high import content and a low percentage of local value-added. The technological and import dependency of these products changed only marginally over the years. It was also evident that the prevailing pattern of industrialization and buildup of production capacities had not been accompanied by a similar development of local technological capabilities. In comparison to countries such as Brazil and India, which were in comparable stages of industrialization, Mexican production of machinery and equipment was very limited. Since machinery production was low, the manufacture of parts and components and other engineering goods also remained limited. A high degree of dependence on foreign technology continued to prevail, and there was little R&D activity by most foreign subsidiaries and affiliates, whose operations tended to perpetuate dependence on imports of technological processes, inputs of materials, and foreign technical services.

With the growth of domestically owned industrial groups and with a growing concern about the extent of control exercised by MNC subsidiaries in several critical sectors of the economy, Mexico made significant policy changes in the early 1970s. During the government of President Luis Echeverria (1970–76), Mexico's industrial development program shifted the emphasis in import substitution from consumer goods production to a wide range of intermediates and capital goods. In the production of durable consumer goods, particularly automobiles, manufacturers were required to rationalize production so as to reduce maintenance imports or to increase exports of vehicles or parts and components to pay the high import bill on this account. Various aspects of the operations of foreign subsidiaries and affiliates began to be scrutinized, and their impact was reviewed in relation to national developmental objectives. A greater degree of self-sufficiency for an increasing range of economic and industrial activities was also sought. National policies were oriented to bring about greater national participation and control in vital sectors of the economy. It is against this background that, in the early 1970s, the government introduced new regulatory measures for foreign investments and technology acquisition.

In 1972, the Law on Registration and Transfer of Technology and the Use and Exploitation of Patents and Trade Marks was promulgated, and in

1973, the Law for the Promotion of Mexican Investments and Regulation of Foreign Investments was brought into effect. In 1976, the Law on Inventions and Trade Marks was enacted, amending major provisions of the then prevailing law on industrial property.[6] Through increased regulation of foreign investment inflow and foreign technology acquisition, this law was intended to exercise greater control over the pattern and pace of industrial and technological development and to strengthen the position of domestic companies and "Mexicanize" the economy. Furthermore, with the screening and evaluation of technology agreements, it was expected that the foreign exchange outflow on this account would decrease substantially. Terms and conditions in such agreements would then be more in consonance with national objectives and priorities. The new law on industrial property was also intended to achieve a greater diffusion of technology and know-how in the economy, particularly in sectors considered vital for national interests. During the 1970s, the technology policy of the country was considerably shaped by these legislative measures, and the pattern and trends in foreign investments and technology have been significantly affected by these laws.

Policies on Foreign Direct Investments

With the close relationship between foreign technology inflow and the operations of MNC subsidiaries and affiliates in Mexico, regulatory policies on foreign technology were adopted in close conjunction with similar regulations on foreign direct investments. The Law for the Promotion of Mexican Investment and the Regulation of Foreign Investment, which was enacted in 1973, had two main objectives.[7] First, it was intended to bring about an increase in Mexican participation in the ownership of companies, particularly in new undertakings involving foreign capital shareholding. For existing foreign-majority subsidiaries in Mexico, the lawmakers sought to reduce foreign shareholding to 49 percent or less, primarily through negotiations at the time of new investments or through major expansions of these companies. Although indirect pressure was often exerted, even prior to this legislation, to increase the extent of Mexican holdings in MNC subsidiaries, the 1973 law gave more concrete shape to the policy of Mexicanization. Second, the law was intended to channel foreign investments to areas of national priority after certain fields for state-owned enterprises and for Mexican-owned companies had been reserved. Certain specified sectors, such as petroleum, basic petrochemicals, nuclear energy, and utilities, were reserved for these state-owned enterprises, and a number of other branches, such as gas distribution, transport, communications, and forestry, were reserved for Mexican-owned companies. In the mining sector, foreign participation was limited to 34 percent ownership. In all other fields, foreign companies could hold up to 49 percent ownership, except in secondary petrochemicals and auto components, where foreign holdings were limited to 40 percent. Existing foreign subsidiaries were required to reduce their foreign holdings to these levels when major new investments or expansions were undertaken, although exceptions could be made by the government.

The screening and evaluation of foreign investment proposals was entrusted to the National Commission on Foreign Investments, with final decisions being made by a cabinet committee consisting of seven ministers from concerned departments. Initially, the Commission on Foreign Investments was quite separate from the Registry for Technology, but later, the two organizations were merged, and at present, the various aspects of foreign investments and those related to foreign technology transfer are examined together.

Although the legislation on foreign investments leaves most fields, except those already mentioned, open to foreign investments, the intention is primarily that MNCs operate through joint ventures with substantial Mexican participation, rather than through foreign-majority subsidiaries. The commission has the discretionary power to evaluate foreign investment proposals, and Article 13 of the law prescribes the criteria that the commission should take into account, including the impact on domestic industry and market conditions, employment creation and training, technological developments of the sector concerned, and the contribution to exports. By and large, however, the commission has followed a policy of encouraging foreign investments in most fields, subject to the prescribed limits of foreign ownership. Even in the matter of foreign holdings, several exceptions have been made, and the policy followed has been fairly liberal. Between 1973 and 1980, 1,724 proposals for foreign direct investments were approved by the commission. Of these 171 wholly foreign-owned subsidiaries were allowed, since their production was entirely for exports. Apart from these, majority foreign holdings were permitted in only forty-four cases.[8]

An important feature of the policy has been the preference given by the regulatory agency to the sale of foreign holdings in bulk to a Mexican group or company when a foreign subsidiary reduces its equity share. Although the sale of shares through the capital market has also been permitted in several cases, proposals for the Mexicanization of some subsidiaries have required the sale of a sizable volume of shares to Mexican partners, rather than the sale or distribution of shares among a large number of local shareholders, as is permitted in most other developing countries. In a number of companies in Mexico, however, foreign subsidiaries with 49 percent equity share have exercised effective control. In these cases, the MNC often sold 2 percent of the shares to local shareholders in such a manner that their effective control has remained ensured. The Mexicanization of foreign-majority companies has also been pursued through various incentives. For example, several fiscal and financial concessions that can significantly improve the profitability of operations have been made available only to companies that have domestic majority holdings. Consequently, a number of former foreign-majority companies have reduced their holdings to a minority position. At the same time, Article 12 of the law gives considerable authority to the commission to influence the operations of existing foreign companies, including those of foreign-majority subsidiaries. Thus, according to the law, new investments by existing companies and their expansion into new product lines are subject to the prior approval of the commission. Through this authority, the commission can significantly influence the growth and diversification of existing foreign-owned companies as well.

Despite the policy of Mexicanization, by 1980, of the 8,820 companies in Mexico that had foreign capital participation, 54.4 percent had holdings of over 49.1 percent, while 38.1 percent of the companies had MNC holdings ranging from 25 to 49 percent, which would also ensure effective control in most cases. Only 7.4 percent of these companies had foreign holdings of less than 25 percent.[9] The introduction of regulatory measures on foreign investments appears to have had little impact on the inflow of foreign capital. From the enactment of regulatory legislation in 1973 to the end of 1982, foreign investments had increased from $4 billion to $10.7 billion.[10] In both 1979 and 1980, the rates of growth exceeded 100 percent. The increase in foreign investments in the latter part of the 1970s can be mainly attributed to the rapid economic expansion that followed the substantial increase in petroleum exports and increased public expenditure. The law has, however, had significant impact on the ownership structure of newly formed companies with foreign capital participation.

Throughout the 1970s and early 1980s, foreign investments have continued to concentrate on a relatively few, mostly technologically advanced industries. At the end of 1980, investments in five sectors of the manufacturing industry accounted for about half of the total foreign investments. These included the manufacture of chemicals (18.5 percent), transport equipment (14.5 percent), electrical and electronics products (9 percent), and nonelectrical machinery (7.4 percent).[11] MNCs from the United States have continued to be the major sources of foreign investments. In 1975, these investments accounted for 70 percent of the total investments; in 1980, they accounted for 69 percent.[12] The continuation of the dominant position of U.S companies in the Mexican market has also been due to the geographical proximity of the countries and the high market acceptance of U.S. products. A noticeable increase has taken place, however, with respect to investments from Japan, albeit from a low base. Such investments increased their share from 2 percent in 1975 to 5.9 percent in 1980.[13]

Policies on Foreign Technology

Until the introduction of legislation on foreign technology in 1972, technology transfer agreements between foreign technology suppliers and recipient Mexican enterprises has been formalized generally by contracts, and there was little governmental control over technology fees and payments to parent companies and other technology licensors. MNC subsidiaries and their parent corporations generally entered into agreements that stipulated specific payments for the supply of technology and know-how. Foreign exchange remittances were made on the basis of the contractual terms specified in the agreement. However, contracts were not evaluated by government agencies from a legal, technical, or economic viewpoint. Subsequent analysis of the contracts entered into before 1972 showed that most of the agreements provided for only a very general, and often vague, description of the services to be rendered by the licensor and the responsibilities for training and other services to be provided to the licensee. This often made it difficult for the licensee to insist on the fulfillment of specific contractual conditions at a later stage. Many of the agreements had indefinite durations or provided for automatic renewal without the licensor being contractually obliged to transfer improvements. Most of the agreements imposed some restrictions on the operations of the domestic licensees. Most frequently, sales of licensee enterprises were restricted to Mexico and, in some cases, Central American countries. A number of contracts incorporated tie-in provisions, particularly for the supply of foreign inputs. It was also common practice to designate the governing law to be that of the licensor's country.

The major objectives of the new legislation were to promote national technological development and thus to provide greater technological support to Mexico's industrialization program.[14] The intention was to regulate and monitor the inflow of foreign technology by the compulsory screening, evaluation, and registration of all technology agreements.[15] By specifying contractual conditions that were prohibited and those that were required in all agreements, the law was intended to improve the bargaining position of national enterprises with foreign technology suppliers. To implement the law, the National Registry of Technology Transfer was created and was empowered to screen, evaluate, and approve contracts. The National Registry, together with the Foreign Investment Commission, are presently part of the Secretariat of National Property and Industrial Development.

The Mexican technology legislation considers technology agreements primarily as purchase agreements, rather than as contracts governing the conditions of use of particular technology. This approach has considerable implications for the usage and application of the technology by licensee enterprises after expiration of the agreement and also for the costs of technology and other general contract provisions. Although this intention is not stated explicitly in the text of the law, several provisions suggest such a view. The National Registry, consequently, takes the stand that after termination of an agreement, the licensee owns all the information on the technology that had been transferred and prohibits all limitations on the licensee to use the information unless it is covered by valid industrial property rights. In a similar way, the licensor is also prohibited from requiring that the licensee keep the information confidential after the expiration of the agreement. In certain cases, however, the registry has made exceptions and has approved contracts specifying a ten-year period for confidentiality following the expiration of the agreement. Such exceptions have mainly involved information on improvements transmitted subsequent to the initial transfer of technical information and know-how.

Regarding remuneration for technology or services, the law is construed in a general manner and does not establish maximum permissible royalty rates or payments. It states, however, that contracts will not be approved "when the price or counterservice is out of proportion to the technology acquired or constitutes an unwarranted or excessive burden on the country's economy."[16] In its evaluation of payment conditions, the registry generally takes into account the nature of technology, the availability of alternatives, the ownership relation between the parties, and the economics of the licensee's operation. Until the 1970s, most technology agreements were limited to a royalty of 3 percent on net sales, although several exceptions were made, particularly in licensing agreements with domestically owned companies. There were also major variations in the royalty rates approved for various industrial sectors. In 1976, for example, the range of royalties approved was 6 to 10 percent for pharmaceuticals, 2.5 to 5 percent for light engineering products and vehicles, and 1 to 3 percent for food products.[17] Since the late 1970s, however, the registry has been more flexible in the approval of payments and in selected priority sectors, such as capital goods and agro-industrial products, has permitted significantly higher royalties than it had previously. The interpretation of the term *net sales,* on which a percentage is calculated as royalty, has been more flexible in Mexico than in India, where several deductions are made on the net sales figure before royalty can be assessed. Provisions for automatic renewals are not allowed, but the registry has permitted extensions if new technologies or significant improvements are transferred during the period of extension.

An important provision of the legislation is contained in Article 7, which identifies the restrictive business practices that are prohibited in agreements. These involve conditions stating the rights of the licensor to intervene in various aspects of the licensee's operation, such as management, domestic and export sales, production, pricing, assignment of personnel, and tie-in arrangements for various inputs, including capital goods. Furthermore, grant-back provisions and jurisdiction by foreign courts are prohibited. If the Secretary of Industry and Commerce considers the technology of special interest to the country, however, the registry has discretionary power to approve contracts even if some of these restrictions are imposed. Such flexibility cannot be exercized if the contract provides for grant-back provisions and limits the R&D activity of the licensee, or if exports are unduly restricted; nor has the Registry the authority to approve agreements with a duration exceeding ten years.

The law had retroactive effect and required the registration of all existing contracts on foreign technology and services within a specified period of time. Since registration could occur only if these agreements complied with the provisions of the legislation or were covered by the provisions relating to exceptions, most existing agreements, which numbered several thousand, had to be renegotiated and then submitted to the registry for approval and registration. Because of the practical difficulties, the period for registration had to be extended, but this requirement did enable all existing technology contracts to be brought within the ambit of the law.

While the Argentinian legislation on technology agreements preceded Mexico's, the Mexican law is more detailed on the prohibited provisions. On certain aspects, such as the prohibition of export restrictions in licensing agreements, the legislation tends to be specific and leaves little room for flexibility in negotiations. At the same time, a clause enables the registry to make exceptions on prohibited provisions if it considers them in the national interest. Since the legislation was brought into effect, the exception provision has been used in a large number of cases and has allowed the degree of flexibility considered necessary.

The enactment of the Mexican legislation on foreign technology and know-how initially drew considerable criticism, mainly from foreign investors and licensors. They believed that the rules of the game had changed and that the flow of foreign technology into Mexico would be severely affected. Except for the initial two-year period after the law was brought into effect, however, the inflow of foreign technology to Mexico does not appear to have been significantly impeded by the regulatory measures. With a growing demand for foreign technology, the number of technology agreements and the volume of technology payments increased considerably in the latter half of the 1970s. In 1979, there were 8,257 contracts registered, which, following Brazil, was the second highest among developing countries.[18] Payments for technology also increased significantly, from $173 million in 1975 to $285 million in 1979.[19] The substantial increase in technology payments was not only due to the greater number of technology agreements, it was also caused by the acquisition of more advanced and complex technologies in high technology sectors, payments for which have generally been higher than average for the manufacturing sector. As a result of the evaluation procedure of the registry, contracts with restrictive clauses have been approved only as exceptions, and the agreements in force show significant improvements in the terms and conditions of acquisition from the viewpoint of licensee enterprises. According to the registry, because of the high royalty and other technology payment conditions, a large number of contracts submitted for approval were either rejected or renegotiated and more favorable conditions obtained.[20] The mandatory registration of agreements already in existence at the time of the introduction of the law resulted in 4,244 contracts being submitted to the registry from January 1973 to May 1975, most of them existing agreements. Over 30 percent of these contracts were rejected by the registry. In most cases, the denial for registration was made on the basis of Article 7 of the law, which pertains to restrictive business practices.[21]

It is difficult, however, to assess the full impact of the law in terms of its effects on foreign technology transfer. This difficulty stems largely from the fact that the predominant proportion of technology transfer still takes place in conjunction with foreign investments. In 1980, for example, 75 percent of the registered technology agreements were between MNC parent companies and their Mexican subsidiaries and affiliates.[22] In these cases, even though the technology agreement may be free of restrictive clauses and otherwise in compliance with the law, in practice, the behavior of the subsidiary and the nature of technology transfer and absorption largely depend on the parent company. In the manufacture of capital goods and intermediate products, for example, where production by foreign subsidiaries still takes place with a relatively low local content, MNC subsidiaries often continue to procure parts and components from the parent company whenever possible, rather than availing themselves of local alternatives. Consequently, even if the technology agreement does not specifically provide for tie-in clauses, the behavior and the operations of MNC subsidiaries follow the global pattern and the requirements of the parent companies.

Most of the technology agreements registered relate to the supply of technical know-how and, in most cases, also include the right to use foreign trademarks. In 1979, only about 20 percent of the agreements involved the use of patents, indicating that foreign technology inflow was more in the form of production know-how than in patent licensing, which is more common among enterprises in industrialized economies. A small proportion of contracts provide for transfer of basic and detailed engineering know-how (11 percent and 8 percent, respectively, during 1979).[23]

Although government policies have aimed at diversifying the sources of foreign technology acquisition from the heavy concentration on U.S. companies, by 1980 approximately 70 percent of the technology agreements in force were with U.S. technology suppliers, and licensors from the Federal Republic of Germany, Switzerland, France, and Japan have accounted for relatively small shares of total agreements.[24] Continued reliance on the United States as the principal source of foreign technology has been largely influenced by the fact that most MNC subsidiaries and affiliates in Mexico are from the United States, and the proximity of the two countries facilitates trade and technology transactions.

In 1982 a new law was passed for foreign technology, amending the legislation enacted ten years earlier.[25] The new law retained most of the key provisions of the 1972 law, such as permissible duration, remuneration, and contractual clauses that were either prohibited or were required, but it also made some important modifications. The major intent of the changes was to widen the regulatory power of the registry and to encourage the assimilation of foreign technology and domestic R&D activities. The new law extended the scope of technology transactions subject to registration and approval. Thus, the border industries, or *maquiladoras,* which were set up primarily for exports and which received various exemptions from regulatory requirements and had been previously exempted from the technology legislation, became subject to regulation. Similarly, consulting and engineering services, if undertaken by foreign individuals and companies, came under the purview of the new law. The law grants considerable power to the Secretariat of National Properties and Industrial Development to guide domestic companies in selecting appropriate foreign technologies and promote their rapid absorption and the development of local R&D capabilities. It also emphasizes the need for domestic companies to look for available domestic technologies and to undertake local adaptation of foreign technology. The 1982 law also gives greater discretionary power to the registry to approve contracts containing restrictive clauses if the technology is of priority to the country. The new law allows greater flexibility in certain restrictive provisions that had been prohibited by the 1972 law. Grant-back provisions, for example, are permitted if there is a reciprocal agreement between the parties for mutual exchange or improvements or if other benefits are provided to the Mexican company. The earlier provision, which prohibited local licensees from being obliged to sell their licensor, was also modified, and the registry may now approve such sales if the Mexican company can prove that the licensor can market the products more effectively abroad. A major new provision of the law relates to the obligations of the licensor, and contracts must provide that the supplier of technology guarantees the quality of the technology and the results of the transfer. The licensor also must assume responsibility for any infringement of the industrial property rights of the third parties. The new law also establishes more stringent penalties for failing to register a contract or for furnishing incorrect information to the registry. For failing to register, the penalty can amount up to 5,000 times the minimum annual wage in Mexico, and for furnishing false information, up to 10,000 times the minimum annual wage.

Impact of Policies

The pattern of industrial development that has taken place in Mexico has resulted in considerable import substitution in consumer goods industries, including consumer durables and intermediate products. The manufacture of various capital goods, such as mechanical, electrical, and transport equipment, has also made significant progress, especially in the 1970s, although domestic self-sufficiency and industrial diversification are considerably below that of Brazil, India, and the Republic of Korea. Although there has been a steady growth of industrialization (except during 1977–78 and 1981–83), domestic technological development has not kept pace. The slow progress of technological capabilities has been closely related to structural elements in the industry—its high foreign ownership and control and the inadequate development of capital goods and engineering goods sectors. In companies controlled by MNCs, particularly in assembly-type industries such as consumer durables, two aspects stand out, as posing major constraints on local technological development. First, the level of domestic content continues to be low in most of these industries, and the local value-added is usually about 40 to 50 percent of the total product value. Although the government has been exerting pressure to increase local content, the pace has been relatively slow.[26] Important limitations have been the inadequate growth of the foundry-forge industry. Also, production of ancillary items for the capital goods sector has lagged substantially behind the local assembly of this equipment, in terms of both quality and quantity. In other branches, also, including various process industries, the dependence on foreign inputs continues to be high. Second, in most industrial sectors, there has been relatively little technological adaptation. This has been particularly marked in the operations of MNC subsidiaries and affiliates that have relied largely on foreign technological inputs and services, but it is also true of most Mexican-controlled companies in both the private and the public sectors.

Although a high degree of dependence on foreign technology has continued in most of the manufacturing sector and indigenous technological innovations have been relatively limited, there are several notable exceptions. Institutions such as the Mexican Institute of Petroleum have made rapid progress in basic and detailed engineering designs, especially for petroleum-based projects. Also, some local consulting engineering companies have developed considerable service capabilities, as in the case of Bufete Industriale for various industrial projects. The sponge-iron process developed by HYLSA (Monterey) has acquired a worldwide reputation. In several other areas, such as food processing, breweries, cement production, and the manufacture of flour-milling equipment and certain types of electrical and construction machinery, Mexican companies have demonstrated considerable technological capability and are increasingly competing in foreign markets.

The regulatory policies toward foreign technology, which have now been in force for over a decade, have created a greater awareness of the need for local technological absorption and adaptation. They have also brought about significant improvements in the terms and conditions of licensing agreements for Mexican licensee enterprises. At the same time, they have had rather limited impact on technological choice and increased use and application of locally developed techniques and processes. Consequently, since the early 1980s, the government has given renewed emphasis to the promotion of R&D activities by local companies, both foreign-owned and domestically owned, and several fiscal incentives have been granted for this purpose. To encourage the development of the capital goods sector, incentives have been made available not only to manufacturers of such equipment but also to purchasers of locally manufactured machinery, provided that they meet the specified local content requirements. During the current plan period and in estimates of the prospects to 1990, with the envisaged growth in local capital goods manufacture and the various incentives for local R&D, it is expected that technological developments in industry will be substantially accelerated.

Notes

1. *Industrial Development Plan 1979–1982–1990* (Mexico City: Secretaria de Patrimonio y Fomento Industrial, 1981), 20.

2. R. Villareal, "Las Empresas Publicas Como Instrumento de Politica Economica en Mexico," *El Trimestre Economico* 45(1978): 213–35.

3. *Investment, Licensing and Trading—Mexico* (New York: Business International Corporation, 1984), 5.

4. F. Fajnzylber and T. Martinez Tarrago, *Las Empresas Transnacionales* (Mexico City: Fonda de Cultura Economica, 1976).

5. R. Newfarmer and W.F. Mueller. *Multinational Corporations in Brazil and Mexico,* Report to the U.S. Senate Committee on Foreign Relations, Subcommittee on Multinational Corporations (Washington, D.C.: U.S. Government Printing Office, 1975), 314–15.

6. A review of these laws is presented in H.H. Camp and C.A. Rojas Magnon, "Recent Developments under the Mexican Foreign Investment Law and the Law Regulating the Transfer of Technology," *Lawyer of the Americas* 8 (February 1976): 1–37.

7. An English translation of the law was published in the *Diaro Oficial,* 9 March 1973. Also see *Law to Promote Mexican Investment and Regulate Foreign Investment* (Mexico City: Secretaria de Patrimonio y Fomento Industrial, 1980).

8. Business International Corporation, *Investment, Licensing and Trading,* 8.

9. *Anuario Estadistico—Inversiones Extranjeras y Transferencia de Tecnologia* (Mexico City: Direccion General de Inversions Extranjeras y Transferencia de Tecnologia, 1981), 6.

10. Business International Corporation, *Investment, Licensing and Trading,* 3.

11. Direccion General de Inversiones Extranjeras y Transferencia de Tecnologia, *Anuario Estadistico,* 11.

12. Ibid., 18.

13. Ibid., 19.

14. "Law on the Transfer of Technology and the Use and Exploitation of Patents and Trademarks," December 1972, effective after January 1973, *Official Gazette of the Federation,* 30 December 1972.

15. Agreements covered by the law include the use of patents and trademarks; the supply of plans, diagrams, models, instructions, formulas, and engineering details for installations; managerial and technical assistance agreements; and consulting and evaluation services. Until 1982, in-bond units were exempted from the law.

16. Article 7/11.

17. Camp and Rojas Magnon, "Recent Developments," 17.

18. Direccion General de Inversiones Extranjeras y Transferencia de Tecnologia, *Anuario Estadistico,* 26. The total of 8,257 registered agreements includes 1,923 agreements among Mexican companies.

19. Ibid.

20. *Recent Developments in the Regulation of Foreign Technology in Selected Developing Countries,* ID/WG.275./8 (Vienna: United Nations Industrial Development Organization, May 1978).

21. Ibid. The most frequently occurring violations relate to Clause 11: "Payments not in relation to the value of technology acquired or constituting an excessive burden on the country's economy which accounted for 22.5% of the agreements rejected."

22. Direccion General de Inversiones Extranjeras y Transferencia de Tecnologia, *Anuario Estadistico,* 37.

23. Ibid., 23.

24. Ibid., 26.

25. "Control and Registration of Technology Transfer and Usage of Patents and Brandnames," *Diario Oficial,* 11 January 1982 effective February 10, 1982. The new law does not have retroactive effect for contracts that had already been registered or for those pending, but parties to such contracts could abide by the terms of the new law.

26. In the early 1980s, there were several decrees that set progressive local-content requirements for various sectors—for example, for automobiles, from 50 percent to a minimum of 55 percent by 1986; for vans, from 65 percent to 70 percent by 1985; for tractors and buses, 90 percent by 1985. See Business International Corporation, *Investment, Licensing and Trading,* 9.

Part IV
Impact, Trends, and Prospects of Technology Transfer through MNCs

13
MNC Activities and Regulation of Foreign Technology

T he foregoing review of technology transfer through MNCs and national policies in Third World countries has dealt with several aspects of MNC activities and their changing relationships with the institutions and enterprises of these countries. In the light of this analysis, it would be useful to assess, first, the overall role and impact of MNCs in technology transfer within the changing environment of developing countries; second, the impact of regulatory policies on technological development; and third, the trends and prospects of technology transfer through alternative forms of MNC participation in these countries. The interaction between national policies and the response of MNCs to them has already resulted in varying patterns of MNC participation in different industrial sectors. These will continue to evolve with changes in the global competitive situation and with increased industrial growth in these countries. Policy measures and institutional and other arrangements in Third World countries are also likely to undergo considerable modification, and these trends should be assessed. In the ultimate analysis, however, the prospects of active MNC participation in particular countries will largely depend on the extent to which the interests of MNCs and the objectives of host countries can be harmonized and suitable mechanisms established for long-term continuing relationships.

Impact of MNC Activities

It is clear from the foregoing chapters that the techno-economic impact of MNC activities has differed considerably from sector to sector and from country to country and has depended on a variety of factors. To the extent that technology has constituted an integral part of MNC investments, the conditions governing such investments have been of basic importance. Although local factor situations and endowments in the form of scarce natural resources, local markets, cost and availability of labor, and the overall investment climate have been critical determinants, host country policies have also had a major impact in shaping the nature of MNC investments and the pace and extent of technology transfer. With programs of industrialization undertaken in almost all Third World countries, there has been considerable scope for MNC investments. Most of these investments, however, have been concentrated in a relatively few developing countries, and in these countries, the nature and extent of technology transfer and the relationship between parent MNCs and local companies have been determined to a great extent by the interaction between national policies and the response of MNCs in this regard.

Important factors that have also had significant impact are the increased global competition in various fields and the availability of industrial technology from a larger number of sources. The entry of Japanese MNCs and their greater flexibility in adjusting to national policies and norms in host developing countries have increased the range of technological alternatives and sources. A number of enterprises from the Third World have also emerged as potential investors, partners, or sources of technology for other developing countries. These enterprises, which range from state-owned companies such as *Petrobras* (Brazil) or Hindustan Machine Tools (India) to a large number of private sector industrial groups from countries such as Brazil, Hong Kong, India, the Republic of Korea, and Mexico, generally have initially acquired technology from MNCs but have now absorbed these technologies and are in a position to transfer industrial know-how in a number of fields. These technologies may often be better suited to the smaller markets and production capacities and other constraints in developing countries.

The changes in competitive structure in most industrial branches and in the investment environment in a number of developing countries have necessitated significant modifications in the strategy of MNCs, particularly in the commercialization of technology and know-how. The traditional pattern of export sales and limited local production through wholly owned subsidiaries is being gradually replaced in several developing countries by varying degrees of MNC participation in ownership and technology licensing arrangements, which are increasingly oriented toward rapid increase in local production and domestic integration in manufacture, together with the assumption of export and other performance commitments in a large number of cases. Wherever possible, MNCs have maintained the traditional pattern of operations through wholly owned subsidiaries, but there has been a growing trend for joint ventures, licensing arrangements, and service contracts. These arrangements have, to a large extent, been based on the commercialization of MNC technology, know-how, and technological services in situations that have involved governmental regulation of MNC operations, mostly since 1960. The initial negative reaction of MNCs to regulatory measures in these countries continues, although there has been much greater acceptance and adjustment over the years. For MNCs from the United States and Western Europe, the adjustment to host country regulations has often involved a fundamental departure from the traditional forms of operation in Third World countries. Operating within national policy parameters and sharing decision-making authority with local partners and licensees, MNCs have often faced major constraints in implementing global corporate strategies and in coordinating joint ventures and licensing arrangements effectively within the MNC system. The sharing of technology with partners in developing countries has, in several cases, been viewed as potentially eroding the proprietary know-how of MNCs and more threatening than investment and licensing arrangements with companies in industrialized countries. MNCs have also generally perceived greater risk in the intervention of Third World host governments in the ownership structure of local subsidiaries and affiliates and also in other aspects of operations, including production levels and product pricing.

Despite their misgivings and concerns, by the 1980s, MNCs generally accepted the fact that joint ventures and licensing constitute the only means of entering the markets of several developing countries, including some of the largest markets and raw-material sources, and of utilizing their factor advantages. The adaptation in the approach of MNCs toward joint ventures and technology licensing has extended to most industrial sectors. This has taken place, however, within an overall framework that ensures global profitability and safeguards the MNC's technology and know-how.

The review of technology transfer in selected industrial sectors brought out the fact that technologies transferred by MNCs to joint ventures have been fairly selective in most fields. At the same time, various control mechanisms have been utilized for the process of transfer. Most of the technologies that were transferred to joint venture had already been extensively utilized and had become fairly standardized. The research programs of parent corporations in their home countries have ensured continuous improvement of products and processes, and there is little evidence that the results of technological research were transferred to joint ventures, except after a considerable period of time. As a result, there have been major differences in the products and production technologies used by parent companies and those used in joint ventures in developing countries. These differences have often arisen because of the smaller scale of operations and because of other constraints and limitations in these countries, including the necessity of down-scaling the technology in certain circumstances. Nevertheless, an important feature has been that the technology transferred to joint ventures and licensees has tended to be frozen at a particular level, while the technologies and processes utilized in the parent company's plant have been subjected to constant improvement and technological breakthroughs. Consequently, joint ventures have seldom posed a major threat to the global competitive positions of MNCs. At the same time, in most developing countries in which local competition is quite limited, the application of technologies that lag behind the latest technological developments or that function at inefficient scales of production have had adequate market acceptance and have ensured the profitability of joint ventures with MNCs.

Although most of the industrial technology transferred to joint ventures has generally involved fairly well-established standard products and production processes, there has also been transfer of complex and advanced technologies, including latest innovations, in several joint ventures. In such instances, MNCs have sought to exercise varying degrees of control over the operations of the joint ventures. The legal protection of industrial property rights has often provided effective means and patents, and trademarks and brand names have ensured MNC control over key elements in joint venture operations. In manufacturing processes involving composition of materials, such as chemicals, or assembly, such as engineering goods, partial production by the joint venture and sourcing of intermediates and components from the parent company have continued over extended periods. The continuing dependence of the joint venture on imported inputs not only has allowed the parent company to exercise control over the joint venture but also has enabled the effective integration of these operations into the MNC system.

The review of technology transfer in various sectors also brought out the fact that there has been a substantial increase in technology licensing by MNCs to unaffiliated, domestically owned companies in developing countries. A major factor promoting such arrangements has been the restrictions imposed by local goverments on foreign direct investments in selected sectors of the economy that were earmarked for development by domestically owned companies. The range of such sectors has varied widely among Third World countries. In some of these countries, state-owned public sector companies are playing a key role in industrial development, and technological participation by MNCs has inevitably taken the form of licensing. A similar situation prevails with large, privately owned companies and industrial groups in these countries, which often prefer licensing arrangements in certain fields rather than joint ventures with MNCs. For both these categories, the technological requirements are often for highly complex and sophisticated industrial technology and know-how. In the majority of cases, however, most of the technological needs of domestic industry in these countries have been for relatively simple technologies for the production of standard industrial products and the application of processes that have already been widely used in developed countries.

In several developing countries, certain industrial activities have increasingly been reserved for domestically owned companies. In others, the small local demand has made MNC investments in such markets unattractive. In several fields of manufacture, especially in the more industrially advanced developing countries, considerable local production has been undertaken by domestically owned companies; this factor not only has lowered profit margins for potential foreign investors but also has made it difficult for MNCs to enter these fields. In such cases, licensing of technology by MNCs to domestically owned companies has constituted the only means of obtaining revenues and entry into these markets.

Although technology licensing to unaffiliated companies in these countries has been increasing, it still accounts for a relatively small proportion of the technology and know-how transferred by MNCs. This is partly because of the preference of MNCs for exploiting their technology through investment channels, which are generally more profitable than pure licensing agreements. A major constraint on the rapid growth of technology licensing has, however, been posed by the inadequate technological infrastructure that prevails in a great number of developing countries. Apart from the most simple technologies, a licensee has to have certain basic technological capabilities in order to utilize foreign technology. The ongoing practice by MNCs of licensing to unaffiliated companies shows that the technical assistance provided within the framework of a licensing agreement to unaffiliated companies is generally much more limited than joint ventures or licensing to wholly owned subsidiaries. Unless the local company has relatively high absorptive capabilities, it is not able to use the licensed technology effectively. Consequently, it has been mostly domestic companies from South and Southeast Asia and some Latin American countries that have been able to take advantage of the increased willingness of MNCs to license their standardized technologies to unaffiliated companies. The limited technological infrastructure for industry in many countries in Africa, and in some of the smaller Latin American and Caribbean countries, has often made it impracticable for domestic companies to acquire foreign technology through licensing agreements without foreign equity participation.

Although MNCs have been engaged in a broader range of activities in developing countries and have entered into new types of contractual relationships, the basic features of technology commercialization by these corporations have remained largely unaffected. As pointed out earlier, adaptations by MNCs to host government policies and regulations have been made only to the extent that global operations and profitability were not adversely affected. In areas where the commercialization of technology would have resulted in a diffusion of key technologies with high market value or would have limited the returns from exploitation of such technology, there has been greater resistance by MNCs to transfering technology. Thus, most advanced production techniques and products incorporating sophisticated technologies—such as several types of machinery and equipment, computers, specialty chemicals, pharmaceutical compounds, and such high-technology fields as microelectronics, genetic engineering, materials technology, and the like—are being developed and produced primarily in the home countries of the MNCs concerned. Regardless of the alternative channels available, the transfer of such technologies to developing countries has been rather rare. Apart from the preference of MNCs to concentrate such production facilities in their home countries, the techno-economic characteristics of production by MNCs often limit the profitability of such manufacture in most developing countries. These products have been manufactured in a relatively few developing countries — and in most cases only partially — so that the production of critical and sophisticated components has not been relocated. This practice has reduced not only the required investment in these markets but also the need for transferring the critical elements of technology.

There has also been some resistance on the part of MNCs to commercializing and transfering technology to Third World countries for the manufacture of certain engineering goods and process industries, even though the technology concerned has been relatively less sophisticated or unique. In such cases, market size considerations have remained the critical determinant for technology transfer. Given the nature of such technologies, the local market in most developing countries has remained inadequate for the manufacture of a wide range of engineering goods and industries. Consequently, although many developing country governments have published extensive lists of industries and specific projects in which MNCs have been invited to participate, these companies have been very slow in responding to incentives and engaging in the production or commercialization of technology. In most cases, MNCs have waited for growth of local markets to levels at which their technologies could yield adequate returns. There have been very few instances in which MNCs have developed more appropriate technologies for the scale and demand of local markets in these countries.

The interaction of host country policies and the response of MNCs on the question of ownership and gradual reduction of foreign-majority holdings is of special interest. As was discussed earlier, host country requirements have been exercized rather selectively across industrial sectors and countries. During the 1970s, the joint venture became an important channel for the commerzialization of technology by MNCs, and measures were implemented in several countries for increases in the national holdings of MNC subsidiaries and in new projects involving MNC participation. Nevertheless, the most common form of MNC participation in most developing countries continues to be through wholly foreign-owned or majority foreign-owned subsidiaries. MNCs have tended to consider joint ventures with local partners the second-best alternative for operating in developing countries. Wholly owned subsidiaries, which ensure the entire profit from an operation and allow full and effective control over operations and the use of technology, have remained the preferred method of operation. For MNCs operating in high-technology areas, this has often been the only acceptable form of participation. In the 1970s, a major exception to this pattern was made by Japanese MNCs, which were generally more willing to participate with minority holdings, and a large number of joint ventures with minority Japanese participation were set up in South and Southeast Asia and, in some instances, in Latin America. These joint ventures were mainly for the manufacture of relatively low-technology industrial products, and the high import content allowed parent companies to retain effective control over production and technological operations. During the early 1970s, this approach was also indirectly supported by Japanese government policies, which did not unduly encourage outflow of investments from Japan. Subsequently, as restrictions on the outflow of investments were eased, new investments by Japanese MNCs were also implemented through wholly or majority-owned subsidiaries in countries in which there were no restrictions. The extent to which full or majority capital ownership has continued in certain sectors and some countries has depended largely on the bargaining strength of the MNCs vis-à-vis the local government and on the overall national policy toward foreign investments. Even where foreign investments have been regulated, considerable discretionary powers have been given to the appropriate regulatory bodies to allow such holdings when a technology or production activity is considered to be of critical importance for national development. MNCs have enjoyed a very strong bargaining position with developing country governments in most fields, but especially in sectors that utilize a more complex and sophisticated level of technology than that available in the local industry. When the availability of technology in any field has been concentrated in one or very few MNCs, these companies may not have undertaken manufacturing operations in developing countries or, when they have initiated local manufacture, it has been through wholly owned subsidiaries.

The preference of MNCs for wholly owned subsidiaries is especially evident in the case of export-oriented manufacture, where joint ventures have been very infrequent. Because of the critical need for exports in most developing countries, export-oriented operations have generally been exempted from joint venture requirements. These operations have consequently been integrated within the production and marketing systems of MNCs, and decision-making powers are not shared with local companies and partners.

The changing pattern of ownership is perhaps most marked in the petroleum and mineral sectors, particularly in petroleum. Since the ownership and responsibilities for petroleum exploration and development have been gradually taken over by state-owned corporations in most oil-producing countries, technology transfer in exploration, processing, and refining through MNCs has mostly—but not entirely—taken place through production-sharing arrangements and service contracts. These arrangements provide remuneration for specific technological operations and services. Although the pace of absorption in the management of petroleum exploration and development has been fairly rapid in most oil-producing countries, the major MNCs in this field and the specialist engineering companies have continued to play an important role in technical operations and in the transfer of operational know-how in specialized oil field activities. In minerals, including aluminum, copper, zinc, tin, lead, and iron ore, MNCs have still retained control over mining and processing activities in some ore-producing countries, although state-owned national corporations have effectively taken over control in many of these countries and are exercising supervisory powers in others. Since mining technology has been relatively stable, technological absorption has not posed any major problems, except at the smelting and processing stages. Negotiations between host countries and MNCs have mainly revolved around the question of revenue distribution.

The requirements of specialized technology tend to be much greater in fertilizers, chemicals, and process industries. As discussed earlier, although operational and maintenance technology has been absorbed in many developing countries, most refineries, and fertilizer and petrochemical plants in these countries, except for India and one or two other countries, continue to be designed and constructed by foreign companies. Since the basic and detailed engineering of such plants is an essential element of technology transfer in process industries, the pace of technological absorption has tended to be slow, except in countries where governmental policies specifically foster the growth of local engineering and consultancy capability.

It is in the manufacturing field, however, that technology transfer through MNCs has been most significant and also most varied in its impact. This field, which extends from the manufacture of consumer goods such as food products, pharmaceuticals, and nondurable and durable consumption products to intermediates and to the production of capital goods, covers an enormous range and variety of products and production technologies. The nature and implications of technology transfer through MNCs in several of these fields were discussed in part II. Although MNCs have been the principal source for foreign industrial technology, national strategies for import substitution and export promotion and policies on MNC investments have had considerable impact on technology transfer and on the development of local technological capability. The technological impact can be assessed in terms of various criteria for different sectors of manufacture, including, first, the development of competitive production capability; second, the levels of domestic integration achieved, especially in assembly industries; and third, the pace of technological absorption and adaptation, including local research capability and application.

A review of MNC activities in various sectors indicates that considerable production and technological capability has been established by MNCs in a number of Third World countries. Some of the technologies transfered have been relatively simple, such as those for agro-processing, beverage products, textiles, clothing, and other consumer goods. MNC control has been exercised in these cases through the ownership of subsidiaries and affiliates or through the use of brand names and trademarks, especially for foods and beverages. Fairly standardized production technology supplied by MNCs has been utilized primarily to meet local market demand. Research activities have been generally concentrated with the parent corporation, and local research has been largely confined to product adaptations to suit local consumer tastes. In branches involving intensive research, particularly pharmaceuticals, technology transfer by MNCs to developing countries has often been limited to formulation and packaging, and only in some countries to the production of intermediates. Research by pharmaceutical MNCs has been undertaken in the very few developing countries where research efforts have been directed toward developing drugs for certain tropical diseases. While there has been considerable growth of indigenous technology and pharmaceutical production in some countries, such as China, Egypt, India, and South Korea, MNCs in this field continue to dominate global production and markets.

Technology transfer through MNCs is undoubtedly of special significance in capital goods manufacture in developing countries, comprising electrical, mechanical, and transport equipment. Most of this production has been confined to a few developing countries that have large internal markets for machinery and equipment and government policies that have specifically concentrated on the gradual replacement of imports in this sector. The extent of such manufacture by MNC subsidiaries has also depended on policies toward foreign investments. In Argentina and Brazil, for example, MNC subsidiaries have played a key role in machinery manufacture, but this is less so in Mexico, where special emphasis has been given to capital goods manufacture since the early 1970s. In India, on the other hand, MNC subsidiaries have played a fairly limited part in such production, which has largely been undertaken by state-owned enterprises and by joint ventures and licensing between MNCs and domestically owned private sector companies. In the Republic of Korea, although MNCs have made considerable investments in other sectors, domestic machinery manufacture was mainly implemented by large Korean-owned companies. In other developing countries in which some machinery production has taken place for import substitution—for example, Egypt, Nigeria, Pakistan, the Philippines, and Turkey—the role of MNC subsidiaries has differed from country to country. In Egypt, for example, production was initially through state enterprises while in most other developing countries, joint ventures are common. In most of these countries, except Brazil and India, foreign subsidiaries have produced mechanical and electrical equipment of certain types and up to limited ranges only and have generally served as sales offices of their parent corporations for machinery in the higher ranges and of greater complexity and not locally manufactured. Initially, most of the local enterprises engaged in machinery production undertook only the later stages of assembly, but over the years, local manufacture of parts and components has increased considerably. In the case of

more complex and heavy machinery and equipment, however, local production has usually stopped short of the manufacture of high-value, sophisticated components, and such items have mostly continued to be covered by
imports, except in some countries, such as Brazil and India. This has led to
the continuing import dependency of production and, perhaps more significant, has limited the scope of the technology transfer that would have been
necessary for the local production of more complex and high-value parts and
components.

The manufacture of capital goods in developing countries has involved a
fairly distinct market division between MNC subsidiaries and affiliates and
those of domestically owned companies. In countries where local companies
were already manufacturing certain types of industrial machinery and equipment, MNC subsidiaries often established production facilities for the higher
ranges, especially in Brazil, although there were also several instances of takeovers of local companies in this field. The entry of MNCs into machinery
manufacture was encouraged by most developing country governments,
except where state-owned enterprises were already set up in this field, as in
Algeria and India. In most other developing countries, MNC subsidiaries
have enjoyed an oligopolistic market position because of the high level of protection and the absence of competition, and in spite of the limited internal
market in most of these countries, they have been able to make substantial
profits. From the viewpoint of technological development and transfer, however, the contribution of MNC subsidiaries has often been limited because of
the relatively low level of integration and the lack of R&D and design capability in most of these companies. Although MNC subsidiaries have produced more complex and higher ranges of equipment with these limitations,
domestically owned companies have largely operated at the lower end of the
technological spectrum in this sector. This has been an important constraint
for technological development in machinery manufacture in these countries.
The established position of foreign companies in these sectors has also discouraged domestic companies from expanding into machinery production, a
field in which foreign companies already enjoyed a dominant position. The
high level of import dependency of foreign subsidiaries in machinery manufacture, however, is also characterized in the operations of domestically
owned companies; it is only in countries in which higher local content has
been insisted upon that there has been an adequate level of domestic integration in manufacture. The role of domestically owned companies in machinery
manufacture has been considerably strengthened when there has been local
production, either by state-owned enterprises, as in India, or by expansion of
large privately owned domestic companies, as in Brazil, Mexico, and the
Republic of Korea.

The nature of transport equipment manufacture, particularly automobiles and trucks, is somewhat different, mainly because most of the automobile production in developing countries has been by foreign subsidiaries. The

large number of automobile models produced in Argentina, Brazil, and Mexico in the 1960s, and the assembly operations set up in several countries in Asian and African countries during the 1970s, highlight the dominant role of MNC subsidiaries in the automobile industry. Import-substitution policies in this industry have concentrated either on a high degree of local integration — as in India, where such manufacture is by local companies — or on phased programs of increased local content — as in the Philippines and Latin American countries. A policy of compensatory exports has been practiced in Brazil and Mexico that requires MNC subsidiaries in this field to meet their import requirements through exports of vehicles or components in accordance with a phased program. In the case of agricultural equipment, particularly tractors, the role of MNC subsidiaries is dominant in most developing countries, with the exception of India. The level of domestic content in tractor manufacture in most of these countries continues to be rather low, however, and is generally around 50 to 60 percent, except in Brazil and India, where tractors and their components are entirely manufactured locally.

Experience of Regulatory Policies

As was brought out in previous chapters, government policies on foreign investment and technology have varied to a large extent across countries and within countries over time. Changes over time have resulted mostly from the inexperience of some countries with policymaking, particularly when adopted measures fail to achieve set objectives and must be replaced with new policies. Modifications in policies have also been undertaken in the light of changes in the internal sociopolitical environment of particular countries and in the international environment, which has affected commercialization of various technologies over time. The dynamic nature of these policies reflects the continuing efforts of governments in Third World countries to adopt a suitable policy framework that will promote the fulfillment of industrial and technological objectives.

The adoption of regulatory measures on foreign technology in Third World countries has been a relatively recent phenomenon. The experience of several countries in which such policies have been adopted over the past decade and more provides substantial material for determining the effects of these measures and the response of MNCs. The regulation of foreign technology and the behavior of MNCs are closely interrelated. On the one hand, it was the limited and often restrictive nature of foreign technology transfer through MNCs that originally gave rise to the need to regulate foreign technology inflow. On the other hand, the response by MNCs to such measures, has played a major role in modifying regulatory policies and measures. Close interaction between MNC behavior and government regulation has been prevalent since the adoption of the initial regulatory measures. It is important to emphasize, however, that the focus of government regulation has changed over time. This has been due partly to the shift in priorities since the introduction of regulatory policies and partly to the greater acceptance by developing country governments of the critical role of MNCs in various fields, particularly of their impact on technological development.

In most developing countries that have adopted regulatory measures, a fairly uniform pattern is discernible in the evolution of regulatory policies and practices. One important trend has been a shift in emphasis from the reduction of costs of foreign technology and outflow of foreign exchange to the broader issue of technological development. A second feature has been the growing sophistication of governments in formulating regulatory measures that deal with the overall process of foreign technology acquisition as well as in improving the implementation of these measures. Third, it is increasingly being realized that besides the regulation and screening of foreign technology, however comprehensive and well planned this may be, other measures are also necessary to ensure the inflow of needed technology in various sectors. This approach is reflected in the exercise of much greater flexibility in the implementation of regulatory measures and in various degrees of liberalization in regulatory control.

An interesting feature of this evolutionary process in countries that have fairly long experience in technology regulation is that while the basic policy focus has changed, the major elements and aspects of earlier phases of regulation have been retained and incorporated within the framework of the new policies. Thus, issues such as reducing direct costs of technology by setting certain sector-specific royalty ceilings and limiting the duration of agreements are still features of regulatory control. Similarly, prohibition of various tie-in provisions, which may increase indirect costs, continues to be part of the more recent regulatory norms and policy guidelines on provisions in technology contracts. Despite the continuance of such norms, greater emphasis has been given to the nature of the technology transferred and its relations to the cost of the technology. Regulatory bodies in developing countries are consequently giving greater attention to the analysis of economic and technological aspects of agreements to determine permissible payments and other contractual provisions. Increased emphasis has also been given to the technical evaluation of foreign technology proposals, and interdepartmental technical committees have been set up to evaluate and review those cases.

It was pointed out earlier that although the trend in developing countries has been toward adopting some degree of control of foreign technology, in several of these countries this still takes place predominantly through regulation of foreign direct investments or, where no foreign investment is involved, through controls over exchange remittances for technology payments according to established ceilings. It is also evident that where direct regulation of foreign technology has been introduced, it has generally—at least in the initial stages—followed a pattern similar to that adopted earlier in India, some Latin American countries, and others. The changes in focus and approach that have occurred have mostly taken place during the 1980s. The effectiveness of technology regulation can be viewed in the context of both the objectives to be directly realized and the broader goal of technological development. This assessment can be based on the experience of countries that have instituted such measures for over a decade. Closely related to this evaluation is the analysis of MNC strategies in various sectors and their adaptation to such measures over time.

Problems of Monitoring

As discussed earlier, the main purpose of regulations on foreign technology has been to improve the terms and conditions of foreign technolog acquisition by domestic companies. By providing norms regarding various contractual conditions in technology agreements, regulatory measures have been primarily intended to strengthen the position of local licensee enterprises vis-à-vis foreign technology licensors. The regulatory process can be utilized as an effective instrument, however, only to the extent that these measures can be implemented. The question to be considered is the extent to which domestic buyers of foreign technology have taken advantage of the regulatory process. Certain regulatory measures, such as limits on royalties or lump-sum payments, have a fairly direct impact. In regard to other norms and guidelines, however, the position often is not so clear-cut. The compliance of local licensees with regulatory norms is influenced by several factors, the most critical of which is the extent of the decision-making authority of licensees versus that of the foreign licensors. In the case of foreign subsidiaries, which are controlled by parent licensor companies, this decision-making authority tends to be very limited. If regulatory norms require conditions for the technology transfer process that are inconsistent with the global objectives of the parent company, foreign subsidiaries would necessarily resolve this conflict in favor of the parent MNC's interest. Even though the technology contract might not specify conditions that are prohibited by regulatory norms, many of the operations or transactions that involve such conflict can be covered by confidential or nondocumented instructions. Such aspects as the sourcing of inputs, the extent of integration, the level of transfer pricing, and the development of export capability to the fullest extent provide considerable scope for deviation between norms and actual practice. For regulatory agencies to monitor such decisions and operations can be extremely difficult and often impracticable. Even in the matter of technology payments, considerable adjustments are possible through the transfer pricing of various inputs, even though the lump-sum payment or percentage of royalty is within approved limits.

In most developing countries, the major share of foreign technology inflow has been company internal — from MNCs to their wholly owned or majority-owned subsidiaries. This channel becomes even more dominant in industrial sectors that utilize relatively complex technologies compared with the level of domestic technological development of the host country. In fact a major feature of MNC strategy has been to transfer relatively advanced technologies primarily through internal channels. Consequently, in most of these sectors, regulatory bodies have limited ability to monitor the actual terms and conditions of technology acquisition through the prevailing system of technology regulation.

It was noted earlier that in several Third World countries, there has been a considerable increase in the number of joint ventures between foreign and domestic companies, since host country policies have aimed at increasing the participation of domestically owned firms in industrialization. In most joint ventures, the contribution of the foreign partner has included transfer of technology to the local operation. Local partners in joint ventures would obviously benefit from technology arrangements that adhere to regulatory norms. Payments for the technology according to established ceilings, complete transfer of improvements, and development of export capability to the full extent would invariably increase the local partners' revenues in such joint ventures. The extent to which the local partners' interests are met, however, would largely be determined by the parties' respective bargaining strength. In cases where the local partner has relatively weak technological or absorptive capacity, the profitability of the operation would depend on the continuous participation of the foreign partner. In fact, access to the technology of the foreign partner provides the basis for such operations. Formation of joint ventures on the basis of unequal technological and managerial capacities has often grown out of government regulations that restrict the participation of MNCs in certain sectors to joint ventures. In these cases, MNCs might well exercise effective control over the joint venture, as they have with local subsidiaries, and could obtain high returns within the framework of regulatory norms. Consequently, the types of technologies that are transferred to such joint ventures and the direct and indirect costs of the transfer continue to be largely dictated by the foreign partner. So long as the operation is profitable, there is a tendency for local partners to accept technological and managerial control by the foreign partners or licensors, including adjustments in the fulfillment of contractual conditions.

It is undeniable that joint ventures have played an important role in the technological development of enterprises in developing countries. However, this has not necessarily taken place to the extent that was envisaged by the imposition of regulatory norms. The relative weakness of local partners has, for the most part, inhibited them from fully availing themselves of the benefits of regulatory norms and more complete technology transfer. On the other hand, when local partners have been large and capable industrial groups, such as the major privately owned industrial companies in Brazil, India, and Korea, the pace of technological absorption and development has been fairly rapid, and regulatory norms and guidelines have been fully utilized by these enterprises. This is largely because their entrepreneurial and managerial capability has given such companies a strong bargaining position in relation to their MNC partners and licensors and thus has enabled them to acquire and use foreign technology under favorable conditions.

In the case of licensing by wholly domestically owned companies, without foreign equity participation, the desire on the part of local companies to adhere to regulatory norms becomes all the more important. Through full ownership rights, local entrepreneurs are able to exercise decision-making power to acquire and use foreign technology according to their best interests to a far greater extent than they can in joint ventures. The extent to which this has taken place has varied, however, with the nature of the technology. In fields where potential licensees can select from several alternative technologies or licensors and are willing to search and negotiate actively, the regulatory framework can be and has been utilized effectively. In sectors where technological alternatives are limited, however, owners of technologies enjoy oligopolistic advantages, costs and terms of transfer become more onerous, and the acquisition of such technology may require acceptance of these terms. Nevertheless, access to these technologies not only would be necessary in various production and service sectors but also would enable profitable operations in domestic markets in which protectionist measures shield local products from foreign competition.

The growing flexibility in the application of regulatory norms in most developing countries provides the necessary policy framework for the licensing of most available technologies. Even in sectors that use the relatively standard technologies available from various sources, as in the manufacture of consumer goods and simple industrial products, well-known brand names and trademarks of dominant MNCs enjoy high market acceptance in developing countries and are of special interest to domestic licensees. Licensees in such cases may also be willing to accept certain restrictive contractual conditions imposed by licensing MNCs. Where such provisions would not be acceptable to regulatory bodies, they are not incorporated in formal agreements but may be left to a tacit understanding between the parties, which cannot be monitored by regulatory bodies. This may well lead to the acceptance of less favorable conditions than would be necessary. The experience of technology licensing practices of domestically owned companies in developing countries also suggests that these companies make rather limited efforts to search for technological alternatives, even in fields where there are several alternative sources. Once licensing arrangements are entered into, there is a high degree of dependence on the specific foreign technology supplier for all technological inputs, including for the expansion of production into new areas. Often, a more extensive search may be hindered by the limited knowledge of domestic companies regarding alternatives, and the high costs that a search would involve tends to reinforce this behavior pattern. Furthermore, familiarity with existing licensors also serves as a strategy for reducing risks to domestic companies.

It should be stressed that, apart from foreign subsidiaries, there may be considerable divergence in the approaches of domestically owned private companies and the socioeconomic and technological objectives embodied in the regulatory norms and guidelines prescribed by national authorities. These differences may relate to contractual arrangements on duration, tie-in conditions for supply of inputs, phasing of integration programs, and various other aspects of operations. They have to be suitably resolved and necessitate periodic monitoring by regulatory bodies. One would expect that in the approach of state-owned public sector enterprises toward acquisition of foreign technology, there would be much greater consistency with regulatory norms. Being ultimately subject to government control, regulatory norms should be implemented by these companies, which are usually fairly large and also enjoy a strong bargaining position with MNCs. Despite these factors, technology acquisition by public sector companies has not always conformed to regulatory norms, and such companies have often sought and obtained exemption from regulatory provisions. There have been several instances of unduly high technology payments by public sector companies, besides continuing maintenance of imports, relatively low levels of integration, and acceptance of export restrictions and other restrictions. The approval of such conditions have, however, been based on the broader industrial and technological objectives that state-owned enterprises intend to fulfill, which often require that these enterprises be exempted from general regulatory norms and guidelines in the public interest.

As can be seen from the preceding discussion, so long as the technology supply arrangements are made by private companies, whether foreign or domestically owned, regulatory bodies face considerable difficulties in implementing and monitoring regulatory norms. As these measures have become more complex, the difficulties have also increased. During the early phases of technology regulation, when government scrutiny focused on the direct costs of technology, the foreign exchange control system could be used rather efficiently to monitor payments. As the scope of control has extended to the various indirect costs of foreign technology and the extent of transfer, effective implementation and monitoring have faced major problems. To the extent that domestic licensees do not or are unable to insist on effective technology transfer on reasonable terms and conditions, it may continue to be necessary for regulatory bodies in developing countries to undertake this function. At the same time, it must be recognized that there are obvious practical limitations to physical monitoring in countries where the number of agreements runs into several thousands. Consequently, alternative monitoring techniques would need to be developed, such as the use of well-defined indicators of technology transfer and absorption in different fields. One important indicator is the level of domestic integration in manufacture, since transfer of technological capability is closely related to progress in production by local licensees and reduced technological dependency over time. As subsequent technology agreements are entered into, they should reflect the progressive localization of production by the licensee enterprise.

The issue of domestic integration in manufacture or local value-added has been a major policy consideration of several governments, since licensees, whether foreign subsidiaries or domestically owned companies, tend to operate with high import content. Consequently, in several countries, policies and import control measures have been intended to increase the use of local inputs by establishing sector-specific patterns of localization in manufacture. The primary focus of these measures, however, has been to reduce foreign exchange outflow and foster local production. It is necessary that such measures be closely coordinated with those relating to foreign technology regulation and monitoring. For measuring the effectiveness of technology transfer, close coordination between import regulation bodies and technology regulation agencies is indispensable. Continuous monitoring of import content of licensees not only would determine whether the technological elements transferred increase significantly over time but would also ensure that the licensee fully obtains those elements for which payments are made to the licensor.

The coordination of import control and technology regulation would undoubtedly enable closer monitoring and assessment of the actual extent of technology transfer. Import control and technology regulation bodies have tended to operate with different priorities, however, and most governments accord higher priority to local manufacture than to the issue of technological development. Although it would seem that the two processes would go hand in hand, in actuality this is rarely the case in most developing countries. In industrialization programs, the primary aim of the government is to establish production in certain identified sectors, and the extent of technology transfer, or its completeness, seldom receives critical attention at this stage. Thus, in the early phases of new industrial projects, the importing of inputs has generally been liberally allowed. Although progressive localization of production has been required in most cases, its follow-up has not been adequate, and the phased schedule of integration has often been renegotiated, resulting in considerable delay in achieving the targeted local content. Several factors have contributed to this practice, including small market size and the higher price—and generally lower quality—of locally produced inputs, and it has been fairly common for import control agencies to repeatedly extend the period of phased local integration. This, however, has reduced the need to acquire a broader range and content of foreign technologies.

MNCs producing technologically sophisticated products, such as automobiles, machinery, and equipment, have resisted government efforts to reduce the import content of their production. In most countries, this resistance has been linked to inadequate economies of scale in the manufacture of various parts and components by particular methods of production. With the growing foreign exchange burden of maintenance imports, certain Third World countries have prescribed export performance criteria for local operations. A good example is the automobile industry in Brazil and Mexico, where foreign subsidiaries have been required to balance their exports and imports. Such a policy inevitably places balance-of-payment considerations ahead of the issue of technological development. By giving up the requirement of increased local content in favor of higher exports, MNC subsidiaries do not have to broaden their technological capabilities to the extent that would be necessary for increasing the depth of local production. In such cases, technology transfer has often stopped short of the manufacture of technologically complex parts and components. Items that have been produced for export have tended to be relatively simple, standard parts and components, which have mostly been sold to other subsidiaries—frequently those located in developing countries. While production for export markets usually requires high-quality products, these products have tended to be low-technology items. Export promotion in place of higher local content has reduced the need to transfer more complex technologies that a rigorous follow-up of local content regulation would have required.

An important feature of technology regulation measures has been the emphasis given to rapid technological absorption and adaptation. This goal is intended to be achieved by restrictions on the duration of contracts and by the granting of permission for renewals and new agreements only if they involve the transfer of new technologies. The implementation of such a policy requires close scrutiny and review of all applications for renewal of technology agreements, and in many cases, it remains questionable whether these measures have been effective. With respect to simple technologies, the usual duration of about ten years is more than sufficient to absorb the technology. For more complex technologies, however, technology agreements usually cover only certain elements or stages of the overall manufacturing process, depending on the extent of local manufacture undertaken. Consequently, the relationship between licensors and licensees has tended to extend over a long period, with continuing agreements and extensions being approved by regulatory bodies. In these cases, the technology elements specified in the agreement may have been absorbed effectively by the licensee, but this absorption may remain partial because of the limited nature of local production, which is governed by broader MNC strategy. The extent of technology transfer is inevitably limited by the scope of the local manufacturing activity. So long as such manufacture remains partial, full absorption of technology does not take place, and, at best, technology for only a few stages of production is absorbed.

Despite the obvious constraints and limitations on foreign technology regulation, it has been an important step for Third World countries toward exercising more control over the process of technology inflow and usage. With the registration and review of all foreign technology agreements, government agencies have more potential opportunity to review and assess the flow of foreign technology over time and for different industrial sectors. The establishment of norms and guidelines and the prohibition of certain practices in technology agreements has increased the awareness of domestic companies regarding the dimensions of the technology transfer process and the conditions of acquisition. Regulatory measures have also set a legal framework within which technology agreements can be entered, which can potentially protect domestic licensees from unreasonably restrictive conditions. This has become increasingly important, since several countries, including the largest developing economies, have adopted similar regulatory guidelines. As a result, foreign technology commercialization by MNCs will take place under conditions that, in many areas, have changed significantly, with licensees exercising greater rights over the use of licensed technology and the costs of acquisition being subjected to scrutiny and review.

At the same time, technology regulation in developing countries has had limited results in most countries from the viewpoint of local technological development; its impact has largely been in the improvement of terms and conditions for licensees in these countries. As discussed earlier, there have been obvious difficulties in administering the relevant laws and guidelines when local licensees, whether foreign subsidiaries or domestically owned companies, choose to avoid compliance with the terms of agreements as approved by regulatory bodies. There have also been problems in directly administering measures for technology regulation. These measures require considerable administrative expertise and legal, economic, and technical knowledge of the issues involved in a number of diverse fields. Where such expertise has been lacking, regulatory measures have served little purpose. A major criticism of technology regulation has been the delay it causes in the planning and execution of industrial projects. This delay may extend to several months—even years in some cases—and leads to considerable frustration and difficulty for both licensors and licensees. There have also been several instances of overzealousness on the part of regulatory bodies and overregulation, leading to difficulties and disputes at the implementation stage. It is only after some years of experience that technology regulating agencies in a few countries have been able to develop the necessary administrative capability to handle this responsibility effectively.

A far greater problem has been the impact of regulatory measures on technological self-reliance and on the inflow of required technology in priority production sectors in these countries. As for MNC subsidiaries and affiliates, their technological dependence on parent corporations has largely continued as before. In most fields, local research by these enterprises, which have continued to operate at the lower end of the technological spectrum, has been very limited. Product models and production processes often have tended to be considerably behind those utilized in industrialized countries, except in process industries. There are undoubtedly several other exceptions, especially in export-oriented fields, but in most instances, the technological level of operations by MNC subsidiaries and affiliates has been much lower in most Third World countries than in industrialized economies. The problem of joint ventures and licensees in developing countries has become even more intensified, since the technological capabilities transferred tend to be frozen at the level of initial transfer. While regulatory norms presume that full and complete access to technological improvements will be provided by the foreign partner or licensor, this is far from being the case, as can be seen in the earlier review of technology in various sectors. Thus, unless and until local research efforts are intensified, both at enterprise level and through closer linkages with research institutions in these countries, the technological gap between parent MNCs and their subsidiaries, affiliates, and licensees in developing countries will continue.

Although technology inflow to countries with regulatory measures, such as Brazil, India, and Mexico, has continued to be quite substantial and has grown (as measured by payments), the latest technologies have been transferred only very selectively, and MNCs appear to be less willing to transfer advanced and innovative technologies to such countries. Regulation of foreign technology has undoubtedly imposed certain constraints on the acquisition of new technologies. This may have resulted in part from competitive considerations, but it is also related to the limitations set on earnings from technology commercialization. With fairly rigid control over payments or fees and royalties, the technology that is transferred to developing countries mostly covers know-how that has already been fully exploited in industrialized economies and is no longer critical to the MNCs' global strategy. Of course, these constraints could well exist even if Third World enterprises paid much higher sums for technology, but the situation does become aggravated when payments (both direct and indirect) are restricted by regulatory measures. This problem becomes even more pronounced in countries where, besides regulation of foreign technology, regulation of foreign direct investments places major restrictions on the permissible equity ownership of MNCs.

14
Prospects for Technology Transfer through MNCs

The experience with technology regulation over the last decade has led to increasing awareness that strict and rigid regulation of foreign technology could result in strong disincentives for the inflow of needed foreign technology. It has also become evident that the regulatory approach, as reflected in the norms and guidelines prescribed for various contractual provisions, has not taken into account the need for substantial flow of technology and know-how in various sectors in which they are urgently necessary. It is also increasingly recognized that in a number of industrial sectors, the access to required foreign technologies and the terms of acquisition are influenced by forces that are beyond the control of governments and that are not necessarily responsive to government policies and measures. MNCs are continuing to play a leading role in technological development in their respective fields, which gives them far-reaching control over specific technologies and know-how.

In fields where technology ownership is highly concentrated, commercialization of technology can take place only on terms and conditions that the proprietors of technology are willing to accept. These conditions would include substantial returns from the local market, protection of worldwide market share, and varying degrees of control over the application of technology. These objectives are usually achieved if the technology is transferred to wholly owned subsidiaries. Where this is not possible, the process of negotiation has to take account of these factors if the supply and transfer of technology is to take place.

Although the bargaining position of corporations for specific products and technologies changes over time with the entry of new competitors or the development of new technologies, these changes almost invariably occur in the industrialized economies—the United States, West Europe, and Japan—and are concentrated in large corporations in these countries. Consequently, in assessing the impact of government policies on foreign technology, it is important to recognize the extent to which regulatory measures can effectively influence MNC behavior in these countries. The imposition of control measures outside such limits may be counterproductive and may prevent the acquisition of needed technologies. At the same time, host country governments have the power to influence the terms and conditions of technology transfer in areas where they enjoy a relatively strong bargaining strength regarding local factor resources, size of market, nature of technology, availability of technological alternatives, and other such aspects.

The recognition of the limitations of technology regulation measures has been reflected in the "new pragmatism" adopted in several of these countries. This approach accepts the fact that MNCs are the principal sources for the acquisition of advanced technologies and that such technologies can be obtained only if MNC operations in developing countries earn adequate returns, both on investments and on the commercialization of technology. This new and pragmatic orientation toward acquisition of foreign technology is being implemented through different policies in various countries. A fairly common element of such policies is that in priority sectors where technology ownership is concentrated, the existing controls on foreign direct investment and technology are lifted or relaxed. This relaxation often takes place in the extent of foreign ownership allowed, including permission to set up MNC majority-owned subsidiaries. In other instances, approvals have been granted for operations with low levels of domestic integration in manufacture and substantial sourcing from imports over an extended period of time. In certain cases involving foreign direct investments, the norms of foreign technology regulation are not applied, and there is substantial relaxation with regard to the imposition of various restrictive conditions on the use of the technology. Besides being granted a larger degree of freedom to determine their ownership structure, form of operation, and conditions of technology transfer, MNCs in priority sectors have also received various fiscal and financial incentives, as well as protection from foreign competition.

Differential treatment of foreign technology agreements according to their importance for the host country has been fairly common since the early phases of foreign technology regulation. In several countries, particularly in Latin America, this flexibility in the application of the law has been considered especially important in facilitating acquisition of critical technology. Technology regulatory norms have been applied rigorously in sectors of less importance for industrialization and in fields with several technological alternatives. With the adoption of more pragmatic and flexible policies by host developing countries, it can be expected that foreign technology flow to Third World countries will be greatly accelerated during the 1980s. The impact of the liberalization of technology regulation has been most marked in the Republic of Korea, where the number of technology agreements doubled between 1981 and 1984. In India, as well, there was a substantial increase in technology agreements during 1984 and the first half of 1985. The necessity for liberalization has become pronounced as development plans have targeted diversification of industrial production into sectors that have more complex technological requirements and where technology ownership is often highly concentrated. New technological needs have also become increasingly evident in existing production sectors, which have often lagged behind international technological developments by decades and have particularly hampered exports. Although the constraints imposed by regulatory measures on inflow of needed foreign technology have been the main reasons for liberalizing these measures, another important factor has been the improved capability of local industrial groups and entrepreneurs to negotiate with foreign technology suppliers directly. With the growth of these capabilities, governmental support through regulatory norms may not be required to the extent necessary a decade or two ago, when these measures and guidelines were introduced.

In several developing countries, the major shift in policies toward foreign technology (also toward foreign direct investments in certain countries) reflects greater acceptance of the role of MNCs and the need for MNC participation in establishing production capabilities in technologically advanced industrial sectors. This change in policies raises several issues about the pattern of industrial development in these countries and the technological objectives that a decade or two ago, led to the introduction of regulatory measures. Incentives for MNC investments in priority sectors will undoubtedly increase foreign penetration in these fields in countries in which MNCs find such operations profitable. A situation may well develop that is similar to the early phase of import substitution, when foreign subsidiaries achieved a dominant position in new industries in several developing countries. Presently, although several host country governments have extensive regulatory tools and measures at their disposal, they are voluntarily not applied in priority sectors of these economies. Instead, MNCs have been given substantial freedom of operations, provided that these operations contribute to the achievement of self-sufficiency in technologically advanced production sectors. Although the field of MNC operations may have changed to more technologically advanced products and processes, the pattern of operations is often similar to that of early import-substitution industries. Most of these activities involve wholly foreign-owned subsidiaries, with partial local production and with MNC control over the terms of technology transfer and its local usage.

The development of production capabilities in technologically advanced sectors through MNC subsidiaries and affiliates, while perhaps necessary in the short term, is likely to pose future problems in adopting policies toward technological development and self-reliance in these countries. With much greater knowledge and awareness of the socioeconomic and technological impact of MNC subsidiaries on host countries, it would be desirable to determine the nature of the relationship between host developing countries and MNCs in high-technology and other fields where their participation is urgently sought. In certain sectors, the conditions for entry of foreign direct investment, including that of wholly owned subsidiaries, may be relaxed, provided that other contributions of MNCs can be agreed upon, such as development of exports, resource allocation for enterprise-level R&D, and increased manufacturing integration within an agreed-upon time span. Rapid technological absorption and adaptation will also undoubtedly constitute criteria for MNC participation. Evaluation of MNC activities, in such circumstances, will focus more on these performances than on ownership, at least in the priority sectors of these economies. At the same time, there can be little doubt that the growth of state-owned enterprises and private, domestically owned companies in Third World countries will lead to a rapid increase in joint ventures and technology licensing agreements. Although these arrangements will also be more frequent in priority sectors in several developing countries, they are likely to constitute the principal channels of technology transfer in sectors of lower national priority. In these sectors, licensing agreements can also be expected to increase with large and medium-sized companies in industrialized countries that are not necessarily MNCs but that operate primarily at a national level in their respective countries.

Developing countries' policies on foreign ownership of local industry must also take account of the growing technological gap between industrialized and Third World countries because of the rapid pace of technological innovation in most industrial sectors, especially in high-technology areas, such as microelectronics, genetic engineering, and materials technology. Technology licensing generally offers access only to those technologies that have already been extensively utilized in industrialized countries. The same situation prevails, though to a lesser extent, in the case of joint ventures, except where technological and managerial control is exercised by the foreign licensor. The latest technological development would be transferred to Third World countries, since they have the necessary factor advantages, primarily through wholly owned subsidiaries. Host countries may well have to choose between the entry or continuance of wholly owned MNC subsidiaries and the undertaking of costly and comprehensive programs for indigenous research to keep pace with technological developments in industrialized countries. With varying degrees of concentration of technological, managerial, and market control among a few MNCs in most industrial branches, the technologies that are transferred to developing countries and the countries to which they are transferred continue to be determined by MNCs to a considerable extent. Despite significant technological diffusion and the development of competitive capability in several developing countries, there continues to be a high degree of technological dependence on MNCs in most Third World countries. The critical policy question for most countries is the manner by which needed foreign technologies can be acquired while reducing technological dependency and the cost that such dependency entails. Pursuit of these dual objectives may necessitate that policies toward foreign technology be incorporated within the framework of a comprehensive technology plan that is fully integrated with national plans for economic and industrial development.

In most developing countries, industrial planning has been adopted for the implementation of economic and industrial objectives. Planning in these countries has also been regarded as critical to the reduction of existing imbalances in these economies, such as the inadequate growth of machine-building industries and the limited local processing of natural resources. The scope and detail of national industrial plans have varied considerably among countries. It has been, however, in only a few of these countries that much greater emphasis has recently been accorded to technology plans covering various aspects of technological development and application. Even in most of these countries, the technology plans have not been integrated with the targets of industrial plans, nor have the elements of technology planning been linked with the achievement of industrial targets. Close coordination of technology planning with industrial plans and targets is essential, however, if industrial development and technological development are to progress in harmony and take place according to identified objectives.

It is the technology plan that has to assess the technological requirements necessary to achieve sectoral targets and identify technological linkages among various industrial sectors. Such plans also must deal with the development of technological infrastructure, which includes the development of human resources and the promotion of indigenous R&D by domestic industry and specialized research institutions. Technology plans would also have to identify the explicit and implicit measures that would be necessary for the growth of local managerial and entrepreneurial capabilities, so that the dominance of MNC subsidiaries and affiliates can be reduced. Despite resource constraints in developing countries, the importance of technology planning must be highlighted as an essential element of economic development.

Through various incentives and regulatory measures, national governments can undoubtedly create an environment in which foreign and local enterprises may undertake industrial activities in accordance with identified priorities. In free-market developing economies, however, investment decisions are made by private sector companies, and there may be considerable deviation between plan targets and actual production levels in different fields. Similarly, in the case of technology plans, established targets may deviate significantly from actual performance. Consequently, besides formulating policies to influence the behavior of private companies, governments have to participate actively to close the gap. To meet the targets of the plan, relevant government agencies would have to allocate significant funds for the development of a technological infrastructure. Through resource allocations for various aspects of industrial and technological development, national governments can also provide broad directions and indicators for national priorities, besides incentives and other measures that have direct impact. Progress toward technological self-reliance requires a fairly long-term horizon and a broad policy framework, which must be provided by national authorities. This can result in patterns of investment and technological development in which the interests of private companies and the longer-term national development objectives are harmonized more closely.

An important role in this regard can be played by state-owned corporations in various industrial and service sectors. Apart from the large number of public sector corporations in several developing countries, the fields covered extend over a wide range of industrial branches and service sectors. These companies have received preferential treatment in resource allocation, technology acquisition, and other operational aspects. Despite their special treatment, state-owned enterprises in the manufacturing sector have not provided the expected technological leadership, and their linkages with local suppliers and ancillary units have remained fairly weak in most developing countries. Because of the limited technological spillover from these enterprises, there has been relatively little impact on the growth of medium-scale industry. Most public sector enterprises have not emerged as centers of local technological growth, and they have assigned low priority to technological adaptation and innovation.

There is no doubt that large state-owned companies can perform a major function in expanding enterprise-level R&D capabilities and building closer technological linkages with R&D institutions and other domestic companies, particularly in the medium- and small-scale sectors, which have limited access to foreign technology. The growth of medium- and small-scale industries is of critical importance in most developing countries. Besides incentives and support, these industrial units require technological linkages that can be provided by the large state-owned enterprises in many of these countries. The medium- and small-scale industrial sectors, which should constitute the bedrock of industrial activities in these countries, have not benefited significantly from growing industrialization and technological development, except in a very few developing countries. In most others, industrial growth has largely taken place either through MNC subsidiaries and affiliates or through large domestically owned companies in the private and public sectors.

The formulation of a technology plan is, to a large extent, a technocratic process. The objectives of the plan and the policies that are adopted to achieve these objectives should ultimately determine the nature and pattern of technological development. Technology plans and policies promote, explicitly or implicitly, certain institutions and certain production and service sectors, some of which often require greater efforts and resources than others. This is an inherent aspect of planning and resource allocation. The nature of this selectivity will, at the same time, have major distribution effects on various groups and institutions of the economy. How countries plan to achieve the distribution of benefits from development is a politico-economic question. Regardless of the system, however, the need of developing countries for advanced foreign technology creates a bias in development toward the growth of large companies and conglomerates. Unless governments specifically provide incentives and support the growth of medium- and small-scale industries with other measures, they will only marginally benefit from development. A continuing polarization in production and technological capabilities between large companies and other segments of the economy is likely to exacerbate existing imbalances in the industrial structure of these countries. This will not only hinder further development but will also result in an uneven distribution of the benefits from development.

Technological development that is wholly or mostly dependent on foreign technology has a tendency to reinforce a dual industrial structure in developing countries and also accentuates the differences between these countries. During the past two decades, the varying access of countries to foreign technology has been a major contributory factor for different levels of industrialization and technological development in Third World countries. In the coming decades, there may be further polarization as the major elements that have shaped the present pattern of industrial development continue to operate. A key element is the strategy of MNCs, and MNC investments in advanced technological sectors will continue to concentrate on a small number of developing countries that have favorable factor conditions. It must also be recognized that although most developing countries seek to progress toward technological self-reliance, the extent to which this objective can be achieved will vary considerably. The financial and technological resource requirements of self-reliant development can be very substantial, for both governments and companies. Consequently, in the relatively few countries that have already established a well-diversified industrial structure and have attained fairly advanced technological skills and capabilities, the potential for pursuing technological self-reliance will be much greater than it will be in most Third World countries. Countries that are at a particular disadvantage are those with small market size and weak production and technological capabilities. These are also the countries in which MNCs are not interested in undertaking major investments in the manufacturing sector, while the weak technological capabilities of domestic companies makes it difficult to make use of foreign technologies. It is also in these countries that other priorities assume greater urgency; these include chronic balance-of-payment difficulties, unemployment, and basic socioeconomic problems that require the immediate attention of the governments concerned. In this process, technological development and the pursuit of technological self-reliance tend to receive low priority.

Index

About the Author

Katherin Marton is associate professor of international business and economics at Fordham University, New York City. She has taught previously at the City University of New York and was visiting professor at the Free University in Berlin. She participated in several field studies in Latin American, Asian, and African countries on industrial and technological development and on the role and impact of operation of multinational corporations in various countries. She has written several monographs and studies, particularly on technology transfer to developing countries in various industrial sectors. Her previous publications also include articles on foreign direct investments in *Host Nation Attitudes towards Multinational Corporations,* edited by John Fayerweather (Praeger, 1982), and, with J.J. Boddewyn, *Comparison Advertising — A Worldwide Study* (Hastings House, 1978).